D0016385

OXFORD HISTORY OF

ENGLISH LITERATURE

Edited by

JOHN BUXTON *and* NORMAN DAVIS

THE OXFORD HISTORY OF ENGLISH LITERATURE

Edited by

JOHN BUXTON AND NORMAN DAVIS

I. Part 1. ENGLISH LITERATURE BEFORE THE NORMAN CONQUEST

Part 2. MIDDLE ENGLISH LITERATURE

II. Part 1. CHAUCER AND THE FIFTEENTH CENTURY (*published*)

Part 2. THE CLOSE OF THE MIDDLE AGES (*published*)

III. THE SIXTEENTH CENTURY (excluding Drama) (*published*)

IV. Part 1. THE ENGLISH DRAMA, 1485-1585 (*published*)

Part 2. THE ENGLISH DRAMA, 1585-1642

V. THE EARLY SEVENTEENTH CENTURY 1600-1660 (*published*)

Second edition 1962

VI. THE LATE SEVENTEENTH CENTURY (*published*)

VII. THE EARLY EIGHTEENTH CENTURY (1700-1740) (*published*)

VIII. THE MID-EIGHTEENTH CENTURY (*published*)

IX. 1789-1815 (*published*)

X. 1815-1832 (*published*)

XI. THE MID-NINETEENTH CENTURY

Part 1. PROSE

Part 2. POETRY

XII. EIGHT MODERN WRITERS (*published*)

XIII. 1880-1930

CHAUCER AND THE FIFTEENTH CENTURY

BY

H. S. BENNETT

OXFORD
AT THE CLARENDON PRESS

Oxford University Press, Walton Street, Oxford OX2 6DP

OXFORD LONDON GLASGOW
NEW YORK TORONTO MELBOURNE WELLINGTON
KUALA LUMPUR SINGAPORE JAKARTA HONG KONG TOKYO
DELHI BOMBAY CALCUTTA MADRAS KARACHI
NAIROBI DAR ES SALAAM CAPE TOWN

ISBN 0 19 812201 2

First published 1947
Reprinted with corrections 1948, 1954, 1958
1961, 1965, 1970, 1979

Printed in Great Britain
at the University Press, Oxford
by Eric Buckley
Printer to the University

PREFACE

THIS book forms part one of Volume II of *The Oxford History of English Literature*, of which part two, under the title of 'The Close of the Middle Ages', has already appeared (1945). In part two Sir E. K. Chambers has dealt with the medieval drama, medieval lyric, popular narrative verse, the ballad, and Malory. The present volume, as its title suggests, has the twofold purpose of attempting to reassess the work of our greatest medieval author and to resurvey the fifteenth century in the light of modern scholarship.

Both parts of this task have been formidable, for different reasons. As long ago as 1870, J. R. Lowell opened his classic essay on Chaucer with these words: 'Will it *do* to say anything more about Chaucer? Can anyone hope to say anything not new, but even fresh, on a topic so well worn? It may well be doubted.' Since then Chaucerian studies have greatly increased in volume and in scope—nowhere more so than in the United States—and we are in some danger of losing sight of the wood for the trees. It is particularly ironic that this most humane of English poets should be in peril of being buried under a mass of erudition. That much of value has emerged from a fraction of such work cannot be denied, but it may well be argued that more is to be obtained from the study of the age of Chaucer and from the events which shaped his career. The age does not make the man, but it contributes much to his making, and the object of the first part of this volume is to show this more clearly than has been done before. At the same time, considerable attention has been paid to the precise poetic means Chaucer used to produce those effects we speak of as peculiarly Chaucerian.

Much that is best known in fifteenth-century literature has been dealt with by Sir E. K. Chambers; in some ways, however, this has been my gain, for it has allowed me to discuss the literature of that century with more attention to its promise than to its performance. The value of the writings of Lydgate, Hoccleve, Pecock, Fortescue, and Caxton can only be assessed as part of the fifteenth century's contribution to the body and continuity of our literature. While the literary value of their work is often small, the importance of these writers, and of many whose names are unknown to us, is real: they tried to satisfy the new demands, made for the most part by a public hitherto uninterested in literature, and in a series of practical, limited treatises they told their first readers not only of love, war, and religion, but also of history, medicine, travel, and practical affairs.

Little is said of the romances in this book since it seemed better to treat of their origins and development as a single story, and not to write merely of their latest days. A full treatment of the romances is given in part two of Volume I.

Texts are normally quoted from first or from authoritative modern editions, such as the 'Student's Cambridge Edition' of Chaucer by F. N. Robinson, with slight modifications for the benefit of the ordinary reader. Thus the medieval ȝ has been replaced by *gh* or other equivalents, and in the short quotations þ has been changed to *th*. Titles are given in their original form in the bibliography and are modernized in the text.

I am indebted to the Executive Committee of the English Association and to the Clarendon Press for permission to make use of my article 'The Author and his Public' which appeared in *Essays and Studies of the English Association*, vol. xxiii (1937), and I owe much to the help given to me by members of the staff of the University Library, Cambridge, and in particular to Mr. H. L. Pink of the Anderson Room.

I must also gratefully record my thanks to the General Editors, Professor Bonamy Dobrée and Professor F. P. Wilson for much help and guidance. Their criticisms and suggestions at various stages of my work were invaluable, and saved me from many blunders. Professor Wilson's conception of the duties of a General Editor has made very great demands on his time and energies. If this book is unworthy of its theme the fault must lie with me and in my inability to profit by all the help Professor Wilson has so generously offered.

H. S. B.

EMMANUEL COLLEGE, CAMBRIDGE

August 1947

CONTENTS

PUBLISHER'S NOTE

THIS book, first published in 1947, was one of the earliest volumes of the series to appear. When the author was invited to prepare a revised edition to take account of later work, he decided that he would prefer to leave the body of the text unchanged except for the elimination of errors of detail, but to bring the bibliography up to date. The present edition therefore presents the original text with minor corrections, but a largely new and reset bibliography and index.

Stanley Bennett died in 1972. He had completed the revision of the bibliography and sent his typescript to the printer, but he never saw a proof. The book has been seen through the press by the General Editors.

I

CHAUCER AND HIS AGE

THE city of London in the fourteenth century, despite the fact that it was incomparably the greatest city of the kingdom, was comparatively small—indeed insignificant when compared with the 'great Wen' of to-day. It was separated from the city of Westminster by a badly paved way—the Strand—on each side of which stood great palaces such as Chester's Inn, or the homes of the lawyers, such as the Temple or Lincoln's Inn. The city itself was surrounded by its wall which ran down to the Thames, and at intervals there stood the gates which gave entrance to the city from various points. Above each of them was the little gatehouse, and in that at Aldgate during the years 1374–86 Geoffrey Chaucer lived. It was not an imposing apartment: it consisted of one large room, with one window looking into the city and another looking outward to the open country. There were also a smaller room and two very small rooms, together with cellars below.

Here, according to his own account, Chaucer pored over his books:

> For when thy labour doon al ys,
> And hast mad alle thy rekenynges,
> In stede of reste and newe thynges,
> Thou goost hom to thy hous anoon;
> And, also domb as any stoon,
> Thou sittest at another book,
> Tyl fully daswed[1] is thy look,
> And lyvest thus as an hermyte,
> Although thyn abstenence ys lyte.

But in less studious moments, as he looked out from his windows, on the one side he saw the road winding out into the open country. The road itself leading from the gate was 'broken and noyous', and more like a miry country track than like anything which we should call a road. To the north, beyond the Bishop's Wood in Stepney, lay the marshes with the Lea meandering through them, and in the farther distance Chaucer could see the heights of the Forest of Epping. Moorgate, and beyond it the

[1] daswed (dazed).

heaths of Highgate and Hampstead, lay to the west, while eastwards stretched the wooded banks of the Thames. It was into some favourite spot ('a litel herber[1] that I have') in this country-side, so near to his home, that Chaucer escaped

> whan that the month of May
> Is comen, and that I here the foules[2] synge,
> And that the floures gynnen for to sprynge,
> Farwel my bok, and my devocioun! . . .
> As I seyde erst, whanne comen is the May,
> That in my bed ther daweth[3] me no day
> That I n'am[4] up and walkyng in the mede
> To seen this flour ayein the sonne sprede,
> Whan it upryseth erly by the morwe.

From his windows which looked down into the city Chaucer saw a very different view, though even so, 'the mass of buildings was not yet sufficient to disguise the natural features of the site. The streets mounted visibly from the river and Fleet Brook to the centre of the city. St. Paul's was plainly set on a hill, and nobody could fail to see the slope from the village of Holborn down the present Gray's Inn Lane. Thames still ran at low tide over native shingle and mud; the Southwark shore was green with trees; not only monasteries but often private houses had their gardens.' At nearer view the medieval streets, with their tall wooden houses overhanging the narrow highway, were in striking contrast to the open country-side without the walls. As Chaucer moved from the Custom-house to Aldgate tower he had to pass through scenes such as those described by Langland:

> Cokes and here knaves[5] · crieden 'Hote pies hote!
> Good gris and gees · gowe dyne, gowe!'[6]
> Taverners until hem[7] · tolde the same,
> 'White wyn of Oseye[8] · and red wyn of Gascoigne,
> Of the Ryne and of the Rochel · the roste to defye.'[9]

The traders had their shops set out on the ground floor; and, in order that prospective customers should know of their whereabouts, they hung out signs of various kinds:

> Somme off hem hang out lyouns,
> Somme eglys and gryffouns,

[1] herber, 'garden, arbour'. [2] foules, 'birds'. [3] daweth (dawneth).
[4] n'am, 'am not'. [5] here knaves, 'their boys'.
[6] Good gris . . . gowe! 'Good pigs and geese! let's go and dine!'
[7] until hem, 'unto them'. [8] Oseye, 'Alsace'. [9] defye, 'digest'.

> Peynted on bordys and on stagys,
> Dyvers armys and ymages
> Wherby men knowe thys craffty men.[1]

But the medieval town, with all its splendid houses and all its squalid lanes and laystalls, is so well known that it need not here be described in any detail. In any case, it has left singularly little impress on Chaucer's work. Hoccleve tells us in considerable detail of his life as a 'young man about town' and of his labours at the Privy Seal Office;[2] Langland has many passages which speak of life in the great town, and of the means whereby 'I live in London and on London both!'; the author of *London Lickpenny* gives a most spirited account of his adventures in the capital where 'For lacke of money, I may not spede'; but Chaucer is almost completely silent. Save for the passages quoted above, he tells us almost nothing of the London of his day: we must be content with a brief reference in the *Nun's Priest's Tale* to the rising in 1381 against the Flemings dwelling in the city, or the memory of a commonplace sight of his day incorporated in

> Have ye nat seyn somtyme a pale face,
> Among a prees,[3] of hym that hath be lad
> Toward his deeth, wher as hym gat no grace,
> And swich a colour in his face hath had,
> Men myghte knowe his face that was bistad,[4]
> Amonges alle the faces in that route?

or of another even more commonplace sight which he witnessed nightly from his Aldgate tower—the closing of the gates at dusk. This he re-creates for us in the moving scene in which Troilus watches for Criseyde the livelong day, until at last

> The warden of the yates[5] gan to calle
> The folk which that withoute the yates were,
> And bad hem dryven in hire bestes alle,
> Or al the nyght they moste bleven[6] there.

Apart from such tantalizing snatches as these, Chaucer, despite a lifetime of experience of London at one of its most interesting periods, tells us nothing. As we shall see, it was not for lack of contact with everyday affairs. Chaucer was no recluse, living remote in an ivory tower, but a man among men,

[1] craffty men (craftsmen).
[2] See below, p. 147.
[3] prees (press), 'crowd'.
[4] bistad, 'in trouble'.
[5] yates (gates).
[6] bleven, 'remain'.

and was more concerned with the rough and tumble of daily life than many poets have been. Civic life, however, did not attract him as potential poetic material—even the *Prologue* deals in rather cavalier fashion with the burgesses and their wives. Nor need we wonder at this. Poets had not yet come to believe that everything was fit matter for poetry, and were obviously much under the domination of a patron or of a limited class of readers. Of this there will be much to say later; here we need only note the fact, and how it predetermined in general the author's choice of subject-matter.[1]

But while Chaucer found little in the way of subject-matter in London and London life in particular, it does not follow that he gained nothing of poetical value from his many years by the wharves and in the streets of London. What it was that he gained cannot be stated exactly, but the enormous specific knowledge of mankind and of its ways that his mature works reveal is the result of a lifetime spent in the midst of his fellow men.[2]

Moreover, Chaucer was not only well versed in the complexities of town life, but also knew from long association the life of the court. London, with its civic pageantry, ceremonial, and ordinances; its trade guilds and fraternities; its rich merchants and poverty-stricken underlings: London, with all its amazing contrasts of rich and poor, of squalor and magnificence, made less impression upon him than did the life of that court which nourished and promoted him through his most impressionable years. The court of Edward III was one of the most brilliant of his time, and life there and in the households of the nobility was full of opportunities for a would-be poet. Chaucer's chance came about 1357 when he was made a member of the household of Elizabeth, wife of Lionel, son of Edward III. As a page he found himself one of a number of youths whose duty it was to be in constant attendance on their masters. They were to be found busy in the hall, serving the various dishes, carrying round the wine flagons, and at the end of the meal kneeling with water-bowl, while their masters washed the fingers which had served them as forks. They attended their masters in their chambers, acting as valets, brushing and polishing their clothes and accoutrements. Much of their time was spent waiting in attendance until something was wanted, meanwhile listening

[1] See below, p. 105.

[2] See below, p. 29.

to the conversation of their betters, or playing one with another, if a lenient discipline so allowed. But there was much for them to learn in their leisure moments: a knowledge of music was particularly important, and a page who valued promotion tried to make himself adept with the viol or other musical instrument, and also studied the art of singing and often attempted to write musical compositions of his own. Dancing, the playing at tables or chess, and other diversions were welcome accomplishments which the ladies admired. For more ordinary occasions the page was required to perfect himself in the formalities of address and to know how to enter the presence or to comport himself before royal or noble guests; the art of conversation in English and in French or other foreign tongues was also important and occupied much of his leisure. Furthermore, there was much to be learnt in the stables and kennels, and hours to be spent in the armoury before any advancement could be hoped for.

Promotion to the rank of valet or yeoman of the king's chamber is perhaps evidence enough that Chaucer in due course was able to satisfy his masters that he had sufficient training in all these matters. His new duties were very similar to those he performed as page: he was one of a small number whose duties are thus described in the Household Book of Edward IV (derived from that of Edward II): 'to make beddis, to beare or holde torches, to sett boardis, to apparell all Chambers, and such other Seruices as the Chamberlaine, or Vshers of Chambre, commaunde or assigne; to attend the Chambre; to watche the King by course; to goe in messages', &c. His further appointment to the rank of squire placed him in the category of those described as 'Esquires of householde', twenty of whom always attended on the king 'in ryding and going at alle tymes'. They served in hall and in chamber, 'and these Esquires of household of old be accustomed, winter and summer, in afternoones and in eveninges, to drawe to Lordes Chambres within Court, there to keep honest company after there Cunninge, in talking of Cronicles of Kinges, and of others Pollicies, or in pipeing or harpeing, songinges, or other actes marcealls, to helpe to occupie the Court, and accompanie estraingers, till the time require of departing'.

Such in bare outline was the life Chaucer led from 1357 onwards for some twenty years. But even when we have filled in all the known details, almost everything of importance escapes us. We can note the black and red hosen, the yearly gift of robes, the daily gallon of beer, or the faggot of firewood which he received as reward for his services, as well as the annuity from John of Gaunt and another from the king. These things have their interest for us, as denoting the satisfaction Chaucer gave to his royal patrons, but they still leave us with none of the essential information we desire as to how all these events shaped, controlled, extended, or enriched his poetic mind throughout these years. Lacking any precise information, we are forced to guess, but we may discipline our guess-work a little by seeing what is known of the court of Edward III and of the lives of the king and his courtiers.

The court of Edward III was unusually interesting, if only for the fact that for some years it contained not only the King of England and his nobles, but also King John of France and many of the greatest peers of his realm who were awaiting the raising of their ransoms. In the meantime they were the honoured captives and guests of their English hosts, and moved about surrounded by much of their accustomed retinue and magnificence. One of the French princes, for instance, had sixteen servants with him; and tournaments and feasts were the constant recreation of hosts and captives. As the royal retinue moved from castle to castle, accompanied by an enormous body of retainers and officers, the masses of treasure ransacked from the French wars were to be seen in palace and hall. Money flowed freely: the extravagance of Edward was only exceeded by that of his grandson, Richard II. Fabulous sums were spent on the royal robes: Edward ordered a tunic for the queen to be worked with birds of gold, each bird being within a small circle of large pearls, while the whole ground was covered with small pearls and silk. The number of large pearls used was 400, besides 38 oz. of small pearls. The beautifully simple dresses of an earlier period gave place to elaborate and ornate creations, stiff with gold and silver and made of tissues from Lucca, or of superfine Flemish cloth, or of rich Italian silks, while over the whole surface birds, animals, heraldic devices, and the like were embroidered in silks and pearls. Banquets and feasts were made the occasion for the prodigal provision of meat and drink, and the ceremonial of banqueting, it has been said, 'reached a dignity almost liturgical'.

Amidst such scenes moved the great lords and princes: Edward III was described by a chronicler as being so refulgent that 'his face shone like the face of a god, so that to see him or to dream of him was to conjure up joyous images', and Froissart tells us that there had been no king to equal him since Arthur. His great strength, his love of war and of martial pursuits, his easy familiarity with his court, his delight in opulent displays and magnificence of all kinds made him *primus inter pares*; but, at the same time, his followers from the Black Prince and John of Gaunt downwards exhibited similar characteristics and helped to make the court of Edward III renowned throughout western Europe. All the splendour, however, had to be paid for. It was all very well for the King of France to laugh at his royal cousin's extravagance, saying 'that he never saw so royal a feast and so costly [as that made by Edward III, on St. George's Day, 1359] made with tallies of wood, and without paying of gold and silver'. But such a method had its limits, and the king and his nobles were always clamouring for money. Hence the court was the scene of much business activity. The great officials of the King's Wardrobe and other departments were for ever receiving manorial seneschals and stewards, while commissioners and special agents came and went on the manifold activities that widespread possessions and incessant requests provoked. The business of keeping alive this court, which dissipated funds, energy, and health with such prodigal eagerness, was a heavy one, and it taxed many of the shrewdest minds of the realm to satisfy the demands made upon them.

Chaucer entered into such a world as this while still in his teens, and many of his most impressionable years were spent mingling with the variety of people that came his way in the course of his daily duties as page and squire.[1] There was obviously much for his quick observant eye to absorb, and much of fascinating interest to the student of life and manners, but all this might have been of little importance to us had not members of the court from the queen downwards shown an interest in literature, so that a writer of parts rapidly found a place for himself, even in the highest circles, if his work was good enough. Froissart writes:

[My first patron was] the good lady who now rots in earth, but who was once Queen of England; Philippa was the noble lady

[1] See also p. 31.

called; God have mercy upon her soul! Truly am I bound to pray for her and to proclaim her largesse; for it was she who made and created me. So also her daughter [in law], duchess of Lancaster, who died fair and young, at about the age of 22 years; gay and glad she was, fresh and sportive; sweet, simple, and of humble semblance, the fair lady whom men call Blanche. And the queen's daughter Isabel, also, lady of Coucy, fervently I must pray for her soul, for I found her of great courtesy. From the earl of Hereford, again, I once had great comfort and from my lord of Mauny, and his son of Pembroke. 'And the great lord Despenser, who spends so freely in largesse, what hath he done for thee?' What? much indeed! for never was he weary of giving to me, wherever he might be; no stones or staves, but horses and florins beyond number.

These generous patrons of Froissart formed part of the potential audience whom Chaucer found awaiting him, and in whose presence he learnt much of the art of poetry. Their tastes were mainly French. The queen's patronage of Froissart is only one indication of the prevalent fashion; a considerable number of French minstrels were in the pay of the king, and indeed there is no clear evidence that he could talk English with any ease. Besides, every one knew that the fountain-head of literature was in France. Ever since the days of the *chansons de geste* and the *chansons d'aventure*, French poetry had maintained an overwhelming superiority to that of England. At a time when the dreary moralizings of the *Ormulum* were the best England could provide, Marie de France, Chrétien de Troyes, Benoît de Ste-Maure, Wace, and many others had produced work of the greatest distinction, and the passage of a century and a half to the days of Chaucer had only emphasized the gulf between the two literatures. Chaucer found in French a wealth of romances, lives of saints, *contes*, *fabliaux*, drama, history, biography, all of great interest and importance. Besides this, the overwhelming influence of the *Roman de la Rose* was still effective, while contemporary (or almost contemporary) poets such as Machaut, Froissart, and Deschamps were providing lovers of poetry with a bewildering variety of verse-forms and of novel methods of treating old subjects. This great body of dead and living authors could not be ignored by one who wished to interest a courtly circle: Gower even went so far as to write a long poem, the *Miroir de l'Omme*, in 30,000 lines of considerable dullness, as well as a number of *balades*, in which he essayed to show his mastery of the prevalent French forms. Chaucer, so far as we know, made no attempt to write in French, but it is significant that among his earliest extant works should be a translation of part of the *Roman de la Rose*—a tribute to a poem which was to remain so valuable a part of his poetic heritage.[1]

Not only French poetry, but English poetry, was also known to Chaucer and was not without merit. When Chaucer was a young man vernacular poetry of several kinds was in circulation. In the first place there was the English romance. Chaucer's keen mockery in *Sir Thopas* serves to emphasize the deplorable nature of much of this kind of verse. What started in its French form in graceful fluent narrative in the course of time suffered from that gradual degeneration which is inseparable from oral transmission. Minstrels did their best, but the heavy burden placed on their memories by a vast repertoire, and the pressure of circumstance which demanded alteration and adaptation of their material, gradually left the romance but a shadow of what once had been its form. In Chaucer's day many of the romances had been given an English form—indeed a large number only survive in fourteenth- and fifteenth-century versions—but often so weakened and corrupted had they become that an artist such as Chaucer realized that their day was nearly over.[2]

Then again there was a considerable body of religious verse, some of which must have been known to him. Professor Carleton Brown's devoted labours in this field have enabled him to collect so much religious verse of before the end of the fifteenth century that two large quarto volumes are required merely to list in brief all that he has found. But students of this material soon find that it is of very mediocre poetic quality, and that even such an anthology as Professor Carleton Brown's *Religious Lyrics of the XIV Century* contains little that would have inspired Chaucer greatly, even had he seen it. His only strictly religious poem extant is a prayer to the Virgin, but this *ABC* is merely a poetic exercise, a free translation of a passage in Deguilleville's *Le Pèlerinage de la Vie Humaine*. Chaucer seems to have delighted in writing 'many a ympne for Loves halidays' rather than in lauding more serious matters.

[1] See below, p. 33.

[2] A full treatment of the romances will be found in Vol. I, Part II, of this *History*. References to romances composed during the fifteenth century only will be found in Section VII of the Bibliography.

The secular lyric of this century survives in so very fragmentary a fashion that nothing of value can be said about its influence on Chaucer save perhaps this. The quality of the lyrics in the well-known manuscript in the British Museum, Harleian 2253, emboldens us to believe that the writing of lyrics in English was much more common than their scanty survival would suggest. Work such as 'Lenten ys come with loue to toune', or 'Bytuene Mersh and Aueril' is not fashioned in a day, or without some tradition. Chaucer tells us of 'many a song and many a lecherous lay' which he had written in an effort to follow in this tradition, and to extend the art of the lyric in the creation of such exquisite works as his own 'Hyd, Absolon, thy gilte tresses clere . . .'

Allegorical poetry again was much the fashion, and Chaucer found plenty of this in an English as well as in a French dress. His contemporary Gower succumbed to its influence in his *Confessio Amantis*, and Chaucer's other great contemporary, Langland, produced his various versions of *Piers Plowman* at intervals during Chaucer's manhood. Chaucer, like his own parson, was a 'southern man', and perhaps like him he cared little, in general, for the alliterative verse descended from the Anglo-Saxons with its '"rum, ram, ruf" by lettre'. In any case the whole tone and temper of Langland's poem would not have appealed greatly to him. There were poets in England of his time, it is true, who could have shown him how to take the best elements of alliterative poetry and to combine them in a highly polished verse-form, making full use of both alliteration and rhyme, but we have no evidence whatsoever that works such as *Pearl* or *Sir Gawain and the Green Knight* ever came his way, or that he could have coped with their difficult dialectical peculiarities even had they done so.

English poetry then made only a small direct appeal among the many things which helped to shape the poet's mind. Yet there is this to be said. The fourteenth century was clearly not so empty as has often been suggested. While we no longer talk of Chaucer as 'the Father of English poetry', we are often inclined to 'assent with civil leer' to any suggestion that there was little or nothing of value before Chaucer wrote. Sir Arthur Quiller-Couch was even content to dismiss *Piers Plowman* as 'the last dying spasm of Anglo-Saxon literature'. This is to ignore the abundant evidence of a living, healthy tradition of writing in

English, and a large body of verse which was in circulation when Chaucer began to write. While, like Dryden, he may have found poetry 'brick and left it marble', yet the brick was there. Chaucer's lost work, no doubt, would be invaluable in helping us to reconstruct the total story of English poetry in the fourteenth century. Without it, we can only guess at the apprentice work which finally led to the early masterpiece the *Book of the Duchess*. The ability to use English rhythms and English diction with the assurance demonstrated continuously by Chaucer and Gower comes to them in part by virtue of their position in the fourteenth century. They flourished at a moment when much hard pioneer work had been done by innumerable known and unknown writers. The authors of the lyrics of Harley 2253, of *Sir Orfeo*, of *Handlyng Synne*, and of many other poems had already blazed the trail: it was for Chaucer, nourished in other literatures and stimulated by aristocratic demands, to make rapid advances on the road of English poetry.

II

RELIGION

CHAUCER's England was Catholic England, and if we wish to understand much of Chaucer's poetry we must know something of the religious beliefs and observances of his time. The majority of people were believers, for although there may have been many like Chaucer's Doctor, whose 'studie was but litel on the Bible', yet few would have been bold enough to declare themselves non-believers, prepared to die without the fold, and in a more desperate state than were infidels or Jews. The world in which Chaucer grew up accepted the Church and its teaching, and such men as Wyclif, however great their ultimate effect, made but little impression on the vast mass of their contemporaries. To most people attendance at church and dependence on their parish priest were axiomatic, and the size and position of the church building, towering over the villagers' petty houses of daub and wattle, or even the larger structures in the towns, served to emphasize the important central position which the Church held in men's lives. Nor did it rest at this, for everywhere as men went up and down the land there were visible signs of the Church's presence, whether it showed itself in the form of a great abbey, or a wayside cross, a cathedral, or a holy well. Similarly, no one could live a day in Chaucer's England without coming into contact with people whose life was bound up in the service of the needs of the Church, both on its spiritual and temporal sides. The village parson depicted by Chaucer ('a poure persoun of a toun'), the parish clerk such as Absolon, a travelling monk or prioress, a number of one of the orders of Canons (such as overtook the pilgrims near 'Boghtoun under Blee'), a wandering pardoner or a victim-seeking summoner were frequently to be seen, as were great ecclesiastics with their imposing retinues, or humble pilgrims in groups or as individuals moving towards a local shrine, or to one of the great shrines, like that at Walsingham or that of 'the hooly blisful martir' at Canterbury. The Church at that time was the Church Universal, and it is no accident that causes members of the Church to figure so frequently in Chaucer's picture of the 'faire felde ful of folke' which forms the *Prologue* to the *Canterbury Tales*. No writer who wished to give a representative picture of England in the fourteenth or fifteenth centuries could have ignored or despised this portion of his material. Hence, both in the *Prologue*, in the *Canterbury Tales*, and in other of his works, Chaucer constantly refers to the Church, its officers, its doctrines, and its powers.

All of these were more or less well known to most of his contemporaries. Of course the degree of knowledge varied, as did the degree of belief, and it is not easy to give any very clear view of the plain man's religion at this time. Most men, however, being believers, never questioned the state of affairs into which they were born. They believed that the Church was 'the mother of us all', and that her divinely appointed officers were her ministers here on earth. Their business was the interpretation of the teaching of the Bible, the saints, and the Doctors of the Church, and was not to be questioned. Every Christian was expected to know the Apostle's Creed, the Ten Commandments, the *Pater*, and the *Ave*. The Seven Sacraments—Baptism, Confirmation, Penance, Communion, Extreme Unction, Ordination, and Matrimony—the Seven Works of Mercy, the Seven Virtues, and the Seven Deadly Sins were also known to a lesser extent, and were brought home to the faithful by a variety of homilies, explanations, stories (*exempla*), and more formal instruction. All this may seem a formidable burden for the ordinary man. It was made more bearable by the practical and definite advice that the Church gave on all these matters. The sacrament of matrimony, for example, was not only explained, but the evils of child-marriage, of 'weddyng withoute frendship', of illegitimate unions without the sanction of the Church, and many other cases were discussed, and advice was clearly given on how a Christian should act.

To enable him to act rightly emphasis was placed on the value of prayer. Both the mystics and the ordinary clergy were alike insistent on the necessity, the comfort, and the spiritual aid given by prayer: prayer, the mystics taught, was not merely a means of asking for God's help, but was in itself a spiritual grace. To the ordinary man it was constantly his way of asking for a solution of practical problems by Divine aid. It was not only Piers Plowman who sought 'to percen with a paternoster the paleys of heuene'. Armed with this knowledge, fortified by the sacraments of the Church, and at one with almost the whole of his fellows in his attitude and belief, the medieval Christian could face the Devil and all his works that were everywhere about him. Erroneous doctrine, although mercilessly suppressed, raised its head from time to time, and often tempted men into wrongdoing. The border-line between religion and superstition was narrow and ill defined, and an ignorant man required guidance lest he should believe that Easter or Whitsun Eve were unlucky days for Baptism, or that Masses were of no avail except on feast-days and the two days following. On the other hand, the Church allowed much that was superstitious to circulate if it tended to promote the interests of religion. Hence the many stories glorifying the sacrament, or lauding the Blessed Virgin and the saints, to be found in collections of the fourteenth and fifteenth centuries. These give us valuable insight into the beliefs of the time, and Chaucer makes magnificent use of one such story in the Prioress's Tale.

While the ordinary man was content to serve God much in the same degree as did his fellows, a minority were touched to finer issues. Some, having a vocation, became monks, friars, or members of religious orders; others became secular clergy, such as parish priests, vicars, rectors, and so on. Something more will be said of them later. In addition, there were those in whom religion was so strong that it was forced to find expression in action and in doctrine. Wyclif is the outstanding example of a man whose zeal for what he believed to be the Truth was expressed in a great many writings in Latin and in English, in his preaching order of 'poore prestis', and in his vernacular versions of the Scripture. 'To be ignorant of the Bible, is to be ignorant of Christ.' This challenging statement came a hundred years too early to be acceptable to authority, but once made, it met with an eager response from those who were able to come by any of the Wyclif translations, and throughout the fifteenth century the 'pestiferous virus' of his teaching was at work, although most of its active exponents had been exterminated or driven underground. While Wyclif was writing, many other indications of the spiritual ferment that marked the second half of the fourteenth century were apparent. A number of mystics, of whom Rolle is the best known, were pouring out treatise after treatise. Rolle died in 1349, but the nature of his writings, with their deep devotion and overwhelming love of God, inspired his followers, and a great many treatises by Hilton,

Nassyngton, Juliana of Norwich, and others testify to the strength of religious feeling and passion felt by them. Strong religious feeling also produced Langland's allegorical poem entitled *Piers Plowman.* It is not an easy poem to understand or to describe briefly, for Langland was careless of poetic art, and careful only to put into the most forceful of words the many ideas that a deep knowledge of the England of his day had impressed upon him. He is satirist, critic, reformer, moralist, and many other things, but all are directed to the creating of a new state of affairs in the realm so that Righteousness and Truth shall prevail. Langland sees no easy solution to this problem; throughout his poem man's pilgrimage is shown to be a hard one, but Grace, Mercy, and Truth are never far away, and the Christian ideals support and encourage him in his quest. A deeply felt conviction underlies the poet's message, and gives power to the wealth of argument, illustration, anecdote, allegory, and realism by which it is conveyed. Langland uses every means in his power, not as a result of conscious art, but as part of his overwhelming anxiety to convince his countrymen of what must be done if England is to be a Christian country.[1]

To be in touch with these great spirits of the age is to see what religion could and did mean to some, gifted enough to express the vision and their hopes, The majority, however, lacked such powers, although the Faith was quick within them. It was the inseparable background of their thoughts, just as the village or town church was the inseparable background where the great events of life—baptism, marriage, burial—were enacted. To the Church they turned for guidance, comfort, and assistance in every crisis, and we can scarcely over-estimate the steady, unquestioning nature with which they accepted the religious *status quo.* Always in our attempts to re-create the world of Chaucer we must remember the great body of the faithful, who have left no record of their unswerving devotion to their parish church and the religion of their fathers.

Having said this, however, we must also recall that as we look back on this period we can see much that was hidden to the humble villager, or even to the most learned or well-informed churchman. The second half of the fourteenth and fifteenth centuries in England were not great ages of widespread religious prosperity; but the cries of Langland and Wyclif were

[1] For full treatment of the mystics and Langland, see Vol. I, Part II.

caught up by many voices as the fifteenth century ran its course. Archbishop Arundel might invoke the temporal arm with its statute *De Heretico Comburendo*, and the Church might disinter the bones of Wyclif, and cast them into the river Swift, but things were moving towards the day of the Reformation in England. The Faith remained, but its institutions needed reform: the faithful remained, but subject to heavy burdens and to superstitious encumbrances which wearied and depressed even the bravest.

With these things in mind we may turn to consider how this deep-seated belief in Holy Church, its ministers and its teaching, was kept alive in Chaucer's day and after, and in what ways they were being questioned. First, the focus of religious life was the church building. Prayers were said at home, and simple explanations made by parent to child, but it was to the church itself that people went for worship, instruction, and consolation. The Wife of Bath tells of her constant attendance at church for preaching, or marriages, or other services, just as the Host speaks of his wife's behaviour if any pressed before her to kiss the pax at the end of the service. The wives of the citizens naturally go to church on the vigil of a saint's day, and the Pardoner sees Thomas's wife there among many others when he preaches after Mass. Langland sums up the matter in his lines:

And up-on Sonedayes to cesse[1] · godes servyce to huyre,[2]
Bothe matyns and messe · and, after mete, in churches
To huyre[2] here evesong · every man ouhte.
Thus it by-longeth for lorde · for lered, and lewede,[3]
Eche haly day to huyre · hollyche the service,
Vigiles and fastyngdayes · forthere-more to knowe,
And fulfille the fastynges · bote infirmite hit made,
Poverte other[4] othere penaunces · as pilgrymages and travayles.

While this may be a counsel of perfection, it is valuable as an indication of the central position held by the church services and the part they were expected to play in men's lives.

Since the medieval service was in Latin, however, not one per cent. of any ordinary congregation could have followed what the priest was saying. The books of devotion of those times could only encourage the faithful to repeat their *Aves* and *Paters* over and over again, while 'the blessed mutter of the Mass' went on at the altar. They joined in the few prayers

[1] cesse, 'cease' [from labour].
[2] huyre, 'hear'.
[3] lewede, 'ignorant'.
[4] other, 'or'.

when they heard the priest intone them, but otherwise were left to make what they could of what was going on. The Church had tried its utmost to help them in this, and in every part of the Mass 'every faculty of man, every property of nature had been captured and subdued for that supreme drama of worship. Music and silence, colour and distance, light and darkness, imagery and gesture, all contributed to the final result. All helped to make real the unseen things that are eternal. Earth was crammed with heaven, and every common bush afire with God.' Besides this they gained something from the wall-paintings which adorned most churches. Here, often in crude colour and with cruder realism, events of biblical history were portrayed. The Last Judgement as it was displayed above the rood-screen, or pictures of the Crucifixion, or some event in the life of the patron saint helped to quicken their imaginations and to convince them of that world to come for which their parson was ever preparing them—a world of which so little was known and from which so much was hoped.

In the greater churches, in addition to the wall-paintings, there was the richly coloured glass, with its portraits and stories to be gazed at and pondered upon. Little was probably learnt from this: the cost of such glass made it rare for any quantity of it to be provided in all but the greatest of churches, and even there it required some knowledge of the Scriptures to interpret it. Thus, in the fifteenth-century *Tale of Beryn* (a continuation of the *Canterbury Tales*) while the Knight and others press forward to the holy shrine:

The Pardoner and the Miller, and other lewde sotes,[1]
Sought hem selfen in the Chirch, right as lewde gotes;
Pyrid fast, and pourid,[2] highe oppon the glase,
Counterfeting gentilmen, the armys for to blase,
Diskyveryng fast the peyntour, and for the story mourned,
And a red it also right as nolde Rammys hornyd:[3]
'He berith a balstaff',[4] quod the toon, 'and els a rakis ende'.
'Thow faillist', quod the Miller, 'thowe has nat wel thy mynde;
It is a spere yf thowe canst se, right with a prik to-fore
To bussh[5] adown his enmy, and thurh the Sholdir bore.'
'Pese!' quod the hoost of Southwork, 'let stond the wyndow glasid!
Goith up, and doith yeur offerynge! yee semeth half amasid!'

[1] lewde sotes, 'ignorant fools'. [2] pyrid faste, and pourid, 'gazed intently'.
[3] also right as nolde Rammys hornyd, 'as accurately as would have old horned rams'. [4] balstaff, 'quarter-staff'. [5] bussh, 'push'.

Nothing could more clearly show the limited nature of what the ordinary man could get from gazing at the great windows of coloured glass. 'The poor man's service book', as they have been called, was almost as hard to read as was its humbler brother written down on vellum—and infinitely more restricted in its variety and information.

For most people, therefore, until reading became a popular accomplishment, religion had to come from such limited means as these, with the all-important aid that came from teaching and preaching. For when all is said, by far the simplest and most efficacious method of inculcating the Christian faith was by direct teaching from the clergy. The parish priest was the mainspring of the ordinary man's religious education, and Chaucer expresses the implications of this clearly in one line—'if gold ruste, what shal iren do?' Hence the emphasis in Chaucer's century, and the fifteenth century, on the spiritual health or lack of health of the clergy, and of the parish priests. Chaucer's celebrated portrait, as has often been said, draws attention not only to his 'poor parson's' good qualities, but also to much about him that contrasts violently with the behaviour of many of his colleagues. The bad example set by many of the clergy constantly outrages a reformer such as Wyclif who speaks of clerics who

> sclaundren the peple bi ensaumple of ydelnesse and wanntonnesse; for comynly thei couchen in softe beddis whanne othere men risen to ther labour and blabren out matyns and masse as hunteris, withouten devocion and contemplacion; and hien faste to mete richely and costly arrayed of the beste, and than to slepe. And soone a-noon to tablis,[1] and chees, and taverne . . . and than speken of lecherie, of depravynge of goode men, that wolen not sue their companye . . . and by these prestis and their wanntonnesse moche peple is brought to lecherie, glotonye, ydelnesse and thefte.

Langland's well-known picture of Sloth the Parson, who had been 'prest and person passyng therty wintere', and who confessed that he could not chant, sing, or read the life of any saint, and preferred the task of finding a hare in a large field to that of construing one clause of the psalm *Beatus vir* or *Beati omnes* is only the best known of his continuous attacks on clerical ignorance and indifference. He condemns priests who wear rich garments unsuitable to their calling, or those 'prechers

[1] tablis, 'backgammon'.

after selver' who refuse the sacraments unless money is forthcoming. Some 'soffren men do sacrifice and worshepen maumettes',[1] others seek chantries in London 'for selver ys swete', while others can say

> I counte namore Conscience · bi so I cacche sylver,[2]
> Than I do to drynke · a draughte of good ale.

Well might men echo Archbishop Peckham's cry of a century earlier than these reformers—'The ignorance of the priests casteth the people into the ditch of error; and the folly or unlearning of the clergy, who are bidden to instruct the faithful in the Catholic faith, sometimes tendeth to error rather than to sound doctrine.'

We must not weight the scales too heavily against the parish priests (Chaucer's one superb portrait should keep us from this), but we cannot ignore the profound effect the failings of priests had on the spiritual health of their flocks. 'As is the shepherd, so are the sheep', and the pages of Chaucer, Gower, and Langland, together with many satirical poems of the fourteenth century, are full of passages that reflect the many abuses of their time. Nor were things better in the succeeding century, and ecclesiastical commentators such as Gascoigne, Chancellor of the University of Oxford, are eloquent in their exposure of the evils of their day.

It was from these priests, good or bad, that the ordinary man obtained most of his instruction in the Faith. Many of them, devout of life and prodigal in good works as they were, could do little more than teach their flocks by good example. They were enjoined to preach at least four sermons a year, and these and simple homilies and explanations of the rudiments of the Faith were as much as they could be expected to give. To help these simple pastors, guides and books of sermons were available. The outlines of the Faith as stated by Archbishop Peckham were in due time translated into English for the benefit of priests who had no Latin. 'Dan Gaytrige's sermon', as the translation was called, was but an early example of clerical manuals, and a work like the *Regimen Animarum* furnished the parson with a very complete vade-mecum based upon ecclesiastical pronouncements. Mirk's *Instructions for Parish Priests* gave

[1] maumettes, 'idols'.

[2] bi so I cacche sylver, 'so long as I receive payment'.

a vernacular translation of part of this, while the same author's *Festial*, or the series of homilies known as *Jacob's Well*, were available for those priests who could come by them.

No one since the production of Dr. Owst's two learned volumes on medieval preaching and preachers will be inclined to underrate the importance of the medieval sermon, and Chaucer makes considerable use of sermon technique or materials. The whole conduct of the *Pardoner's Tale*, with its series of illustrative references from history, sacred and profane, and its superb *exemplum* of the three revellers who found death on a heap of gold, is derived from pulpit practice of the time, and something of the same method is followed (and ridiculed) in the *Nun's Priest's Tale*. Again, the *Wife of Bath's Prologue* owes a great debt for much of its subject-matter to the pulpit. More important still is Chaucer's insistence on the part played by preachers and preaching in the ordinary man's life. He shows us how the Pardoner prepares to preach, and of the methods he uses:

> I stonde lyk a clerk in my pulpet,
> And whan the lewed peple is doun yset,
> I preche so as ye han herd bifoore,
> And telle an hundred false japes moore.
> Thanne peyne I me to strecche forth the nekke,
> And est and west upon the peple I bekke,[1]
> As dooth a dowve sittynge on a berne.[2]
> Myn handes and my tonge goon so yerne[3]
> That it is joye to se my bisynesse.

He notes how the friars used the Lenten season to exhort the audiences to repentance by their violent preachings ('But precheth not as freres doon in Lente, To make us for olde sinnes wepe'); and how they can persuade folk to give to their Order:

> And specially, aboven every thing,
> Excited he the peple in his preching,
> To trentals,[4] and to yeve, for Goddes sake,
> Wher-with men mighten hooly houses make.

They tell of the pains of hell, and how

> Ful hard it is with flessh-hook or with oules[5]
> To been y-clawed, or to brenne or bake.

[1] bekke, 'nod'. [2] berne, 'barn'. [3] yerne, 'eagerly, actively'.
[4] trentals, 'series of 30 masses for the dead'.
[5] oules, 'spiked irons for tormenting men'.

Chaucer was wise in placing these and many more passages in his picture of English life, for all contemporary writers bear witness to the importance of the sermon, and to its use and abuse by the various types of preacher. Some of these, as Wyclif says, 'in her prechinge fordon[1] prechinge of Crist, and prechen lesyngus[2] and japes plesynge to the peple'; or as Langland protests, 'prechinge the peple for profyt of heore wombes,[3] Glosynge the gospel as hem good liketh'; or as Chaucer's other contemporary Hoccleve complains:

> The oynement of holy sermonynge
> Hym loth is upon hem for to despende;
> Som person is so threde-bare of konnynge[4]
> That he can noght, thogh he hym wys pretende,
> And he that can, may not his herte bende
> Therto, but from his cure he hym absentith.

These few examples, and the remembrance of the 'povre persoun' ('That Cristes gospel trewely wolde preche; His parisshens devoutly wolde he teche'), must suffice to remind us how universal and lively a topic of conversation and comment the medieval sermon and preacher provided.

The lives of many of these preachers, as we have already seen, did not escape without comment, not only by reformers such as Wyclif and Langland, but also by the anonymous satirists, who wrote the *Complaint of the Ploughman*, or the *Song Against the Friars*, or *Jack Upland*,[5] and many other poems. Chaucer, in accordance with his tolerant view of the world about him, does not hit out so fiercely, but his pages contain many a shrewd blow, which his contemporaries would have relished, and so shall we, if only we take the trouble to understand the religious conditions of the times. 'Freres and feendes ben but lyte asonder', says Chaucer, and the judgement implicit in this line is the judgement of Wyclif, Langland, and the satirists. But where Langland uses the cudgel, Chaucer prefers the rapier. If we read any of Langland's vehement outbursts against the friars, and then turn to such a passage as the opening lines of the *Wife of Bath's Tale*, we cannot fail to note how the urbane ironic thrusts of Chaucer are more deadly than the

[1] fordon, 'forsake'.
[2] lesyngus, 'lies'.
[3] heore wombes, 'their bellies'.
[4] konnynge, 'understanding'.
[5] See below, p. 155.

blows of Langland, despite the hurly-burly of words which accompany the latter's efforts. The description of the Pardoner in the *Prologue* ('perhaps the one lost soul on the pilgrimage', as Professor Kittredge terms him), the boastful account he gives of his own tricks and devices in the prologue to his tale, and his final barefaced attempt to thrust his self-discredited relics on the pilgrims are a continuous commentary on one of the religious scandals of Chaucer's day. What Chaucer says in the fourteenth century is said more plainly by the fifteenth-century Chancellor of Oxford who wrote: 'Sinners say nowadays, "I care not how many or what evils I do in God's sight, for I can easily and quickly get plenary absolution and indulgence granted me by the Pope, whose written grant I have bought for 4d or 6d or have won as a stake for a game of tennis [with the pardoner].' An understanding of such matters as the theory of indulgences, the doctrine of the Treasury of Merits, and the powers of the Pardoner conferred on him by Pope or bishop is essential to our full appreciation of Chaucer and his contemporaries.

The use of the word 'essential' may be questioned, but it is true to say that the more complete our knowledge of Chaucer's times can be made, the more clearly we discern his whole purpose. It cannot be too often stated that his writings were primarily for an educated and sophisticated audience, quick to take an allusion and well aware of the state of affairs which existed in political, social, or religious life. The way in which Chaucer develops the characters of the Prioress, the Monk, or the Friar illustrates the point very clearly. What Chaucer was doing in his sketch of the Prioress has been discussed by many critics, who are in general agreement that the subtle ironical nature of his portrait shows 'the delightfully imperfect submergence of the woman in the nun'. The Monk is also depicted as something of a worldling. Chaucer notes his many horses, his bridle which jingles gaily in the whistling wind, as clear and loud as does the bell of his chapel. He owned swift greyhounds, wore supple boots and rode on a brown palfrey, and loved the chase of the hare above all field sports. At home he loved best of all a fat swan, and as a result of his continuous feasting was very fat, with bulging eyes which gleamed like the furnace under a cauldron. In addition he was well dressed, with expensive fur at his wrists, and a gold pin to fasten his hood with a love-knot at one end of it. Who could recognize in such a man the monk sworn to the *tria substantialia* of Obedience, Poverty, Celibacy with the accompanying reinforcements of labour, claustration, and a quasi-vegetarian diet? As they heard Chaucer's description, many of the audience must have recalled monks of a like nature whom they saw riding about in their country-side, and who also held the text 'A monk out of his cloister dies spiritually, like a fish out of water' not to be worth a straw. Some of the audience, indeed, must have known either in detail or in general terms the attitude of the ecclesiastical authorities to such behaviour. Councils had inveighed against it: claustration was commanded, fur was prohibited, gold ornaments were strictly forbidden, the pleasures of the table were anathema—many knew all this, and how constantly the Church campaigned against such worldlings as the Monk; and some knew of the visitations of bishops to monastery and nunnery, and of their attempts to stamp out all kinds of behaviour and of living which departed from the strict Rule. Such a man as William of Wykeham, whom Richard II made Chancellor in 1389 and who was therefore in close attendance at court, had met men like the Monk during his visitations of his diocese as Bishop of Winchester. Within a year of the time that Chaucer was writing the *Prologue*, Wykeham visited the priory of Selborne, and there he found a state of affairs almost identical with that which must have existed in the monastery which from time to time housed Chaucer's Monk. As a result of his visitation, Wykeham deplores the custom of some of the inmates who absent themselves from their cloister, or ride to their farms and manor, under pretence of inspecting them, and stay away as long as they please. The bishop finds many of them to be hunters and sportsmen, keeping hounds and attending hunting matches, while some are reprimanded for the fine quality of their hose and shoes, for wearing garments edged with costly furs, for lack of due attendance at the canonical services, and for indulging in frivolous conversation. Injunctions such as these, or the mass of evidence presented in Bishop Alnwick's visitation of his diocese of Lincoln in the first half of the fifteenth century, are the raw materials, so to speak, used by Chaucer to create his portrait. It had little or nothing that was imaginary in it: on the contrary, as his audience knew, it was all too true, and the writings of men such as Wyclif, Gower, or Langland only afford additional evidence of the widespread knowledge of monastic decay. Thus Langland can write:

> Ac[1] now is Religioun a ryder · a rowmer bi stretes,
> A leder of louedayes[2] · and a lande-bugger,[3]
> A priker on a palfray · fro manere to manere,[4]
> An heep of houndes at his ers · as he a lorde were.
> And but if[5] his knave knele · that shal his cuppe brynge,
> He loureth on hym and axeth hym · who taughte hym curteisye?

and Wyclif argues that 'four or five needy men might well be clothed with one cope and hood of a monk, and that large cloth serveth to gird wind and prevent him to go and do his deeds'. He denounces the 'possessioners', as he calls them, and says (with considerable exaggeration) that the whole population of England could be maintained out of their income, which instead they wasted on gluttony, gay clothes, hawks, and minstrels.

> Wyclif's invective spared none [writes Dr Workman]; he discriminated between the [religious] orders only to condemn them more effectively. Monks with their 'red and fat cheeks and great bellies', who 'do not the office of curates, neither in teaching nor preaching nor giving of sacraments, but set an idiot for vicar', are but squanderers of national wealth better bestowed on the poor. 'Instead of desert places they have chosen cities', where they live 'a lustful life to feed the flesh', and 'eat up what would keep many families'.

Writings such as these, or Gower's diatribes in the *Miroir de l'Omme*, or the *Vox Clamantis*, which he says are the opinions of all Christian folk, since 'it is the voice of the people which dictates these words of mine', are perhaps sufficient to suggest the background against which the poet's creations must be viewed.

But whatever were the failings of the monks, the friars far outstripped them in winning opprobrium and derision for their orders. 'Ravishing wolves', and 'members of the devil', Wyclif terms them, while a popular proverb ran, 'This is a friar and therefore a liar'. Langland's hostility to them was constantly expressed in unmeasured language. Their greed for wealth, their unscrupulous practices, their indulgence in the pleasures of fine living and fine clothing, their easy penances are all

[1] Ac, 'but'.
[2] louedayes, 'days for settling disputes by arbitration'.
[3] lande-bugger, 'land-buyer'.
[4] manere, 'manor'.
[5] but if, 'unless'.

continuously in his mind. Collectively and individually he has nothing but contempt for the

> freres alle the foure ordres,
> Preched the peple · for profit of hem-selven,
> Glosed the gospel · as hem good lyked,
> For coveitise of copis[1] · construed it as thei wolde.

He gives us pictures such as that of the friar in Beton's tavern, or of the friar who was a Doctor of Divinity, and who after preaching on continence, made his way through the crowd of pilgrims and beggars to sit down at the chief table and astonish everyone by his trencher-work.

Chaucer accepts this view, characteristically minimizing its more repulsive elements, but nevertheless allowing the full weakness of the type to be apparent. Both in the *Prologue* and in the *Summoner's Tale* he reveals point after point which made the friars a byword in his time. To take one example only—that of confession. Everyone knew how necessary it was: to die unshriven was to die damned:

> But and[2] thei dye a sodeyne dethe
> With-outen shrefte or penaunce,
> To helle they gone withouten lese[3]
> For they can chese none other chaunse.

Everyone also knew that his parish priest was always there, and ready to hear the confessions of his parishioners. He knew their personal history and their difficulties in a way that no one else could know them. At the same time, these very things were the greatest obstacles to some penitents, who preferred to speak with a stranger. Now when this stranger was such a one as Chaucer's Friar, who 'was an esy man to yeve penaunce', since 'Ful swetely herde he confessioun, And plesaunt was his absolucioun', and when in addition he had power of confession greater than that of the parish priest, what wonder if men ran to him on his advent to the village, and left their own parson deserted? If the parish priest was prone to curse offenders (as popular opinion believed he was), then the friar was only too ready to make up for this by his leniency, and 'in stede of wepynge and preyeres, Men moote yeve silver to the povre freres'. In Wyclif's words, 'any cursed swearer, extortioner, or adulterer will not be shriven by his own curate but go to a flattering friar that will

[1] copis (copes). [2] and, 'if'. [3] withouten lese, 'without lying, truly'.

assoil him falsely for a little money by the year, though he be not in will to make restitution, or to leave his cursed sin'. A full appreciation of all these points is clearly in Chaucer's mind, and he draws his portraits accordingly.

These are the lines on which we must proceed if we wish to comprehend Chaucer's purpose, and to estimate his success as an artist or as a moralist. A careful reading of almost any of his *Canterbury Tales* will reveal the wealth of observation and criticism they contain of religious theory and practice in his day. Often Chaucer merely mentions some matter in passing, and assumes everyone's understanding: the names of the various services, compline, trentals, vigils; the payments such as God's halfpenny, or mass penny; ceremonies such as processions or kissing the pax. At other times he is simply giving a straightforward statement of current custom: the celebration of marriage *ante ostium ecclesiae* ('housbondes at chirche dore she hadde fyve'); the allocation of a certain area to an individual friar ('Noon of his brethren cam ther in his haunt'); the practice of collecting tithes and of cursing defaulters ('Ful looth were hym to cursen for his tithes'). Often, however, they are more than this, and contain within themselves a criticism of the person or institution. Thus when Chaucer writes of the Prioress, 'But sikerly she had a fair forheed', he not only draws attention to the lady's beauty, but also reminds us that as a religious her forehead should not have been thus visible. Such nakedness was fashionable and might pass among the worldly, but in a nun! So again when he tells us that the merchant's 'cousin', Dan John, came to the house bearing with him a jug of malmsey and another of red wine, the material conditions under which monks lived (despite their Rule) are quietly suggested, just as the moral conditions of some parishes are indicated by the behaviour of Absolon, or the Wife of Bath; or the frequent contemporary evasion of canonical law is hinted at in the line, 'The person of the toun hir fader was'.

In spite of many references to its failings, Chaucer accepted the religion of his day, without question, as far as we can tell, and therefore felt little difficulty in exposing its weaknesses and the fallibility of its institutions and officers. Perhaps, like Wordsworth, he believed that in religion as in nature there is

> Central peace subsisting at the heart
> Of endless agitation.

On one religious matter there was certainly 'endless agitation'. From the earliest times the problem of determinism and of man's free will had occupied theologians, and the question was very much alive in Chaucer's time, for, while he was a youth, Bishop Bradwardine in his *De Causa Dei* had stirred the troubled waters afresh. In the *Nun's Priest's Tale*, and in the revised version of *Troilus and Criseyde*, Chaucer shows his interest in the matter, although he characteristically shrugs his shoulders and declares that he must leave it to schoolmen 'to bulte it to the bren'.[1] Here he was wise, for the finest minds had found it difficult to reconcile God's foreknowledge of events with man's free exercise of his will. 'What free will had man?' it was asked, as people viewed the disastrous effects of plague and war, which the Church frequently declared to 'falle by the ordenaunce of God for mannys synne or for to shewe his might and his worshippe'. Yet that man had such free will and was responsible for his actions was firmly held by most churchmen. 'Because God foreknows what will come to pass', they said, 'it does not follow that he wills it to be so. It is true that if God foreknows that a man will do a certain thing, e.g. go for a walk, he will inevitably do so, but the decision to go for a walk is man's and man's alone.' This was called 'conditional necessity', and was in no way constrained by God's foreknowledge. 'Simple necessity', on the other hand, dealt with unavoidable things, i.e. the rising and setting of the sun, and came about as part of the general plan of the Universe.

These subtle arguments were not easily apprehended, but had a similar attraction for thoughtful men to those raised in our own day by relativity or dialectical materialism. Few are fitted to understand these things, but that does not preclude many from trying. Chaucer and his contemporaries exercised their minds on this baffling problem as part of their attempt to understand the ways of God and the place of man in the scheme of things. Few men who considered this problem seriously were unaware of its treatment in one of the great books of the Middle Ages, the *De Consolatione Philosophiae* of Boethius. Chaucer was immensely influenced by it. He translated the whole of it into prose, and constantly made use of its ideas. The doctrine of *gentilesse*, the nature of chance, the problem of free will are all dealt with by Boethius and helped to form Chaucer's thought

[1] to bulte it to the bren, 'to sift the corn from the husks, i.e. get at the truth'.

on these matters, and to guide him in some of the deepest passages of the *Knight's Tale* and *Troilus and Criseyde*. The *Consolatio* with its nobility and serenity of outlook made a great impression on the men of the Middle Ages. In its pages they found a refuge from the tempestuous, troubled world about them. Boethius taught them how to bear the strokes of Fortune, to realize how unstable she was, and how to seek a happiness independent of her. The supreme Good is shown not to reside in wealth, official dignity, power, or pleasure, but only in God, the supreme and all-inclusive good. Despite outward appearances, Boethius insists that it is only the good who really achieve their ends, and 'just as righteousness is the reward of the righteous, so is wickedness the reward of the wicked'. Further, men have it in their own hands to make their own fortunes, for good or ill, for all beings are endowed with reason and have the power of choice. God's foreknowledge of what will happen does not preclude this.

The teaching of Boethius supplemented the teaching of the Church and gave men something to hold fast to in the midst of a difficult, turbulent, changing world. True happiness (*felicitee*) was shown to come from within: despite the misery inflicted by tyrants, or the worst that malice and injustice could inflict, happiness was still to be won only by self-mastery and a recognition that things of the spirit were always available to those worthy and ready to receive them.

> That thee is sent, receyve in buxumnesse,[1]
> The wrastlyng for this world axeth a fal.
> Her is non hoom, her nis but wildernesse:
> Forth, pilgrim, forth! Forth, beste, out of thy stal!
> Know thy contree, look up, thank God of al;
> Hold the heye wey, and lat thy gost[2] thee lede;
> And trouthe thee shal delivere, it is no drede.[3]

[1] in buxumnesse, 'submissively'. [2] gost, 'spirit'.
[3] it is no drede, 'without doubt'.

III
CHAUCER
I

GEOFFREY CHAUCER was a product of that fourteenth-century world of affairs which produced such a wealth of good business men throughout this and the next century. The East Anglian counties were their headquarters, and the Chaucer family first come before our notice as vintners living in Ipswich. There the poet's grandfather, Robert Chaucer, his step-grandfather, Richard, and his father, John, were all vintners—that is wine-merchants—on a considerable scale. The evidence available all goes to show that they were a flourishing family with substantial wealth and property, and had by marriage acquired further property in London. Indeed, Chaucer's father, John, was evidently an important person in the civic life of London, for his name frequently occurs in the city documents and he was also an officer of the customs (as his father and stepfather before him) charged with the office of collecting the duty on wines at various south coast ports.

Into such a family Chaucer was born. We do not know the exact place or date of his birth. The assertion that he was born in London in 1340 seems to be based only on the fact that his parents had property in London (as well as in Ipswich), and that at the Scrope-Grosvenor trial in 1386 Chaucer testified that he was then 'forty years old and more' (*et plus*)—a vague statement which leaves it possible that he was born at any time between 1340 and 1345.

More important is the consideration of what it meant to the growing boy to be the son of John Chaucer, the vintner, in the reign of Edward III. Another vintner's son, John Ruskin, has told us in *Praeterita* what such a background meant to a youthful Victorian. He makes us realize the immense part played in his life as a boy by the French and Spanish connexions of his father's firm, and how deeply they influenced him. So too, we may imagine, with Chaucer. The daily life of the busy wharf was no mystery to him. There he saw at intervals the ships come to port, bringing the hogsheads from Guienne, or 'the wyn of Spaigne that crepeth subtilly', or 'whyte wyn of Oseye and red wyn of Gascoigne, of the Ryne and of the Rochel'. As all these cargoes were landed, tallied for, and stored away in the cellars, Geoffrey had abundant opportunities to watch these men from overseas and to listen to their strange talk and stranger ideas. Even if at this time his fluency in the French tongue was small, yet he was certainly absorbing much which, but for the happy accident of his father's calling, would have been denied him. We have only to recall the restricted possibilities which were all that Langland or Lydgate had to see what this meant. Langland, for example, found much material in the 'fair field full of folk' as he went about England, but it was material which he could shape only in a certain way—a way determined by his own limited education and opportunities, which had left him very insular in many ways. The very form of his verse—descended from the old Anglo-Saxon alliterative measure—or his reliance on a comparatively limited range of reading, or his violent, passionate attitude at times all stand in sharp contrast to Chaucer's eager metrical experimentation, his considerable learning, and his wide, tolerant outlook. The urbanity of one, favoured by fortune, who had 'seen many men and many cities' is the more striking when placed in juxtaposition with the *saeva indignatio* which so often overwhelms his contemporary who had spent all his life at the miserable business of a hireling mass-priest, 'singing for simony, for silver is sweet'. Chaucer's poise comes in part from the wider outlook which was his from those early days upon his father's wharf.

Not that we need imagine that such a position put Chaucer in any completely care-free class. No such class existed at that time—if ever. The Chaucer family had had some experience of the violence inseparable from medieval life. Chaucer's father as a boy of twelve had been kidnapped by some of his relatives in order to marry him to one of their daughters for the sake of his property. Again, only a few years before Chaucer's birth, his great-uncle was killed in an affray which arose between him and a neighbour with whom he quarrelled in the high street after dinner. The neighbour's son, observing the quarrel, 'took up a door-bar, without the consent of his father, and struck Simon Chaucer on the head, and on the left hand and side', and of these blows Simon died. Prosperous and well-to-do though the Chaucer family certainly were, we may remember these two incidents (together with certain adventures which befell Chaucer himself) when we are inclined to over-estimate the 'bourgeois respectability' of Chaucer's youth and up-bringing.

Of his more formal education during these years nothing is known. There were three schools available to him, all very near his Thames Street home, but there is no evidence that he went to any one of them. Professor Rickert has shown that the list of books left in 1358 by a schoolmaster of St. Paul's Almonry School for the use of the scholars 'parallels to an extraordinary degree the hypothetical list of those which Chaucer, from internal evidence, seems to have read in his youth'. But, as Professor Rickert warns us, this is no more than 'a pleasing possibility'.

We shall probably do better to remind ourselves that throughout this early period of Chaucer's life London was his school—or rather was many schools to him. As Professor Lowes puts it, 'Chaucer's London was his own vast House of Rumour—a house "ful of shipmen and pilgrimes, With scrippes bret-ful of lesinges, Entremedled with tydinges".' Here he was in constant touch with life from overseas, and especially with the highly cultured south of France. Cosmopolitan ideas, and men holding such ideas, were part of his daily life, and it was among such people and such opportunities that Chaucer grew to early manhood.

In April 1357, however, we find Chaucer moving in a very different world. The merchant's son appears with others among the recipients of rewards from Elizabeth of Ulster, wife of Lionel, son of Edward III. Chaucer was evidently a page in her service, and from time to time received gifts of clothing or money 'for necessaries'. The account book which records these payments also shows that Elizabeth took part in such great ceremonies as the Garter Feast on St. George's Day, 1358, or visited the Dowager Queen Isabella, or the Queen of Scotland in the same year, while in 1359 she was at the wedding of John of Gaunt and Blanche of Lancaster. Events and society such as he encountered in the train of Elizabeth gave the youthful Chaucer much to observe and to reflect upon. The service of ladies and the elaborate ceremonial of the royal circle called for qualities only partly exercised in Thames Street. Those duties of hall and bower described in an earlier chapter now became part of his everyday life. His education was further advanced when in the autumn of 1359 he was part of Edward's invading army in France. Here he distinguished himself no better than by being taken prisoner, for he was captured in a skirmish near Rheims. The king and others ransomed him in 1360, the king contributing £16 towards the sum, and he returned to England with the royal party in May of that year. The same autumn he was again in France, and then after this brief view of his activities our information once more ceases and we hear no more of him till 1367. But these glimpses are sufficient to enable us to see how wide and rich an experience went to the making of the poet.

The years between 1360 and 1367 are Chaucer's 'lost years' and remain unexplained. Some think he stayed with Lionel and his wife, and point out that Lionel's tour of duty as the King's Lieutenant in Ireland very nearly coincides with this period. Others imagine him in the service of John of Gaunt, while more recently Professor Manly has revived an old tradition which saw Chaucer as a member of one of the Inns of Court. No contemporary records now remain to prove this, but there is some supporting evidence. Students of the Inns of Court at that time were not all necessarily in training for the law. As Chief Justice Fortescue pointed out a few years after Chaucer's death, the inns were a place of study for those who hoped to be administrators of lands, officials, diplomatists, and the like. Chaucer's Manciple had a heap of such learned men in his Temple, few of whom seem to have been destined for the law. A course of study at the Temple would be a fitting prelude to the career which lay before him, and would fill in the vacant years very well.

We are on firm ground once more in June 1367, when Chaucer received a pension as a yeoman or groom in the king's household, and a little later he is described as *dilectus vallectus noster*. A recently discovered document shows that he was sent abroad on an unknown mission in July 1368—the earliest so far as is known at present of many missions he was to undertake for his royal master. A little earlier the poet was married to Philippa, sister to Katherine Swynford, sometime wife to John of Gaunt. Philippa was in the queen's service, and both she and Geoffrey were among the mourners at various royal funerals. Of their married life, or any personal details about Philippa, we know nothing.

The details we have so far been able to give of Chaucer's life would be of little importance were it not that they are the abstracts of his time and experience. The vintner's son would not have written the poems he did had it not been for the variety of experience which his life so far had given him. True that by 1370 he had by no means mastered his experience: much of it was as yet fresh and unassimilated, but at the same time his daily life for some ten or fifteen years past had directly turned his thoughts and energies towards the creation of English poetry of a courtly kind. When towards his end Chaucer asks forgiveness for 'many a song and many a lecherous lay', and for worldly vanities 'that sownen into[1] synne', he is in part thinking of the products of his pen (mostly lost to us) which belong to these early years. For in these apprentice years he had learnt, as his own squire had done, how to compose both words and music of his songs, and also how to sing them so as to win the favour of the ladies. It was probably during this apprentice period that Chaucer was interested in translating the *Roman de la Rose*. Just how much of the fragment which has survived is the work of Chaucer is still in debate. Since Kaluza's work of 1893 most scholars have adopted his view that the poem falls into three fragments. Fragment A (lines 1–1705) is accepted as containing nothing that prevents it from being by Chaucer, but fragments B and C (lines 1706–5810; 5811–7696) are regarded as suspect, and probably not by Chaucer but a continuation (in Chaucerian vein) by a northern author. Whatever the truth of the matter, there is nothing surprising in believing that Chaucer attempted a translation. The original was composed in the thirteenth century by two authors. Guillaume de Lorris was the originator of the plan of the poem, and between 1225 and 1230 wrote the first part in 4,067 lines. His work is a dream-vision, a story of courtly love in which the lady is symbolized in the rose which the lover would pluck, and which is so closely guarded. His work is of a gentle, poetic nature: woman is exalted, idealized, and the quest is conducted in gardens of unsurpassed beauty by a devoted, reverential lover. Between 1268 and 1277 Jean de Meun took up the story from where Guillaume had left off, and completed it in a poem of 22,047 lines. The quest of the rose is continued, but in place of reverence is satire, and within the allegorical form de Meun develops a number of

[1] sownen into, 'tend toward'.

disquisitions on current theological and philosophical matters. A harsh realism replaces the idealist pictures of the earlier part of the poem: the devotion of the believer is displaced by the cynicism of the unbeliever. The dual nature of the poem achieved for it great popularity, and for more than two centuries it was the most important and admired single poem in French or English. It certainly influenced Chaucer more than any other work he read; for, in common with all men, he found in it something to suit every mood. The influence of de Lorris was strong upon him throughout all his earlier poems: when he came to write the *Canterbury Tales*, however, he found both method and models in the unsparing, realistic, satirical work of de Meun. As a young poet he could not have been better employed than in getting fully acquainted with the *Roman*, and by putting part of it into the graceful easy translation in octosyllabic couplets. This he probably did between 1360 and 1368, and it forms an admirable prelude to what was to come, for in September 1369 the Duchess Blanche, first wife of John of Gaunt, had died, and Chaucer composed his elegiac poem within the next few months. The *Death of Blanche the Duchess*, as Chaucer calls the poem in the *Legend of Good Women*, is a revealing work. In the first place it shows how dependent Chaucer still was on his French and Latin models. Almost everything in the poem is derivative, yet English critics have rightly refused to regard it as being little more than a 'servile imitation of Machaut'. It is true that Chaucer takes over much of the paraphernalia of the allegorical dream poem with its artificial conventions and its set formulae, but at the same time he does not allow these to control his treatment of the theme. Allegory disappears, and while he retains the dream-vision, he uses it in a new (if not novel) way to bring out the pathos of his story. Chaucer was always fascinated by the subject of dreams, and perhaps felt that here was an opportunity to demonstrate that the strange unconnected things that happen in dreams could be fashioned into poetic material for an elegy.

Chaucer begins by a relation of his sleepless state, and says that to beguile his wakeful hours he read the 'romance' of Ceyx and Alcyone—Ovid's story of the death of Ceyx, and of Alcyone's endeavours to learn of his fate. This leads her to pray to Juno, who sends a messenger to Morpheus ordering him to break the news to Alcyone—and at the mere mention of the god of Sleep the author makes rich promises to Morpheus, could sleep only come to him, and 'sodeynly, I nyste how, Such a lust anoon me took To slepe, that ryght upon my book Y fil aslepe'.

Such is the machinery by which Chaucer carries us to the threshold of his poem, and it is a much more complicated engine than would appear at first sight. Scholars have shown how much reading went to its making: the eleventh Metamorphosis, Machaut's *Dit de la Fontaine Amoureuse* and his *Le Jugement dou Roy de Behaingne*, and Froissart's *Paradys d'Amours*, among others, 'and as he retells the story, the three blend into a fresh and delightful *quartum quid* which is at once all of them, yet none of them but Chaucer'. Professor Lowes continues: 'one has only to read the tale as Ovid, Machaut, Froissart, and Chaucer respectively tell it to see what all the books and lectures ever written can never show—the unmistakable, individual stamp which Chaucer, even at this early day, set upon everything he touched'.

In the dream which follows we are at once in the well-known world of romance: the inevitable May morning, the song of birds, the bedroom with its painted scenes from the *Romance of the Rose*, and the bright sunshine streaming on his bed through the coloured glass. 'Blew, bright, clere was the ayr', and as he lies there he hears the hunter's horn, and rapidly makes his way to where he finds 'a great rout of hunters and foresters'. With them he follows the chase, until 'the forloyn'[1] was sounded, and then finds himself

> Doun by a floury grene wente[2]
> Ful thikke of gras, ful softe and swete,
> With floures fele,[3] faire under fete
> And litel used, hyt semed thus.

And so at last we come to the real subject-matter of the poem; for wandering thus, the dreamer comes upon a Man in Black, sitting with his back against an oak, and composing a complaint—the most piteous and sorrowful ever heard.

In the remaining two-thirds of the poem Chaucer describes how the Dreamer learns from the Man in Black of the death of the 'goode faire white'. In his classic exposition of this poem Professor Kittredge has taught us how we are to watch the

[1] forloyn, 'recall'. [2] wente, 'path'. [3] fele, 'many'.

rather obtuse Dreamer at his task of elucidation. Little by little we are shown him cross-questioning the highly sophisticated Man in Black, and winning from him the story of his love-making and of the perfection of his lady, and of her end. The Dreamer's intelligence (dulled perhaps by long lack of sleep) only slowly absorbs what seems so obvious to us, and it is with some relief that we find him at last asking, 'Sir, where is she now?' The direct question shatters the elaborate world of make-believe. The leisurely dialogue gives place to a terse, rapid exchange of sentences:

> 'Allas, sir, how? What may that be?'
> 'She ys ded!'
> 'Nay!'
> 'Yis, be my trouthe!'
> 'Is that youre los? Be God, hyt ys routhe!'

The change is most striking: Chaucer gives this brief taste of his power in writing dialogue, but fails to develop his theme or to exploit its possibilities. Instead, he turns back to the hunt again:

> ryght anoon
> They gan to strake forth;[1] al was doon,
> For that tyme, the hert-huntyng.

So with the break up of the hunt the poem comes to an end as the Dreamer awakes to the sound of the tolling bell ringing at noon, the book of Ceyx and Alcyone lying by his hand.

In the *Book of the Duchess* we may find much to praise, although much is derivative and crude. Structurally it has serious faults: the poem of Ceyx and Alcyone is developed at too great length; the prolix nature of the Man in Black's speeches, together with his pedantry, is not easily justified. The story drags before it reaches its climax, and once there Chaucer rapidly abandons his theme as if the detailed treatment of so profound an experience was as yet beyond his powers. Again, there is much that is hackneyed—the personified abstractions of Love and Nature, the May morning, the dream-convention, the sleepless reader—all these, allied to an absence of any profound emotion, or any piercing thought, limit our admiration of the poem and must be weighed against its merits. Yet it has merits. It is penetrated with Chaucer's growing knowledge of

[1] strake forth, 'return home from the hunt'.

life: his reading had provided him with useful accessories and models, while the death of the duchess gave just the personal touch that fired his poetic imagination and enabled him to fuse the whole into an elegiac poem which gives so sympathetic a picture of the husband's grief—a grief we are made to feel so strongly by Chaucer's superb portrait of the duchess—her beauty, her womanly nature, and the happiness that radiated from her. And the more strongly we feel this, and accept the perfect union of Blanche and the Man in Black, the more moving shall we find the background against which the poem has its setting, with its concert of birds and streams; its glades lively with buck and doe; and (like an anticipation of his poetical son, Spenser) the sound from afar of the waterfall which comes

> rennynge fro the clyves adoun,
> That made a dedly slepynge soun.

2

Had Chaucer died in 1370 the most that could have been said of him was that here was a poet of brilliant promise. Into something less than thirty years he had crammed a wealth of experience gained from his daily encounters with all sorts of people in the king's court, among the merchants of London, or in the rough and tumble of the warrior's camp. As well as this his more formal learning had not been neglected. His schooling would have introduced him to Latin and Latin authors, and some of these such as Virgil and Ovid, together with outstanding classics of medieval Latin such as St. Jerome on marriage, the *De Planctu Naturae* of Alanus de Insulis, the *Nova Poetria* of Geoffrey de Vinsauf, for example, he had read and studied to advantage. And long before 1370 he must have considered the various ways of poetry open to a poet at that time which have already been mentioned.[1] Undoubtedly his mind most inclined to the French forms of poetry so commonly in circulation among the court. The work of Machaut attracted him in particular; and, as Professor Manly has well shown, Machaut's contributions to verse technique, to the union of music and versification in the lyric, and to the establishment of new poetical forms, were immense. In Machaut Chaucer

[1] See above, p. 8.

found a master and an example, and his early years we may well imagine were spent in making those 'ballades, roundels and virelays' which have long since disappeared. The result of all this experimentation and poetic exercise, however, is to be seen in the *Book of the Duchess*. It is the fine flower of Chaucer's apprenticeship to France.

The years 1370–80 were in many ways the most critical of Chaucer's life. He was now an Esquire of the Royal Household, and as such was in a peculiarly interesting position. The court of Edward III was the intellectual and social focus of the kingdom. The great officers of the household were among the most influential men of the day, and in some ways resembled the present Secretaries of State. Besides these, many others whose high birth or service to the State gave them access were to be seen at the court. Further, there was the constant coming and going of judges, bishops, great officials, and a thousand lesser men in their train—all of them full of interest and instruction to the king's esquire.

Throughout his long public career [writes Professor Manly] Chaucer came into contact with most of the men of importance in London as well as with continental diplomats and rulers. The list of those with whom he appears to have had frequent dealings includes the great merchants Sir William Walworth, Sir Nicholas Brembre, and Sir John Philpot, and a number of ambassadors and officials of various sorts—Sir William de Beauchamp, Sir Guichard d'Angle, Sir John Burley, Sir Peter Courtenay, Walter Skirlawe, Bishop of Durham, and the so-called Lollard Knights—at one time followers of Wyclif—Sir Lewis Clifford, Sir William Neville, Sir John Clanvowe, and Sir Richard Sturry. To these men, whom the records show to have been in one way or another associated with Chaucer, may be added, on the evidence of his own writings, Sir Philip de Vache, Clifford's son-in-law, and one of the Bucktons.

This is a brilliant circle of courtiers and men of affairs, and from them Chaucer must have derived some of that specific knowledge of humanity which is so characteristic a part of him.

Life at court we may well believe not only widened his experience of men and affairs but gave him ample opportunities to show his own parts. To succeed at court required the constant exercise of one's wits: if it was not necessary to be all things to all men, it was at least expedient to create this illusion in their minds. The fullest exercise of a man's talents was required: an ability 'to dance and well purtreye and write', as well as more sober qualities were called for at times. Chaucer had to show all those qualities which went to the making of a squire, and the description of them given in an earlier chapter must suffice to suggest how much of Chaucer's time was spent at court. One important aspect of the squire's life, however, was omitted—the service of ladies. This was particularly important: 'to stonden in his lady grace' was the desire of every youthful aspirant, and in her service he did everything he could to further that end. The young lover in Gower's *Confessio Amantis* gives us chapter and verse for the way in which a man should behave. We learn how he accompanies his lady to Mass, lifts her into the saddle, or rides by her carriage; how he delights to be present in her chamber, or to sing or read to her, or even to sit and watch her long fingers at work at her weaving or embroidery. When she will not stay with him he plays with her dog or bird, or converses with the page of her chamber, making any excuse to await her return. How far Chaucer adopted such conventional attitudes we do not know, but the constant meeting with well-bred women gave him that intimate knowledge of good society of which he made full use in his innumerable feminine portraits. His women characters have a lifelikeness and poise sadly lacking in many of the heroines of romance, of whom Léon Gautier, the panegyrist of that age, has to admit: 'The girls, it must be confessed, are too often little monsters.' Chaucer knew from first-hand observation and daily contact the way in which a lady of breeding would behave: he was not a mere adventurer or a flunkey whose knowledge of 'high life above stairs' was limited to fugitive and partial contacts. Hence, in as early a composition as the *Book of the Duchess*, the portrait of the lady Blanche is the outstanding feature of the work, for Chaucer has here combined literary conventions and models with knowledge of life to produce something hitherto unknown in romance. Chaucer's originality of treatment arose from the fact that he was depicting a character that he knew very well, not something viewed from afar or only read about in books. He was to show many striking examples of his observation and understanding of women in his future poems.

But it was not his presence at court which made this decade

so decisive a period of Chaucer's life, but rather his absences. We have already seen that in 1368 he was sent abroad on an unknown mission. In 1370 he was abroad on another piece of unknown business for the king. From December 1372 to May 1373 he was sent to Genoa with two colleagues on business negotiations. Between 1376 and 1381 he was employed on several missions abroad—in France and Flanders, and most important of all, in May 1378, he went in the train of Sir Edward de Berkeley to Lombardy to negotiate with Bernabò Visconti, Lord of Milan, and Sir John Hawkwood, 'for certain affairs touching the expedition of the King's war'. This journey lasted until September 1378.

France, Flanders, Italy—these all contributed immensely to Chaucer's knowledge of life and letters. France, as we have already seen, was known to him both by travel and still more by the fact that he had grown up in a court in which French culture was all-prevailing and in which French literature was all-important. Flanders and Italy had also their several parts to play. To a citizen of the world, like Chaucer, the Flemish cities were a fascinating study. In them he saw a flourishing democracy (so far as democracy was possible in the fourteenth century). The cities of Bruges and Ghent were centres of a busy commercial life: the weavers of Ghent and Ypres were famous. In the shops of the artisans remarkable works of applied art were being manufactured—witness the Flemish brasses. The busy trading-world of London with which he was becoming once again closely acquainted must often have been compared to its disadvantage with the much greater and busier cities of Flanders.

It was to Italy, however, that Chaucer was to owe most. Even if we agree with Professor Manly that 'when one deliberately sums up Chaucer's direct debt to the Italians it is surprisingly small', we must never forget his all-important corollary: 'Yet it is probable that but for the Italians Chaucer would not have become the great artist that he did become.' Just how this was brought about is part of the strange process which makes one man a poet and leaves another at best a poetaster, but we can see something of what Italy had to offer to a poetic imagination by trying to re-create as best we can the physical and intellectual world which Chaucer found in Italy in 1372–3 and 1378.

To enter Italy for the first time is still a land-mark in a man's life, and it certainly was not less so in Chaucer's day. The grinding climb up over the northern slopes of the Alps was made the more fearful for the medieval traveller by his belief that these waste spaces were the especial abode of the creatures of the Devil, and he must have reached the upper passes and turned his face towards Italy with some relief—a relief often quickened by the dramatic nature of the change that even now greets the traveller. The gloomy overshadowing rocks and their attendant mists seem to close down as one ascends to the topmost col, and then at a turn of the path the southern slopes of the Alps flash before one, and the whole landscape falls away in fold upon fold of sunlit splendour. Whether or no Chaucer felt, as Ruskin felt, that 'the best image which the world can give of paradise is the slope of the meadows, orchards, and cornfields on the sides of a great Alp with its purple rocks and eternal snows above', it is impossible to say. In Chaucer's day landscape only formed a conventional background, and seemed but little valued for itself. Yet it is hard to believe that the rich Italian country-side, with its great woods of chestnuts and walnuts on the lower mountain slopes, followed by the olives and vines and the carefully cultivated fields of the plains, was passed by with indifference.

But with whatever eye Chaucer looked on the Italian country-side, we may be certain that the Italian cities, their inhabitants, and their civilization all filled him with interest and even excitement. For Chaucer's Italy was an exciting land. In the first place he saw past and present mingling as he had never done before. The cities still kept something of their Roman origins: everywhere he went he would see the walls and buildings with many centuries of history behind them. Even more exhilarating was the vast wealth of new buildings and artistic endeavour which he saw on every side. Dr. Coulton thus describes the scene:

Everywhere he would find greater buildings and brighter colours than in our northern air. The pale ghosts of frescoes which we study so regretfully, were then in their first freshness, with thousands more which have long since disappeared. Wherever he went, the cities were already building, or had newly built, the finest of the Gothic structures which adorn them still; and Chaucer must have passed through Pisa and Florence like a new Æneas among the rising glories of Carthage. A whole population of great artists vied with each other in every department of human skill—

'Qualis apes aestate nova per florea rura
Exercet sub sole labor.'

Giotto and Andrea Pisano were not long dead; their pupils were carrying on their great traditions; and splendid schools of sculpture and painting flourished, especially in those districts through which our poet's business led him.

While the artist in him was revelling in all this architecture, sculpture, and painting, the man of the world was also absorbed by the drama which was going on wherever he went. For Italy was no united country, but a confusion of small states each fighting for its existence and each hammering out its own destiny. Tyrants arose and overthrew the existing semi-democratic governments of city and state: Chaucer must have felt that England was a quiet and well-governed country when he saw the fierce strife of faction and tyrant prevalent in Italy. On his second embassy he came into close contact with one of the most powerful of Italian tyrants—Bernabò Visconti, whom he apostrophizes as

Off Melan grete Barnabo Viscounte,
God of delit, and scourge of Lumbardye

and a brief account of him will help us to realize the violent life of Italy in the midst of which Chaucer found himself. Bernabò was a member of the great family of Visconti who gradually usurped the whole of Lombardy from other tyrants, and he was perhaps the cruellest of them all. His edict that anyone caught conspiring against him was to be tortured for forty-one days in succession before being put to death, or the fact that he kept 5,000 hunting-dogs—any one of which it was death to touch—are perhaps sufficient evidence of his state of mind. He was immensely ambitious, and offered one of his daughters as a wife to Richard II, while he married his niece Violanta to Lionel, son of Edward III. He finally overreached himself in trying to oust his nephew Gian Galeazzo from his father's inheritance, first by poison and then by other means, and was cunningly tricked by his nephew, incarcerated, and made away with somehow in prison. The power, ambition, and immense personal prestige of individuals like these Visconti were common gossip in fourteenth-century Italy and must have come to Chaucer's notice. Moreover, his stay in Florence acquainted him with something of the stormy history of that city, and of the Guelphs and Ghibellines who strove there, while the wealth and power of the great Florentine guilds gave him cause to reflect on the difference between them and those of London.

3

If some may regard all this as idle theorizing, it is otherwise when we come to discuss the Italian authors then being read. Dante, Petrarch, and Boccaccio all had their part to play in Chaucer's story. When and how he learnt Italian we do not know. Professor Manly has pointed out that it would not have been impossible for him to have learnt it from one of the many Italians resident in London, and it may have been because he already knew Italian that he was sent to Genoa in 1372. Certainly it seems to explain why he was sent to investigate some affair concerning a Genoese vessel at Dartmouth the next year. By the time of his second visit to Italy, in 1378, we may assume that he had a competent knowledge of the language.

When he first reached Italy, Dante had been dead for fifty-one years, while Petrarch had only two and Boccaccio three more years to live. Whether Chaucer ever met Petrarch or not remains an undecided question, although most scholarly opinion inclines against their having met. The relation between Chaucer and Boccaccio is obscure. We have nothing to assure us that they ever met, and much as Chaucer takes from the Italian, he not only never mentions him by name, but when he has to quote him directly he says the passage is by 'Lollius' or some writer other than Boccaccio. These are points of small importance, however, weighed against the fact that on his return to England manuscripts of Dante and Boccaccio were in his baggage. We may imagine him devoting what leisure he had to a careful study of the Italian writers, and it was this, combined with the sights and experiences which Italy had provided, which eventually made of him 'an artist in a sense in which the word can be used of no other English poet before him, and of none after him until the sixteenth century brought English men of letters again into close communion with Italian poetry'.

The qualification 'what leisure he had' is necessary, for

apart from his various embassies abroad Chaucer had by now become an official in the city. From 1374 until 1386 he held the office of Controller of the Customs and Subsidies on wool, hides, and sheep-skins in the port of London, on condition that he should write the rolls with his own hand. This post gave him a considerable salary with additional rewards from time to time, and also brought him into contact with some of the greatest business men of the city. The award of a daily pitcher of wine, of a pension from John of Gaunt, of the controllership of the petty customs on wines and other merchandise, and a rent-free house above Aldgate are all evidence of the esteem in which he was held, and of the constant demands upon his time which were recognized and recompensed. A number of other records of the period 1374–86 all show him as a man of considerable standing, and enjoying the favour both of the court and of the city. As such he was in a peculiarly favourable position to learn much of what was going on.

We need constantly to remind ourselves [writes Professor Lowes] of the degree to which in Chaucer's day communication had to be by word of mouth. And so the people whom he knew were also channels through which came to him news of his world—news not only of that 'little world' which to Shakespeare's John of Gaunt was England; not only of that 'queasy world' across the Channel; but also of that now looming, menacing, always mysterious world beyond, which was the Orient.

Not much imagination is required to see how Chaucer used all this. The court and the city, as we have seen, gave him manifold opportunities of meeting men whose business and pleasure took them through the length and breadth of the country. Truth and fiction travelled with them and was thus easily at the service of so experienced a man of the world as Chaucer. The affairs of Europe were likewise known to him as he had speech with returning knights and their followers. The freemasonry of knighthood allowed a knight to take service with many princes from time to time, and he thus obtained a superficial but lively knowledge of various parts of Europe. Chaucer's Knight is the result of a lifetime spent by his creator in listening to men's adventures in the three great theatres of war of his day—against the Turks, the Tartars, and the Moors. Merchants and shipmen, together with pilgrims and others, had adventured to the farthest limits—even 'to the Drye Se, And come hoom by the Carrenar', and these 'fadres of tydinges', as Chaucer calls them, enriched his store of knowledge and legend.

Between 1374 and his retirement from office in 1386 Chaucer's time was thus spent in diplomatic and business journeys at home and abroad and in daily labours at the Custom-house. At the same time he was steadily practising his craft as a poet. There, in his lodging at Aldgate, he spent what leisure he had turning over the pages of his French and Italian authors and trying to shape into English verse the stories from them which had so absorbed him. For, as he tells us, once his work on the wharves was done he turned to his books, and read until he was in a daze.[1] The result was some of his finest poems: the *House of Fame*, the *Parliament of Fowls*, and *Troilus and Criseyde*. To these we may add the less important *Legend of Good Women* and *Palamon* (slightly revised later as the *Knight's Tale*) and a number of translations and paraphrases, such as *Anelida and Arcite*, numerous 'Complaints', the lost 'balades, roundels, virelays', and the prose Boethius. In addition he wrote the *Life of St. Cecilia* (afterwards used as the *Second Nun's Tale*), together with much of the work now known as the *Monk's Tale*. The exact order in which Chaucer wrote these works is still in doubt. Poems such as *Troilus and Criseyde* or *Anelida and Arcite* which are based on Italian originals are obviously to be dated after Chaucer's first visit to Italy, while the date of the *House of Fame* or the *Parliament of Fowls* depends largely upon our interpretation of the occasions thought to have given rise to them.

To begin with the *House of Fame*. Chaucer refers in Book II to his daily reckonings at the Customs, which places the date between 1374 and 1386. The various suggestions concerning the occasion of the poem would place it between 1378 and 1384, while on general stylistic grounds there is much to be said for a date round about 1380. Throughout the years 1380–90 Chaucer was influenced by Boccaccio's long poems, and turned more to them than to France for inspiration. Moreover, his growing poetic technique was showing him the limitations of the octosyllabic couplet, and leading him to the rhyme royal and the decasyllabic couplet. All this, we may imagine, slowly became clear to him between the two Italian visits, so that the

[1] See above, p. 1.

end of the seventies found him between two worlds. He was still much at home in the old world of French poetry, but was already eagerly exploring the new Italian world. For a time, therefore, his output was of a mixed nature, and this is clearly seen in the *House of Fame.*

Here Chaucer returns again to the dream-vision. Once more he makes great use of French poetry and to a lesser extent of certain Latin poets. A new influence, however, is apparent—that of Italy, although many critics have exaggerated or mistaken the nature of it. Chaucer, it is true, imitates the *Divine Comedy* in a few places in the *House of Fame,* most continuously in the invocations to Books II and III, but the works are of so widely different a nature that little direct imitation was possible. What Chaucer got from Dante was a glimpse of the possibilities open to poets outside the charmed circle of French erotic poetry. Once he had broken out from that circle a great step forward had been taken, and it is in this sense, rather than in the indebtedness for this or that line or detail, that we may consider that Chaucer learnt from Dante.

As in the *Book of the Duchess* Chaucer's new poem is shot through and through with snatches from his reading of many authors. Scholars have shown the variety of works which Chaucer had seemingly at his finger-tips—Ovid, Virgil, Macrobius, Alanus de Insulis, Froissart, Dante, Boccaccio—but the use that he makes of them is all his own, for in the *House of Fame* he has written one of his most original works. Many attempts have been made to find an explanation for the poem in terms of Chaucer's personal affairs, or of those of the royal family. The 'man of gret auctorite' mentioned in the last line of the poem may have had tidings to tell Chaucer once he had reached the House of Fame, but as the poem breaks off at this point we shall never know what they were. Indeed, the whole purpose of the poem is obscure. Chaucer tells us that in his dream an Eagle caught him up by order of Jupiter so as to carry him to the House of Fame where he could hear 'tydynges of Loves folk'. Despite this, what he hears most about concerns Fame, either in the sense of 'rumour' or of 'renoun', and the vicissitudes of Fame. Little seems to have been gained by the continuous attempts of the critics, either to find a satisfactory allegorical or personal interpretation of the poem, or to explain how Chaucer meant to finish it.

The poem, however, may be enjoyed even if (or perhaps because) we ignore all these matters. It is one of the most charming of dream-visions. In Book I we have the scenes in the Temple of Glass and the epitomized account of the *Aeneid.* All this is well done, but perhaps at unnecessary length for modern readers, and certainly delays our introduction to the great comic character of the poem—the Eagle. Once he has arrived, he takes charge of Chaucer and of the poem, and talks away to the laconic (and terrified) poet with a verve and raciness of expression not easily matched elsewhere except in Chaucer's works. The characteristics of the two protagonists may be seen from one extract:

'Telle me this now feythfully,
Have y not preved thus symply,
Withouten any subtilite
Of speche, or gret prolixite
Of termes of philosophie,
Of figures of poetrie,
Or colours of rethorike?
Pardee, hit oughte thee to lyke!
For hard langage and hard matere
Ys encombrous for to here
Attones; wost thou not wel this?'
And y answerde and seyde, 'Yis.'
'A ha!' quod he, 'lo, so I can
Lewedly[1] to a lewed man
Speke, . . .'

Arrived at the House of Fame Chaucer is at his imaginative best. He describes the castle itself, and how it is full of statues of minstrels, musicians, jugglers, and others, and how in a magnificent hall adorned with statues of great writers there sits the lady Fame. In this hall the poet watches group after group of aspirants for fame approach the throne. Some are granted their requests, others rejected, and the decisions are announced by Aeolus on the two trumpets of Fame and of Slander. But the poet has come for 'tidings of love, or such things glad', and is finally conducted by a stranger to the Laborintus. This is some sixty miles long, made of twigs, and is constantly whirling around so that to enter its ever-open doors is not easy. Here the invaluable Eagle comes to the

[1] Lewedly, 'unlearnedly'.

rescue, and sets the poet down in the Laborintus where he hears all kinds of people discussing tidings, and at last sees in a corner of the hall men rushing and scrambling over one another to hear tidings of love which were being told by 'a man of gret auctorite'. Here, unfortunately, the poem breaks off. The excitement and bewilderment which beset the poet are vividly expressed. A profusion of ever-changing detail and of amusing and shrewd observation is constantly before us. Chaucer's contemporaries must have found all this much to their taste. The retelling of the story of the *Aeneid*, with special attention to Dido, revived many memories, while the constant employment of detail suggestive of the old French romances pleased and fascinated his cultivated audience. Then again there was the brilliant reproduction of the Eagle's conversation, the descriptions so full of detail and gusto of the Houses of Fame and of Rumour, all expressed in easy-moving supple octosyllabics, which helped to make up a poem unlike anything that had previously appeared in English.

Anelida and Arcite, a poem belonging to this period, is a charming but incomplete piece of work. The story in the main comes from Boccaccio's *Teseide*, despite Chaucer's claim that 'First folowe I Stace, and after him Corynne', and briefly relates how Anelida was deserted by the false Arcite. This leads on to the heart of the poem, 'The Complaint of Anelida', a piece of highly elaborate writing in which Chaucer shows a remarkable control of lyric form. Various stanzas and intricate rhyme schemes are employed with seeming ease and a fluidity of movement which marks an advance on any earlier work, while the whole poem seems an attempt to frame the conventional French 'complaint' poem in a setting of a heroic nature. Chaucer broke off the poem after adding a few lines at the end of the 'Complaint' in which Anelida goes to the temple of Mars. The promised description of the temple (taken from the *Teseide*) did not follow, but was used later in the *Knight's Tale*. No exact date can be assigned to the fragment, but its combination of French and Italian forms and its metrical ability suggest that it was written between 1380 and 1386—the years in which Chaucer was mastering his new Italian material.

In the *Parliament of Fowls* (written about 1382) Chaucer takes up once again the dream-vision. All the old concomitants reappear: the preliminary reading, the sleep, and the dream arising from the subject-matter of the book, the adventures of the dream, the strange figures, natural and supernatural, that appear and disappear. As before, Chaucer draws on a widely selected variety of material from his reading matter and subdues it magnificently to his purpose. Scholars have shown in detail how French, Latin, and Italian authors have all been laid under contribution, and yet here, even more than in the *Book of the Duchess*, the result is something quite new. Chaucer seems by now to have mastered the art of felicitous borrowing: his mind stored with much reading produces what is required on demand—sometimes his own, sometimes borrowed, but always new. Take the opening lines as an example. *Ars longa, vita brevis*—the tag goes back to Hippocrates, but Chaucer, following the rhetorical method of beginning with a *sententia*, gives us his arresting and novel version:

> The lyf so short, the craft so long to lerne,
> Th'assay so hard, so sharp the conquerynge,
> The dredful joye, alwey that slit so yerne:[1]
> Al this mene I by Love.

Similarly with his treatment of the subject. The first few hundred lines relate how he has been reading Cicero's *Somnium Scipionis* where the young Scipio dreams that he is taken by Africanus into the heavens and is shown the life to come. Then in his sleep Africanus appears to the poet also, and takes him to the beautiful park wherein he sees 'Nature the vicaire of the almyghty Lord', and the gathering of birds on St. Valentine's Day. This is conventional enough, and owes its life solely to the highly individual treatment it receives from Chaucer. From this point, however, the work is more original, and is devoted to the choosing of mates by the various kinds of birds. An unsubstantial subject perhaps, but treated by Chaucer with such variety and freshness that every phrase is alive. When the birds come to choose their mates the three royal eagles each make protestation of their love for the formel eagle, but take such a time over it that the lesser breeds get impatient and make the woods ring with their cry 'Have don, and lat us wende!', while the goose, the cuckoo, and the duck cried 'Kek kek! kokkow! quek quek!', and such a clatter is set up as requires

[1] slit so yerne, 'passes away (slides) so quickly'.

all Nature's authority to control. The ultimate arrangement whereby the various birds make their views heard is a piece of comedy quite outside anything hitherto known in English literature. Chaucer is complete master of the scene, and is able to give the various birds a racy and individual existence. The goose's platitudes, the sparrowhawk's sarcasm, the lady-like turtle-dove, the common sense of the duck—all are suggested with an economy and variety that show a master-hand. And then to conclude, Nature decrees a year's respite, while the formel eagle considers the claims of her lovers, and the lesser birds choose their mates ('And, Lord, the blisse and joye that they make!'), and so the vision ends:

> But fyrst were chosen foules for to synge,
> As yer by yer was alwey hir usaunce,
> To synge a roundel at here departynge,
> To don to Nature honour and plesaunce.
> The note, I trowe, imaked was in Fraunce,
> The wordes were swiche as ye may heer fynde,
> The nexte vers, as I now have in mynde.
>
> 'Now welcome, somer, with thy sonne softe,
> That hast this wintres wedres overshake,
> And driven away the longe nyghtes blake!'

The noise made by the birds as they fly away wakes the dreamer and the poem ends.

An examination of the poem makes clear the lines on which Chaucer was progressing. In the first place the somewhat limited octosyllabic measure with its rapidly recurring rhymes ('lyght and lewed') has been displaced by what was to become so supple a vehicle for Chaucer's poetry—the seven-lined decasyllabic stanza. A new music arises as Chaucer finds himself with more room within the line and within the stanza. We have only to compare the description of the forest in the *Book of the Duchess* with the description of the garden here to see what this extra freedom (together with an increased skill in his use of his materials) could mean. And with this we can see elements which we think of as peculiarly Chaucerian. The various orders of birds—birds of prey, birds feeding on worms, others on seeds, and birds living in the water—all these are given life and individuality, and are the early version of the immortal Chaunticleer and Pertelote. They may be thought of as representing some of the orders of society. Chaucer's growing concern to reflect contemporary life and ideas in his poetry is shown by the rough treatment given to the ideals of courtly love, as put forward by the eagles, and his tolerance in the way in which he holds the balance evenly between the various participants in the Parliament. His serene detachment, so characteristic of the mature Chaucer, is evident throughout, and he allows the birds to disperse with no decision taken.

Much ink has been spilt in the attempt to decide what occasioned the writing of the poem, but no circumstances have yet been found which exactly satisfy all the conditions. May we not accept Professor Manly's solution that the poem follows the lines of the conventional *demande d'amours* in its central idea, and that about this Chaucer has grouped this charming picture with its temple and gardens, its vivacious fowls with their sentiment and comedy and its underlying criticism of the social order and perhaps even a little criticism of the ideals of courtly love?

4

The new conceptions which Chaucer had acquired from his Italian journeys did not fade away on his return to England. He brought back manuscripts of the *Divina Commedia* of Dante and of the *Teseide* and *Filostrato* of Boccaccio. There is no evidence that he knew more of Petrarch's poetry than the 88th Sonnet which he paraphrases in Book I of *Troilus and Criseyde.* He was not long content merely to translate passages from these poets into English, but soon faced the task of giving the whole of one of the larger Italian pieces an English form. Of these writers Boccaccio had most in common with Chaucer. Dante he undoubtedly admired greatly, yet he realized that Dante's mind sounded depths and passed to heights beyond his understanding.

The writings of Boccaccio, however, presented fewer difficulties to Chaucer, and he evidently studied two of these, the *Teseide* and the *Filostrato*, with great care. His version of the *Teseide*, under the title of 'Palamon and Arcite', appears in the list of his works in the Prologue to the *Legend of Good Women.* At a later date it was slightly adapted and became the *Knight's Tale.* The *Filostrato* gave him the subject-matter for *Troilus and Criseyde.*

Chaucer learnt much from Boccaccio. The Italian writer's sense of narrative structure, whether displayed in the epic story of Theseus or the swift-moving story of the passionate lovers, revealed new possibilities to Chaucer. Boccaccio managed the great length of the *Teseide* with skill, so that, in spite of long descriptions and some digressions, the main epic story steadily advanced. The *Filostrato*, on the other hand, moved with the rapidity of the early action of *Romeo and Juliet*: Boccaccio keyed his work so as to express with great force the joy and sorrow of the lovers. Chaucer's poetic tact at this time is shown by his treatment of these two works. The *Teseide* he reduced from 9,896 lines to 2,250; the *Filostrato* he expanded from 5,704 lines to 8,239. In so doing he eliminated from the *Teseide* much mythological machinery, and many lists of names and battles, descriptions and episodes, which impeded the action. The *Knight's Tale* as it finally emerged was a splendid romance. The *Filostrato*, on the other hand, contained material which Chaucer realized needed both careful selection and expansion if the full humanity of its three leading characters was to be revealed. Some 2,730 lines of the *Filostrato* only are followed, but no doubt he soon recognized the firm architectonics of the poem, and saw that here was a power of narrative hitherto unknown to him. The detailed working out of the story with its episodes and organic movement must have been a revelation to him, but more than that, he saw in the three chief characters the makings of his own version. His wide experience of the world helped him here: the outward formalism of courtly life was well known to him, but equally well known was the strong passion and individuality which pulsed beneath the conventional attitudes and conversations. As he brooded over Boccaccio's pages he gradually saw how to turn this clear-cut southern story of faithless love into something rich, and full of the interplay of light and shade which is life. Criseida, Pandaro, and Troilo had, it is true, a life of their own, but it was all so patterned and convention-ridden. Troilo was the idle, spoilt young 'man about town', passionate, dissolute, with no further vision than the obtaining of his immediate desires. Criseida was a beautiful young wanton: like Shakespeare's Cressida, 'a daughter of the game'—shallow, treacherous, and faithless. Pandaro, Creseida's cousin, was another idle young 'man about town', whose greatest duty was comprised in the business of aiding his friend to get the woman of his desires. The lover, the faithless beloved, and the confidant: there was little new in all this in substance, but it was all dealt with by Boccaccio with such fire and with so firm a handling of the essential action that Chaucer realized its possibilities and began his own version.

From the outset he goes his own pace, makes his own diversions, and proceeds to write an original work. Boccaccio had concentrated on the story: Chaucer carries on the story, but is clearly absorbed by the leading characters whose individuality becomes more interesting as scene after scene portrays their many-sided natures. The simple creatures of Boccaccio give place to the immensely subtle and highly sophisticated creations which are Pandarus and Criseyde. Even Troilus is much more than his prototype in the *Filostrato*. It is a grave misreading of the poem which sees in him only 'an undeveloped love-sick youth'. Such a one would not be worth a poem of some 8,000 lines and, more important, would fail to call forth any of that intense pity with which Chaucer charges the finale of his poem. It is essential that we should recognize in Troilus a warrior among warriors, and from time to time he is brought before us in this guise, never more dramatically, perhaps, than at the critical moment in Book II, when Criseyde is drawn to her window to see ride by the man whose fortune her uncle has just been pleading:

So lik a man of armes and a knyght
He was to seen, fulfilled of heigh prowesse;
For bothe he hadde a body and a myght
To don that thyng, as wel as hardynesse;
And ek to seen hym in his gere hym dresse,
So fressh, so yong, so weldy[1] semed he,
It was an heven upon hym for to see.

His helm tohewen was in twenty places,
That by a tyssew heng his bak byhynde;
His sheeld todasshed was with swerdes and maces,
In which men myght many an arwe fynde
That thirled[2] hadde horn and nerf and rynde;
And ay the peple cryde, 'Here cometh oure joye,
And, next his brother, holder up of Troye.'

This is one aspect of Troilus we must never forget. It is true that there is another aspect—and it is precisely because it is so

[1] weldy, 'active'. [2] thirled, 'pierced'.

different from this that it is so significant. For the very greatness of the man, his seeming security, and his jeering diatribes againts love are no protection. The god smites whom he will: the great warrior falls, and once smitten his behaviour is axiomatic. We may not understand this state of affairs without trouble, but it is of the first importance if we are to understand the poem. For *Troilus and Criseyde* is a medieval poem, and it is based upon medieval conventions—the conventions of courtly love. We may approve or disapprove of them—but we must not deny them, or else we must abandon the book, just as the first hearers or readers of the poem would have had to do. They knew well enough that the days of the chivalric code were past—that marriage, or at least betrothal, was the easiest of matters in the medieval world, a matter requiring neither priest nor witnesses for its validity, and one constantly employed by themselves and their friends in their everyday life. Nevertheless, that did not prevent them from suspending their disbelief for the time being, and accepting the code, with its rules which laid down that love could not exist between married people; that whom one loved was a matter of destiny; that love must be secret; that lovers must be ever faithful—fidelity was all. And it is in obedience to this code that Troilus despairs, agonizes, is sleepless, lies 'weary as water in the weir', suffering from the 'lover's malady of Hereos'. But all the time the other Troilus is there, and at intervals we are made to realize this. It is part of Chaucer's success in this poem that he is able to convince us that below the conventional attitudinizing a man lies hid.

When we turn to Criseyde and Pandarus we have no difficulty in realizing that we are dealing with complex human beings. Chaucer was never greater than when he turned the comparatively shallow light-o'-love Creseida into the many-sided lady of his poem. Her reserved, dignified bearing at the feast of the Palladium, with its elements of timidity mingled with a consciousness of her own status ('What! may I not stonden here?')—all these are part of this woman who seems on a first sight to Troilus 'a thing immortal . . . as doth a heavenish parfit creature'. She is alone in Troy, her father Calchas has deserted to the Greeks, and only her uncle Pandarus is left to advise and comfort her. We see her in her own home, happy and surrounded by her maidens, their greatest joy the teasing of Pandarus or the quiet reading of the *Siege of*

Thebes. Once she had a husband, but he is dead, and Criseyde lives her life in part happy, in part fearful of the perils of the outside world and of her doubtful position as a traitor's daughter.

Such was the situation when first Pandarus came to broach ever so delicately the sad case of his friend who had seen her, and fallen madly in love with her, at the feast of the Palladium. His circumspection was so overwhelming that it aroused the greatest apprehension in this timid creature, and the clearer his meaning became, the more agitated her condition, until the 'peynted proces' is fully revealed, and she bursts out:

> O lady myn, Pallas!
> Thou in this dredful cas for me purveye;
> For so astonied am I that I deye!

'Criseyde, which that wel neigh starf[1] for fere, So as she was the ferfulleste wight That myghte be' was little able to cope with the situation she found herself in, for her uncle's life seemed in the balance, while fears as to what action the prince Troilus might take against her in her equivocal position should she refuse him, and fears of love itself, all filled her heart with uncertainty and dismay. Driven thus into a corner, 'of harmes two, the lesse is for to chese', she agreed to see Troilus, 'myn honour sauf', and so Pandarus took his leave. Criseyde's reflections after he has gone are broken by the passage of Troilus under her window, a scene which left her saying 'Who yaf me drinke?'—what love potion is this? Chaucer then analyses with wonderful subtlety the way in which Criseyde's mind moves to and fro—brooding over what has taken place: for, as he is eager to have us note, she does not fall in love at first sight, but only inclines towards Troilus, moved both by his manhood and his devotion. Yet, as she thinks of him, her timid spirit reasserts itself. Is he not a prince of Troy, and may he not, therefore, do her some harm unless she falls in with his desires? Her reflections at this point present a complex study: not one side, but twenty, of her character are revealed as she ponders her situation—her pride that Troilus should choose her of all Troy; her secret thought that after all she is the most beautiful woman in Troy, and should not such a one love where she list? But will not the very act of loving put her precious freedom and sovereignty in peril? She sees this in others, and how wicked tongues wag against

[1] starf, 'died'.

them, and how hard it is for them to keep their lovers and to cajole the gossips to keep silence. On these, and other topics, the uneasy mind of Criseyde reflects before she goes to her chamber to sleep, while without

> A nightingale, upon a cedir grene,
> Under the chambre-wal ther as she lay,
> Ful loude song ayein the moone shene,
> Peraunter,[1] in his briddes wise, a lay
> Of love, that made hire herte fressh and gay.

Once she has got even thus far, the remainder of the journey for one of her temperament is almost certain. Little by little, circumstances so wind themselves about her tender amorous spirit that she surrenders, and is the more ready to do so since she finds in Troilus 'a wal of steel, and sheld from every displesaunce'. 'Hang there like fruit my soul, Till the tree die' she might have cried, for once her love was given she felt sure

> That first shall Phebus fallen fro his spere,[2]
> And everich egle ben the dowves feere,
> And everi roche out of his place sterte,
> Er Troilus out of Criseydes herte.

Chaucer's triumph is complete: he has taken us step by step so that we have understood throughout the situation in which Criseyde found herself, and have been allowed to see the day-to-day moods and changes which have gradually led her to her lover's arms. The rapid consummation desired and effected by a Troilo and Criseida is replaced by this lifelike history in which this lovely, affectionate, timid lady slowly surrenders her whole being into the protection of the strong prince Troilus.

Could it have rested there we might well have believed that 'they lived happily ever after', for so far nothing in either character has gainsaid it. But though their world was one in which the chivalric code had authority, there was still a large world whose authority was even more powerful. When the chances of the Trojan war exchanged Criseyde for the warrior Antenor, a vital blow was struck at the lovers' happiness. For once Criseyde was removed from the sure shelter of her lover's arms, all those elements of fear and uncertainty she had shown hitherto reassert themselves. 'How sholde I live, if that I from him twinne',[3] she cries, and her constant asseverations of faith-

[1] Peraunter, 'perhaps'. [2] spere (sphere). [3] twinne, 'separate'.

fulness are all part of her attempts to reassure herself as well as Troilus. The unknown world of the Greek camp frightens her, but she says she will be back within ten days. So she firmly believes when she parts from her lover at the gate, but from the moment the 'sudden' Diomede takes charge of her everything is to do—and no one to assist her. Her father Calchas refuses to help her to escape; she fears to be taken as a spy in no-man's-land, or worse to fall into some wretch's hands, while Diomede harps on the impending fall of Troy and the destruction of all therein. Turn where she will Criseyde sees no hope: she evades Diomede for a time, but he knows his quarry, and gradually wears down her resistance. At last, she gives way. Her weary mind has pondered over every possibility: she knows her weak nature well enough at the last to see that Diomede's position and her need of help point out one way of escape from the intolerable burden she bears alone. With a last attempt to mitigate the painful impression her complete surrender brings with it she cries, 'To Diomede algate[1] I wol be trewe', and so ends her struggle. Once in Diomede's power her deterioration is rapid indeed. She writes characteristically tender but deceitful letters to Troilus and even gives his brooch to Diomede. Henceforth, her life and that of Troilus each go their several ways:

> Criseyde loveth the sone of Tideüs,
> And Troilus moot wepe in cares colde.

Chaucer does not bring his story to this conclusion without pain. The lovely figure of Criseyde that he builds up in the first three books works its spell upon him, and he turns reluctantly to what he knows has to be done. In the remaining two books the story of Criseyde's faithlessness seems to be wrung out of him with slow pain. Again and again he says that he does but follow his authorities, and

> Allas! that they sholde evere cause fynde
> To speke hire harm! and if they on hire lye,
> Iwis, hem self sholde han the vilanye.

But the tale must be told, and Chaucer tells it, defending her and mitigating her offence wherever possible, for as he says:

> Ne me ne list this sely[2] womman chyde
> Forther than the storye wol devyse.
> Hire name, allas! is punysshed so wyde,

[1] algate, 'always'. [2] sely, 'hapless, wretched'.

> That for hire gilte it oughte ynough suffyse,
> And if I myghte excuse hire any wyse,
> For she so sory was for hire untrouthe,
> Iwis, I wolde excuse hire yet for routhe.

The story of Troilus and Criseyde, as Chaucer saw it, was a story in which a woman such as he has depicted Criseyde to be—'this sely womman', 'slydyng of corage'—has to encounter the force of circumstances which are sufficient to test the strongest character. Her timid, amorous, dependent nature cannot stand the burden: she is no Juliet, no Imogen—far less a Cleopatra—but Chaucer would not have her pass into history as a shameful example of the faithless lover.

Any judgement, however, which we feel inclined to make concerning Criseyde must be influenced by the part played by Pandarus in her fortunes. He is her uncle—not the mere young gallant of Boccaccio—and, as Criseyde herself says, should have protected her from lovers, not urged their claims. And herein lies her misfortune. For he is placed in an impossible position—a double loyalty is demanded of him, and in the event he surrenders his niece to his friend. Pandarus is no simple character. His garrulous, easy-going nature makes him everywhere welcome. He can be grave or gay; tell stories or relate his own misadventures; plead a friend's cause or prattle on about nothing unendingly. No one can be out of temper with him for long: he is experience itself, and his experience is at your disposal in almost embarrassing quantities. We must not think of him as a 'battered man of the world'—or at least, must admit that the battering has had little effect on his resilient good temper. He is still able to look about the world with unflagging spirits and resourcefulness. His friend's despair or his niece's humours are things to be overcome—and to their overthrow he brings in equal parts a pleasure in pleasing and a delight in his own skill. There is another side to Pandarus, however. The chivalric code seldom had a more devout servant than he shows himself to be. Whatever else in life he takes lightly, it certainly is not the service of Love and all that goes to its making. He himself has been a lover these many years, and has had but little success. Indeed, his failure here has made him a standing jest to his friends. But his enunciation of the faith within him has lost nothing of its fire, and the fact that a man has served his lady for twenty years unrewarded, as he tells us, does not alter matters:

> What? sholde he therfore fallen in dispayr,
> Or be recreant for his owne tene,[1]
> Or slen hymself, al be his lady fair?
> Nay, nay, but evere in oon be fressh and grene
> To serve and love his deere hertes queene,
> And thynk it is a guerdon,[2] hire to serve,
> A thousand fold moore than he kan deserve.

So it is that, once he is convinced that Troilus is in love, he is doubly his servant—first because Troilus is his friend, and then because the service of Love is a duty to which he is sworn. We see him, therefore, weeping with Troilus; so moved that 'the teres braste out of his iyen' while he pleaded with Criseyde; and always associating himself with his friend's cause, so much so that at the last desperate moments, when Troilus is casting about how to keep Criseyde from the Grecian tents, he is prepared to sacrifice himself and his kindred in a futile defiance of the king.

Against such a man Criseyde fights a losing match. We need not imagine her powerless or without her own weapons, but Pandarus is full of reasonableness and resource. She plays the game of love as one who knows its arts full well, yet even so her uncle is far better instructed and sticks at little to bring about his ends. He swore to her that she need have no fear in coming to his house, and that Troilus was out of town, just as later on he tells her that Troilus has just arrived and 'into my chaumbre com in al this reyn'. He is complete master of the situation which follows: full of suggestions and practical advice; now bringing a cushion, now discreetly retiring to the fireside or stealing from the chamber. Well may Criseyde greet him the next 'merry' morning, when he asks how she fares,

> 'nevere the bet for yow,
> Fox that ye ben! God yeve youre herte kare!
> God help me so, ye caused al this fare,
> Trowe I,' quod she, 'for al youre wordes white.
> O, whoso seeth yow, knoweth yow ful lite.'

It was the history and characters of these three people that fascinated Chaucer as he elaborated Boccaccio's story. 'The

[1] tene, 'grief, trouble'.
[2] guerdon, 'reward'.

double sorwe of Troilus . . . how his aventures fellen Fro wo to wele, and after out of joye, My purpos is', he declares, and to do this he must show us something of the world in which Troilus was placed. The story of Troilus and Criseyde, therefore, has for its background the events and personalities of the Trojan war. Just as the gracious Hector raises the suppliant Criseyde in the opening scenes and bids her 'dwelleth with us, whil yow good list, in Troie', so from time to time the warriors and the rival camps are made part of the story, and as we have seen, we are made to realize the heroic stature of Troilus, and his manly part in the great scene of war. For it is the Trojan war that holds everyone in its grip. Little by little the ineluctable pressure of events sweeps away the secret refuge of the lovers, and compels Criseyde to leave Troy. Once in the Greek camp, almost the strongest of those influences which persuade her to abandon her lover is the constantly reiterated 'Troy is doomed'.

The 'star-crossed lovers' can no more prevail against these conditions than could Romeo and Juliet against theirs. They cannot control their fate, and this was predetermined when the God of Love caused Troilus to look at Criseyde at the feast. Troilus knew this: neither the toils of Love, nor those more austere workings of the Parcae, to whom he appeals, can be evaded:

> O fatal sustren, which, er any cloth
> Me shapen was, my destine me sponne.

So he and Criseyde go their way. It is not a way in which the harsh notes of war are the only accompaniment of the lover's journey. Much of it takes place in serene and lovely settings, where the nightingale sings and maidens play and read in sheltered gardens. An air of chivalric courtesy is everywhere present: Hector's conduct to Criseyde at the first is sustained in his pleas to retain her as a guest of the city when the Trojan parliament clamour for her exchange. The gathering in the house of Deiphebus with its stately ceremonial and polite manners, or the scene in Criseyde's garden where her three nieces and her women were walking in the shady bowers, or the hush while Antigone sang her Trojan song—all these things remind us of the 'ampler aether, the diviner air' in which the tragedy has its setting, and in which Chaucer develops his story.

The manner in which Chaucer does this has long been recognized as a triumph of narrative art by those critics who have rightly understood Chaucer's purpose and have had knowledge enough to realize his difficulties. Just as a knowledge of the conventions of chivalric love is an essential to any comprehension of the poem, so to a lesser degree is it necessary for us to realize that much in the poem which we could wish away is the result of the demands of the court of Richard II for which Chaucer was writing. The long discussion on predestination in Book IV, for example, need not be looked on as the doctrine governing the whole action, but rather as an exposition by Chaucer (perhaps at inordinate length to one way of thinking) of a doctrine which was then a burning question, not only among 'high-brows', but also in political and clerical circles. Once we are clear about this, we shall give it less weight in our second or third reading of the poem. Similarly with much of the wearisome and detailed descriptions of the love-sufferings of Troilus. 'Something too much of this' is the feeling of most readers, even when they have appreciated that it is all part of a recognized ritual. This and other manifestations of the love-code clog the action for modern readers. Again, Chaucer elaborates and gives us in full detail the ebb and flow of conversation—an attempt on his part to recapture the delight aroused at his time by the arts and graces of polite discourse. He also 'amplifies' his original in many places by using the devices of the rhetoricians. *Descriptio*; *circumlocutio*; *expolitio*; *exclamatio*, and the rest are all employed at length, according to the best medieval theory and practice. These and other difficulties confront us, and we shall serve Chaucer best by frankly recognizing them as matters mainly of medieval and not of permanent interest. Once that is done there will still remain the major part of the poem intact—the classic example of Chaucer's narrative skill.

Looking back we can see how formidable was the task which Chaucer had set himself. His purpose was not only to tell a story which had its roots in a convention of courtly love which had but little reality for most of his audience, but also to deal with his material in such a way that the innermost feelings of the chief characters would be revealed. Mr. C. S. Lewis has sufficiently shown that as the poet of courtly love, Chaucer is concerned with both the 'mirthe and doctrine' of the code. At times, therefore, when some point of doctrine is being discussed we feel a certain tedium, since it is matter more suited to the medieval than to the modern mind. At other times the movement is slow because Chaucer is determined to show every facet of the characters of his actors. Until that is done he will return to his point in stanza after stanza, and unless we allow ourselves to follow him in this spirit, much of his total intention will be lost. In our zeal for mirth we must not eschew doctrine.

This attitude is particularly necessary when we come to the closing stanzas of the poem. In these Chaucer sounds depths seldom fathomed by him, for in some of the most moving verses he ever wrote he implores 'yonge fresshe folkes' to turn from worldly vanity to the love of Christ, and to abandon earthly love for heavenly love. Although he has lavished so much care and skill on his poem depicting the erotic code in action he is not deceived by its meretricious attractions. The overwhelming passion of the lovers and their adherence to the courtly code are shown for what they are when compared with the love of Christ that

> Upon a crois, our soules for to beye,
> First starf, and roos, and sit in hevene above.

From the 'eighth sphere' Troilus looked down and laughed at those weeping for his death, and condemned men's ways which follow the 'blinde lust,[1] the which that may nat laste'. The 'tragedy' of Troilus and Criseyde is 'a ditee of a prosperitee for a tyme, that endeth in wrecchednesse'. Chaucer from the first knew that 'evere the latter ende of joye is woe', and emphasizes again and again the evanescent nature of human happiness. He does not deny—rather he extols—the delights of earthly 'felicitee', but he realizes that there are more important considerations. It was in this attitude of mind that he first set to work to transform Boccaccio's comparatively slender story of an amorous intrigue into a work which would pay homage to worldly pleasures but at the same time would see them in their right perspective when viewed *sub specie aeternitatis*.

5

By the time that *Troilus and Criseyde* was completed Chaucer was nearing his grand conception of the *Canterbury Tales*. Before (or while) these were being written and assembled he turned

[1] lust, 'pleasure'.

once more to the love-vision, and in the *Legend of Good Women* takes his farewell of this kind of poetry which had so fascinated him from his earliest years. On this account alone the *Legend* would have its importance in the canon of his work, but he preludes his 'lives of Cupid's saints' by a personal revelation in a Prologue, fascinating alike for its fresh sincerity and for what it tells us of the poet's devotion to the daisy, and of his delight in the hours spent in the fields. The date of the poem has caused much controversy. The legends themselves, it is generally agreed, were written about 1386. The date of the *Prologue* is more difficult to decide, since it exists in two versions; one of these (the F version) has survived in eleven manuscripts, the other (the G version) only in one. Each has independent passages and merits of its own. The G version was thought to be the earlier by Skeat and Pollard among others, but most scholars now believe F to be the earlier. A careful examination of this version shows that it is not so well constructed as the G version; that a number of weak metrical lines are improved in G; and that the reference to the queen at Shene in F (which is omitted in G) is explicable only if F is the earlier, for the queen died in 1394, and Richard II ordered the destruction of the palace there. The omission of the reference to Shene in the G version was a tactful gesture by Chaucer. We may, therefore, believe it likely that the F version dates from about 1386, and the G version not earlier than 1394. Of the legends themselves Chaucer soon wearied and left his series but part finished. The continued harping on one string seems to have bored him: the theme was to serve Gower better in the *Confessio Amantis*, and no doubt it was gradually superseded by the individual tales for his new Canterbury pilgrimage.

The Prologue to the *Legend*, however, is another matter. It serves as a means whereby Chaucer can tell us of his long hours spent in delighted contemplation of 'thise floures white and rede, Swiche as men callen daysyes in our toun', and of his sleep afterwards in his little arbour where a vision of the God of Love and of the Lady Alceste appears to him. Chaucer is condemned by the God of Love as a heretic—has he not written against women in his *Troilus* and in the *Romance of the Rose*? He is saved by the pleading of Alceste, and is ordered as a sign of repentance to write a legendary of good women—that is, of women whose faithful love had never been put in doubt. Into this Prologue Chaucer has put some of his most intimate and charming poetry, mingled with some of his most felicitous adaptations from his French and Italian authors. Of them he writes:

> For wel I wot that ye han her-biforn
> Of makyng ropen, and lad awey the corn,[1]
> And I come after, glenyng here and there,
> And am ful glad yf I may fynde an ere
> Of any goodly word that ye han left.

Chaucer's powers of 'glenyng' and of making something of his own from his labours are brilliantly shown in the Prologue. His borrowings are not in the main general or vague: his memory was full of passages from his reading and at times he clearly had his author open before him. Thus in lines 40 to 65 of the Prologue he most skilfully makes a mosaic from his French reading. He calls on no less than four of Froissart's poems for help: *Paradys d'Amours*, *Prison Amoureuse*, *Dittié de la Flour de la Margherite*, and *Le Joli Mois de May*; on two from Deschamps: *Lay de Franchise* and a *Ballade*; and also takes a few lines from Machaut's *Dit de la Marguerite*. After this wholesale borrowing he may well pen his acknowledgements in the lines quoted above. A little farther on he makes a more extended borrowing when he follows closely the opening stanzas of the *Filostrato*, a passage unused in his *Troilus*, deftly catching up several phrases from the French 'marguerite poetry' as he writes. Even more interesting than this 'felicitous borrowing' is the masterly use of verse that he here exhibits. Chaucer uses this medium with such skill that it is difficult to believe that this is his first attempt (and so far as is known the first attempt in English) to use the decasyllabic couplet. We are almost unaware that the trammels of verse are holding him just sufficiently to give form to his ideas. At the same time the natural, easy manner in which he writes gives a directness and intimacy to his work. Take, for instance, the passage:

> I, knelyng by this flour, in good entente,
> Abood to knowen what this peple mente,
> As stille as any ston; til at the laste
> This god of Love on me hys eyen caste,
> And seyde, 'Who kneleth there?' and I answerde

[1] 'For I fully understand that you have reaped the field of poetry, and carried away the sheaves.'

> Unto his askynge, whan that I it herde,
> And seyde, 'Sir it am I', and com him ner,
> And salwed him. Quod he, 'What dostow her
> So nygh myn owne floure, so boldely?'

Simple, unforced narrative writing such as this shows how considerable were Chaucer's powers. The way in which the scene is created, and still more the graceful way in which the dialogue is introduced into the narrative, are characteristic of the directness of Chaucer's method. The very ease with which it is done, the perfect naturalness, may deceive us into believing it to be less remarkable than it really is. Chaucer, of course, is actually using all the art that a long tradition of French poetry and a highly cultivated audience of courtly patrons made possible and necessary. In the hands of a less experienced artist the simplicity of sentence structure and of language would only have produced an empty and lifeless jingle. In the Prologue, as this passage sufficiently shows, Chaucer is the complete master: the verse moves without effort from line to line, carrying on the ideas without any feeling of constraint, or of the exigencies of rhyme or verse-ending impeding its progress. And at the same time it is all so good-mannered: there is no apparent striving for effect—the limpid flow of the lines serves just sufficiently to clothe but not to obscure the thought. If we want to explain what we mean by style, it is to be seen here.

6

While the poems we have just been discussing (*The House of Fame*, *The Parliament of Fowls*, *Troilus and Criseyde*, and the *Legend*) were being written, Chaucer was mainly occupied, as we have seen, by his controllership, and by other embassies and services for the king. The various records of him that have been discovered all show him to have been a man of importance and of some substantial financial means. He was allotted wardships; acted as surety and received gifts from the royal household. There was a change in his fortunes some time in 1386, when Chaucer no longer held his controllerships, and went to live in Kent. He was made a justice of the peace in 1385, and a member of Parliament for Kent the next year. We have little information concerning him during these years. It is thought that he lost office and favour when the Duke of

Gloucester took charge of the realm in 1386 and removed 'the John of Gaunt gang' from power. Be this as it may, it was not till Richard II came of age and recovered his position that Chaucer began to receive new appointments.

In 1389 he was given one of the most important offices he was destined to hold. The Clerkship of the King's Works gave him charge of the Tower, Westminster Palace, and eight other royal residences, hunting lodges, mews, gardens, ponds, mills, &c., and to these was added St. George's Chapel, Windsor, in 1390. About the same time he was made a member of a commission to look after the walls, ditches, sewers, roads, &c., along the Thames between Greenwich and Woolwich. In these various capacities Chaucer found himself with considerable powers: he could impress workmen, purvey materials, or imprison those who impeded him. At the same time his responsibilities were great. Under his direction the scaffolds for the great tournaments at Smithfield were erected: the Chapel at Windsor was repaired, and he was forced to go from place to place on the king's business. It was at this time that he was assaulted and robbed three times within four days (September 1390). This experience comes at the end of his service, for in 1391 he resigned, and in due course settled his accounts and was formally discharged. Various reasons have been given to account for his retirement, but it was probably not due to any lack of the royal favour, for early in 1391 he was appointed deputy forester of the royal forest of North Petherton, Somerset. This office involved the management of a vast estate, and it seems reasonable to suppose that Chaucer spent a good deal of his time in this last decade of his life in Somerset. The records show, however, that he was in London from time to time: almost every year we find mention of his receiving gifts of money or of robes or of wine. The accession of Henry IV brought the poet a renewal of his annuity of £20 and his hogshead of wine and a further annuity of forty marks. A few weeks later Chaucer took a fifty-three-year lease of a house within the garden of Westminster Abbey, but only occupied it for a short time. The last pension payment made to him was on 5 June 1400, and soon afterwards he died—probably, as his tombstone says, on 25 October 1400.

This recital of the main events of the life of Chaucer leaves us lacking much that we would know. Chaucer *en pantoufles* is never before us: we know nothing of his married life, his habits, his interests—all that side which might help us to understand him better. Yet that must not encourage us to belittle what we have. Chaucer's official life may mean less than nothing to the aesthetic critic; but, nevertheless, is it not a short-sighted view that leads us to ignore all this information that is available? For it is not mere information but material which enables us to see how it was that the poet of the *Canterbury Tales* came by much of his knowledge of men and women. As we rehearse the many phases of Chaucer's life—vintner's son, page, esquire, ambassador, controller of customs, clerk of works, surveyor of sewers, sub-forester—we cannot but realize the many-sided world which had been set out before him. The wonderful Italian landscape became part of his inheritance, as did also those pearly greys and cool greens that are the quiet beauty of the English country-side. The humdrum daily routine at the Custom-House must often have been contrasted in his mind with the more violent life he saw in Florence or Milan. Those long quiet rides in the forest at Petherton gave him ample opportunity to reflect upon the panorama of life that had unrolled itself before him during the past fifty years. English faces and scenes, we may well believe, predominated: there seems to be no side of English life with which he had not come into contact at some period, and all these had left their mark. Chaucer, says Blake, numbered the classes of men 'as Newton numbered the stars, and as Linnaeus numbered the plants'. He owes a large part of his greatness to his superb understanding (based on a lifelong daily acquaintance) of every variety of the human scene. If this point of view is accepted, then the critics who make so much of Chaucer's reading and divide his works up into three periods—the French, the Italian, and the English—are placing the emphasis wrongly. Books were an undeniably important factor in Chaucer's life: his study of French and Italian literatures enabled him to devise new forms and metres, and gave him a wider artistic outlook, but these things in themselves would have remained comparatively sterile had not Chaucer's immense experience of men and women put life and movement into them.

About the time (1386) that Chaucer surrendered his controllership and retired to his Kentish home the idea of the Canterbury pilgrimage seems to have come to his mind.

Despite the energetic efforts of scholars to find a definite series of 'frame-stories', or series of tales, which served as a model to Chaucer, nothing has yet been found. There is no evidence that he knew the *Decameron*, nor is there any proof that he was acquainted with Sercambi's collection of tales. The work of his contemporary Gower—the *Confessio Amantis*—was probably not completed before 1390, two or three years too late to be of use to Chaucer. In any case, Chaucer's conception differs fundamentally from any of these, for his tales are told mainly for amusement, by a very mixed company, as they ride on their leisurely way to Canterbury, just as he could have observed pilgrims constantly passing by his residence near the great pilgrim road.

The idea of a pilgrimage was masterly. Since 'pilgrimes were they alle' Chaucer was able to assemble the greatest possible variety of people, all linked by a common purpose, and to allow them to jog forward with a certain loosening of the stricter rules of etiquette and precedence which divided them in everyday life. As the hours proceed they mix together, lose their shyness, and in intercourse, or rivalry, or sheer exhibitionism reveal themselves, and often much more than themselves—the whole social *milieu* which contains them. We are privileged, in short, to see this group of fourteenth-century men and women, not as in a picture, or in the stiff attitudes of a tapestry, but as they laughed and talked, unconscious that the sharp highly trained eye of Geoffrey Chaucer was upon them. The result is not the story, but the *drama* of the *Canterbury Tales*.

Scholars have naturally asked themselves how Chaucer meant to present his material, given the idea of a story-telling pilgrimage. They have tried to estimate how many days were to be spent on the pilgrimage, and have investigated the fourteenth-century records to see what was commonly done by pilgrims and travellers on the Canterbury road, in the hope of understanding what Chaucer might have had in mind. They have endeavoured to reconcile various statements concerning the number of pilgrims and how many tales each of them was to tell. Most important of all, they have tried to arrange the tales in what they believe to have been the order which Chaucer meant them to follow one another. On none of these matters has there been general agreement.

The manuscript evidence does not help us, for there is no

manuscript that exhibits any arrangement having Chaucer's sanction. When he died it is probable that a complete set of pieces which now make up the *Canterbury Tales* was in his possession, but these were in various states of revision and preparation. Copies of some tales, or groups of tales, may also have been in circulation, but none of these gave authority for any particular arrangement. The task which faced the earliest editors was to collect all the material they could and to arrange it according to their own ideas and from such indications as the pieces and links gave them. These assembled texts have a limited and varying authority, since they were made by various editors, each with his own materials and his own views.

The order of the *Tales* is greatly simplified by the presence of the links. These are passages of narrative and descriptive matter which come at the end of many tales and lead on to the next tale. Thus the *Prologue* leads straight on to the *Knight's Tale*, and the dialogue which follows that provokes the *Miller's Tale* and the *Reeve's Tale*. These in their turn lead the Cook to begin his tale which is broken off unfinished. There are other groups (B to I) similarly held together, and something of Chaucer's plan can thus be discerned. What is impossible to discern clearly is the order of the groups, one to another. Skeat adopted as his basis of arrangement the assumptions that allusions to time and place were to be taken into consideration and so produced the order adopted in his standard edition and accepted by the editors of the Globe edition, and no rival order has as yet won general approval.

Rather more sympathy has been shown for the view so attractively stated by Professor Kittredge that whole blocks of tales are concerned with a single problem. He shows how the groups D, E, and F, beginning with the *Wife of Bath's Prologue* and continuing without a break until the end of the *Franklin's Tale* are almost entirely concerned with one problem—the relations between husband and wife—and it has been argued that Chaucer may well have meant to develop other central ideas as the controlling features of other groups of tales.

That the work was never completely planned, and that final decisions and corrections had not been made, is clear. There are several passages which betray this. For instance, the Man of Law tells us in his Prologue that he will speak in prose, yet his tale is in a seven-line stanza. The *Shipman's Tale* contains lines which show the speaker to have been a woman; conversely, the Second Nun alludes to herself as an 'unworthy son of Eve'. The narrator of the *Merchant's Tale* is a cleric, while discrepancies between the *Cook's Tale* and the *Prologue* show that Chaucer had changed his mind at some point. Miss Hammond has also given grounds for her belief that the reeve, miller, summoner, pardoner, manciple, and Chaucer himself were an afterthought. Some of these discrepancies, like that in the *Second Nun's Tale*, are obviously due to the fact that Chaucer is intercalating stories previously written which he had by him; the *Cook's Tale* variants arise from changes of plan while the work was in progress; and, if Miss Hammond's theory is valid, Chaucer enlarged his group of pilgrims to give himself greater scope in his general plan.

This general plan was originally conceived on an optimistic scale. Each of the pilgrims was to tell two stories on the outward and two on the homeward journey. The Host was constituted as master of the ceremonies and as absolute ruler and arbiter. If any were so bold as to dispute his judgement the culprit was to pay the entire expenses of the whole company—a staggering fine. Whatever happened the Host, Harry Bailly, was to come well out of it, for the prize for the teller of the best story was a supper at the expense of his fellows at the Tabard Inn. Whether this implied a narrative relating the events of the supper, or whether Chaucer contemplated an account of their devotions and amusements at Canterbury similar to that attempted in the Prologue to the *Tale of Beryn* we do not know. It is clear, however, that the original scheme provided for 120 stories (four by each character) and probably four in addition by Chaucer. Besides this, an essential part of the plan was the narrative links which were designed to join one tale to another, and to give verisimilitude to the continuous story-telling.

At whatever point in his deliberations the above scheme commended itself to Chaucer, he found it impossible to carry out in its fullness, and many modifications can be noted. The dramatic arrival of the Canon and his Yeoman, followed by the even more dramatic departure of the Canon, was the only addition Chaucer made to his pilgrims and to the number of stories necessary. His other changes were rather in the nature of reducing his labours. The statement in the Parson's head-link, 'Now lakketh us no tales mo than oon', suggests that Chaucer was demanding but one tale from each of his pilgrims, and Professor Manly has even suggested that the *Parson's Tale* may come at the close of the home journey and not as they neared Canterbury. It is clear that if the 'Retraction' which follows the *Parson's Tale* is genuine (and the weight of modern critical opinion inclines in that direction), and if it is in its right place immediately after that tale, then when it was penned Chaucer had evidently given up any idea of a farewell supper. But however we reduce the work required to complete the scheme, even on its most slender basis, Chaucer never lived to carry it out, for besides the incomplete tales of the Squire and the Cook, nine other pilgrims (or seven if we omit two of the nun's priests) make no contribution.

Whatever may be the order of the groups of tales, the brilliance and originality of the connecting narrative material has been widely recognized. Here Chaucer is at his best. Once the first choice has been made and the Knight has begun his story, what happens after this seems to be as natural and as haphazard as life itself. Even Harry Bailly, strong man that he is, cannot always overcome the chances and forces which suddenly rise up against him. Thus, when the Knight has finished his tale, and all have agreed that it was 'a noble storie, And worthy for to drawen to memorie', the Host turns to the Monk for the next tale. But here the Miller, 'that for-dronken was al pale', intervenes, and insists on having the ear of the pilgrims. Chaucer manages the scene that follows so that it appears to be a transcript from life, and the characters of the Host and the Miller emerge more fully realized than before. This artistic method is a remarkable change from the common medieval fashion such as that adopted in *Handlyng Synne* or the *Confessio Amantis*. Here the scheme is all-important, and stories and characters are made to fit into its Procrustean bed.

These connecting passages are found throughout the *Tales*, and they give life and vivacity to the work. The *Miller's Tale* so provokes the Reeve that he breaks into a long-winded harangue which is abruptly terminated by the Host who bids him get on with his story—a story against a Miller. This done, the Cook takes up the running; and, after an exchange or two with the Host, gets to his tale. Throughout this first section of the *Tales* (the A group) one tale follows the other linked together by these passages of comment and character revelation. The

Host above all comes to life as the pilgrims ride on. He rebukes his flock with little respect to their status if he thinks that they are boring their fellows or taking too much on themselves. The *Monk's Tale* he characterizes as 'nat worth a boterflye'; Chaucer's tale of *Sir Thopas* makes his ears ache, and he tells him to change his 'drasty rhyming' for something in prose. He gives careful instructions to the Clerk as to the kind of tale he is to tell, and praises the Squire's wit after hearing his tale of Cambuscan. As he proceeds we learn much of his wife and of her temper, and of his own difficulties in keeping the peace when she is roused.

A mere description or running analysis of the various stories that make up the *Canterbury Tales* would be to little purpose. It is not only (or even principally) the variety of tales with which we are concerned, but the immensely varied ways in which Chaucer deals with his material. Dryden's remark: 'Here is God's plenty', is still the predominant impression left with the reader. A more careful scrutiny only serves to deepen this, for it shows us that much of the medieval scene is portrayed by Chaucer. It is true, however, that certain sides of life and whole sections of the community are not present in his work save at infrequent and unimportant moments. 'The wo of these women that dwelleth in cots' is only represented by the widow in the *Nun's Priest's Tale* whose home and garden form so picturesque a setting for the adventures of Chanticleer and Reynard. The peasant and the life of the fields which formed so large a part of medieval England are absent. Such scenes as the night in the woods at the beginning of the *Parliament of the Three Ages*, the many pictures of peasant life in *Piers Plowman*, or the unforgettable vignette in *Pierce the Ploughman's Creed* of the ploughman and his wife at work in the icy fields, while their infants 'crieden alle o cry[1]—a carefull note. The sely man sighede sore, and seide: "children, beth stille!"'—all these come from a side of medieval life Chaucer does not choose to depict in detail. He is content to allow a few members from the villages and townships to appear, but they are usually the aristocracy of the village—the miller, the reeve, or the carpenter. Similarly, the 'solemn and grete fraternite' of citizens receives meagre treatment, which is strange when we remember that Chaucer was born and bred in their midst, and that the part played by the

[1] crieden alle o cry, 'all cried the same cry'.

great merchants and the great city companies must have been constantly before his eyes.

With this *caveat* in mind we may agree that here is 'God's foyson'. Chaucer has given us something of every variety of medieval story. The romances are represented by the *Knight's Tale*, and the *Squire's Tale*, while their decadence is satirized in the *Tale of Sir Thopas*. Medieval delight in lives of saints and of miracle working is satisfied by such stories as those of the Prioress, the Second Nun, and the Monk. The tales of the Man of Law or of the Clerk, of Melibeus or of the Franklin, dealt with various attitudes to life full of interest to Chaucer's audience. Again, the *Wife of Bath's Tale* delighted them with a story of 'faerye', and the *Nun's Priest's Tale* and the *Pardoner's Tale* amused while they instructed. And besides these Chaucer gave, in good measure, that body of 'churl's tales' which bring us so close to 'l'homme moyen sensuel'. In the tales of the Miller, Reeve, Shipman, Summoner, Merchant, or Friar the brilliance of the telling makes us condone the coarse nature of the tale.

Chaucer uses this variety of material to the utmost advantage, keeping his audience constantly uncertain of what next was in store for them. For example, the Wife of Bath's very worldly prologue is followed by her tale of the days of King Arthur, and when this is told the Friar's lewd tale follows and provokes one equally lewd from the Summoner. Then Chaucer (in the guise of Harry Bailly) firmly directs the Clerk to tell him 'som murie thyng of aventures' which will not send them to sleep by its dullness, nor be couched in terms too difficult for them to understand. In the story of Griselda which follows, the Clerk provides an admirable contrast to the overwhelming 'masterie' of the Wife, or the earthy humours of the Friar and Summoner. The patience and devotion of Griselda are thrown into sharp contrast with the wifely behaviour of May as described by the next narrator—the Merchant. This done, the *Squire's Tale* provides an interlude of romance, and this is followed by the Franklin's narrative, with its mixture of magic, romance, and the supernatural. So throughout the *Canterbury Tales*, grave and gay, worldly, supernatural, or elemental—all have their turn and mingle together in our memory to make up the world that is the *Canterbury Tales*. Chaucer's claims to fame are based on the continuous level of excellence which he maintained in reproducing in verse this human comedy. His poetic sensibility, combined with an immense understanding of men and women, enabled him to survey the life about him with such imaginative insight and power. No detail was too small for him to observe, and from it he would frequently draw, or suggest, conclusions which would have escaped many. Thus he sees the seaman, unskilled in horsemanship, who 'roode upon a rouncy[1] as he kouthe',[2] and brings out something of the reeve's sly nature by his remark, 'And evere he rood the hyndreste of oure route'. The Knight's devotion to religion and indifference to worldly show is suggested when Chaucer tells us that he rode, 'Al bismotered with his habergeon,[3] For he was new ycome from his viage', just as the Pardoner's nature is indicated by his goat voice, and 'Swiche glarynge eyen hadde he as an hare'. Similarly, a single reading of Chaucer's description of the Summoner's face is enough to warn us of what to expect when he comes to tell his tale. Men's actions are ever betraying their character in Chaucer, and the comfort-loving nature of the Friar is revealed in those few lines which tell us how he lost no time on coming into a house, but

> 'fro the bench *he droof awey the cat*,
> And leyde adoun his potente[4] and his hat,
> And eek his scrippe, *and sette hym softe adoun.*'

Much of Chaucer's success is due to the way in which he builds up his characters by an accumulation of closely observed significant detail. The *Prologue* is the most famous example, but the tales themselves are well stored with characters minutely observed and described. 'Hende[5] Nicholas', that lively clerk, is clearly put before our eyes: not only as a musician, but as a scholar in whose chamber might be seen

> His Almageste,[6] and bookes grete and smale,
> His astrelabie,[7] longynge for his art,
> His augrym stones[8] layen faire apart,
> On shelves couched at his beddes heed;
> His presse ycovered with a faldyng[9] reed;

[1] rouncy, 'nag' or 'great, strong horse'.
[2] as he kouthe, 'as best he could'.
[3] bismotered . . . habergeon, 'besmutted with marks made by his coat of mail'.
[4] potente, 'staff'. [5] hende, 'gentle, pleasant'.
[6] Almageste, 'the name given to Ptolemy's treatise on astronomy, and applied loosely to works on astrology'.
[7] astrelabie, 'astrolabe'. [8] augrym stones, 'counters for calculation'.
[9] faldyng, 'coarse woollen cloth'.

And al above ther lay a gay sautrie,[1]
On which he made a-nyghtes melodie
So swetely that all the chambre rong;
And *Angelus ad virginem* he song.

Even more detailed is his description of Alison: eighteen years of age, a gentle and slender creature. Chaucer notes her silk-striped girdle, her gored snow-white apron, her white smock with its black-silk embroideries, and the broad fillet of silk upon her head. She had black arched eyebrows, plucked as was the fashion. A leather purse ornamented with silk and metal hung by her side, and her low-cut collar was held together by a brooch as large as the boss of a shield, while her shoes were laced high on her legs. No wonder 'She was moore blisful on to see Than is the newe pere-jonette tree', since in addition to this outward finery, 'Wynsynge she was, as is a joly colt, Long as a mast, and upright as a bolt'—in fact, he sums up, 'she was a prymerole, a piggesnye'.[2] Nor is the portrait yet finished: he emphasizes her abundant healthiness as he describes the ease of her movements, her loud and eager singing, and the glowing radiance of her countenance. As a result we know that we have no Constance or Griselda to deal with, nor on the other hand so overwhelming a woman as the Wife of Bath, but one who enjoyed life and took it as she found it, especially when it came in the attractive guise of a Nicholas.

This controlled use of elaborate description is well illustrated by Chauntecleer. His whole appearance is magnificent, and Chaucer relishes presenting it to us. Chauntecleer's comb is

redder than the fyn coral,
And batailled as it were a castel wal;
His byle was blak, and as the jeet it shoon;
Lyk asure were his legges and his toon;[3]
His nayles whitter than the lylye flour,
And lyk the burned gold was his colour.

It is essential, however, that we should realize that Chaucer does not invent this merely as a delightful piece of descriptive writing. Chauntecleer's behaviour is closely connected with his own appreciation of his outstanding beauty, and we must see it

[1] sautrie, 'a kind of harp'.

[2] prymerole, 'primrose'; piggesnye (pig's eye), 'a flower and then a term of endearment'.

[3] toon, 'toes'.

through his eyes and those of Pertelote if we are to savour the mock-heroic story to the full.

Chaucer frequently gets his effects by more indirect means. Young May, the wife of January, is put before our eyes in these words:

> Mayus, that sit with so benyngne a chiere,
> Hire to biholde it seemed fayerye.
> Queen Ester looked nevere with swich an ye
> On Assuer, so meke a look hath she.
> I may yow nat devyse al hir beautee,
> But thus muche of hir beautee telle I may,
> That she was lyk the bryghte morwe of May,
> Fulfild of alle beautee and plesaunce.
> This Januarie is ravysshed in a traunce
> At every tyme he looked on hir face.

This is sufficient for Chaucer's purpose: we think of May, benign, fair as the May morning, so that to look on her was to be ravished and translated into a world of faery. So she seemed, not only to January, but also to his squire Damian when first he saw her enter the hall—so much so that her beauty inflamed him and thus began the action of the *Merchant's Tale*. Similarly, the characteristics of Griselda ('hir vertu, passynge any wyght Of so yong age, as wel in chiere as dede'), or of Constance ('To rekene as wel hir goodnesse as beautee, Nas nevere swich another as is shee'), or of Emelye ('that fairer was to sene Than is the lylie upon his stalke grene') are rapidly made sufficiently clear for us to realize their importance in their several stories. These descriptions are all part of Chaucer's desire to put living people before us, and not conventionalized lay-figures. From his first great success—the *Book of the Duchess*—to the *Canterbury Tales* this purpose was never lost sight of. Blanche the Duchess, Criseyde, Dorigen are individuals, although they come from a conventional type, and when convention is less heavy upon him, Chaucer can do even better, and create the Wife of Bath or Madame Pertelote. He was never willing to conform to the common medieval method of cataloguing a woman's charms, 'item, two lips indifferent red', and so on. His early attempts in the *Book of the Duchess* show him struggling to break away from the stereotype, and in *Troilus and Criseyde* he gets his effect, in general, not by any detailed description (despite the formal 'portraits' of Book V) but by saying of Criseyde that 'So aungelik was hir natif beaute, That lik a thing immortal semed she, As doth an hevenyssh perfit creature'. Similarly, in *Anelida and Arcite* he sees Emelye as so fair 'That al the ground about her char she spradde With brightnesse of the beaute in her face', or makes Palamon cry out on his first sight of Emelye 'I noot wher she be womman or goddesse, But Venus is it soothly, as I gesse'. He can, if occasion demands, be more explicit. Venus is seen 'Naked fletinge in a see', or Beauty 'withouten any atyr', while the centre of *Troilus and Criseyde* is made up of a series of stanzas describing the consummation of love in frank, sensuous, and passionate verses.

But Chaucer never made the mistake of thinking of women in terms of angels, or of men as paragons of virtue farther than the strict necessities of his story demanded. 'Grisilde is deed, and eek hire pacience', and it is of men and women as immensely fallible (and the more human for it) that he writes. In doing so he frequently gives rein to witty, ironic comment, and is then often at his most characteristic and best. It was this strain in him which produced the Eagle in the *House of Fame*, or Pandarus, or Harry Bailly, and which also enabled him to emphasize the irony of situation and character which is revealed in many of the *Canterbury Tales* and of their narrators. This ironical quality which informs so much of his writing is all part of his omnipresent sense of humour. Chaucer seldom allows any topic, however serious, to extinguish his realization that even here laughter may have its place. It is not the harsh, tortured laughter of Swift but more akin to that of Shakespeare. The Wife of Bath and Sir John Falstaff would have understood one another. Chaucer's sense of humour enables him to relish the vulgarities of his churls, the attitudinizing of the Miller and his wife, or the pretensions of the learned. He can laugh at himself when he feels he is getting too portentous, or falling into a medieval commonplace. His catalogues of men, places, authorities; his appeals to gods and to the learned; his detailed accounts of the minutiae of astronomy and alchemy all require careful scrutiny before we can be sure that Chaucer is not mocking at us—and himself.

Indeed the *visage de bois* is his favourite guise. The most seemingly innocent line may hold a wealth of meaning for the instructed, and it was to them that Chaucer appealed. When he alludes to the Prioress as 'simple and coy' he was aware that these words had a long ancestry in medieval romance which gave to them associations not at all fitting for a nun, just as to note that the Monk's sleeves were 'purfiled[1] at the hond With grys,[2] and that the fyneste of a lond' was to draw the attention of those with more knowledge than their fellows to this infraction of a papal decree, barely fifty years old. Chaucer's ironic, humorous gaze fastened on all he saw with great accuracy and directness. He seldom leaves us in doubt of what he wants us to understand, whether it is the widow's sooty bower and hall and the little yard where Chauntecleer strutted so proudly, or the gay appearance of the Squire, or of Absolon, or the 'grisly feendly rokkes blake' on the Breton shore. The brass horse of the *Squire's Tale*, for all that 'it was of Fairye, as the peple semed', is likened to a steed of Lombardy, or a courser of Apulia, and the preparations for the tourney in the *Knight's Tale* are described in terms as technical and precise as they are full of colour and movement. Chaucer liked his pictures with clear edges, just as he liked a 'manly man' or one who 'so swatte that it wonder was to see', or a 'horsly horse'. His images are curiously simple and direct. They are for the most part introduced with nothing more than a 'like to', or 'as', and cover all phases of human activity, and make their effect by their homely and immediate appeal. The bells on the Monk's bridle ring 'in a whistlynge wynd als cleere, And eek as loude as dooth the chapel belle': the exiled Arcite grows lean and 'drye as is a shaft': the trumpet sounded 'As swifte as pelet out of gonne, Whan fyre is in the poudre ronne': Alisoun 'sproong as a colt dooth in the trave'[3] when Nicholas came too near to her. A man is 'as dronken as a mous', or looks angry as 'a wylde bore', or 'as a grym lyoun', or a 'cruel tygre'. He sleeps 'no more than doth a nightyngale', and is 'murie as a papejay' when he goes wooing 'a prymerole, a piggesnye'.

With this directness of imagery goes an equally direct appeal which was gained by Chaucer's use of proverbs and of maxims drawn from past writers. Chaucer realized that much of this proverbial lore which had its origins in the folk had a clear, unpretentious atmosphere which he valued highly. Hence he uses this material more constantly and with far greater felicity than any author before or since with the possible exception

[1] purfiled, 'trimmed at the edges'. [2] grys, 'costly grey fur'.
[3] trave, 'wooden frame for holding horses'.

of Shakespeare. Sometimes proverbs are used as a means of characterization, as in *Troilus and Criseyde* ('A fool may ek a wis-man ofte gide'), or in the *Wife of Bath's Prologue* ('With empty hand men may none haukes lure'); sometimes they prepare the reader for a new stage in the narrative, as in the *Nun's Priest's Tale* ('Evere the latter ende of joye is wo'); sometimes they comment on a situation, as in the *Knight's Tale* ('who may been a fool, but if he love'). The continuous appearance of proverbs and of proverbial lore helped to give to the poems something of that contact with life which even his most fanciful works maintain. This perception of the beauty of people and of things naturally sharpened in Chaucer that feeling so strong and so widespread among medieval people—a sense of the evanescence of human existence, and of the transitory nature of our life on earth. The Franciscan's *Love Rune* of a century earlier, with its deep-felt warning cries—

> Hwer is Paris and Heleyne,
> Þat weren so bryht and feyre on bleo?[1]
> Amadas and Ideyne,
> Tristram, Yseude, and alle þeo?[2]

—is the theme of the great stanzas at the end of *Troilus and Criseyde*, and is explicit in the *Knight's Tale*: 'This world nys but a thurghfare ful of wo, And we been pilgrymes, passynge to and fro'. The Reeve's recognition of the coming of old age is wonderfully expressed in his Prologue, as is January's refusal to recognize it in the *Merchant's Tale*. 'The tap of life', as Chaucer calls it, is turned on at birth by Death, who awaits the emptying of the vessel of Life—and such is man's lot on earth, 'Now with his love, now in his colde grave, allone'. Just as he realizes the overwhelming emotions associated with death, so his sensitive imagination played about other human experiences, and few have excelled him in depicting simple states of feeling. The story of Griselda, with its appealing lines:

> O goode God! how gentil and how kynde
> Ye semed by youre speche and youre visage
> The day that maked was oure mariage.

leads up to the moving conclusion:

> 'O tendre, o deere, o yonge children myne!
> Youre woful mooder wende stedfastly
> That crueel houndes or som foul vermyne

[1] bleo, 'hue'. [2] þeo, 'those'.

Hadde eten yow: but God, of his mercy,
And youre benyngne fader tendrely
Hath doon yow kept'—and in that same stounde
Al sodeynly she swapte adoun to grounde.

Passages such as this, or Constance's 'Pees, litel sone, I wol do thee noon harm', or Dorigen's lament for her absent husband, 'Is ther no ship, of so many as I se, Wol bryngen hom my lord', or Ugolino's young son's questions: 'Fader, why do ye wepe? Whanne wol the gayler bryngen oure potage', or the cry of the deserted Troilus, 'Who shal now trowe on any othes mo?'—such passages illustrate Chaucer's favourite line 'But pity renneth soone in gentil herte'. The full force of these poignantly simple lines, however, is only felt by reading them in their contexts. In the *Monk's Tale* the terrible passage from Dante of the suffering Ugolino and his sons is divested of the terror with which Dante charged it and is replaced by pity. Chaucer makes us feel the full pathos of the scene by the direct, simple language which he uses, culminating in

And after that, withinne a day or two,
They leyde hem in his lappe adoun and deyde.

This last line might well have served Arnold as one of his 'touchstones': it is certainly far more Chaucerian than is the mere vocative of Arnold's choice: 'O martir, sowded to virginitee'.

This deliberate portrayal of pity rather than terror is characteristic of Chaucer. His reading of life inclined him to take the easier way. Constantly he refers us to learned authorities if we would go deeper into problems. As he modestly says:

But I ne kan nat bulte it to the bren,
As kan the hooly doctour Augustyn,
Or Boece, or the Bisshop Bradwardyn.

For him the surface of life provided so much of interest that he seldom attempted to plumb its depths. To some extent it seems that he did not consider the deeper aspects of human existence as fit matters for poetry. His great contemporaries Wyclif, Gower, and Langland all devoted much of their energy to such topics, and Chaucer left it to them to frighten and persuade people to the good life, by picturing the wickedness and depravity of the world. His own view did not entirely shut out evil or the effects of evil; he recognized the presence of wrongdoers in the world, but refused to castigate them severely or to investigate the reasons for their wickedness very fully. His tolerance had its limits—witness his description of the Summoner, or the unsparing detail of his portrait of old January—but tolerance, moderation, and pity are the abiding notes which help to keep Chaucer's poetry level with life. Where his contemporaries raged he was content to smile. His friend Gower could not mention an abuse without getting angry about it, while Langland and Wyclif were easily roused to violent outbursts by the mention of any one of their *bêtes noires*—the monks, the friars, the idle beggars, and the like. Chaucer's detachment and tolerance are evident as we turn the pages of the *Canterbury Tales* and see the variety of men and women pictured there with all his immense zest for life. The relish with which he details the domestic history of the Host or of the Wife of Bath, or shows the Pardoner at work, or describes the activities of Pandarus carries us away and we accept his characters, as he himself accepts them, without being shocked or wishing to judge them. Chaucer, in brief, had something of Shakespeare's ability to receive whatever came his way, and to regard it without prejudice or disgust, however alien it may have been to his own outlook. Life in all its forms fascinated him, and there, perhaps, we might well be content to leave the matter, adding only Professor Lowes's summary: 'He had, to be sure, no "message". But his sanity ("He is", said Dryden, "a perpetual fountain of good sense"), his soundness, his freedom from sentimentality, his balance of humorous detachment and directness of vision, and above all his large humanity—those are qualities which "give us", to use Arnold's own criticism, "what we can rest on".'

7

If we 'can rest on' these things, which seem so patent, it is because Chaucer has made them so by his skill as an artist, that is by his ability to communicate his ideas in terms of words, rhymes, rhythms, and stanzas. It is no longer possible to think of 'naïve Chaucer' writing in a 'misty age'. On the contrary, as Professor Ker has taught us, 'the latter half of the fourteenth century was more consciously artistic, more secure in command of its resources, than any other period till the time of Pope'; and further Chaucer was the greatest and most resourceful English poet of that period. The long apprenticeship he underwent as an eager student of French and Italian models we have already seen. What he became he became as the result of a deliberate choice and of an unflagging determination, for his decision to study Machaut's poetry was made in the face of other and easier choices.[1] He might have gone on in the long-established tradition, best exemplified in *The Owl and the Nightingale*, or he might have been attracted by the newly revived alliterative poetry, with its splendid possibilities of development, as in *Pearl*. He turned, however, to the new school of French poetry, headed by Machaut, and studied eagerly their experiments in form, in music, and in ideas. So in due time he came to his study of the Italians; and new conceptions of form and new possibilities of story-telling became clear to him. Apprenticeship such as this made him able to convey his ideas and emotions with clarity, ease, and exactitude. Hence it is that our reading of Chaucer, once we have mastered a few matters, is so seemingly easy. Indeed, it is often fatally easy, for the eye runs on delightedly line after line, and much of the true Chaucerian nuance is missed. There is a limpid freshness about it all: page succeeds page of simple eloquence, and unforced, natural dialogue and description. It is in the creation of such a medium that Chaucer shows his skill as an artist and his own peculiar quality.

It would be foolish to think that we can describe this peculiar quality in set terms, but we can see how it was created if we study carefully Chaucer's diction and versification. First, as to diction. Chaucer wrote in an age when words were still limited in their associations. Often, indeed, no word was available which would express Chaucer's exact meaning, and he had to coin a word, or more generally to take one over from a Latin or French source. Of the four thousand and odd words from Romance languages used by Chaucer more than one thousand have not been found in earlier writers in English. No doubt many of them were in use in social and literary circles, but it is to Chaucer's credit that he used, whenever he felt they were wanted, such words—now so common—as administration, comedy, digestion, erect, galaxy, indifferently, moisture, philosophical, policy, secret, tranquillity, and voluptuous. One example must serve to show that they are used effectively. Criseyde tells Troilus that if he leaves her, men will say it is for

[1] See above, p. 37.

shame and 'That love ne drof yow naught to don this dede, But lust *voluptuous* and coward drede'. Chaucer deliberately chose the word 'voluptuous' so as to express the highly sensuous nature of Troilus's action, and its place in the line and its long-drawn-out-character emphasize Chaucer's intention.

Apart from the use he made of newly imported words, Chaucer mainly relied on a large vocabulary which has been estimated at just over 8,000 words, derived in almost equal proportions from Germanic and Romance sources. Gower's vocabulary was little more than half that of Chaucer, and something of the monotony of the *Confessio Amantis* may arise from this fact. (Shakespeare had a vocabulary of some 24,000 words.) But while Chaucer had this large and varied vocabulary on which he could draw, he could not get from his words those 'peripheral overtones' which have meant so much to later writers. Critics have made great play over the pathos of Arcite's farewell cry, 'Allone, withouten any compaignye', but this phrase had little of the evocative effect that it has for us with centuries of association behind the word 'alone'—associations magnificently called on by Coleridge in

> Alone, alone, all, all alone,
> Alone on a wide wide sea.

Chaucer relies for his effect, not on association, but on the position of the line in his narrative, that is by the cumulative effect produced as the passage proceeds, and secondly by the speed, weight, and meaning of the actual words themselves. Thus, in the *Knight's Tale*, Arcite cries:

> Allas, myn hertes queene! allas, my wyf!
> Myn hertes lady, endere of my lyf!
> What is this world? what asketh men to have?
> Now with his love, now in his colde grave
> Allone, withouten any compaignye.
> Fare wel, my sweete foo, myn Emelye!

In this passage the emotional pitch is steadily raised by Arcite's cries and questions to the moment when he contrasts man's earthly felicity with his solitary after-life, and the effectiveness of the line, 'Allone, withouten any compaignye', is immensely enhanced by this building-up of the emotional pitch. Secondly, the appeal this line makes to us is greatly dependent on the skill with which Chaucer uses his diction and varies the pauses and the length of the phrases. The whole passage has a solemn and plangent note: the lines move with dignity, and the monosyllabic character of many of the words emphasizes the slow, deliberate nature of the speech. The antithesis, 'Nów with his lóve, nów in his cólde gráve Allóne' is greatly strengthened by the way in which Chaucer has contrived to stress the words, and by the way in which the tempo is slowed down while the voice lingers over the words 'colde grave Allone, withouten any compaignye'.

Any doubts which might be felt about his deliberate artistry in this passage may be set at rest by turning to the *Miller's Tale* where the line 'Allone, withouten any compaignye' occurs again:

> This clerk was cleped hende Nicholas.
> Of deerne[1] love he koude and of solas;
> And therto he was sleigh and ful privee,
> And lyk a mayden meke for to see.
> A chambre hadde he in that hostelrye
> Allone, withouten any compaignye,
> Ful fetisly ydight with herbes swoote.

Here it will at once be felt that the whole movement is lighter and more rapid. The poet is concerned in setting Nicholas and his chamber clearly before us, and when he wants to express the fact that Nicholas (most unusually at that time) had a room to himself, he does so without holding up his narrative in any way, using the words, 'A chambre hadde he in that hostelrye Allone, withouten any compaignye', and adding that it was bedecked with sweet herbs. Clearly, the whole weight given to the phrase in the *Knight's Tale* is lacking here, and it is lacking because the narrative does not warrant or require its application. In the same way, the movement is such that the verse is kept light and continuous. The emphatic solemnity of 'his colde grave Allone' is absent, and the clear, simple diction is in keeping with the simplicity of the speech and rhythm.

Chaucer's diction, therefore, owes little to the past in the sense that we speak of a modern poet's indebtedness to his predecessors, whose poems have helped to build up the overtones and associations which now cling about certain words and phrases. He is, of course, indebted to earlier writers, not only for actual words, but also for set phrases and collocations which were part of the poetic stock-in-trade, and especially useful for

[1] deerne, 'secret'.

rhyme-tags and for padding out a line. Thus he takes over from the common stock such things as 'rose-red', 'silver-bright', 'snow-white', 'grey as glass', 'soft as silk', 'still as a stone', 'jangled as a Jay', 'digne[1] as water in a ditch', 'brown as a berry', and many others, and uses them at his discretion. Nevertheless, this does not give these phrases any very definite associative value; and indeed, Chaucer's words for the most part have a clear-cut and limited meaning and that close contact with actuality which was part of his method. It is this that makes him liken the Pardoner in his pulpit to a 'dowve sittynge on a berne', or mention the burdock-leaf which the canon's yeoman put under his hood, 'For swoot, and for to keep his heed from heete. . . . His forheed dropped as a stillatorie'. The Clerk is said to ride 'as still and coy as doth a mayde, Were newe spoused, sitting at the bord', while Alisoun's complexion glowed more brightly 'than in the Tour the noble yforged newe'. Such phrases as these are surely Chaucer's own.

This is not to deny, however, as has been admitted above, that Chaucer made use of rhyme-tags and padding material. All medieval writers drew upon a large rag-bag full of tags, alliterative and stock phrases to save themselves trouble, to give their listeners time to absorb some fact or interesting detail, or to drive home the importance of a statement. 'There is no more to say' is only the medieval poet's way of saying what a modern person means when he declares, 'That's all there is about it', or more colloquially, 'That's that!' As for alliterative phrases, they were to be heard on the lips of the people as well as on those of poets and minstrels. Chaucer recognized the vital, racy nature of many of these, and he was right, for some two-thirds of the alliterative phrases used by him have survived in modern English. Such phrases as 'busy as bees', 'fish and flesh', 'friend or foe', 'horse and hounds', 'mirth and melody', 'sigh and sob', or 'weary or wet' are as common now as in Chaucer's time, and these he used with others, such as 'herde ne hyne', 'looth or lief', 'swelten and swoonen', or 'wanen and wenden', which are no longer in common use.

Besides alliterative phrases there were many stock phrases at his disposal. It is not always easy nowadays to give them any specific meaning; but, as Mr. Kenneth Sisam has made clear, they 'have their importance in the economy of spoken verse,

[1] digne, 'worthy'

when a good voice carried them off. They helped out a composer in need of a rime; the reciter on his feet compelled to improvise; and the audience who, lacking the reader's privilege to linger over close-packed lines, welcomed familiar terms that by diluting the sense made it easier to receive.' Such welcome aids were not to be disdained by a poet of Chaucer's temperament, and accordingly we find his poems punctuated by such stock phrases as 'all and some', 'bright and clear', 'deep and wide', 'more and less', 'old and young', 'dance and sing', 'ride and go', or 'weep and cry'. These, with tags like 'out of doubt', 'I dare wel seyn', or 'as olde bokes seyn', or 'sothly to telle', were useful for filling up lines and often for eking out his rhyme.

8

Chaucer's major preoccupation, however, in his efforts to express his poetic ideas most fittingly, was to find what metrical pattern would best meet his purpose, and his surviving works show how ardently he experimented with stanza and metre with this in view. It was obviously right for him to try his hand at the staple French octosyllabics, for these had by his time become almost as common in England as in France, and we have two outstanding poems in this metre—the *Book of the Duchess* and the *House of Fame*, to say nothing of the *Romance of the Rose*. The merits of octosyllabics had been well tested: it is an excellent verse for a quick-moving, conversational type of poem. It is not so well adapted to convey emotion as it is to convey information or description, and the line nowhere seems long enough to allow much freedom to the writer, or any undue elaboration. The rhyme-words seem to bustle along, and a tendency for the verse to break into a jog-trot, or even a gallop, is not easily restrained. Chaucer uses this verse with considerable skill, and essays with some success to overcome its difficulties. Thus he employs run-on lines, at times only within the couplet, but sometimes over-stepping even this. He ends a paragraph on the first half of the couplet, and gets welcome variation by a reversal of the first foot as in '"Blythely", quod he, "com sytte adown"'; or by omitting the first syllable of the line altogether. He splits a couplet between two speakers and occasionally splits a line between them. By these devices, and some skill at varying the pause in the line, throwing it very early, as in 'To hym, to loke wher I myght wight', or ignoring it and running on to an early pause in the next line, as in 'But which a congregacioun Of folk, as I saugh rome aboute'—by such means Chaucer made a lively measure of octosyllabics.

But he was aware of its serious limitations, and a large number of verse-forms, such as the eight-line decasyllabic stanza of the *A.B.C.*, or the nine-line decasyllabic stanza of the 'Complaint' in the *Complaint of Mars*, together with the 'pot-pourri' of verse forms which go to the making of *A Complaint to his Lady*, are evidence enough of Chaucer's experimental ardour. In the course of his efforts he gradually found that the decasyllabic line was most congenial to him, and that in using this line two forms were of outstanding importance. These were the seven-line stanza—the rhyme royal—of *Troilus and Criseyde*, or the *Parliament of Fowls*, and the decasyllabic couplet, as used in the *Legend*, and afterwards in most of the *Canterbury Tales*.

It is important to notice, however, that Chaucer's tact is shown not only by his selection of certain verse-forms, but even more by the remarkable way in which he used and developed them. He was never satisfied to use the form in too regular and unvaried a fashion. Indeed, he rapidly learnt that variation was one of the great secrets, and much of his outstanding superiority to his contemporaries is due to this. The norm, to him, was not something sacrosanct, to which a poet must adhere slavishly, so that the principle that 'language should always seem to *feel*, but not to *suffer from*, the bonds of verse' was fundamental to him. Hence he seldom allows the metrical pattern to be over-emphasized, and his ten syllables may melt to nine, or swell to eleven or twelve at will to meet the exigencies of his ideas. Similarly, the five accents required by metre are frequently lost sight of when the rhythmical pattern only requires the stressing of three of four syllables or words in the line. In these, and a number of other ways to be explained, Chaucer obtained variety, and the result was a flexible, easy-moving form of verse, the like of nothing any of his contemporaries could produce. At its best it has what Arnold called a 'divine fluidity of movement'.

Much of this he undoubtedly owed to Italy. There he was able to study, principally in the works of his beloved Boccaccio, such technical devices as enjambment and the variation of phrase length, or the skilful employment of rhythmic emphasis to support and suggest a fitting emphasis of the idea. But wherever he obtained his models and inspiration, he acquired in time an understanding that freedom of flow was all-important, and that this freedom is the resultant of a number of devices and modulations which chiefly depend upon a constant adjustment of the claims of speech rhythm and metrical pattern.

> In the finest specimens of versification [says Coventry Patmore] there seems to be a perpetual conflict between the law of the verse and the freedom of the language, and each is incessantly, though insignificantly, violated for the purpose of giving effect to the other. The best poet is not he whose verses are the most easily scanned, and whose phraseology is the commonest in its materials, and the most direct in its arrangement; but rather he whose language combines the greatest imaginative accuracy with the most elaborate and sensible metrical organisation, and who, in his verse, preserves everywhere the living sense of the metre, not so much by unvarying obedience to, as by innumerable small departures from, its *modulus*.

We cannot expect to find the greatest imaginative accuracy in Chaucer's diction and imagery, but we can and do find a 'perpetual conflict' between language and versification owing to his understanding of 'the living sense of the metre'.

To illustrate this we may usefully investigate Chaucer's mastery of his narrative verse. In part, his undoubted excellence in this kind of verse is due to his mastery of form, and his ability to keep a firm grasp on the essentials, however wayward at times the vagaries of his narrators. He generally exercises a close control over episodic matter, and uses his illustrative detail to develop and enrich his central themes. Whatever value there is in his narrative as poetry, however, rests on the versification and diction. If these are too regular, wooden, or conventional, the result will be a failure. The nicest tact, arising from a delicate ear and a sensitive feeling for words, gives Chaucer's work its own particular stamp, just as the work of every considerable poet is signed by his power to control these things. Now in narrative poetry a constant variation of the tempo has to be combined with an easy unbroken movement. One of the greatest difficulties of the greatest of English narrative poems, *The Faerie Queene*, arises from the continuous series of momentary breaks which come at the end of each stanza with the Alexandrine. Chaucer avoids this, both in his seven-lined stanza (rhyme royal) and still more in his decasyllabic couplets, for he keeps his verse on the move, save for moments when the needs of his story require a pause to be made. More important, perhaps, is his skill in the use of non-emphatic words and phrases when he wants to hurry his story along, or to give a light, conversational passage after one more heavily weighted for descriptive or reflective purposes. His conservative usage of the final *e* for many words was a great help here, as it gave him many extra syllables for 'filling out' his verses without adding very much to the weight of the line, as, for example, in 'I deemé that hire herté was ful wo' (E 753), where the final *e* of 'deeme' and 'herte' are just sounded, but add nothing to the line's emphasis or weight. In similar fashion, lines such as 'Pekke hem up right as they growe and ete hem yn' (B 4157), or 'Or breke it at a rennyng with his heed' (A 551), or 'And ay the peple cryde, "Here cometh oure joye, And, next his brother, holder up of Troye!"' (*T. and C.* ii. 643–4) obviously are constructed so as to carry on the narrative without delay, while others, such as 'O hateful harm, condicion of poverte!' (B 99) or 'The shepne brennynge with the blake smoke' (A 2000) are equally meant to be recited slowly, so that their due effect may be experienced. In short, Chaucer was a conscious artist with a clear sense of the effect he wished to produce, and of how best he could produce it. The more we investigate Chaucer's work, the more clearly this establishes itself. We shall reach no vital results, however, so long as we are content to examine his work in single lines, and to discuss his variations within the line or the couplet. We must escape from the line, as Chaucer did, and see the wider movement and the way in which sentences and paragraphs were built up. Moreover, we must remember that Chaucer required his verse to be supple enough for every purpose: it had to convey the pathos of Constance as well as the humour of Pandarus, the bawdy reminiscences of the Wife of Bath as well as the knightly adventures of Palamon and Arcite with equal ease and fidelity. An examination of several passages of verse will best make clear how successful Chaucer was in these matters, and how his paragraph and sentence structure, with other poetic devices, contributed to this end. First we may take his work in rhyme royal and look at a passage in which a sense of considerable emotion has to be conveyed:

The lyf so short, the craft so long to lerne,
Th'assay so hard, so sharp the conquerynge,
The dredful joye, alwey that slit so yerne:[1]

[1] slit so yerne, 'passes away so quickly'.

Al this mene I by Love, that my felynge
Astonyeth with his wonderful werkynge
So sore iwis, that whan I on hym thynke,
Nat wot I wel wher that I flete[1] or synke.

Now while it is true, as Professor Manly points out, that this passage is an example of the rhetorical method of beginning a poem with a *sententia*, it is even more important to observe how Chaucer has given the bare idea a life and emotion of his own. In the first place the movement of the whole stanza is admirably controlled. The first three lines describe, in language so expressive of the feelings provoked, the lover's hopes and difficulties, while the remaining four lines portray the lively emotions a contemplation of such a state of affairs produces in him. Chaucer builds up the first three lines with six balanced phrases, all closely knit into one inseparable whole, and their sum is triumphantly stated in the fourth half-line, 'Al this mene I by Love'. And having said this, the stanza runs on without pause, elaborating on the effect produced by the many-sided nature of Love, to its final conclusion, 'Nat wot I wel wher that I flete or synke'. The whole stanza is, therefore, conceived of in two units, which are closely held together by the 'chain-method' employed in the first part, and the movement of the verse in the second with its run-on lines and its shifting caesuras. A firm sense of structure is thus obtained. This general impression is greatly aided by the controlled use of language throughout. The monosyllables of the first and the last line are weighty and dignified: the speech stresses fall regularly on the metrical accents and give a sense of certitude. So in lines 2 and 3 Chaucer keeps his metre regular, but gives life and interest by such things as 'dredful joye' and the forcefulness of 'slit', but in line 4 everything gives way as the voice hurries on to the key-word of the stanza—'Love'. In this, and in the next two lines, 'the perpetual conflict' is seen, for while the underlying metrical pattern is clearly there when we look for it, the voice does not stress so many or the same syllables as those a strict scansion would demand, so that in line 5 only the three important words are given full value, and even so, 'wonderful werkynge', with its alliterative quality, demands that the main stress should fall on the first syllable of each word only and not, as in the metrical pattern, upon 'wónderfúl werkýnge'.

[1] flete, 'float'.

This same stanza-form was also used to convey the wide variety of moods, the philosophical reflections, the discussions and conversations, as well as all that ebb and flow of story and circumstance that went to the making of *Troilus and Criseyde*. Naturally it is not equally well suited to express all of these, although it is remarkable how supple Chaucer makes this noble and firmly articulated stanza. He seldom allows any run-on between one stanza and another, so that each stanza forms a little unit by itself and gives, as it were, an internal structure for the poet's thought. This most frequently results in the first four lines forming one unit, and the remainder of the stanza continuing or developing the thought therein expressed; but it is more important to notice that the limited space keeps the ideas under control, yet gives the poet scope enough with his combination of seven lines, five feet and a nicely interwoven rhyme-scheme (a b a b b c c) to get that movement and variety of tone and verbal contrasts which are so distinctive of this stanza. It is seen at its best, undoubtedly, in conveying such emotions as those expressed by Troilus when he rides past the empty house of Criseyde:

> Then seide he thus, 'O! paleys desolat,
> O hous of houses whilom best ihight,[1]
> O paleys empty and disconsolat,
> O thow lanterne of which queynt[2] is the light,
> O paleys, whilom day, that now art nyght,
> Wel oughtestow to falle, and I to dye,
> Syn she is went that wont was us to gye![3]
>
> O paleis, whilom crowne of houses alle,
> Enlumyned with sonne of alle blisse!
> O ryng, fro which the ruby is out falle,
> O cause of wo, that cause hast ben of lisse![4]
> Yet, syn I may no bet, fayn wolde I kisse
> Thy colde dores, dorste I for this route;
> And farwel shryne, of which the seynt is oute!'

The corresponding passage in the *Filostrato* is thus rendered by Professor Gordon: 'He said "Alas! What a place filled with light and joy thou wert when thou didst contain that beauty who held all my peace of mind in her eyes; now, lacking her, thou art left in darkness; nor do I know if thou art ever destined to possess her

[1] ihight, 'called'.
[2] queynt, 'extinguished'.
[3] gye, 'guide'.
[4] lisse, 'solace, joy'.

again."' From this simple account Chaucer built up his moving apostrophe. It is, of course, rightly thrown into a rhetorical pattern, and the reiterated 'O paleys' and its variants serve to drive home the wealth of associations Troilus had to recall (it is worth while to notice that in Boccaccio it is called simply 'la casa' or 'la magione'). So it moves forward in its stately progress, line by line, building up an overwhelming sense of loss, and bringing us to Chaucer's magnificent final image 'And farwel shryne, of which the seynt is oute!' The words 'light', 'joy', and 'darkness' of the original are all caught up by Chaucer and given full poetic expression, while he enriches his picture by the images of the extinguished lantern, the lost ruby, and the empty shrine, which help to create the sense of universal loss felt by Troilus. The simplicity of structure used in these two stanzas is emphasized by an equal simplicity of language. Here again, Chaucer employs monosyllabic words with great effect, as in the last lines of each stanza, but knows when to use such sonorous words as *disconsolat* and *enlumyned* to help convey the sense of loss or of dazzling light that their contexts require. Alliteration, again, is sparingly but effectively used, while the musical flow of the passage is the result of Chaucer's admirable handling of his open vowels.

The day came, however, when Chaucer could no longer disguise from himself that, despite all his mastery of its possibilities, the rhyme royal could not accomplish the heavy demands he wished to make on verse in order to express the many phases of life that were to form the *Canterbury Tales*. The Wife of Bath, the Reeve, the Miller, and many others who were to tell their 'churl's tales' would have found their words and thoughts sadly out of place in the dignified sobriety of rhyme royal. Chaucer could not return to octosyllabics, and he found a metre ready to his hand in the decasyllabic couplet—a form which he had in one sense been using every time he wrote the two concluding lines of a rhyme-royal stanza. The merits of the decasyllabic couplet are many—as its continuous use in English verse from Chaucer's time onward attests—and we need only remind ourselves here of its immense flexibility and power to express all kinds of emotion, description, conversation, or reflection. Chaucer did not, of course, know all of its possibilities, but an example or two will show what use he made of it. Its narrative power is shown in the following extract:

And so bifel it that this kyng Arthour
Hadde in his hous a lusty bacheler,
That on a day cam ridynge fro ryver;[1]
And happed that, allone as she was born,
5 He saugh a mayde walkynge hym biforn,
Of which mayde anon, maugree hir heed,[2]
By verray force, he rafte hire maydenhed;
For which oppressioun was swich clamour
And swich pursute unto the kyng Arthour,
10 That dampned was this knyght for to be deed,
By cours of lawe, and sholde han lost his heed—
Paraventure swich was the statute tho[3]—
But that the queene and other ladyes mo
So longe preyeden the kyng of grace,
15 Til he his lyf him graunted in the place,
And yaf hym to the queene, al at hir wille,
To chese wheither she wolde hym save or spille.

In this passage, at line 26 of the *Wife of Bath's Tale*, it will be noticed that Chaucer's unit is one of no less than seventeen lines; yet the complex sentence shows no sign of distress. The semicolons of the editors distinguish clearly the three sections which make up the whole; and these increase in length as the poet captures the ear of his audience and is able to convey more and more of the necessary preliminaries of his tale. So clearly did Chaucer envisage the whole paragraph that he is able to keep it flowing easily along, and we are scarcely conscious of the artist's hand which is continuously varying the line. As a result, the number of instances in which the speech stresses coincide with the metrical accents is less than half. The necessity for running on without pause at the end of the first line, for example, throws the stress on '*Hadde* in his *hous*', with a consequent inversion of the first foot, and this device is adopted again in other lines. Indeed, the whole passage 'feels, but does not suffer from the bonds of the verse', and it is this power of counterpointing the speech rhythm against the metrical pattern that helps to give Chaucer his command of an easy, flowing, narrative style. This counterpointing is done in various ways, not probably as a result of any very conscious design on Chaucer's part, but because his sensitive ear could register the various rhythms and was not satisfied for long by the simplicity of a

[1] fro ryver, 'from hawking (near the banks of a river)'.
[2] maugree hir heed, 'in spite of all that she could do'. [3] tho, 'then'.

regular, unvariegated metrical pattern. Hence the position of the pause is varied constantly; the speech stresses are thrown on unaccented syllables; a number of the rhyme-words are unemphatic and easily passed over, while the weight of the various lines is continually changing. Add to these the varying length of the phrases, now some two or three words long only, now running on for two or even three lines—the sum of these uneven parts gradually building up the whole paragraph.

With such a diversity of parts it might well be thought that the metrical pattern would be completely lost. This does not happen, however, for several reasons. First, there is the constant steadying influence of the rhymes. However lightly some of them may be stressed (and this licence must not be abused), yet there they are, and must be taken into account by the poet, and to that extent continually remind him of his norm. Secondly, the stresses may come on the metrical beat or may not, but the stresses are not so varied that the ear loses its sense of the underburden of the metre and its decasyllabic norm. Thus the line, 'That dampned was this knyght for to be deed', can only have speech stresses on *dampned*, *knyght*, and *deed*, although the line can be scanned with its perfectly normal five accents: 'That dámpned wás this knýght for tó be déed'.

More than narrative was required by Chaucer from this verse form, and the following passage from the *Summoner's Tale* will illustrate the way in which it was made to reproduce conversation and to suggest character. The Friar on entering salutes his host and speaks of his recent sermon:

'And there I saugh oure dame,—a! where is she?'
'Yond in the yerd I trowe that she be,'
Seyde this man, 'and she wol come anon.'
'Ey, maister, welcome be ye, by Seint John!'
Seyde this wyf, 'how fare ye, hertely?'
The frere ariseth up ful curteisly,
And hire embraceth in his armes narwe,
And kiste hire sweete, and chirketh as a sparwe
With his lyppes: 'Dame,' quod he, 'right weel,
As he that is youre servant every deel,
Thanked be God, that yow yaf soule and lyf!
Yet saugh I nat this day so fair a wyf
In al the chirche, God so save me!'
'Ye, God amende defautes,[1] sire,' quod she.

[1] defautes (faults).

'Algates,[1] welcome be ye, by my fey!'
'Graunt mercy, dame, this have I founde alwey.'

Little need be said in explanation of the technique of this passage, as many of the means employed in the passage from the *Wife of Bath's Tale* are again used here. The light, conversational tone is admirably suggested by the wealth of monosyllables which carry each line rapidly forward, and may well be compared with the slower moving lines which describe the Friar's first movements on the wife's entry. In the dialogue speed, however, is all-important, and to this the diction makes a notable contribution. Otherwise the run-on lines, the break of the couplet so that each character has one line of it, the numerous inversions at the beginning of the lines, the varying position of the pause, the interplay of speech rhythm and metrical accents seem to give to these lines the actuality of speech, and with this actuality something of the speaker's own character.

These four passages may serve to illustrate some of the characteristics of style which give Chaucer's writings their own peculiar character and flavour. 'The wordes moote be the cosyn to the dede', he tells us, and our analysis has shown how closely Chaucer's thoughts and words go together, and how from this union there results a body of poetry which gives expression to his world of men and women. This world, rich as it is, is nevertheless limited, not only, as we have already noted, in the way in which certain sides of contemporary life are almost excluded, but also in its limited recognition of certain attitudes to life. Arnold's view that Chaucer lacked 'high seriousness' is so beside the mark that we may question whether he had read *Troilus and Criseyde*; yet it would be idle to pretend that Chaucer's mind moved easily or constantly in the most difficult and complicated spheres of thought and speculation. 'Of heaven and hell I have no power to sing'; it was the human comedy which fascinated him, and which he so vividly reproduced in his poetry. That is not to say that the serious side of life meant nothing to him—there are many poems to show that it did—but rather that this most humane, most lovable of poets was at his most characteristic and happiest when dealing with the lighter emotions and with the kaleidoscopic movement of the human scene as he saw it about him, or mused over it among his beloved books.

[1] Algates, 'nevertheless'.

IV

THE FIFTEENTH CENTURY

The death of Chaucer in 1400 deprived England at a blow of her one outstanding author. His successors are to be found in a host of imitators at the head of whom stand Hoccleve and Lydgate; a body of Scottish poets who owe him some allegiance but have their own virtues; a number of anonymous writers of verse whose inspiration is more difficult to trace, and who sang in the remote country-side, and for 'upland men' far from Court or baronial halls. The fifteenth century is by no means as barren of poetry as it used to be fashionable for critics to believe; nevertheless, the glory had departed, and the story of fifteenth-century poetry in England is largely the story of 'the shade of that which once was great', though momentary flashes reveal the fires underneath.

In surveying this poetry we may distinguish between two main classes. First there is the poetry that can absorb and even improve on European models as did the student of Machaut and friend of Eustache Deschamps, Geoffrey Chaucer. Secondly, there is the popular poetry which follows native tradition. In the fifteenth century the first of these kinds of poetry was deficient in England, if not in Scotland; the second kind flourished, and the century is rich in ballad and popular narrative, carol, lyric, and drama.[1] It is to be noted that much verse of this second group is of an accentual rather than a syllabic structure, and that accented metres, where the syllables can take care of themselves, are not so subject to the decay which sets in in the more difficult decasyllabic line.

Nothing is more difficult than to attempt an explanation for the lack of great literature at any point of time. It is not enough to say that this arises from the lack of great poets. *Poeta nascitur non fit* to be sure, but this is not the whole truth. The poet is made or marred to some extent by his age, and still more by the accident of his birth or upbringing which contributes so largely to the growth of his poetic sensibility. Milton's early training at Cambridge and Horton, Wordsworth's life in the Lake country, Byron's unhappy heritage, Tennyson's

[1] For these, see Vol. II, Part II.

Lincolnshire origins--all these had a direct effect on the poet which can often be clearly discerned. Less obvious, but strongly operative, we have also to admit the 'form and pressure' of the age: all those influences, spiritual, material, intellectual, which make up the 'climate of opinion' in which we live. Even the most individual poet cannot altogether dissociate himself from such influences, and they were as important in the fifteenth century as they are to-day. We must not hope to explain the weakness of Lydgate and others solely in terms of the 'spirit of the age', but, on the other hand, we are not entitled to ignore it. The wise plan would seem to be to make an effort to appreciate the peculiar conditions which obtained throughout the fifteenth century, and then to see how these were likely to help or hinder any kind of writer who sought a public for his wares.

One thing is clear. In the fifteenth century England was constantly engaged in war and the business of war—both in France and at home between the houses of York and Lancaster. The early years of the century until the death of Henry V were on the whole bright with promise. Henry IV consolidated his kingdom, and afterwards the young king, his son, rapidly won the affection and esteem of his people. Agincourt, and all that flowed from it, swept the king to the highest point of fame, but after his death in 1422 there followed the long, chequered reign of Henry VI. The burning of Joan of Arc illustrates the sour, revengeful temper which gradually gained the upper hand as our forces were steadily driven back from lands which we had recently conquered, as well as from others held by English kings for centuries. There was little enough in all this to call for national enthusiasm, while on the other hand the constant drain of men and money left the whole country impoverished and commercial expansion seriously curtailed.

At home affairs were no better. The civil war was as disastrous in its effects as was that in France. To see in the Wars of the Roses only a series of fights between a few great lords and their retainers is to take a superficial view. It may well be that the majority of the people of England were not called upon to take up cudgel, or knife, or bow on behalf of the participants; but no student of the period can ignore the effects produced by civil war upon all grades of society. Certainly the example set by these encounters encouraged a lawless spirit among all classes. The Paston family, for example, three times in a few years found themselves besieged in their houses by armed bands, once by Lord Moleyns, once by the Duke of Suffolk, and lastly by the Duke of Norfolk. The last took Caister Castle, 'a rich jewel' recently built and left to the Pastons by Sir John Fastolf, by means of a force 3,000 strong, and when asked to give it back replied that 'the King should as soon have his life as that place'. What wonder that when the greatest lords of the realm so behaved lesser men exercised what power they could, and that as a result England in the fifteenth century was a very unsettled place to live in. Whether we look at official records, at private letters, or at contemporary verses, all alike are constantly recording outrages and lawless deeds of the most flagrant nature. The *Early Chancery Proceedings*, the *Proceedings of the Privy Council*, the *Rolls of Parliament*, the *Coroners' Rolls* all tell the same tale. Civil war: private wars between local lords or factions: gangs of cut-throats and robbers wandering from place to place: everywhere naked force was asserted as argument. These, then, were the material conditions which prevailed over wide areas and long stretches of time in the fifteenth century. A contemporary chronicler puts the condition of England very clearly before us:

> In euery shire with Iakkes and Salades[1] clene
> Myssereule doth ryse and maketh neyghbours werre;
> The wayker gothe benethe, as ofte ys sene,
> The myghtyest his quarell wyll preferre, . . .
> Thay kyll your men alway by one and one,
> And who say ought he shall be bette doutlesse;
> For in your Reme[2] Iustyse of pese bene none
> That darr ought now the contekours[3] oppresse . . .
> The lawe is lyke vnto a Walshmannes hose,
> To eche mannes legge that shapen is and mete;
> So mayntenours subuerte it and transpose,
> Thurgh myght it is full low layde vndyr fete.

The weakness of the central administration was unable to check these abuses, and the old saying, 'man without lord is ill provided for', seemed to be more true than ever as the great nobles with their bands of retainers moved from place to place, asserting their authority ruthlessly, since they knew that they were able to back it by force if necessary.

[1] Iakkes and Salades, 'coats of mail and head-pieces'. [2] Reme, 'realm'.
[3] contekours, 'quarrellers'.

The life of the country was strong, however, and the commercial activity centred in the towns was not easily brought to a standstill. Energetic traders had sent their vessels far and wide: they were to be seen in Ireland and in the distant harbours of Iceland: the whole European coast from Norway to Greece was visited in search of commodities, and many a mariner, besides Chaucer's shipman,

> . . . knew alle the havenes, as they were,
> Fro Gootlond to the cape of Fynystere,
> And every cryke[1] in Britaigne and in Spayne.

The fifteenth century saw much of this trade brought almost to a standstill; nevertheless such names as those of Cely, Bushey, Forteys, and others remind us of the flourishing wool trade between the Cotswold hill villages and the Low Countries, just as the Conynges of Bristol recall the busy carrying trade associated with their name. The Springs of Lavenham, the Tames of Gloucester, and others all form part of that sturdy, industrious middle-class that was making such headway at this time. While the aristocracy killed one another, they lent money to these foolish warriors and took every advantage that the situation gave them. Many civic bodies were similarly active: London got two new charters from Edward IV, and several other towns did likewise. On all sides the records show us men eager for the advancement of themselves, their families, or their towns. The Pastons and the Stonors, for example, illustrate the unending fight that a country gentleman had to make to maintain, or to increase, his position in the county. John Paston spent his life fighting in the courts, or at the sessions, and often used dubiously honest devices to get what he wanted, even resorting to downright violence when it suited his purpose. Thus one of his agents writes to him: 'I lay in wait upon him on the heath, as he should have come homewards, and if I might have met with him I should have had Betts [his prisoner] from him; but he had laid such a watch that he espied us before he came fully at us . . . and he took his horse with his spurs and rode as fast as he might ride.' Such actions were all in the day's work: a bribe to a justice, a threat of force to an unwilling neighbour, a hard bargain over a marriage settlement, a skilfully devised delaying action in the law courts: these and a thousand other devices

[1] cryke (creek).

showed that these fifteenth-century folk were not easily intimidated or persuaded against their wills, and that life conducted on such terms left but little time for the arts or for the deeper things of life.

Yet the deeper things of life were not entirely forgotten. That preoccupation with the hereafter, which we saw to be so strong a factor in fourteenth-century life, was still operative. Indeed, in some ways it seemed to be even stronger. *Timor mortis conturbat me* was an ever-insistent refrain beating in man's inner ear, and perhaps the many visitations of the plague in western Europe between 1348 and 1450 gave special force to such fears. Hence the popularity of the Dance Macabre both in its written and in its plastic forms. The evanescence of human life and the levelling nature of death are both strongly stressed therein, and throughout the fifteenth century such thoughts as these reminded men of the world to come. Their acknowledgement of a world beyond this world is to be seen in the splendid series of perpendicular churches, with their wealth of glass and carved woodwork. How far they fall short of the inspired craftsmanship of the best of Gothic need not be argued here: the fine, substantial proportions of their naves and aisles, with their magnificent bell-towers, are evidence enough that these very merchants who fought with every means within their power for their own advancement still had time to remember that there were other and higher values, and spent their money accordingly, *ad majorem honorem Dei*.

Other signs of an interest in the less material things may be seen in the progress of education during this century. Mr. A. F. Leach, perhaps the most learned student of the history of schools, writes: 'So far as education is concerned, the fifteenth century was not one of decadence, but of progress. A great development of educational foundations took place, alike in the re-endowment and enlargement of old schools and the erection of new schools and colleges.' And with this progress went one vital innovation—the introduction of the layman. As early as 1432 William Sevenoaks, a London grocer, provided by will for a school at Sevenoaks to be taught by 'a master, an honest man, sufficiently advanced and expert in the science of [Latin] grammar, *but by no means in Holy Orders*'. From this it was a simple step to the provision of instruction in reading and writing in the vernacular, and to the production of pupils able to cast accounts and to be of use to tradesmen and merchants. What was coming to be thought necessary is explicitly stated in Archbishop Rotherham's foundation charter of his school in 1483: 'Thirdly, because that country-side [of York] brings forth many youths endowed with the light of keen wit, and not all of them wish to attain to the lofty dignity of the priesthood, we have ordained a third master knowing and skilled in the arts of writing and keeping accounts, in order that such youths may be rendered more capable for the mechanic arts and other worldly affairs.'

The spread of the vernacular was assisted by the numerous injunctions to chantry priests to employ part of their time in teaching the alphabet and reading, while little schools for this purpose were to be found about the country. A growing ability to read and even to write in the vernacular manifests itself throughout this century, although we must be on our guard against accepting *in toto* Gairdner's over-confident assertion that 'no person of any rank or station above mere labouring men seems to have been wholly illiterate'.[1] Further interest in education was shown by the number of grammar schools and colleges founded in this century. 'Henry VI, far more than Edward VI, deserves to be remembered as a founder of English schools', and names such as Eton, Magdalen College School, Ewelme, and Rotherham remind us of some typical fifteenth-century foundations. Similarly, the universities were enlarged in a remarkable way at this time, Cambridge especially benefiting by the desire of pious founders to dedicate part of their revenues to the aid of learning. Thus, King's College was founded in 1441 by Henry VI; Queens' College in 1448 by Margaret of Anjou, and refounded in 1465 by Elizabeth Woodville, consort of Edward IV. St. Catharine's College dates from 1473, Jesus College from 1496, and Christ's College, a refoundation of 1505, was originally founded in 1439 by Henry VI. Whatever we may think of the type of education given in these grammar schools and colleges (and they certainly suffered as inheritors of an outworn tradition), we cannot ignore them when considering the way men's minds were turning in this century.

Yet it must be admitted that, new foundations notwithstanding, learning and higher education were content in this century to live on the past. Only the smallest changes in the university

[1] See also p. 115.

curriculum are to be observed; for the most part, things remained as they had been for generations. Wyclif was 'the last of the schoolmen', and his successors, whether supporters or opponents, left intellectual matters much where they found them. English philosophers of the fifteenth century are almost unknown: indeed, Professor Sorley calls the period 'a blank'. The most important signs of intellectual life were the attempts of Pecock to discuss matters philosophical in the vernacular in such a way that they could be understood by the layman, or the attempt of Fortescue to formulate political theory.

It is true that what Mr. C. L. Kingsford calls an 'intellectual ferment' was at work, but it was limited in its scope and in its agents. Humanism only made its appeal slowly, and men responded to it for different reasons. Great lords such as Humphrey and Tiptoft were patrons of 'the new learning', and as such built up great libraries, stored with manuscripts brought from Italy which introduced new authors and new works to the medieval store. Others, such as Sellyng, Grocyn, and Linacre, studied in Italy, and returned to teach in their own universities, bringing with them their new-found enthusiasm for Greek and many precious manuscripts as well. This ferment must not be ignored, but it did little to leaven the mass. In the universities the old learning slowly ran down as the teachers droned on and on. It was not until the end of the century that the process of fermentation began to give results when men such as Erasmus, Linacre, Grocyn, Colet, and More set up new standards and ideals.

While philosophy and scholasticism were at this low ebb it was unlikely that any other intellectual pursuits would forge rapidly ahead. The history of science, for example, in this century is an uninspiring one. No great English doctor arose to take the place of the famous fourteenth-century surgeon, John of Arderne. Science in the fifteenth century contented itself with making available in the vernacular his works and those of others. Many copies of Arderne's various treatises were made, as were versions of the works of famous surgeons such as Guy de Chauliac or Lanfranc. Works on particular diseases or on special topics broke little fresh ground. For example, we have three fifteenth-century manuscripts which deal with diseases of the eye, but they are all translations of the work of Benevenutus Grassus, a surgeon of the mid-eleventh century. The most flourishing science was alchemy, especially in the latter part of the century. Ripley's *Compound of Alchemy* is only the best known of many works written by him and by his contemporaries, and the study had the support both of Henry VI and Edward IV. Astrology was also popular. The nature and influence of the planets was discussed in innumerable treatises, yet as they were almost entirely based on earlier works of Ptolemy, Alexander, Alkindi, and others, they were of small value and did little to advance knowledge.

The advancement of knowledge, learning, and religion, we must confess, seems to have been pursued with no overwhelming zest at this time, but it is impossible in our present state of knowledge to tell what proportion of the population felt any interest for things of the spirit, or what effect war, riot, lawlessness, trading avarice, and a thousand and one other details had on fifteenth-century life and thought. The historians have no agreed answer to give us: two generations have elapsed since Denton and Thorold Rogers took up diametrically opposite views on the state of England in this period, and most modern historians are content rather to pose the various problems than to attempt to solve them. In this, perhaps, they are wise: the problems of the first half of the century are not those of the second, and detailed researches are but slowly making clear the wide range of economic and social changes that were in progress. The break-up of the old manorial system, the decline of chivalry, the comparative lethargy of the Church once the Lollard heresies had been checked, the decline of overseas trade for a while, the isolation from the Continent caused by the Hundred Years War, the rise of a prosperous middle class, the growing interest in Humanism, the increasing ability to read and write in English—things such as these helped to make the century a notable one, albeit puzzling, full of divided aims and lacking in much that encourages great literature.

Unfortunately, no great artist was forthcoming with sufficient vitality and creative power to overcome these obstacles. The genius of a Chaucer, a Donne, a Wordsworth gave fresh impetus and direction to the stream of English poetry, despite all the influences of the times. A lonely genius, such as Blake, or Gerard Manley Hopkins, will make itself felt, alien though it may be to its age, and although its due recognition may have to await posterity. Failing outstanding merit, the poets of a lesser magnitude require the stimulus of certain conditions, chief of which are a sympathetic cultivated audience and a living tradition of matter and form. Given these, they may achieve work of secondary worth, and have provided a great part of English literature, both prose and verse. The death of Chaucer at the end of the fourteenth century came at an untoward moment. The *Canterbury Tales* are evidence enough of his powers of inclusiveness: there, in one series of stories, he combined past and present, the native with the European tradition, the aristocratic and the *bourgeois*, the romance and the *fabliau*, the elevated and the coarse. The sureness of touch with which he dealt with this diversified material and the unequalled technical accomplishment which he possessed—to these he left no heir. The new tradition he had created had had no time to root itself firmly in the few years between the writing of the *Tales* and his death, and it was easier to see how to imitate the formal qualities of his poems than how to capture their spirit or to emulate their range. His greatness was accepted without question, and every poet conceived his task to be to follow in 'the parfitness and trace' of his dear master. Hence the fifteenth century is filled with 'Chaucerian' poetry. The same measures, the same stanza forms, the same subjects, the same devices are used: it is as if the perfect pattern were available for all to use—'a common greyness silvers everything'. Here, indeed, was tradition, but it was lifeless and empty; and, while it strove to preserve the form, lost almost every trace of the spirit.

V

THE AUTHOR AND HIS PUBLIC

BEFORE we attempt any detailed survey of the poetry and prose of the fifteenth century we may turn to consider the effects of the changes outlined above on the public for whom they were composed, and the problems facing the writer who wished to get a hearing for his work. To take the latter problem first: readers of Monsieur Jusserand's delightful *English Wayfaring Life in the Middle Ages* will not need to be reminded of the difficulties of travel in medieval England, and students of our early literature may well pause on reading his pages to reflect upon the results of such difficulties so far as they affected the creation and dissemination of literature. We must, perhaps, be on our guard against exaggerating these difficulties, for when all is said people did travel in medieval England not only 'from every shires ende. . . . The hooly blisful martir for to seke', but also on the more prosaic errands that the king's officers, the monastic authorities, or the desire for gain commanded. The roads of medieval England were peopled with a motley crew: we may see something of them in Langland's pages clearly enough, and need only remind ourselves of their existence. Every township and village saw the passing stranger: friars on their rounds, the plausible performing beggar, the haughty king's messenger, the trader upon his lawful occasions—a variety of men from whom they learned of what was happening in the great world or, at least, that fraction of what was happening which was known to the traveller or that he was willing to divulge.

Yet even when we have made full allowance for the variety of people to be met with on the road, and have given due weight to their ability and willingness to disseminate such information as they had, the difficulties facing the would-be author were formidable. He only knew by accident what was being written elsewhere, and had no certain means of any kind whereby he could find out if the work which he proposed to do was already done, or in process of composition. So we find the story of the Passion related in both a northern and a southern version; no less than three versions of Mandeville's travels were produced within a brief period, and two versions of the *Seven Sages of Rome*, of *Parthenope of Blois*, of *Sir Launfal*, of *Octavian*. The list could be extended indefinitely. The medieval author, it is clear, was working in the dark; but this did not matter so much then as it would now, for if his knowledge of what was happening elsewhere was limited, so was that of his potential audience, and therefore his version of *Octavian* was *the* version, for all intents and purposes, in his part of England. Authors had a parochial outlook: few of them hoped for much more than a local reputation, and perhaps some of them were wise enough to understand the dilemma which beset Caxton at the end of the fifteenth century when he came to print his materials and could expect to reach a much wider public. In a well-known passage he complained that what was easily understood in one part of England was hard reading or even unintelligible in another part.

> That comyn englysshe that is spoken in one shyre varyeth from a nother. In so moche that in my dayes happened that certayn merchauntes were in a shippe in tamyse, for to have sayled over the see into zelande; and, for lacke of wynde, thei taryed atte forland, and wente to lande for to refreshe them. And one of theym named sheffelde, a mercer, cam into an hows and axed for mete; and specyally he axyd after eggys; And the good wyf answerde, that she coude speke no frenshe. And the marchaunt was angry, for he also coude speke no frenshe, but wold have hadde egges and she understode hym not. And thenne at laste a nother sayd that he wold have eyren; then the good wyf sayd that she understod hym wel. Loo! what sholde a man in thyse dayes now wryte, egges or eyren? certaynly it is harde to playse every man by cause of dyversite and chaunge of langage.

'Egges or eyren'—the dilemma which perplexed Caxton towards the end of the fifteenth century in this preface to *Eneydos* was one which must have been present in the minds of authors throughout that century, and more so earlier. Chaucer was well aware of the difficulties which beset authors whose works were likely to command more than a local circulation as he notes in his verses at the end of *Troilus and Criseyde*:

> And for ther is so gret diversite
> In Englissh and in writyng of oure tonge,
> So prey I God that non myswrite the,
> Ne the mysmetre for defaute of tonge.
> And red wherso thow be, or elles songe,
> That thow be understonde, God I beseche!

Here is indication enough that a widespread circulation demanded much co-operation from readers and listeners, especially if the work was slightly unusual in form or content. Most writers, therefore, perhaps realizing something of all this, found themselves forced to write for an audience within a limited area, and in general for some one person or group of persons. The simplest choice for an author was to write for a patron who would support him and whose tastes and desires he would study to satisfy. Unless he could get such a patron, or had a patrimony of his own, or was a member of some religious fraternity, he was in the unenviable position of a Rutebeuf or a Villon, compelled to make a living as best he could, and often forced to those ignoble tricks and accomplishments, so well recognized as part of the minstrel's stock-in-trade, which called down on his head the vituperations of Holy Church. Rutebeuf voices the common experience of these authors without patrons when he writes:

Chill are my loins when the east-wind blows; it comes and blows through and through me. God so tempers His seasons to me that black flies bite me in summer, and white flies in winter. I am like the wild osier, or like the bird on the bough; in summer I sing, and in winter I weep and make lament. . . . The dice that we buy at the dice-makers have spoiled me of all my garments; dice are my death. . . . I lack food and have lacked it long; no man offers, no man gives to me. I cough with cold, I gape with hunger, whereby I am consumed and maltreated; mattress I lack, bed I lack. My ribs know well the taste of horse-litter; straw bed is no bed, and on mine lies naught but straw.[1]

The life of an author who had a patron was immeasurably better than this, but even he had his difficulties, although they were of another kind. Even so great an author as Chrétien

[1] Et froit au cul quant bise vente.
Li vens me vient, li vens m'esvente.
Diex me fet le tens si à point:
Noire mousche en esté me point,
En yver blanche.
Issi sui com l'osière franche
Ou com li oisiaus seur la branche:
En esté chante,
En yver plor et me gaimante . . .
Li dé qui li détier ont fet
M'ont de ma robe tout desfet;
Li dé m'ocient, . . .
(*De la Griesche d'Yver*)

Vivres me faut et est failliz.
N'uns ne me tent, n'uns ne me baille:
Je touz de froit, de fain baaille,
Dont je sui mors et maubailliz.
Je suis sans coutes et sans liz;
Mes costeiz connoit le pailliz
Et liz de paille n'est pas liz
Et en mon lit n'a fors la paille.
(*La Povretei Rutebeuf*)

de Troyes found this was so when his good lady, Marie of Champagne, ordered him to write on a theme which (good moralist that he was) he found highly distasteful. Nevertheless, he took pen and began his story of Lancelot thus:

Since my lady of Champagne wishes me to write a romance, I shall very gladly do so, being so devoted to her service as to do anything in the world for her, without any intention of flattery. . . . I will say, however, that her command has more to do with this work than any thought or pains that I may expend on it. Here I begin my book about the knight of the cart (Lancelot). The material and the treatment of it are given and furnished to me by the Countess, and I am simply trying to do her will.[1]

And as with Chrétien so with many a lesser man. His patron's desire was his driving force, and it may well be that much of the dreary pedestrian verse which disfigures the fourteenth and fifteenth centuries would never have been written save to flatter the vanity or to please the wretched taste of some rich patron.

Let us not be unduly hard on the patron, however, since he was the only prop and stay of most authors. What patronage could mean may be seen in the career of Froissart. In his youth he found a patron in the Count of Namur, and later he came to England to the court of Edward III, bringing with him letters of recommendation to the queen, who came from his own country of Hainault. She made him one of her *ditteurs*, and for some years Froissart stayed under her protection. After her death he was without a patron for a time and was forced, therefore, to return to his native Valenciennes, and to endure a bleak period of service *dans la marchendise* from which he was rescued by an old friend of his London days, who was a cousin of Queen Philippa, and who was able to bestow on him a vacant living at Lestines. There, in a comfortable rectory, Froissart had leisure and money enough to begin writing his

[1] Des que ma dame de Chanpaingne
Viaut que romanz a feire anpraingne,
Je l'anprandrai moult volantiers,
Come cil qui est suens antiers
De quanqu'il puet el monde feire,
Sanz rien de losange avant treire....
Nenil, je n'an dirai ja rien,
S'est il voirs maleoit gre mien;
Mes tant dirai je que miauz oevre
Ses comandemanz an ceste oevre
Que sans ne painne que j'i mete.
Del *Chevalier de la Charrete*
Comance Crestiiens son livre;
Matiere et san l'an done et livre
La contesse, et il s'antremet
De panser si que rien ni met
Fors sa painne et s'antancion.

imperishable chronicles. So we might continue the story of how his patron advanced him to the canonry of Chimay, or sent him to visit the great Comte de Foix to get new materials for his chronicles, with the result that under such princely patronage his collection of materials grew apace. Let us hear him on some of his patrons:

> To the duke and duchess of Brabant owe I great thanks; for they have always been such to me that I have found them and their friends and their household liberal and courteous to me. The duke Albert hath always received me gladly, and also the lords of Blois, and the good lord of Beaumont and the lord of Moriaumé. . . . I know not if I have named Amedeus, count of Savoy: but in Milan, in Lombardy, the good count gave me a cote-hardie worth twenty golden florins. Reason I have to tell the praises of the noble king of Cyprus, &c.[1]

Not all authors had such good fortune, but whatever chances came their way, we of later times must remember with gratitude (exceptions notwithstanding) the services rendered to literature by the patron in the Middle Ages.

Changing conditions in Chaucer's time and after, however, made it increasingly difficult for men to find it worth while to devote their whole time to writing. Their main work lay elsewhere, and it was only for part of the day, or in leisure moments, that they could turn to their literary work. For such men the hermit's cell, the monastery, the counting-house, or the office stool was their daily lot—literature was reserved for leisure and 'off-duty' hours. The part played by the Church throughout the Middle Ages in providing a competence for authors can scarcely be over-estimated. We have seen how Froissart was made free of money troubles by his livings at Lestines and at Chimay, and we may take it that some ecclesiastical office was the support of most medieval writers in the fifteenth century. Lydgate, Capgrave, Bokenham, Awdley, Pecock, Walton,

[1] Le duc et la ducoise aussi
De Braibant, moult je regrasci.
Car il m'ont tout dis esté tel
Que euls, le leur et leur hostel
Ai je trouvé large et courtois.
Le duc Aubert premièrement
M'a à toute heure liement
Recoeillié, . . .
Et aussi mes seignours de Blois . . .
Et le bon seignour de Beaumont . . .
Et le seignour de Moriaumés. . .
Amé, le conte de Savoie,
Je ne sçai se nommé l'avoie,
Mès à Milans, en Lombardie,
Une bonne cote hardie
Me donna de vingt florins d'or
Et c'est raisons que je renomme
De Cippre le noble roy . . . .
(*Biographie de Sire J. Froissart.*)

and many lesser men were all ecclesiastics. Thus freed from the economic pressure which weighed on the ordinary man, they were able to write in the peace of the monastic scriptorium or the tranquil comfort of their parsonage. As they wrote their seemingly interminable lives of the saints, or devotional homilies, or turned into French or English the learning of the schoolmen and the Fathers, the days passed quickly enough, only disturbed by the ringing of the monastery bell for the daily offices, or by the day-to-day duties which the parish priest had to perform. No doubt, as soon as they had acquired some local reputation, much of their work was done to meet an express desire, or at the command of an ecclesiastical superior; and even when this was not so, the chances were that some devout soul would be glad to purchase the work, or that, if the worst came to the worst, the monastic library would be richer by yet another volume. Yet even monastic bodies had limits to their patience, the space in their libraries, and the extent to which they were prepared to watch one of their number passing his days in endless composition. Hence we sometimes find them seeking about for someone to relieve them of their burdens, and encouraging their writers to obtain outside help and patronage.

John Lydgate, monk of Bury, may well serve as a horrid example of the worst that this system could evolve.[1] Born at Lydgate, near Bury St. Edmunds, he entered the monastery as a novice while still a boy; in due time took the monk's frock and spent the remainder of his life within the cloister walls of Bury or of Hatfield Broadoak. While Bury was one of the most important monasteries in England, and was exceptionally rich with a library of more than 2,000 volumes of sacred and profane literature, yet that was not enough in itself to produce poetry. Lydgate lacked any 'precious experience of life', and this lack is reflected in his work. Unfortunately, he showed distinct powers of welding together words and phrases into colloca-

[1] John Lydgate (*c.* 1370–1450) was born at Lydgate in Suffolk. He was early in life taken into the service of the great Benedictine abbey at Bury St. Edmunds; and, after passing through his novitiate, was professed a monk and by 1397 was also a priest. From then on, until 1415, we lose sight of him. He evidently knew London well, but in 1415 was back in Bury. In *c.* 1421 he seems to have been in Paris, and in 1421 was made Prior of Hatfield Broadoak, Essex, where he remained until 1432. He then received permission to return to Bury, where presumably he passed the rest of his days and died, probably in the autumn of 1449.

tions which had all the appearance of verse, and he had an intolerable glibness and an indomitable energy, which enabled him to essay tasks which a more sensitive man, or one 'charged with children and chief lordes rent', would not have dared to attempt. Hence, in the quiet of the monastic scriptorium, he turned out works in the utmost profusion and of the greatest variety. Nothing seems to have been beyond him: 'a mumming by London merchants before the Lord Mayor, a "letter" to accompany Christmas gifts to the King, an explanation of the Mass for a pious Countess to keep in her chamber, a set of stanzas to serve up as a "subtlety" at a banquet, a complaint for a love-sick squire to offer his lady, the "histories" to accompany figures in a fresco or tapestry, a colossal translation of Boccaccio's "tragedies" . . .'—all went through the same process, and the same dreary tale of verses poured out.

Lydgate's importance, it will perhaps be obvious, is not because of the quality of his work, but by reason of the conditions which enabled him to gratify his literary fecundity. Much of his work is not of a predominantly ecclesiastical nature, and he was frequently employed by a number of patrons to write on various subjects. His translations, made to satisfy some patron's desire, were voluminous. His history of the Trojan wars (the Troy Book) runs to some 30,000 lines, and was commissioned by Henry V while Prince of Wales. Again, his translation of Deguilleville's *Pèlerinage de la Vie Humaine*, made for the Earl of Salisbury, occupies 25,000 lines, while his translation of a French version of Boccaccio's *De Casibus Virorum Illustrium*, made for that prince of patrons, Humphrey, Duke of Gloucester, has the correspondingly princely length of 36,000 lines. His smaller works, such as those already mentioned, were obviously *pièces d'occasion*, and no doubt were paid for by the London merchants, or the pious countess, or the love-sick squire at rates satisfactory to the poet. Hence in the course of an industrious lifetime Lydgate turned out about 145,000 lines of verse.[1]

Patronage did not often achieve such elephantine success, but Lydgate's career shows how a man with a safe harbourage, coupled with the support of rich patrons, was able to increase the literary output of his time. Lydgate is only an outstanding example of what was a widespread practice. The fifteenth-

[1] See also below, p. 138.

century Augustinian friar, Osbern Bokenham, who translated into English verse a number of lives of the saints, furnishes us with another instructive example of how literature was evolved.[1] Fortunately Bokenham tells us a good deal about his literary methods and about his patrons. For example, he says that the life of St. Margaret was written at 'the importune and besy preyere Of oon whom I loue wyth herte entere, ... Whos request to me is a comaundement'. He did not, however, at first assent to this prayer and request, but finally on the 17 September 1443, after pondering the matter, he decided to translate the life of the blessed saint. Another friend, the Lady Katherine Denston, and her husband John persuaded him to do the same for the life of St. Anna, and the humble supplication of John and Isabel Hunt produced yet another saint's life. He is even more explicit concerning the origin of his life of St. Mary Magdalene. He tells us that he was in the presence of the Lady Bourchier at a time when her four sons, all dressed in fresh array, like a meadow bedecked with blue and green flowers, were dancing with their friends in her chamber. The lady talked with him of the many legends which he had turned into English, and added that she long had had a peculiar affection for the blessed Mary Magdalene, and desired him to render her life in English. Bokenham was (or professed to be) doubtful of his poetic ability; but finally, after obtaining a respite while he made a pilgrimage to St. James of Compostella, agreed to do what she wished. It is evident that these patrons had learned by popular report of Bokenham's poetic ability, and persuaded him from time to time (no doubt accompanied by a suitable reward for himself or his friary) to write something for them. Their own special devotion to a particular saint furnished a subject, and provided the poet with a good reason

[1] Osbern Bokenham (1392?–1447?). Little is known of Bokenham's life save what can be gathered from his writings. His birthplace is unknown—villages in Surrey, Lincolnshire, and Norfolk have all been suggested—and all he tells us is that his rude English comes from 'the barbarisme of the soyle the wych I haue be fostryd & brought forthe yn of youthe'. He was an Augustinian friar of Stoke Clare, and a Doctor of Divinity, who had travelled in Italy and in Spain. In addition to his verse translations of the 'Lives of Holy Women' he also wrote a geographical account of England in prose known as the *Mappula Angliae*, translated from Higden's *Polychronicon*. He tells us that he also compiled a collection of legends from the *Legenda Aurea*. Nothing is known of the whereabouts of this work, which was presumably a larger volume to which the 'Lives of Holy Women' may have been an addition.

to English yet another of these lives. When we find also that all these people whose names are mentioned in the poem were friends or relations, or lived fairly close together, the deduction is clear that here we have a local writer with a reputation, whose works were sought after, and whose fame was well appreciated within a certain area, and yet a writer whose livelihood was assured by none of these things but by his religious vocation.

From these ecclesiastics we may turn to the laymen—a growing body of writers in the late fourteenth and fifteenth centuries who indulged in literary composition only 'out of hours'. We so constantly think of Chaucer solely as a poet that we are apt to forget how, in the course of a very busy life, he filled a variety of royal offices which must have exacted much time and energy for their discharge. His career illustrates the immense benefits to be gained by an eager alert mind as it moves from place to place on official business, and stores up impressions of men and manners, all of which are the raw materials upon which the artist will work when the time comes to call them forth from their resting-place.

Thomas Hoccleve furnishes us with another good example of the 'part-time' literary man. He entered the office of the King's Privy Seal when he was about twenty, and there he remained. In his leisure he wrote verse, much of it of an autobiographical nature, and from this we can learn a great deal about the life of a gay 'young man about town' of the late fourteenth century; but, more to our purpose, we can learn something of the difficulties which beset a man who probably turned to literature as a means of supplementing a slender salary irregularly paid. We find him looking in all directions for wealthy and influential patrons, among whom he names in various works Henry IV, Henry V, Humphrey, Duke of Gloucester, the Duke of Bedford, the Duke of York, John of Gaunt, and many others less important. Among his extant poems are a number which were composed (like similar works of Lydgate) solely to exhort various officials, such as the Lord Chancellor, or the Under-Treasurer, or various patrons, such as Henry V, to make money payments to him.[1] The desirability of having a patron or patrons, despite the fact that he had a permanent office, was clearly constantly before Hoccleve's mind, and may help us to

[1] See also below, p. 148.

remember how dependent literature still was on the private generosity of rich patrons.

Evidence such as this suggests that medieval authors depended upon patrons unless they had some assured source of income or other certainty of a livelihood. Literature had flourished under the patronage of the Church and of the aristocracy. These two bodies had paid the piper and the tunes had been fashioned to meet their wishes. Once they had been satisfied there was no reason why their followers and dependants should not participate in enjoying the romances, tales, legends or saints' lives which the minstrel could bring to them, but it was to the Church and the aristocracy that writers of Chaucer's day still looked for patronage. As time went on the part played by the Church grew less and less important,[1] but throughout the fifteenth century and beyond the court and the aristocracy continued to act as patrons of literature. Late in the fourteenth century Gower relates how he met Richard II while rowing on the Thames, and how he was commanded to enter the royal barge. After some talk the king ordered him to write 'some newe thing', and as a result we have the *Confessio Amantis*, made as Gower tells us 'for King Richardes sake'. Many earlier examples might be quoted to show the prevailing practice of this century.

The coming of the fifteenth century saw no rapid change, and indeed the number of works dedicated to the aristocratic patron who had commissioned the work seems to increase, and the Lydgates, Hoccleves, Bokenhams, and the like were able to continue their labours; yet at the same time a new class of reader was slowly forming. Its formation was immensely accelerated by the establishment of English as the recognized medium of official correspondence, of the law courts, and of our own literature. When Chaucer was born, French was still the language of the court, and Gower's work in French as well as in English is evidence that French still retained something of its former importance as a literary medium even late in the century. But the tide had turned; and during Chaucer's lifetime it became abundantly clear that English and not French was henceforth to be the language of the aristocracy. For a long time French had been the official language; but in 1356 it was ordered that English should be spoken in all cases in

[1] See below, p. 151.

the London sheriffs' courts. Six years later the law courts followed suit, and in 1363 the Chancellor opened Parliament in English. Once the long-drawn-out battle between French and English had been settled, the rapid decay of French was notable. Trevisa, in 1385, says that 'nowadays boys know no more French than their left heel', while in 1404 two ambassadors to France admitted that they were 'as ignorant of French as of Hebrew'! Henry IV 'challenged in Englyssh tonge' before the Parliament; the earliest known will in English was made in 1387; a proclamation of the City of London appears in English in 1383, and that some ability to write in English had already been gained is shown from a letter of Sir John Hawkwood in Florence, written to Thomas Cogesale. It runs:

Dere S. I grete you wel and do you to wytyn þ[t] at the makyng of þis lettre I was in good poynt I thank God. I send Johan Sampson bryngere of þis lettere to you enformed of certeyn thyngs quiche he schal tellyn you of mouthe. Querfore I preye you þat ye leven hym as my persone. Wrytyn at Florence þe viii day of Novembre [1392]. John Hawkwode, chivaler.

Increased facilities for education enabled more and more people to read and write in English. As we have seen, grammar schools and colleges for the study of Latin were a feature of the fifteenth century, but there went side by side with these a setting up of 'petty schools' called ABC's and Song (*petytis vocatis Apesyes et Songe*). Here the elements of reading and writing in the vernacular were taught with the result that in 1533 Sir Thomas More asserted that over half the population could read. This seems to have been an over-estimate, even in 1533, and a century earlier it would certainly have been a gross exaggeration. Nevertheless, literacy was on the increase in the fifteenth century, and we may accept Mr. C. L. Kingsford's considered view that

there has been too much readiness to undervalue the culture and civilisation of the age. Certainly capacity to read and write was no longer an accomplishment confined to the clerical class. The wives and sisters of country gentlemen could often write as well as their husbands and brothers, and both they and their servants could and commonly did keep regular household accounts. In a merchant's office a capacity to read and write must long have been required.

Hence a new public was awaiting the writer. He was no

longer forced to depend mainly on the generosity of one person, or on one small group of persons, but could begin to cater for the great body of rising middle-class men and women of England who, with money in their pockets and a little learning in their heads, were asking to be instructed and amused. So by the middle of the century, wherever we turn, the evidence is all of a piece; a new public has been created, and writers are busy satisfying its needs.

2

The career of John Shirley illustrates the change. Here we have a man who, in the course of his ninety-year life, found that his interest in the works of Chaucer, Lydgate, and others was shared by many. He also realized that these were folk who were not rich enough to follow the old fashion, and to ask for a poem or history to be copied for themselves; still less could they hope ever to commission books to be written for their exclusive use. Nevertheless, they were eager to read whatever they could get hold of, especially the works of certain authors whose fame was a matter of common repute. Shirley tried to satisfy this demand. When he died in 1456 he was the tenant of a large house and four shops which he rented from St. Bartholomew's Hospital, and it has been strongly argued that these were the headquarters of his 'publishing business'. There are extant enough manuscripts written by Shirley, or partly copied from his work, for us to realize that they were compiled to satisfy an existing public; and these manuscripts contain not single pieces but a number of items to satisfy a variety of tastes. Thus, in one volume of his (now Brit. Mus. Additional MS. 16165) we find Chaucer's translation of Boethius, Trevisa's translation of Nicodemus' *De Passione Christi*, the second Duke of York's *The Master of Game*, Lydgate's *The Complaint of the Black Knight*, the *Regula sacerdotalis*, Chaucer's *Anelida*, Lydgate's *St. Anne* and his *Departing of Chaucer*, the Earl of Warwick's poem to Lady Despenser, and a number of short 'litel balades, complaintes and roundelles'. That these were intended to be read and in due course returned by his customers appears from his prefatory verses:

þe prologe of þe Kalundare of þis little booke

If þat you list for to entende
Of þis booke to here legende

Suche as is right vertuous
Of maner of mirthe nought vicious
As wryten haue þees olde clerkes
þat beon appreued in alle hir werkis
By oure eldres here to fore
Remembraunce ellys were forlore.
Wher fore dere sirs I you beseche
þat ye disdeyne not with my speche
ffor affter þe symplesse of my witt
So as feblesse wolde suffice hit
þis litell booke with myn hande
wryten I haue ye shul vnderstande
And sought þe copie in many a place
To haue þe more thank of your grace
And doon hit bynde In þis volume
þat boþe þe grete and þe comune
May þer on looke and eke hit reede.

He goes on to enumerate the pieces which follow, adding remarks on their authors ('by *Geffrey Chaucier* Which in oure wolgare hade neuer his pere Of eloquencyale retorryke') or on the subject-matter ('The notablest story of huntyng That euer was made to fore this day'); and, after warmly praising the authors and their works, he concludes with a piece of practical advice:

And whane ye haue þis booke ouerlooked
The right lynes with þe crooked
And þe sentence vnderstonden
With Inne youre mynde hit faste ebounden
Thankeþe þauctoures þat þeos storyes
Renoueld haue to youre memoryes
And þe wryter for his distresse
Whiche besechiþe youre gentylesse
þat ye sende þis booke ageyne
Hoome to *Shirley* þat is right feyne
If hit haþe beon to youre plesaunce
As in þe reedyng of þe romaunce
And alle þat beon in þis companye
God sende hem Joye of hir ladye
And euery womman of hir loue
Prey I to God þat sitteþe aboue.

Explicit.

A number of manuscripts still exist, containing what has been described as his 'bookplate'—that is to say, a single stanza recording his ownership of the volume and recommending its pleasurable contents. It runs:

> Yee þat desyre in herte and haue plesaunce
> Olde stories in bokis for to rede
> Gode matieres putt hem in remembraunce
> And of the other take yee none hede
> Bysechyng yowe of youre godely hede
> Whanne yee þis boke haue ouer-redde and seyne
> To *Johan Shirley* restore yee hit ageyne.

Shirley's efforts to interest and instruct his readers are also to be seen in the long rubrics with which he introduces some of the poems. These often provide the only external evidence for ascribing certain poems to Chaucer or Lydgate. *A Mumming for the Goldsmiths of London* is thus described by Shirley:

> And nowe filowethe a lettre made in wyse of balade by Ledegate Daun Johan, of a mommynge,[1] whiche the goldesmythes of the Cite of London mommed in right fresshe and costele welych desguysing[2] to þeyre Mayre Eestfeld, vpon Candelmasse day at nyght, affter souper; brought and presented vn to þe Mayre by an heraude, cleped Fortune.

In addition to Shirley's acknowledged manuscripts, a number of others survive which are derived from Shirley's texts or are the work of scribes able to put their hands on Shirley manuscripts. These may well be the work of one scriptorium, and the obvious inference is that this was the purpose for which Shirley rented the four shops above mentioned. Among disseminators of literature in the fifteenth century Shirley will always hold an honoured place.

3

But the newly born 'reading public' of the fifteenth century was not to be satisfied merely by borrowing books. Naturally, as the ability to read became more widespread, so did the desire to have books of one's own. The itinerant minstrel had been a most welcome visitant in the past. His repertoire was immense, and while he was at hand no one need go for long without hearing romance, ballad, story, or religious narrative as their taste demanded. But once he had left the hall, only a few tantalizing scraps of his repertoire remained in the memory,

[1] mommynge (mumming).
[2] costele welych desguysing (costly Welsh disguising).

and men longed for a written record which would recreate the whole whenever they so desired. To meet such a demand manuscripts began to multiply, as more and more copies of poems or prose works were made, and each in its turn became the propagator of yet more copies. The survival of so many manuscripts of such things as *Piers Plowman*, the *Canterbury Tales*, the *Brut*, or the writings of Rolle, Hilton, Love, or Lydgate is evidence of their great popularity, and of the fact that people liked them well enough to go to the trouble and expense of getting a copy for their own use.

The fifteenth century was not an age of great creative literature, but it was not without interest in literature. Although their aims were limited, pragmatic, and uninstructed, writers and scholars cultivated almost every province of knowledge. Religious literature had always held a predominating position from the earliest times, and the fifteenth century saw the tradition still upheld. The widespread interest in sacred legend was met by such vast compilations as the prose translation of the *Golden Legend*, or by smaller collections such as those of Lydgate or Bokenham. The pious tale or *exemplum* had a great vogue, and was collected in volumes such as the *Gesta Romanorum*, the *Alphabet of Tales*, or the *Book of the Knight of La Tour Landry*. Allegory, again, survived from preceding centuries, and blossomed out in *The Assembly of the Gods*, *The Pilgrimage of the Life of Man*, or *The Quatrefoil of Love*. The most original contribution of the century, however, was in books of systematized religious instruction: Love's *Mirror*, the *Lantern of Light* or the translation of à Kempis. Sermons and homilies were collected in such works as Mirk's *Festial*, *Jacob's Well*; or Pecock's *Rule of Christian Religion*, the *Donet*, and the *Follower to the Donet*. Then again numerous works appeared as practical helps to those attending the services of Holy Church. The *Lay Folks Mass Book* and the *Lay Folks Prayer Book* are both of the fourteenth century, but works such as the *Merita Missae* (attributed to Lydgate), *Of the Sacrament of the Altar*, or Mirk's *Instruction for Parish Priests* are good examples of fifteenth-century attempts to provide clear and definite help to the practising Christian. Lastly, we must not fail to notice the great body of religious lyrics which the century produced—a mass so skilfully reduced and edited for us in Carleton Brown's *Religious Lyrics of the Fifteenth Century*.

While religious needs were thus satisfied secular literature was becoming more and more important. We may readily admit that, for the most part, it was not 'a literature of power'. It has too often in the past been considered only from such a point of view, and as such rightly condemned. But if we will but be content to see in it a literature vital to the education of a newly created public, and to observe how it tried to meet the varied needs of that public, we shall understand it better and arrive at a truer estimate of its value. First, however, we must note that the traditional literature as written by 'court poets' continued with growing feebleness throughout the century. Lydgate at the beginning and Hawes at the end of the century may serve for the moment to indicate the kind of work that is meant. The poetry which they wrote was in the main traditional: its types, its stanza forms, its diction, its ideas—all were stereotyped, and the results disappointing. Translations, allegories, devotional works, didactic works were still the main output of these followers of tradition, and such works as *The Flower and the Leaf*, *The Assembly of Ladies*, *The Cuckoo and the Nightingale*, *The Court of Love*, *Reason and Sensuality*, or *The Temple of Glass* show how strongly entrenched the 'courtly' type of poetry remained.[1] The uneducated, or partially educated, palates found little here to their taste. For them, however, a considerable output of the utmost variety was available.

To a public newly aware of its powers and anxious to consolidate its position, literature of an informative nature was an obvious need. Works were written to advise parents on the upbringing of their children, such as *How the Goodwife taught her Daughter*; or to instruct would-be aspirants to professional knowledge, as in John Russell's *Boke of Nurture*, or in the *Boke of Curtasye*; or to teach children, as in the 'lytyl reporte' of how young people should behave, known as *The Babees Book*, or *Urbanitatis*, or *The ABC of Aristotle* (to give them the titles of Furnivall's edition of them in *Manners and Meals in Olden Times*). Again, the delights of the chase or of gardening are described in the second Duke of York's *The Master of Game*, and in Jon Gardener's treatise on gardens. The world of knowledge as contained in Bartholomew's *De Proprietatibus Rerum* was put into English by John Trevisa in 1398; culinary science was made available in the *Liber Cure Cocorum* and other fifteenth-

[1] See below, p. 130.

century cookery books. John of Arderne's medical works were translated while works like the 'Dietary' attributed to Lydgate served as guides to health, and the *Book of Quinte Essence*, an early treatise on 'natural science', contained much strange information.[1]

Matters of ecclesiastical, social, and political interest were constantly dealt with by various writers in verse easily understood by ordinary people. A violent attack was made on the many semi-religious activities of the friars in *Jack Upland*, to which the *Reply of Friar Daw Topias* is an answer. *Against the Lollards* voices popular feeling against the followers of Wyclif. *The Libel of English Policy* sets out in vigorous fashion current ideas on commercial policy, the importance of a navy, and the need to keep clear the narrow seas. The wars in France naturally furnished much matter for comment, and the *Battaile of Agincourt*, the *Siege of Calais*, or 'Verses on the popular discontent at the disasters in France' reflect various phases of these campaigns. Suffolk and his unpopular colleagues were the occasion for a number of satires, culminating in verses celebrating his execution: 'For Jack Napes soule, *Placebo* and *Dirige*'. The fortunes of 'York and Lancaster's long jars' are mirrored in such poems as *The Ship of State*, *The Bearward and the Bear*, *The Rose of Rouen*, *A Political Retrospect*, *The Recovery of the Throne by Edward IV*, or *The Rose of England*. These and many other subjects are dealt with in vigorous if unpolished verse, and reflect the intense popular interest in the themes they describe.[2]

Historical writings of a more formal nature also abound. Until the fifteenth century nearly all history had been written in Latin. After the Anglo-Saxon Chronicle ceased to be written at Peterborough in 1154, the only attempts at historical writing in the vernacular were such works as Layamon's *Brut*, Robert of Gloucester's *Chronicle*, Mannyng of Brunne's *Story of England*, Barbour's *Bruce*, and the Chronicles of England known as the *Brut*. Far outweighing these in importance as historical records and as literature were the writings in Latin of the great chroniclers, William of Malmesbury, Geoffrey of Monmouth, Matthew Paris, and many others. In the fifteenth century all this was changed. Instead of English history being written for the most part in Latin, and possibly translated for those who

[1] See below, p. 156. [2] See Vol. II, Part II, for popular narrative verse.

could not understand Latin, the only continuous chronicle of the fifteenth century was actually composed in English, and afterwards translated into Latin for those who clung to the ancient tradition. So great was the demand for the vernacular version that Dr. Brie has listed no less than 121 copies of the *Brut*, and tells us that this list is by no means complete. Even more significant than the wide diffusion of the *Brut* in manuscript and (between 1480 and 1530) in print is, as Mr. C. L. Kingsford observes, 'the fact that through the London Chronicle and the *Brut*, a narrative written in English speech for popular use for the first time takes rank as a leading contemporary authority. Viewed simply as a literary production it is of no great merit, though passages of a good, forceful kind are not lacking. However, the immaturity of its style is of small moment as compared with the fact of its existence.' What the *Brut* did for national history a series of local chronicles did for the towns. The English chronicles of London were first put into the form in which we now have them about 1414, and various versions and additions continued to appear for the next half-century. In the same way a number of chronicles were written to set forth the history of various towns, and the many existing manuscripts of these and of the London chronicles all strengthen the evidence afforded by the *Brut* that there was a growing and widespread demand for historical matter in English during the fifteenth century.

Works of an instructive nature were not the only secular reading the fifteenth century required. To this century we are indebted for the earliest texts of some of our ballads and for many a romance. Lyric poetry—religious, occasional, amatory—is much more widespread than in the fourteenth century; the religious drama made great strides in response to popular demand and a growing secular control; the humorous tale, so superbly handled by Chaucer, finds many practitioners, whilst the fable flourished, as is seen in collections by Lydgate, Henryson, and Caxton.[1]

In these various ways the writers of this period responded to the demands made upon them. The extent and urgency of these demands must remain a matter on which we are very imperfectly informed, but some indication of the growing interest in books in manuscript is shown by an examination of

[1] See below, p. 161.

the wills of laymen of this century. Bequests of books (and these not exclusively of a religious character) begin to be made in wills. Country gentlemen and merchants now feel that the possession of a few books at least was a thing demanded by their position. Old Sir John Fastolf, who was no reader himself, owned many a book in French and English, and the Paston family, with a greater interest in reading, collected many volumes. Anne Paston had a copy of Lydgate's *Siege of Thebes* of her own; Walter Paston had the *Book of the Seven Sages*, and John Paston was the owner of a book containing 'The Meeting of the Duke and Emperor'. His elder brother, Sir John Paston, was an enthusiastic bibliophile, and was ever anxious to acquire new works, or to have copies of old ones made for him. He had, for example, a volume which contained 26 pages of writing concerning the Coronation and the duties of Knighthood; a 120-page treatise on War in four books; an 86-page treatise on Wisdom; the rules of Chivalry set out in 28 pages; and at the end the *de Regimine Principum* in 90 pages. Among other composite volumes Sir John had one in which were *La Belle Dame sans merci*, *The Disputation between Hope and Despair*, *The Parliament of Fowls*, and *The Life of St. Christopher*. Many other works were in his possession, some bound up into collections as the above, some in single volumes, and some existing only in quires—that is, just as they came from the scrivener. Finally, as soon as the new-fashioned printed book became available, Sir John bought one of these—*The Game and Play of Chess* 'in preente', as the inventory of his library puts it.

The mention of print brings us to the beginning in 1476 of a new era. But by the time that Caxton set up his press at Westminster in 1476 there had been created this new body of readers to whom authors found they could increasingly turn for appreciative support. Manuscript copies of their work could be multiplied in limited numbers by the scriveners, but do what they would author and scrivener could only reach a relatively small public. Once, however, the possibilities which the printing press could offer became available literary wares were at the command of modest purses, so that a little more than a hundred years were to elapse before the quarto editions of Shakespeare's plays were to be bought for sixpence apiece—the price of a draught of canary or a can of sack.

VI

FIFTEENTH-CENTURY VERSE

From what has already been said it will be evident that fifteenth-century literature is deserving of far more respectful attention than it has received from literary historians in the past. The qualified nature of its claims we have already admitted, but even such claims have hitherto not been clearly set out. Both verse and prose have suffered, for the extent and variety of a valuable material in both forms has been very inadequately recognized. In verse the emphasis in literary histories has been on 'courtly' poetry, and Lydgate and his followers —the so-called 'Chaucerians'—have had most of the critical attention, while the whole body of writers of 'non-Chaucerian' verse have been fobbed off with a few condescending paragraphs of mild commendation. Dr. A. W. Pollard has been an honourable exception here: as early as 1903 he was calling attention to the mass of poetry of a 'non-Chaucerian' or 'non-courtly' nature that was available, and after quoting some verses from the *Nut-Brown Maid* declares: 'to say that English poetry was dead when verse like this was being written is absurd. It was not dead, but banished from court.'

Anyone who follows the advice implicit in this statement soon comes to realize that there is a great body of fifteenth-century verse available. Some of this is purely religious: indeed Professor Carleton Brown tells us in his Introduction to *Religious Lyrics of the Fifteenth Century* that 'the volume of extant fifteenth-century religious poetry, contrary to the impression which one receives from handbooks of literature, is many times larger than that of the preceding century'. Not only religious poetry, but political, satiric, and occasional verse of many kinds was being produced—most of it mediocre, but generally bearing about it something lacking in the 'courtly' poetry—a something which we may conveniently summarize as a lively contact with life. This is the vital dividing line between the two great streams of fifteenth-century poetry, and we must distinguish sharply between them. Throughout much of the century there was still a demand for the old 'courtly' type of poetry, a demand encouraged by the chivalric renaissance of the court of Edward III. Edward had reanimated the chivalric world; his new Order of the Garter, his love of jousts and tournaments, the martial exploits of his son and his nobles all encouraged the propagation of a literature in which knightly prowess and the love of ladies could be celebrated. This interest was kept alive by the exploits of Henry V, and it is significant that a large number of the romances have been preserved for us by the care of fifteenth-century patrons. Some of these patrons no doubt were moved by their love of these tales and of the life which they reflected, while others, perhaps, collected these and other forms of literature because it was the 'right thing' to do. As we have seen, Sir John Paston may be regarded as a representative of the former class, while Sir John Fastolf may stand for the latter.[1]

The demand for 'courtly' poetry, therefore, encouraged many poets to fashion their verses in the old tried forms, and to elaborate themes which had been old centuries before. Gradually a crushing weight of tradition was created which no 'courtly' poet was strong enough or audacious enough to defy. The two leaders of poetry in the early decades of the century were Lydgate and Hoccleve, who untiringly acknowledged their indebtedness to Chaucer and their determination to follow in his footsteps. But who can draw the bow of Ulysses? Both these writers could only take over the verse-forms, the diction, and the conventions used by Chaucer, and in their turn hand them on to their successors and pupils. The degradation of verse which was brought about by this progressive in-breeding can be estimated by reflecting on the implications of Hawes's profession that he tries

> To folowe the trace, and all the perfitnes
> Of my master Lydgate.

Whatever vitality Chaucer had imparted to his themes and metrical patterns was utterly exhausted during the century, for unless constantly renewed their strength rapidly becomes formalized and emptied of delight. This was the history of the ambitious 'courtly works' of the fifteenth century. It was the hey-day of the poetaster, who, with little feeling for verse and no intellectual powers of any consequence, beat out his numbers with growing incompetence.

[1] See above, p. 123.

These writers slavishly followed traditional forms and themes, and clutched eagerly at any device which they thought might help them. Hence they took over ready-made the dream-convention, and began their poems by dozing over their books, or by allowing the author to read and to fall asleep over his book; or by a description of the time of year, in imitation of Chaucer's *Prologue*; or by a prologue explaining their deficiencies and how they came to write at all. They exploited every technical device, such as telling of their story by 'cloudy figures', or by 'veiled discourse', or by the elaborate use of the 'rhetorical colours', or by a reliance upon allegory. They employed the metres, forms and diction which had descended from the time of Chaucer, and hoped by so doing to merit for themselves the title of poet.

I

To illustrate all this in detail would be tedious, but an understanding of what was wrong with this 'courtly' poetry depends upon a realization of how widespread the canker of servile imitation had become. Take, for example, the idea of prefacing a work by a prologue. We have plenty of examples in Chaucer's work, or in the *Confessio Amantis*, or the *Parliament of the Three Ages* to remind us how effective this device may be. It is otherwise with many fifteenth-century prologues. In the general prologue to his *Legends of Holy Women* Bokenham follows scholastic tradition with his careful statement of the four causes of his work: material, formal, final, and efficient. Fortunately, in the prologues to the separate legends he gives a more lively and gossipy account of their origin, and despite much conventional self-abasement, his prologues remain the most readable part of his work.[1] Other writers use the prologue to excuse themselves or to put in a claim for the indulgence of their readers or their patron. Lydgate luxuriates in these introductory grovellings, which at times he couples with entreaties for money. Walton apologizes for his 'Insuffishaunce of cunnyng and of wit, Defaut of langage and of eloquence'. The anonymous translator of *Palladius on Husbandry* devotes a prologue of 128 lines to the praise of the patron, Humphrey of Gloucester, while Ridley dedicates his *Compound of Alchemy* to

[1] See above, p. 112.

Edward IV in an introduction of 240 lines. Hawes is little briefer in the *Pastime of Pleasure*, where he apologizes to his 'Ryght myghty prynce and redoubted souerayne' Henry VII because his work is 'opprest with rudenes Without rhetoryke or colour crafty'.

The 'colours' of which Hawes speaks were among the technical devices used by all medieval poets. In the pseudo-Ciceronian treatise *Ad Herennium* will be found a list of the various *exornationes* of formal speech. Later writers enlarged on these, and Brunetto Latini in his *Livre dou Trésor* lists Ornament, Circumlocution, Comparison, Exclamation, Fable, Transition, Demonstration, and Repetition as 'colours' or embellishments of style. Medieval rhetoricians, like Matthew of Vendôme, Geoffrey de Vinsauf, and John de Garland greatly expanded the categories of 'colours', while French poets such as Chaucer's contemporary Deschamps discussed at length the many problems of form and style that were so living a matter for them.

Fifteenth-century poets expected more, perhaps, from these 'rules' than it was possible to obtain, and they are constantly pleading their inability to conform to the rules, or to the practice of great followers of the rules (as they thought) such as Chaucer. But here they misunderstood what had happened. Chaucer began by being the servant of rhetoric but ended by being its master. No fifteenth-century 'courtly' poet laughed at 'Gaufred, deere maister soverayn'; yet no poet could profit from works like Geoffrey's *Nova Poetria* who took them too seriously and regarded rhetoric as an end in itself. Thus the author of the *Court of Love* apologizes for his work, since in it 'Ne craft of Galfrid [Geoffrey] may nat here sojorne', while *La Belle Dame sans Merci*, its author tells us, 'Standeth ful destitute Of eloquence, of metre, and of colours', whereas it ought to be written, as Walton regrets he cannot write, 'With wordes set in colour wonder wel, Of rhetoryk endited craftily.'

Despite such disclaimers, most authors endeavoured to use the rhetorical 'colours' so far as they could, since they enabled the writer to exhibit his *expertise*, and powers of amplification. But they were a double-edged weapon, which had to be used with a clear knowledge of the effect they were designed to obtain. Used clumsily, or excessively, they only resulted in boring or annoying the reader; and in the main, fifteenth-century writers used these devices in a lifeless, unenterprising way.

Even with such aids, these poets never tired of proclaiming their own incompetence. One and all they repeat with wearisome unanimity that they never slept on Parnassus nor drank of the Muses' well, have never been inspired by Clio, or Melpomene, or Calliope, and have failed to garner any wisdom from Tully, Quintilian, Virgil, or other 'laureate clerks'. Benedict Burgh's comprehensive disclaimer may well illustrate this trick:

> Of tullius frauncis[1] and quintilian
> fayne wolde I lere. but I not conceyve can
> The noble poete virgil the mantuan
> Omere the greke and torqwat[2] sovereyne
> Naso[3] also that sith this worlde firste began
> the marvelist transformynge all best can devyne
> Terence ye mery and plesant theatryne
> porcyus[4] lucan marcyan[5] and orace
> stace Juvenall and the lauriate bocase.[6]

Their timidity of outlook and lack of enterprise also betrayed itself in the way in which they clung to forms, such as allegory. Where Langland had used it as a vital part of his poetic method and as a means to an end, a host of lesser writers found in it an end in itself. Hence much fifteenth-century verse is disfigured by allegorical conceits which lie heavy and lifeless upon such ideas as the poets have. To men who had laughed at the 'churls' tales' of Chaucer, with their homely realism and frank acceptance of men as men, the insistence on allegorical interpretations, on personified abstractions, and the continual emphasis on moral and philosophical considerations rapidly became tedious. Some men might still be willing to work their way through such instructive works, but long before the end of the century it became clear that this form of poetry was losing its appeal. Men were no longer content to accept the medieval, Christian view, that for poets, 'Ther chieff labour is vicis to repreue With a maner couvert similitude'. By the end of the

[1] tullius frauncis, 'Marcus Tullius Cicero, Francis Petrarch'.
[2] torqwat, 'Torquatus Severinus Boethius'.
[3] Naso, 'Ovidius Naso'.
[4] porcyus, 'Persius'.
[5] marcyan, 'Martianus Capella'.
[6] bocase, 'Boccaccio'.

century Hawes reiterates this as the proper doctrine, but is forced to admit that

> rude people, opprest with blindnes
> Against your fables, will often solisgise
> Suche is their minde, such is their folishnes
> For they beleue, in no maner of wyse
> That vnder a coloure, a trouth may aryse
> For folyshe people, blynded in a matter
> Will often erre, when they of it do clatter.

'Courtly' poets were also servile in their use of stanza forms and in their diction. This may be seen by noting the volume of verse written in Chaucer's rhyme royal. Hoccleve and Lydgate also use rhyme royal, though Lydgate especially makes use of other metres. Many a later writer, however, uses rhyme royal for the most unlikely purposes—in a treatise on agriculture, or one on alchemy, or to introduce one on economic policy—as well as for poems of a more traditional kind, such as *The Pastime of Pleasure*, *The Ship of Fools*, or *The Garland of Laurel*. It is perhaps worth noting that Skelton realizes the unsuitable nature of the stanza for his *Garland*, and in places bursts out into a tripping, singing measure that offers the reader much needed relief. For even with Chaucer's verses before them as a model, the work of these poets is void of metrical pleasure. There is a prosodic incompetence about it which is wellnigh omnipresent. A few writers show some feeling for verse—the anonymous writers of *Palladius*, or of the *Lover's Mass*,[1] for example—but for such writers as Lydgate, Hawes, and Barclay we can only regret that they were misguided enough to think that they could use Chaucer's verse form. A reader who tries to read them aloud halts and stumbles as he endeavours to make the lines scan or run with any ease. The incompetence of these poets cannot be entirely explained in terms of the elimination of the final *e* and other changes in syntax and pronunciation which were in process at the time. Hoccleve and Lydgate were both men of thirty and over when Chaucer died, and were both admitted followers of Chaucer, yet their verses are halting and rhythmically insensitive to a degree. In common with their contemporaries and successors, Hoccleve and Lydgate failed to understand what constitutes easy-moving verse. The ordinary laws of scansion hardly obtain

[1] See Vol. II, Part II, p. 119.

in many places, and words are stressed or coined to suit the author's purpose in a most unexpected fashion. Lydgate must bear much of the blame for the disastrous example he set, and much of what has been said above will be illustrated in detail in a consideration of his work.

Their diction is as lacking in freshness and enterprise as their use of verse forms. 'So all my best is dressing old words new', writes Shakespeare, but these writers use old words without making them new. Within some fifty lines the author of the *Court of Sapience* uses *heavenly* to help describe *sound*, *a wood*, *a voice*, *colours*, and *paradise*. Words such as 'golden', 'sugared', 'angelic', 'lusty', and many others are worked to death and there is a resulting flatness and lack of originality. As offensive is the 'aureate' language[1] which more and more came to be thought necessary, so that Hawes could declare it to be the poet's duty to tell

> the tale in termes eloquent
> The barbary[2] tongue it doth ferre exclude
> Electynge wordes whiche are expedyent
> In latyn or in englysshe after the entent
> Encensynge out the aromatyke fume
> Our langage rude to exyle and consume.

2

The best examples of 'courtly' poetry in fifteenth-century England are to be sought among those poems for long accepted as the genuine works of Chaucer. The ascription of these poems to Chaucer, and their inclusion in the Chaucer canon, gave to them a wider publicity than they have had since Skeat and other editors consigned them to the Chaucer apocrypha. Dryden modernized *The Flower and the Leaf* and Wordsworth *The Cuckoo and the Nightingale*, Keats borrowed a title from *La Belle Dame sans Merci*, and Hazlitt in his lecture on 'Chaucer and Spenser' quoted nine stanzas from *The Flower and the Leaf* to illustrate the gusto of Chaucer's descriptions of natural scenery. 'They have a local truth and freshness, which gives the very feeling of the air, the coolness or moisture of the ground. Inanimate objects are thus made to have a fellow-feeling in the interest of the story; and render back the sentiment of the speaker's mind.'

[1] For this, see Vol. III, Chap. I.

[2] barbary (barbarous)

The earliest of these poems is *The Cuckoo and the Nightingale*, written about 1403 by Sir T. Clanvowe, a member of a Herefordshire family, and well known at the court of Henry IV. It follows the familiar pattern in which the poet, after reflections on the power of Love and the influence of May upon lovers, leaves his sleepless bed and wanders into the fields to hear the nightingale. Soothed by the song of birds, and by the running water, he falls asleep, and in his dream hears the debate of a nightingale and a cuckoo. The cuckoo laughs at Love and its victims, and makes light of the nightingale's praise of Love's gifts to men. The nightingale weeps with exasperation, and the dreamer drives the cuckoo away. He is thanked by the nightingale, told not to believe the cuckoo, but to worship the daisy and listen to the nightingale's song. She assembles all the birds of the vale, asks for their support against the cuckoo, which they give, and agree to hold a parliament at Woodstock outside the queen's window on St. Valentine's Day. The loud triumphant song of the nightingale wakes the dreamer and ends the poem. There is little here that is new, and the poet excites little surprise by his handling of the theme. His five-line stanza is not very firmly controlled: 'headless' lines are comparatively frequent, while there are a number of lines with faulty metrical patterns. There is, however, a certain freshness in the way that the poet extols the May morning

> whan they mowe here the briddes singe,
> And see the floures and the leves springe,
> That bringeth into hertes remembraunce
> A maner ese, medled with grevaunce,[1]
> And lusty thoughtes fulle of greet longinge.

The country-side is 'a launde of whyte and grene' in which the birds sing and debate, and leave far behind them a world in which Love and the troubles of lovers have to be dealt with in more business-like ways. While we read the poem we are still in that well-known country so favoured by the 'courtly' poet, and known for centuries as his homeland by 'every wight that gentil is of kinde'.

The strong hold which this 'courtly' poetry had is shown by the way it persisted through the century. Throughout the period of the Wars of the Roses every now and then someone thought it worth while to commission, or to get copied out

[1] medled with grevaunce, 'mixed with sorrow'.

for themselves, one of these poems. *La Belle Dame sans Merci*, for instance, belongs to the middle years of the century and is a translation by Sir Richard Ros of a poem by Alain Chartier written about 1424. The core of the poem consists of a long debate between a lover and lady. He is ardent, she is cold. Her matter-of-fact replies to his enthusiastic outbursts are an interesting commentary on how *amour courtois* was regarded by some fifteenth-century people. To the lover's assertion that 'Who sonest dyeth, his care is leest of alle', she answers: 'This sicknesse is right esy to endure, But fewe people it causeth for to dy', and says plainly, 'Who secheth sorowe, his be the receyt!' She concludes by telling the lover that:

> My hert, nor I, have don you no forfeyt,
> By which ye shulde complayne in any kynde.
> There hurteth you nothing but your conceyt . . .
> Ye noy me sore, in wasting al this wynde.

Against such a matter-of-fact attitude the lover can make no progress. He states his case with zeal and orthodoxy. 'Resoun, counsayl, wisdom, and good avyse Ben under love arested everichoon', he cries, but it is all of no avail. The lady is adamant, and the poet departs: 'And in him-self took so gret hevinesse, That he was deed, within a day or twayne.'

Though the matter is translated and conventional there are some noteworthy things in the poem. As in *Troilus and Criseyde*, the courtly dialogue had an interest of its own for a contemporary audience. There is the medieval delight in the pursuit of a word, and one speaker often takes up a word or phrase coming at the end of the previous stanza and makes it the subject of his new utterance. There is a skill in this word-play that was fascinating to the original readers of the poem. We, unfortunately, feel but little of this. The word-spinning nature of the dialogue requires a leisure and a sympathetic understanding of conventions which are very remote to us. *La Belle Dame*, therefore, refuses to come to life, although the poet is well in command of his form, and handles his eight-line stanza with fluency and ease:

> In-to this world was never formed non,
> Nor under heven crëature y-bore,
> Nor never shal, save only your persone,
> To whom your worship toucheth half so sore,

But me, which have no seson, lesse ne more,
Of youth ne age, but still in your service;
I have non eyen, no wit, nor mouth in store,
But al be given to the same office.

Perhaps the best-known poems of a 'courtly' nature written in the fifteenth century are *The Flower and the Leaf* and the *Assembly of Ladies*. They both belong to the second half and probably to the end of the century. Scholars have been unable to agree as to their authorship: Skeat thought they were both by one author—a woman—but his conjecture has not been accepted, nor have those guesses which attribute *The Flower and the Leaf* to Lydgate, or even to Chaucer. The unknown writer of *The Flower and the Leaf*, however, was a poet of distinction: as we have seen, Hazlitt used a passage from this work to illustrate Chaucer's outstanding merits, and the whole poem is gracefully contrived. It tells how the poet, a woman, unable to sleep, wanders afield and takes up her station in an arbour from where she can see and hear the nightingale and the goldfinch. After a time a 'world of ladies' and of knights and men at arms, all in white garments, appear. These are the followers of the Leaf, who worship the laurel. Another band of lords and ladies arrive, clad in green, who dance, and then kneel in praise before the daisy—the followers of the Flower. While the former party rest in the shade of a laurel tree, the company of the Flower suffer from heat, are buffeted by hail and rain, and present a bedraggled appearance to those beneath the laurel. The latter succour them, anoint their blistered limbs, and provide them with 'plesaunt salades', and in good time

They passed al, so plesantly singing
That it would have comforted any wight.

The poet asks a conveniently belated member of the Leaf party to explain the meaning of all she has seen. The followers of the Leaf, she is told, are those who have been chaste, brave, and steadfast in love, while the followers of the Flower are those who have loved idleness, and cared for nothing but hunting, hawking, and playing in meads. The party of the Leaf are led by Diana, of the Flower by Flora.

The value of this poem cannot arise from any novelty of subject-matter. All its concomitants—the orders of the Flower and the Leaf, the white and green costumes, the cult of the daisy, the astronomical reference, the spring setting, and the rest—can be traced to one or more earlier poems in French or English, but the poem's distinction lies in the ease and grace with which they have been adapted to the author's purpose. For unlike its models, *The Flower and the Leaf* is no straightforward example of the ordinary 'courtly' type. The chaste, brave, and constant in love are set against the idle, frivolous, and casual. The knightly amusements of the chase or the pleasuring with ladies 'down by the river or up in the forest' are pastimes of the party of the Flower, which wilt and suffer under the blasts of everyday life. The life of devotion and restraint is opposed to one of pleasure and indulgence. Yet both are so much a part of life as we know it that the poet, while expressing a preference for the Leaf, does not exile the Flower, and the story ends with the departure of the two parties to sup together. The whole is a pleasing little morality: the blacks are not really very black, while the whites are not too self-conscious of their own virtues. It marks the beginning of a change: the appeal seems no longer to be to ecclesiastical or 'courtly' standards, but rather to a common-sense morality which might commend itself to the changing age it sought to amuse and instruct.

The instruction is half-concealed, partly by the allegory of the Leaf and the Flower, and partly by the graceful accomplishment of the verse. Although much of the imagery and diction are conventional, the poet gives us many charming pictures of the goldfinch on the medlar, or the entry of the supporters of the Leaf with 'so greet a noise of thundring trompes blow', or of the ladies with their chaplets of 'leves fresh and grene'. Bright, clear colours abound: the greens of the 'benched arbour' or the robes of the Knights of the Flower are contrasted with the white surcoats and horse-harness of the Knights of the Leaf. Country sights and sounds are with us throughout, and the simple cadences in which the poet describes the scene and its action make a harmonious accompaniment which allows us to enjoy this unforced contribution to the allegory of Love. Among all fifteenth-century poems written in this genre it well deserves the high place it has held since its earliest appearance in print in 1598.

The *Assembly of Ladies* belongs to this group of poems. Skeat's view that it was by the same author as *The Flower and the Leaf*, although of a later date, has not been strongly supported, for much of the material that is common to the two poems is the stock-in-trade of the 'courtly' poet. Allegory has laid a heavy hand on the *Assembly*; and, in place of the charming groups which gathered about Flora and Diana, we are confronted with such stock characters as Perseveraunce, the usher; Countenance, the porter; Largesse, the steward; Remembrance, the chamberlain; and many others who are servants to the Lady Loyalty, dwelling at Pleasant Regard.

The story is simple and inconclusive. The narrator and four of her friends are summoned to appear before the Lady at her council, and there to present their petitions. We follow their preparations to this end, and finally find ourselves in the presence-chamber of Loyalty, who receives the petitions, and then adjourns the sitting, postponing her answer till 'within short tyme our court of parliment Here shal be holde', when their grievances shall be remedied. All this is a dream which comes to the writer (supposedly a woman) and is as unsatisfying as dreams often are. The machinery has creaked and groaned to no purpose. The writer clearly makes use of the allegorical form because it is there at hand, and is the conventional method of expressing one's ideas. But Perseveraunce, Loyalty, and all the rest are very shadowy figures: Loyalty never comes to life, and never assumes any individuality of her own. She is fully described: her beauty is such

> That, in ernest to speke, withouten fayl,
> For yonge and olde, and every maner age,
> It was a world to loke on her visage.

Even so, both she and her court remain but lay-figures. What life there is in the poem comes from the writer's frank interest in the ceremonial of princely courts, the behaviour of cultured people, and the conversation that such places and people implied, and the fresh simplicity of the writing.

Thus the opening stanzas are admirable in their economical description of the garden and of the conversation between the lady and a knight:

> He asked me ayein—'whom that I sought,
> And of my colour why I was so pale?'
> 'Forsothe', quod I, 'and therby lyth a tale.'

'That must me wite', quod he, 'and that anon;
Tel on, let see, and make no tarying.'
'Abyd', quod I, 'ye been a hasty oon,
I let you wite it is no litel thing.'

Throughout the poem there are constant touches which enliven the dull wastes of the allegorical landscape: the description of Pleasant Regard ('a very paradyse'); the asides or last-moment thoughts of the characters, as when the dreamer remarks that 'long to sewe, it is a wery thing', and asks her friend if her gown is becoming: 'It is right wel', quod she, 'unto my pay:[1] Ye nede not care to what place ever ye go'—an opinion which is enforced later by the tribute of Diligence: 'Sister', quod she, 'right wel brouk[2] ye your new'. The etiquette and intrigue of courts are cleverly suggested in a few phrases, and the reader is constantly aware of the bifocal vision of the author. At moments we are asked to see at long distance (as it were) the movement of the story and characters as parts of the allegory: at other moments at short distance, and much more clearly, we get touches of life or of lifelike material. Hence the poem cannot be considered a success: the handling of the fable is uncertain, and is not redeemed by any poetic vision of life, or by any mastery of technique. Despite some memorable passages, much observation and a sense of dialogue, the *Assembly* remains a museum piece.

Few medieval institutions have excited more speculation than the so-called Courts of Love, said to have been held by such ladies as Eleanor of Aquitaine or Marie of Champagne. Their fame and influence early became a matter of first-rate importance to poets, for the decisions of these courts, and the rules of love on which they were based, are at the root of most courtly poetry. The action of the lovers in *Troilus and Criseyde*, or of the lover in *La Belle Dame*, as we have already seen, is in conformity with the classic rules of love as stated by Andreas Capellanus, and as interpreted by the Courts of Love. Consequently it is no surprise to find among 'Chaucerian poems' one entitled the *Court of Love*. Its author and the date of its composition are unknown. It exists in one manuscript only, said to be of the early sixteenth century; its use of some linguistic forms show that they are archaisms and that it was written at a period when the final *-e* was seldom sounded. We may

[1] unto my pay, 'to my satisfaction'. [2] brouk, 'enjoy'.

reasonably consider it to be the work of a writer well read in Chaucer and Lydgate, and fully conversant with the body of poetry, both French and English, which made use of all the paraphernalia of courtly love.

The poem tells how Philogenet appears at the Castle of Love, is sent by Admetus and Alceste into the temple where the oath of allegiance and of obedience to the twenty commandments of Love (which are recited in full) is administered. Philogenet is introduced to the Lady Rosiall, who in due course confesses her love for him and tells him he may stay until the first of May, when the festival of Love is celebrated. The poem concludes with this festival, when the birds sing the praises of the god.

This poem serves as a good example of the debilitating effect of a tradition that has lost its vigour. All the materials common to the type are here. The twenty statutes of Love and their discussion take us back to Andreas Capellanus, while the detailed description of Rosiall and of her dress, the May-day song of the birds, the numerous allegorical figures, the court of Admetus and Alceste—all these had flourished for centuries, but had little importance at a time when Henry VII and Henry VIII were fashioning the new Tudor England. The poet of the *Court of Love* is skilful, ingenious, and a versifier of some power: he has some pretty fancies, is fluent, and carries us along with the buoyant enthusiasm of his 'little Philobona' and the ardent lover; the dialogue in places is well contrived and managed with great skill. If we have to class this poem with the *Assembly of Ladies* as a *tour de force* we must again remind ourselves that a good deal of poetic talent is here stultified, because it is content to pad round in the traces of a thousand predecessors, and has not courage and strength enough to break away and risk failure in new unaccepted forms.

3

From these 'Chaucerian' poems we turn to scrutinize the works of others who called Chaucer their master, and at their head stand Lydgate and Hoccleve. An examination of their poems will emphasize what has been said in the opening paragraphs of this chapter, and will explain why many critics after reading in their works have impatiently pronounced a general condemnation of the poetry of the century.

Lydgate's career has already been briefly described, and emphasis has been laid on the fact that his life was 'above the battle'.[1] We know little of his early life, but he tells us himself how he entered the abbey of Bury St. Edmunds while still a boy, and was a novice there, passing his days idly and little inclined to listen to his teachers, or to abstain from 'ryot or excesse', until in his fifteenth year

> holdyng my passage
> Myd of a cloyster, depicte upon a wall,
> I saugh a crucifix, whos woundes were not smalle,
> With this word 'Vide', wreten there besyde,
> 'Behold my mekenesse, O child, and leve thy pryde.'

From that day he dated his real conversion, and the rest of his life was spent mainly in the cloister at Bury or nearby at Hatfield Broadoak. Life passed him by while he spent endless hours in the scriptorium turning out verses on very many subjects, so that, despite the inevitable losses, there still remain 145,500 lines of verse to testify to his energy.

While his energy cannot be gainsaid, the value of his work as poetry has been a matter of much dispute. Ritson, *more suo*, speaks of him as 'a voluminous, prosaic, and drivelling monk', and one of his recent editors tells us that 'it cannot be too clearly asserted that as poetry Lydgate's works are absolutely worthless'. From this we may pass to the opposite point of view strongly advanced on several occasions by Churton Collins that Lydgate was a poet of genius, most musical, with a style and verse of exquisite beauty at its best, and great powers of pathos.

Before surveying his work we must admit that its volume raises doubts concerning its quality, and the fact that so much of it was written to order adds to our uneasiness. The long poems on which his contemporary reputation was based were all commissioned work, as was also much of his occasional verse.[2] To whatever demands were made on him Lydgate willingly responded, and his prodigious output has been a heavy legacy for generations of students. A brief examination of some of his chief works must precede any attempt to estimate their value.

An early piece from his pen, *Reason and Sensuality*, a poem in octosyllabic couplets, was written about 1408, and is one of the more readable of Lydgate's works. It is translated from the French *Les Échecs Amoureux*, and its theme is chastity. Here is

[1] See above, p. 110. [2] See above, p. 111.

much of the familiar apparatus of the allegorical convention: Spring, gardens, Nature, the Goddesses, together with the Forest of Reason and the Garden of Pleasure. Having reached the Garden of Pleasure the poet watches a game of chess, and then begins one himself with a fair maid; but before they have got far the poem breaks off. There is some freedom in Lydgate's use of his octosyllabics, despite much tiresome padding, and he has not yet lapsed into his practice of over-lengthy description and trite moralizing.

A few years later Lydgate began one of the longest of his compositions—*The Hystorye Sege and Dystruccyon of Troye*, as Pynson styled his edition of 1513, or the *Troy Book* as it is more generally called. The poem was begun in 1412 at the command of Henry V while Prince of Wales, and was not finished until early in 1421. It consists of decasyllabic couplets, with a prologue and epilogue in addition, and follows closely the version of Guido delle Colonne's *Historia Troiana*. Few readers will have patience to read much of this uninspired translation: here and there, however, the social historian will find full-length descriptions of medieval life, such as the account of the workmen and of the building of New Troy, or that describing the powers of the 'nigromancer'. There are also occasional poetic moments when Lydgate describes the Spring, or strikes out lines such as 'With swiche colour as men go to her graue', or 'And saue the eye atwen was no message'. While still working on the last stretches of the *Troy Book* Lydgate put in hand his *Siege of Thebes*. It may, perhaps, be regarded as his tribute to his master Chaucer. Written in the autumn of 1421, or early in 1422, it is composed in decasyllabic couplets. The story has been adapted from an unknown French prose romance —itself a redaction of the verse *Roman de Thèbes*—with garnishings from the writings of Boccaccio added by Lydgate. The *Siege of Thebes* is the most readable of Lydgate's epics, since here he has not indulged unduly in his characteristic enlargements and adornings. Even so, it is far too long: the preparation for the siege takes up three-quarters of the poem, and although the poet has the fortunes of Oedipus at his disposal, we are never absorbed by the story. The most interesting part of the poem in every way is the prologue, in which Lydgate represents himself as joining the pilgrims at Canterbury, and being invited to ride with them towards London, and to tell a tale. Here

Lydgate appears 'almost as Chaucer's ape', writes Ten Brink, and we have only to read the two prologues side by side to realize the gulf between master and pupil.

A few years after he had completed his *Troy Book* Lydgate was at work again on another lengthy enterprise, *The Pilgrimage of the Life of Man*. This time it was a work undertaken at the bequest of Edward, Earl of Salisbury, and was begun in 1426. The original of Guillaume de Deguilleville, entitled *Le Pèlerinage de la Vie Humaine*, and Lydgate's version are of a monkish, allegorical, and didactic nature, which Lydgate's stylistic limitations do nothing to make more palatable. Mr. C. S. Lewis has remarked that 'the poem is unpleasant to read, not only because of its monstrous length and imperfect art, but because of the repellent and suffocating nature of its content'. We share with him 'a heartfelt relief' in turning to other work even of Lydgate.

The longest of Lydgate's commissioned works was the *Fall of Princes*. This was composed between 1431 and 1438 for Humphrey, Duke of Gloucester, and is mainly written in rhyme royal. It is a translation, based on Laurent de Premierfait's second and enlarged version of Boccaccio's *De Casibus Virorum Illustrium*, and is a long-winded affair, in which Lydgate embroiders at will on the French rendering, and there is much in his version that is alien to Boccaccio's work. Lydgate sees in the Fall of Princes material from which he can draw clear-cut moral lessons. Wickedness is punished here and now; tragedy results from the evil-doing of men, for poetic justice overtakes them. 'Remembreth pleynli, yif ye be vertuous, Ye shal perseuere in long prosperitie' is his constant theme. Yet at the same time, Fortune is playing her incalculable part;

> Fortunis wheel by reuolucioun
> Doth oon clymbe up, another to discende.

Lydgate shares with many medieval writers a belief in the 'unwar strok' which may fall on even the most innocent. Arthur, bravest and most famous of men, was destroyed by Fate and Fortune, and so were Alcibiades, Hector, and scores of others. The monk in Lydgate wallows in relating these woes, and sees no hope for men unless they retire from the world and its mutable affairs. Lydgate's treatment of his material is almost unbearably prolix, and the modern reader will find that much judicious skipping is necessary if he wishes to reach the end.

These are large-scale works, and a reader interested in statistics may like to know that *Reason and Sensuality* runs to 7,042 lines, the *Troy Book* to 30,117, the *Siege of Thebes* to 4,716, the *Pilgrimage of the Life of Man* to 24,832, and the *Fall of Princes* to 36,365 lines, so that these five works contain nearly three-quarters of the surviving verses of Lydgate. In addition he wrote many shorter poems on religious and didactic themes. He tells us that the chief office of poets is 'vicis to repreue', and whatever they write they should always 'on vertue ay conclude'. With this in mind he wrote such poems as his versions of Aesop's *Fables*, or the tales of *The Horse, Goose and Sheep* and *The Churl and the Bird*. *London Lickpenny*, a vivid and satirical commentary on London life and on lawyers, is now generally denied to Lydgate. The current taste for saints' lives was gratified by his *Life of St. Margaret*, and later by the *Lives of St. Edmund and St. Fremund*. These now rank among the most lifeless of his works. His religious lyrics have more to be said for them—especially the *Testament of Dan John Lydgate*—for in these his real religious fervour gives some excitement to his verse.

This vast volume of work was not written without the author having some sense of its imperfections. Despite the high esteem in which Lydgate was held by his contemporaries, almost every poem of any length warns us that he is aware of his feeble poetic powers. He bemoans his dullness and the fact that the Muses did not preside at his cradle. He laments that he never slept on the hill of Parnassus, and that he is ignorant of the flowers of Tully and that he lacks metrical skill. These things soon become apparent to the reader. The plain grammatical meaning of passage after passage only becomes clear on a second or third reading, and then often only at some violence to syntax or grammar. At the same time the reader finds himself in the midst of a spate of words which seem to be doing very little, while the development of the argument or the narrative appears to be in abeyance. A closer scrutiny reveals various reasons for this. First, we may notice Lydgate's own views on narrative technique, expressed fairly late in his career in the General Prologue to the *Fall of Princes*. There he writes:

> Ffor a stori which is nat pleynli told,
> But constreyned vndir wordes fewe,
> Ffor lak off trouth, wher thei be newe or old,
> Men be report kan nat the mater shewe.

Thes ookes grete be nat downe ihewe[1]
Ffirst at a strok, but bi longe processe;
Nor longe stories a woord may nat expresse.

In his comments on this passage Thomas Gray said:

These 'long processes' indeed suited wonderfully with the attention and simple curiosity of the age in which Lydgate lived. Many a 'stroke' have he and the best of his contemporaries spent on a sturdy old story, till they had blunted their own edge and that of their readers; at least a modern reader will find it so: but it is a folly to judge of the understanding and of the patience of those times by our own. They loved, I will not say tediousness, but length and a chain of circumstances in a narration. The vulgar do so still: it gives an air of reality to facts, it fixes the attention, raises and keeps in suspense their expectation, and supplies the defects of their little and lifeless imagination; and it keeps pace with the slow motion of their own thoughts. Tell them a story as you would tell it to a man of wit, it will appear to them as an object seen in the night by a flash of lightning; but when you have placed it in various lights and in various positions, they will come at last to see and feel it as well as others.

This is well said, but we must not impute the whole of Lydgate's long-windedness to the 'spirit of the age'. The root fact is that Lydgate was a man with a timid, limited, unenterprising mind. His life in the cloister did nothing to bring out other qualities which may have been latent in him, and his knowledge of men and women was sadly handicapped through lack of personal contacts. Even the little he knew of life was coloured by his ecclesiastical prejudices; and, as a result, his work is almost entirely derivative, often no more than direct—if diluted—translation. Unfortunately, the limitations of his mind were coupled with an overwhelming facility of utterance and a very imperfect understanding of the problems of form and style.

Lydgate's limited poetic gifts show most clearly in his diction and the use he makes of words and phrases. An examination of Chaucer's diction has already shown us how we must look at the medieval poet's use of language, and in Lydgate even more than in Chaucer we shall find that words have but a limited associative value, and are not rich in 'overtones'. Phrases like 'her sonnysh hair', or the 'restless stone' of Sisyphus, are rare: Lydgate uses them in the strict sense of the language

[1] ihewe (hewn).

from which he takes them—generally French or Latin. He extends our vocabulary of abstract terms—dismay, infallible, solicitude, tolerance—but he does little to use language in an imaginative or stimulating fashion. This comparative 'deadness' of language is to be found everywhere in Lydgate: he had little feeling for the poetical value of words. The *mot juste* meant nothing to him. Indeed the most outstanding feature of his style is repetition—both of word and phrase. He sought to obtain his effects, not by selecting the most suitable word or phrase, but by heaping up a series of synonyms and relying on their cumulative effect. Thus he writes 'synge and make melodye'; 'for veray joye and gladnesse', 'ruthe and pitie'. Simple adverbs such as 'nowhere' are evaded by phrases: 'neither in borgh or toun', or 'withinne nor withoute'. Phrases or sentences are even more full of potentialities for him: 'Pertynent to thy voyage' is followed by 'And nedful to thy pylgrimage'; while 'In al hast when I was clad' he thinks requires 'And redy eke in myn array' to make it clear. This itch for repetition is carried to greater excess, as in:

Thorient
Which ys so bryght
And casteth forth so dire a lyght,
Betokeneth in especiall
Thinges that be celestiall
And thinges, as I kan diffyne,
That be verrily dyvyne.

Wherever we turn this verbiage is to be seen: in pleonasms—'togedir yferre';[1] 'suffise enowgh'; in periphrases—'thy hevenly emperesse', 'this noble goddesse honurable'; in a delight in intensives for their own sake—wel, passingly, pleynly, sothely; or in the constant use of rhyme tags and padding formulae.

All medieval poets are fond of verbal formulae, but with Lydgate they are carried to outrageous lengths and are an outstanding feature of his style. They have been classified as 'those which make some appeal to, or assertion of the good judgement and intelligence either of the reader or of the poet, such as "As thou wel wost", or "as to myn intent". Secondly, phrases that are strongly confirmative of some preceding point —"It is no doubt", or "yiff I shal not lye". Thirdly, those that contain reference to authority—"as the phylisofre seyth", or "as

[1] yferre, 'together'.

clerkys teche". Fourthly, such expressions as, "In substaunce", or "shortely to specefye", and lastly, certain adverbial expressions of place and time—"erly and late", "both este and weste" or "at eve and eke at prime".' We may classify these things, but that does not justify their use, nor does it illustrate fully 'the deep damnation of their taking off'. Phrases like 'Ther nis namor to seye', or 'In al the haste he may', are constantly used by Lydgate to fill up his lines, and he will go even farther, so that 'in al the haste he may' in one line can provoke the equally feeble 'withoute more delay' in the next. 'Yf I shal nat feyne' is not to be taken at its face value, but as a convenient line-filler to be followed by 'They be set lyk hornes tweyne', and this principle leads to such couplets as

> I am the same, thys the cas,
> Off whom that whylom wrote Esdras

or

> That Malebouche, yt ys no lye
> Ffledde ffyrst out off Normaundye.

This slackness of control and inability to resist the easy, empty tag or phrase or rhyme is characteristic of Lydgate's work. In the face of tens of thousands of lines disfigured by such blemishes, the limited number of lines where Lydgate rises above correctness to something nearer poetry cannot be considered as sufficient to justify the claims made by Churton Collins and others on his behalf.

But it is not on these grounds alone that any such claims must be resisted. Lydgate's sense of syntax was as uncertain as his feeling for words. He has no rules to guide him in the construction of the sentences; indeed he often seems to start out with no clear idea of where his sentence will lead him. Clauses and phrases in apposition are frequent, the main thread is picked up again with 'I mene', or some such phrase, only to be followed by many qualifying phrases and dependent sentences. 'His clauses run headlong, shuffling and entangled in proportion as the idea is intricate.' And as with the smaller units, so with the greater. The verse, the paragraph, the section—these were but dimly apprehended units to Lydgate. He seldom looked far ahead, and had little notion, apparently, of the relation between the parts and the whole. Size was to him what it is to a child with a box of bricks—the larger the better. So his works ramble on with little attempt to tell their story clearly and economically. Even when he is translating, he finds it necessary to expand his original to inordinate lengths. His mind is at the mercy of innumerable side issues, any one of which may start him off on a heap of verses which have little connexion with his theme. The mention of the gods, of the heroes of antiquity, of the saints, or of any one of the many stock subjects of the Middle Ages elicited from him a stock response which often meant the pouring out of all his knowledge and miscellaneous reading, or gave him an opportunity for trite and dreary moralizing with a seemingly unending series of examples. The 'catalogue method' of describing a woman's charms or the beauty of a May morning had no more determined adherent than Lydgate, while the unending line of historical personages, such as we get in the *Fall of Princes*, fascinated him, and encouraged the production of his monumental series of 'tragedies'—a poetic blunder realized by Chaucer when he left part told the *Legend of Good Women* or interrupted the Monk's 'tragedies' with the Knight's 'good sire, namoore of this'. These many weaknesses are made the more exasperating by Lydgate's peculiar versification. While it may be untrue to say that he cannot write three consecutive lines without offending the rules of metre, the fact remains that even with the best modern 'edited' texts the scansion of innumerable lines of Lydgate is performed only with difficulty. Professor Schick adopted for Lydgate's decasyllabic line a scheme whereby he divided the lines into five principal types, differentiated according to the number of their syllables. Whatever merits this scheme may have for reducing Lydgate's prosodic practices to some system, it does little to make his lines more tolerable to the eye or ear. More recently Mr. C. S. Lewis has invited us to overcome these difficulties by reminding us that Lydgate was 'comparatively heedless of the number of syllables and generally attentive to stress', and that Chaucer's tradition of writing in true decasyllables was very soon lost. It was therefore possible for Lydgate to write lines many of which can be tortured into a decasyllabic pattern of sorts, but which in reality are what Mr. Lewis calls 'fifteenth-century heroics'—that is a series of lines 'each divided by a sharp medial break into two half-lines, each half-line containing not less than two or more than three stresses'. Many of Lydgate's lines can be read as four-stress lines with a movement like that of the fables in the *Shepherd's Calendar*, in which critics have supposed Spenser to be imitating the 'riding rhyme' to Canterbury. Even if all could be so read, the necessity of emphasizing the stresses and slurring the intermediate syllables breeds, in a poet with no gift for rhythm and musical phrasing, an unbearable monotony. But many cannot be so read, and the ear dithers between two or more systems of versification and rests in none.

Even if we admit that Mr. Lewis is Lydgate's Tyrwhitt, there remain the many weaknesses when some larger unit than the line is considered. Where we saw Chaucer working by the large paragraph unit, with a full understanding of 'the perpetual conflict between the law of verse, and the freedom of language', Lydgate moves forward hesitantly line by line, and frequently his metrical peculiarities only serve to direct our attention to words that have no claim to special consideration. When Chaucer writes: 'Tróuthe and honóur, frédom and cúrteisie', the stresses are so placed as to bring out the force of the four stressed words. When (following his master) Lydgate writes: 'Pées and qúyete, cóncorde and v́nyte', the stresses only serve to draw attention to the tautologous nature of the coupled terms. When Lydgate tries to use the larger paragraph there results a lamentable confusion in which sense and rhythm are both swept away. A good example may be seen in the prologue to the *Siege of Thebes*, where Lydgate opens his poem with a sentence of 78 lines modelled on the *Prologue* to the *Canterbury Tales*. But where Chaucer controls his paragraph with reiterated *Whan* followed in due course by 'Than longen folk . . .', Lydgate begins, then begins again and accumulates a series of clauses and phrases for at least 78 lines without reaching a principal verb, while his versification also is lacking in Chaucerian suppleness and rhythmic flow.

4

To turn from Lydgate to his contemporary Hoccleve is to turn from the cloistered tranquillity of Bury St. Edmunds to the bustle and movement of London. The recluse gives way to the man of the world, and the larger part of the interest that Hoccleve has for us comes from the social rather than poetical reason that his many autobiographical passages re-create in vivid fashion the London of his day. There apparently he lived throughout his working life, and much of his poetry is the direct result of his experiences as a clerk in the Privy Seal office by day and a 'man about town' by night.

Hoccleve's constant gossiping about himself, together with entries in official documents, enable us to get a clear picture of his life. He entered the office of the Privy Seal about 1378, and there he seems to have stayed until 1425. His merits were recognized by a yearly pension (first granted in 1399) of £10, but this was raised to £13. 6*s*. 8*d*. at Michaelmas 1408. These payments were not always forthcoming, and several of Hoccleve's poems are appeals to 'my lord the Fourneval', or Sir Henry Somer, or some other official, begging him to expedite payment. Save for this annuity, and whatever the Keeper of the Privy Seal paid the clerks out of the 20 shillings a day which he received, Hoccleve had only a slender private income of £4 a year. When he first entered the Privy Seal he had no intention of remaining there, and hoped for a benefice. But,

> I gasyd longe firste, and waytid faste
> After some benefice, and whan non cam,
>   By proces I me weddid atte laste.
> And, god it wot, it sore me agaste
>   To bynde me where I was at my large;
>   But done it was: I toke on me that charge.

We may well understand Hoccleve's unwillingness to bind himself when we turn to the story he has to tell of his bachelor life. Out of office hours he had been accustomed to lead a gay life; eating and drinking riotously, strutting about in his wide-sleeved cloak, and taking boat from his rooms in Chester's Inn (Somerset House) up to his office in Westminster. He gave generously to the watermen who flattered his vanity and called him 'Master', while he was held 'a verray gentil man' by the taverners and cooks at Westminster Gate. His evenings were uproarious: no one in the Privy Seal office drank as late as he did, nor was so loath to rise in the morning, for he haunted taverns, drank deeply when he had the money, and frequented the company

> Of venus femel lusty children deere,
> That so goodly so shaply were, and feir,
> And so plesant of port and of maneere,

And feede cowden al a world with cheere,
And of atyr passyngly wel byseye,
At Poules heed me maden ofte appeere,
To talke of mirthe, and to disporte and pleye.

Ther was sweet wyn ynow thurgh-out the hous,
And wafres thikke, for this conpaignie
That I spak of been sumwhat likerous,
Where as they mowe a draght of wyn espie,
Sweete and in wirkynge hoot for the maistrie
To warme a stomak with ther of they dranke.
To suffre hem paie, had been no courtesie;
That charge I tooke to wynne loue and thanke.

This was an expensive way of living, and Hoccleve found himself with nothing between him and poverty but a small income and his pension (when it was paid). His 'skittish youth' was over; no benefice seemed forthcoming, and God sent him a wife 'for his own good'. They married for love, dwelt humbly in 'a poore cote', constantly fretted by his lack of money, and at one time they were almost overwhelmed by a five-year 'wylde infirmytie . . . whiche me owt of myselfe cast and threw'. Hoccleve recovered, but friends cut him and said he would go mad again. Nevertheless, he returned for a while to his office labours, despite the pains they gave him. Copying, he tells us, is hard work: it injures eyes and health, and calls for incessant attention. Others can talk and sing at their work: the scribe's eye, hand, and mind must work together. At last he was relieved from his desk at the Privy Seal, for a pension was found for him from the funds of the Hampshire priory of Southwick, and we may hope that this grant brought him a happy release from toil and provided for him until his death.

Hoccleve's financial position was as different from Chaucer's comparative affluence as it was from Lydgate's economic security as a member of one of the greatest of English abbeys. As soon as he was aware of his literary powers he must have realized that they might augment his income considerably, if only a patron could be secured. Hence he turned from one noble patron or government official to another, and hoped that they would look favourably on his verses: in 1406 he wrote *La Mâle Règle*, which ends with a petition to Lord Furnivall, the Treasurer, to pay his overdue annuity. In 1411 or 1412 he translates the *De Regimine Principum* of Aegidius Romanus for

Henry, Prince of Wales, and in 1421 says that he will append to his *Dialog* a story to please the Duke of Gloucester, and to this end translates the *Gesta Romanorum* story of Jereslaus' wife. He presents a *Balade* to the Duke of Bedford, and another to the Duke of York, who once asked him to send all the *Balades* that he had by him. Among other patrons he mentions the Duchess of York, John of Gaunt, the Lord Chancellor, the Countess of Westmorland, Lady Hereford, as well as lesser folk.

His works, despite this number of patrons, are much more limited in character than those of Lydgate. They are in the main of a moralizing, didactic nature, plentifully interspersed in the large works by refreshing personal anecdotes and reflections. We are always in touch with the poet: we do not feel that his poems are mechanic exercises, but the reflection of the poet's own ideas and personality. That does not give his verses value, for on the whole Hoccleve has not a sensitive alert mind. He is an egoist, and the naïve outpourings of his own hopes and fears are presented to us in all their crude immediacy. What his mind thought his pen set down without much preliminary attempt to control or refine his matter in a clear picture: yet his dialogue gives the illusion of life: we feel something of the give and take of conversation in such passages as:

> 'The book concludith for hem is no nay,[1]
> Vertuously my good freend dooth it not?'
> 'Thomas, I noot,[2] for neuere it yit I say.'[3]
> 'No, freend?' 'No, Thomas.' 'Wel trowe I, in fay;
> Ffor had ye reed it fully to the ende,
> Yee wolde seyn[4] it is nat as ye wende.'[5]

This immediacy gives what little value may be found in Hoccleve's work. He does not pierce far below the surface, nor has he a very poetic view of life, but his poems move to their conclusions without the padding and syntactical confusion of Lydgate. Hoccleve never rises to any heights—even such a passage as Lydgate's verses on his conversion is beyond him, and he has no feeling, or liking, apparently for nature. Fortunately he never tries to cover up his poetic weaknesses by

[1] no nay, 'without doubt'.
[2] noot, 'know not'.
[3] say (saw).
[4] seyn, 'see'.
[5] wende, 'thought'.

the use of 'aureate' language, but is content with a limited vocabulary which he occasionally uses to good effect by the inclusion of some colloquial phrase, such as 'ryse up and slynge hym down', or 'I told him so'; or by a striking line—'Excesse at borde hath leyd his knyf with me', or 'For rethorik hath hid fro me the keye', or 'There never strode yet wyse man on my fete'. His control of rhythms and the verse forms which he adopts is very imperfect, but at times he gets beyond a mechanical counting of syllables and marking of stresses. On the whole, however, the Chaucerian music, which he tried to imitate, eluded him completely. He has every reason to ask his friends to correct his work

> If that I in my wrytynge foleye,
> As I do ofte, (I can it nat withseye,)
> Meetrynge amis or speke vnfittyngly,
> Or nat by iust peys[1] my sentences weye,
> And nat to the ordre of endytyng obeye
> And my colours sette ofte sythe awry.

Hoccleve, then, cannot claim any high place in the poetic heavens. Indeed, this 'crimeless Villon', as Saintsbury calls him, survives mainly for two reasons. First, because his devotion to Chaucer endears him to all lovers of poetry. He rises to something near eloquence when he speaks of his 'master deere and fadir reuerent' who 'fayn wolde han me taght, But I was dul, and lerned lite or naught', and tells how he has had Chaucer's likeness painted in the manuscript of his *Regiment of Princes*:

> That hei that haue of him lest thought and mynde,
> By his peynture may ageyn hym fynde.

Secondly, Hoccleve's work is full of interest for the student of social history. The extravagant costumes of his time; the debauchery and riotous behaviour of the 'man about town'; the starvation endured by those broken by the wars; the decay and partiality of justice; pluralism and absenteeism; the abuses of child-marriages—these and many another topic find expression in the pages of Hoccleve, and help to create the picture of the world in which the poet lived, and in which poetry could hope for but a casual and fugitive hearing among the many distractions of the times.

[1] peys, 'weight'.

5

Hoccleve and Lydgate were only two of the many writers of long religious or didactic poems in this century. Devout authors tried to interest and instruct at the same time, and improving narratives in verse, or saints' lives, or portions of the Psalms, were produced from time to time. There is nothing surprising in this: the Church was still immensely powerful, and a concern for things spiritual was ever close to men's thoughts whenever they paused from their getting and spending of things material.

A typical example is Brampton's *Seven Penitential Psalms*. This is a competent piece of versifying, but is uninspired and contains nothing that cannot be paralleled in many a poem written by Lydgate and his followers, and well represented in Carleton Brown's *Religious Lyrics of the Fifteenth Century*. The lives of a number of saints or legends of holy women by Osbern Bokenham are of greater interest. They have already been discussed[1] in view of the light which they throw on the relation between author and patron, but something more may be said about this characteristic fifteenth-century author and his work. Bokenham was a Suffolk man, an Augustinian friar of the convent of Stoke Clare, and appears to have lived mainly in Suffolk. He was born about 1392, and died in or just before 1447, and his *Legends* were 'doon wrytyn in Canebryge[2] by his soun Frere Thomas Burgh'. He translated his *Legends* from various Latin sources, and kept closely to his text. In common with many others he was a great admirer and disciple of Chaucer, and like them seems forced to write in verse, despite his limitations. He apologizes from time to time for his lack of skill, and asks his friend not to mention his name in Cambridge, 'where wythys[3] be manye ryht capcyous and subtyl'. He composed at a good speed when in the vein, for he tells us that he wrote the life of St. Katherine, which runs to 1,064 lines, in five days. His method of translation was that commonly adopted by medieval writers, namely to follow his author not word by word but sentence by sentence. The most pleasing parts of his work are the introductory and connecting passages, where he prattles away about the reasons for undertaking the work or indulges in 'poetical' passages, such as that in the Prologue to the life of St. Mary Magdalene, where

[1] See above, p. 112. [2] Canebryge, 'Cambridge'. [3] wythys, 'wits'.

the date is indicated in a sentence of twenty-three lines. He betrays his naïve pleasure in his own powers, in spite of his conventional outcries that he lacks the 'cunnyng and eloquens' of Gower, Chaucer, and Lydgate; and 'as euere crystene man owyth to do', he utterly rejects the elaborate eloquence of some writers, and cries for help to Christ and not to the Muses. His telling of the saints' lives never reaches any distinction: when he is held by his source material he is able to control his verse better than when he is free to go his own way. He uses the staple measures of rhyme royal and decasyllabic couplet in the main, although some of his prologues and the stories of Christina and Elizabeth employ an eight-line stanza, and generally he confines himself to the accepted vocabulary of his age. His narrative lacks individuality or even the well-mannered ease of much of Gower; and if read continuously the seemingly endless barbarities and cruelties which confronted these holy women become unendurable.

One of the most learned men of his day, John Capgrave, also turned from his voluminous prose works in English and Latin to write the *Life of St. Katherine* in verse.[1] He tells us that the work is a translation from the Latin, just made by an English priest, but that it was not easy to understand because of the 'derk langage' that he used. Capgrave rewrites it to make it more plain, and after a confused appeal to God, Apollo, and Saint Paul begins his poem. This consists of 8,372 lines in rhyme royal. Dr. Furnivall speaks of the poem as 'worthless', and this is very nearly the truth. Capgrave's work, like many other lives of the saints, has little to commend it as poetry. It might equally well (or better) have been written in prose, for its slow-moving pedestrian verse does nothing to reconcile us to the *longueurs* of the narrative, the credulous recital of the impossible, and the long-drawn-out descriptions of torture and mutilation, in spite of Capgrave's plea:

[1] John Capgrave (1393–1464) was a native of Lynn in Norfolk, and probably studied at Cambridge. At an early age he entered the Augustinian Order (of which there was a famous house at Lynn) and was priested in 1418. He is reputed to have been a Doctor of Divinity of Oxford, and soon after taking this degree he became Provincial of the Augustinian Friars in England in 1456. Capgrave's chief patron was Humphrey, Duke of Gloucester (till Humphrey's death in 1447), on whose behalf he went to Rome and to whom were dedicated some of his works. He was a distinguished philosopher and theologian and wrote a great deal in Latin and English. Much of this is lost, but a number of English works remain.

And if ye dowte, ye reders of þis lyffe,
Wheyther it be southe, ye may well vndyrstande:
Mech þing hath be do whech hath be ful ryue[1]
And is not wretyn ne can neuer to our hande,
Mech þing eke hyd in many dyuerse lande;
Euene so was þis lyffe.

The writing of saints' lives represents one side of didactic versification in this century. Another is admirably illustrated by the works of John Walton, Canon of Osney, who in 1410 translated into verse the *Consolations of Boethius*, and from the comparatively large number of surviving manuscripts (twenty-three in all) it is clear that his version provided his readers with an acceptable account of this work which so fascinated the medieval mind. The interest of Walton's work to modern students, however, is not so much in his restatement of Boethius' ideas as in his skilful management of his materials. Chaucer had attempted a version in prose: Walton uses an eight-line stanza for his first three books, and rhyme royal for the last two. Both writers lose by abandoning the plan of their original, for Boethius alternated his prose sections with lyrical passages, thereby giving relief and variety to his reflections. Walton undoubtedly had Chaucer's version before him, but makes his own translation and exercises a good control over his matter, and at times is astonishingly successful in reproducing the ideas of Boethius—no easy task for a poet, especially when it is remembered that Walton's endeavour was to keep to the words of his original 'as neigh as may be broght where lawe of metyr is noght resistent'. His abandonment of the eight-line stanza at the end of Book III is evidence of his tact. Walton must have realized that the rhyme requirements of his stanza invited padding, for when he comes to deal with the problems of Fate and Providence, of Destiny and Free Will, he eliminates one line of his stanza, and so tightens his verse unit and rids himself of the extra rhyme. Even so, he feels that

Lo of so hye a matre for to trete
As aftir þis myn auctour doth pursue
This wote I well my wyttes ben vnmete[2]
The sentence forto saue (in) metre trewe
And not forthi[3] I may it not eschewe.

[1] ryue, 'evident'.
[2] vnmete (unmeet), 'insufficient'.
[3] not forthi, 'nevertheless'.

Walton's translation lacks much of the conciseness of his original, but it is a workmanlike, honest attempt to render his author in a readable and flowing verse, as shown in the following passage:

> Bot here þou makest this obieccioun:
> 'If goddes science[1] may be changed so
> Right as myne owne disposicioun,
> And when I now this and now þat m[ay] do,
> Than may I enterchaungen to and fro
> His hye science be stoundes[2] of my wille?'
> 'Nay, nay, forsothe, þat myght þou not be skille,[3]
>
> For-why þe knowynge of devyne sight
> It goth bifore þat þing þat schall be-falle,
> And right before his propre presence right,
> Lo of his knowyng he retorneth all
> That euer was or ben here-after schall.
> Ne as þow wenest he alterneþ noght
> His presence be stoundes of þi þoght,
>
> As now þis þing and now þat þing to knowe,
> Bot he, beholdyng euery wyt, compaseth
> The chaunginge of þi þoghtes all arowe.[4]
> With o syght all at ones he enlaceth;
> He goth also before and all embraceth.

Another aspect of didactic poetry in its most forbidding form is found in the *Court of Sapience*, a poem of about 1470. Its authorship is still in dispute: it was long attributed to Lydgate, but critical opinion now is more in favour of Hawes, although his claims have not been fully established. Whoever wrote it was a man well versed in medieval education and theology, and his learning is poured out in a fashion little to the modern taste. The work is in two books. In Book I we read of how the fate of man is debated and disputed by the Four Daughters of God—Peace, Mercy, Righteousness, and Truth—and is decided by the taking of human form by Christ. This leads to the reunion of the Four Daughters, and is related by Sapience to the author. In Book II he accompanies her on a journey to her court, meeting with many wonders on the way, and there meets Dame Philosophy, with her seven ladies, representing the seven arts.

[1] science, 'knowledge'.
[2] stoundes, 'movements'.
[3] be skille, 'by knowledge, reason'.
[4] arowe, 'in succession'.

Philosophy leads him into the courts of Dame Science, Dame Intelligence, and Dame Sapience herself. We are next treated to a long account of the parlours 'ful of Blys' occupied by Dame Grammar and the other heads of the Trivium and the Quadrivium. The wearied traveller is then led to a tower where he finds the Apostles, and there we leave him learning from them the articles of the Christian faith.

Despite the heavily didactic nature of this poem, the reader is lured on by the considerable skill with which the writer uses the rhyme royal. He has a real feeling for verse; and occasional phrases, such as 'she gan unlace her tressyd sonnysh here', or 'the swerde of sorow ran oute thurgh myne hert', are attractive. Certainly the author is here far more capable than Hawes in the *Pastime of Pleasure*, or any late fifteenth-century writer in this genre, to express himself clearly, although his story is greatly overladen with detail and digression. Contemporary readers would find in it a convenient epitome of much current knowledge and belief, and were not deterred by the unpoetical way in which this was expressed.

At any rate these limitations did not deter Stephen Hawes from taking a good many hints from the *Court of Sapience* when he was composing the *Pastime of Pleasure*. In it Hawes attempts to give new life to two outmoded and decaying expressions of medieval thought—chivalry and scholasticism. He obstinately clings to both of these, although he wrote after the Wars of the Roses and in the first great days of the New Learning. The poem is a depressing specimen of very early sixteenth-century versifying, and what interest it has is more for the student of literary history than for the lover of poetry.[1]

There is satirical and controversial verse as well as devout. The vigour and excitement generated by such poems as Hoccleve's *Reproof to Oldcastle*, or the anonymous *Against the Lollards*, testify to the zeal of their authors even though they add little to their reputation as poets. There is but little poetry in the diatribe known as *Jack Upland* and its accompanying pieces. *Jack Upland* is a vigorous (not to say violent) attack on the friars, which is answered by the *Reply of Friar Daw Topias*, and followed by Jack Upland's *Rejoinder*. Only the *Reply* is really in verse, and its writer is capable of a crude alliterative line (modelled perhaps on *Pierce the Ploughman's Crede*), but attempts to find a

[1] For a fuller treatment of this poem, see Vol. III of this series.

metrical system for the other two have not succeeded.[1] The real interest of all these works (apart from their importance as documents in religious controversy) lies in their use of popular and alliterative phrases and snatches of proverbial wisdom. We hear of 'that wicked worm Wyclif' from one who himself is spoken of as 'lewed as a leke', and who in turn tells Jack Upland that 'thou wost no more what thou blaberist than Balames asse'. Jack likens him to 'blynde Bayarde [that] berkest at the mone, or as an old mylne dog when he begynnith to dote'. We learn that 'on old Englis it is said unkissid is unknown, and many men spekyn of Robyn Hood ond shotte nevere in his bowe'.

Side by side with the 'courtly' poetry there was a growing output of verse written to satisfy the demands of a new reading public. Chaucer's 'churls' tales' to some extent reflect his response to this demand, but its growth made poetry, long the handmaid of the Church and the nobility, also the maid of all work for those who wished to inculcate manners, amusement, instruction, popular wisdom, and the like in a palatable form.[2] 'How the Wise Man taught his Son', or the *Libel of English Policy*, are poor enough stuff as verse, but are precious indications of a growing determination to induce poets to write on themes other than those hallowed by centuries of use. Naturally the nobility and the clergy still exercised a considerable control, but the pressure of the fifteenth-century *bourgeoisie* may be said to have brought to an end an era in which literature had so limited a contact with any readers except a privileged minority.

It is not surprising, therefore, that social behaviour rather than religious belief is the theme of much minor verse of the fifteenth century. From its opening years we have a series of poems which set out correct behaviour in some detail, and instruct the young in matters of ceremonial and etiquette. Even now manuscripts containing such poems survive in considerable numbers, and they must have circulated widely throughout the fifteenth century. Their merits as poetry are non-existent: verse is used merely as a convenience to throw into story and couplet instruction often taken from a Latin or French source. In the main they are undoubtedly meant for the 'bele babees' of the aristocracy and the well-to-do. These are admonished not to imitate the uncouth manners of the rustic 'felde men', and

[1] See Vol. I, Part II. [2] See above, p. 119.

when at table to sit where they are told. 'To embrace thi jawis with breed, it is not dewe', says one manual, and adds 'pyke not thi tethe with thi knyfe, ne spitte thou not over the tabyll'. They learn how to enter and leave a chamber, and how to behave while there; how to walk in the streets, to avoid scandal, and not to be 'to noyous, ne to nyce, ne to new fangylle'.

More elaborate treatises, such as John Russell's *Book of Carving and Nurture* (*c.* 1440) explain to the pupil in considerable detail the duties of a butler, pantler, chamberlain, and carver. Russell had been 'sum tym seruande with Duke Umfrey of Glowcetur, a prynce ful royalle, with whom uschere in chambur was y, and mershalle also in halle', and his book is a mine of detailed information, invaluable to those who would know what is meant by Chaucer's commendation of Harry Bailly as one fit 'for to have been a marchal in an halle'. Other books of a similar nature, such as the *Book of Courtesy* (*c.* 1460) or Hugh Rhodes's *Book of Nurture* (*temp.* Henry VII), help to fill out the picture.

Another series of poems concern themselves more with the relations between people than with table manners and the like. One of the most popular of these was 'How the good wife taught her daughter'—a work full of practical wisdom concerning the getting and keeping of a husband, the treatment of strangers and of her own children and household. At home, at church, in the street, or in the ale-house, decorum is advocated: 'if thou be ofte dronken, it fallith the to grete schame'. The work is an epitome of common sense, and may be paralleled by 'How the Wise Man taught his Son' (*c.* 1430) in which similar good advice, but of a more general nature, is given, or by 'A Father's Counsel to his Son', 'A Father's Instructions to his Son', or 'A Good Wife's Counsels to her Daughter'. A short work in alliterative alphabetical verses, known as *Aristotle's ABC*, epitomizes a great deal of worldly wisdom and advice:

> To Amerous, to Aunterous,[1] ne Angre the nat to muche;
> To Bolde, ne to Besy, ne Bourde[2] nat to large;
> To Curteys, to Cruelle, ne Care nat to sore;
> To Dulle, ne to Dredefulle,[3] ne Drynke nat to offte; . . .

This work is sometimes attributed to Benedict Burgh, but it was actually written by a certain Benedict of Norwich. A version of

[1] Aunterous, 'adventurous'. [2] Bourde, 'jest'. [3] Dredefulle, 'fearful'.

the *Disticha Catonis*, an ever popular work in the Middle Ages, was made by Benedict Burgh. It is in two parts: 'Cato Major' in 111 stanzas, and 'Cato Minor' in seven stanzas, both of rhyme royal. It has little merit as verse, but gives a convenient summary of precepts:

> Sith manys liff is fulle of miserie,
> Whilom in mirthe and aftir in myscheef,
> Now in the vale, now in the mont on hihe;
> Now man is poore and eft richesse releffe;
> The shynyng morwe hath ofte a stormy eve—
> To this policie take heed and entend:
> Look thou haue lucre in thy labours eende.

Yet another series of these little verse treatises deals with matters of bodily health. Lydgate's *Dietary* was the most popular of them all, and survives in forty-six manuscripts. Other widely circulated works were little books on blood-letting, or of medical recipes in couplets, or a series of versified herbals which gave simple advice to the layman.

At the other end of the scale in length stands Peter Idley's *Instructions to his Son*. This is a long work of 1,108 stanzas of rhyme royal written between 1445 and 1450. It is almost entirely derivative—a fact which commended it to the age, for not only does it incorporate the kind of advice given in many of the short treatises mentioned above, but it also draws its material from two longer works by well-known authors. Book I is based on the Latin treatises of Albertanus of Brescia entitled *Liber Consolationis et Consilii* and *De Amore et Dilectione Dei*. In this book Idley sets out a collection of instructions on a miscellany of subjects. It is full of worldly wisdom—much of it highly unsuitable for the boy of six to whom it was ostensibly addressed. In Book II 'the counsels of the world' give place to 'the exhortations of the Church' and Idley uses Mannyng's *Handlyng Synne* and Lydgate's *Fall of Princes* as a supplementary source of information, and begins a detailed exposition of the usual kind —the Ten Commandments, the Seven Deadly Sins, and so on.

No doubt when manuscripts were expensive and learning difficult to come by, Idley was very much to the taste of some sober spirits of the time, but he makes dull reading now. Idley had little skill as a versifier ('I have non vteraunce for this cheffare Sauffe oonly nature whiche doith me leede'); he seems unable to decide whether the staple line is one of eight or ten syllables, and even when we have allowed for this difficulty, the lack of rhythmical movement makes the reading of his verses a tiring, vexatious feat. His diction, also, is contaminated with 'floresshed eloquence', so that he turns the simple English of Mannyng's 'To thefte wyl y neuer go' into 'That occupation shall I never assent unto', or 'Abraham ne graunted hym noght' into 'Abraham wold not enclyne to his peticioun'.

The subject-matter is equally unrewarding. We have read it all before done by more accomplished writers. The interest of Idley resides in the personal touches in his work which reveal something of the man and something of his times. He advises his son to 'ride on the right of a stranger bearing a spear: on his left if he wears a sword'; regrets that 'a man shall not now kenne a knave from a knight', and still worse, that it is hard to tell 'a tapester, a Cookesse, or a hosteller's wife fro a gentilwoman', since they are all so painted, and 'with wymples and tires wrapped in pride'. With religion it is no better: 'Now it is harde in all a towne To ken a secular man froo a priest', while 'to see a preistly preist it were grete deyntee'. As with all moralists, Idley looks back to the Golden Age when true religion flourished, and God and the king were honoured as they should be. It is a relief to escape from this for a brief minute into the country-side of fifteenth-century England where the village wife and daughter go out into the fields:

> Vnto a preuye place wher they wold be,
> Wher was a fresshe sprynge vndre a banke
> In a secrete place whiche that she knewe,
> With grete hauthorn busshes, roughe and ranke.
> The water was clier and fresshe of hue.

Idley is of interest to us also as one among many laymen who were working quietly in their several spheres to educate their children and friends—often from worldly motives it is true, but also with a deep conviction of the part each of them had to play in the service of the Church and the State. Peter Idley's *Instructions* are the verse analogues of innumerable passages in the letters of such typical fifteenth-century characters as the Stonors and the Pastons, and his latest editor, Miss Charlotte D'Evelyn, does well to remind us that Idley's work can be compared

> with that most poignant of fatherly instructions, the letter written by the first Duke of Suffolk to his son on the eve of his banishment,

April 30, 1450. Composed under circumstances so different and written in a compass so much more compact, the letter is nevertheless an epitome of his counsels. Dread of God, knowledge of his laws and commandments, loyalty to the King, respect for his mother, caution in the choice of counsellors: these are the subjects of the Duke's farewell admonitions.

To fifteenth-century fathers these were still the all-important subjects of paternal advice.

One other work of advice requires brief mention, the *Libel of English Policy.*[1] It is a work of some 1,200 lines of verse which set out the author's view of 'the trewe processe of Englyshe polycye'. This is, in brief:

> Cheryshe marchandyse, kepeth amyralté
> That we bee maysteres of the narowe see.

The author gives an account of the commodities and exports of various countries from the Mediterranean to the Baltic and argues that the true interests of England lay in developing this trade and in ensuring permanent supremacy at sea.

> Kepe than the see, that is the wall of Englond,
> And than is Englond kepte by Goddes sonde.[2]

The English domination of the Channel is essential: secure that, says our author, and all nations, including the troublesome Flemings, will be forced to cultivate our friendship if they wish to pass through English waters. As poetry the work has no merits: as a vigorous patriotic outpouring of one desperately anxious to uphold his country's prestige (and trade) it is an interesting and significant work. To students of literature perhaps its greatest importance is in the evidence which it furnishes of the fifteenth-century tendency to use verse for works of information, whether on politics, husbandry, etiquette, travel, or alchemy.

6

As we look back on Idley's moralizings and most of the verse dealt with in this chapter we may well cry, 'Not here, O Apollo, are haunts meet for thee!' and turn to the lyrics and popular verse

[1] The work is anonymous, but Sir George Warner in his edition of the poem has given reason for the belief that it was written by Adam Moleyns, Clerk of the Council of Henry VI (1436–41). He became Bishop of Chichester in 1446, and died 1450.

[2] sonde, 'dispensation, grace'.

of the century.[1] Lyric poetry of this period is not so devoid of interest as many writers have suggested. True it has lost the first freshness of 'Lenten is come with loue to toun', but in place of that it has acquired control over form, ability to use technical devices, and a considerable metrical agility. It avoids the use of 'aureate' diction for the most part, and at its best is capable of outstanding works which reach their height in *Quia amore langueo* or 'I syng of a mayden', or 'Adam lay i-bowndyn, bowndyn in a bond'.

The religious lyric still predominated, and poems on many phases of Christian life and faith were composed for the edification of the ordinary worshipper. They generally reach no great heights, but present in an attractive and easily followed form songs to the Blessed Virgin, to the Trinity, or for the various Church seasons. Others again tell of man's mortality: 'Farewell, my frendis! the tide abideth no man: I moste departe hens and so shall ye', or lament the untimely death of youth:

> Of lordis lyne and lynage sche was, here sche lyse!
> Bounteuus, benigne, enbleshed[2] wyth beaute,
> Sage, softe and sobre an gentyll in al wyse,
> fflorishyng and fecunde, with femenyn beaute,
> Meke, mylde and merciful, of pite sche bar þe prise.

The carol also comes to its fullest perfection in this period. As well as the work of old blind Awdelay, who wrote

> As I lay seke in my langure
> In an abbay here be west,

or of the Franciscan, James Ryman, there is that of many anonymous authors. The carols, with their characteristic refrains—'Hey now, now, now', or

> Now let us syng and mery be,
> For Crist oure Kyng hath made us fre,

—and their fresh, singing note won a wide popularity. There were carols not only for Christmas, but for many other moments in the Christian year. There were also the secular carols, the combats between the Holly and the Ivy, the ceremonial entry of the boar's head, or the convivial and amorous carols. The secular lyric was far from dead. The *Nut Brown Maid* is the best-known and perhaps the finest of these fifteenth-century lyrics, but it had many companions of merit. Love-songs

[1] For full treatment see Vol. II, Part II.

[2] enbleshed (embellished).

predominate, though the border-line between earthly and heavenly love is often extremely hard to define. They range from the sophisticated to the simple, and express the courtier's ardours as well as the homely realistic passion of the countryman.

Other lyrics come closer to the ordinary people. They tell of everyday affairs, and express the homely wisdom, shrewdness, fears, affections, and amusements of the folk. *London Lickpenny* with its caustic refrain 'For lack of money I myghte nat spede' has its counterpart in a series of poems on the same theme expressed more tersely. The amorous songs and love plaints are replaced by the caustic realism of the husband's cry, 'I dare not seyn, whan she seith "Pes"!' The life of the tavern is re-created in songs with the refrain:

> Brynge vs home good ale, ser; brynge vs home good ale,
> And for owre dere Lady love, brynge vs home good ale.

Other events have their chronicles in verse as is seen in the realistic account of the pilgrim's sea voyage to St. James of Compostella in Spain:

> Men may leve alle gamys
> That saylen to Seynt Jamys,
> Ffor many a man hit gramys,[1]
>   When they begyn to sayle;
> Ffor when they have take the see
> At Sandwyche or at Wynchylsee,
> At Brystow, or where that hit bee,
>   Theyr hertes begyn to fayle.
>
> Anone the mastyr commaundeth fast
> To hys shypmen, in alle the hast,
> To dresse hem[2] sone about the mast,
>   Theyr takelyng[3] to make;
> With 'Howe! hissa!' then they cry;
> 'What, howe! mate, thow stondyst to ny,
> Thy felow may nat hale the by';[4]
>   Thus they begyn to crake[5] . . .
>
> 'Hale the bowelyne! now, vere the shete!
> Cooke, make redy anoon our mete;
> Our pylgryms have no lust to ete,
>   I pray God yeve[6] hem rest.'

[1] gramys, 'grieves'.
[2] dresse hem, 'busy themselves'.
[3] takelyng (tackling).
[4] hale the by, 'haul by thee'.
[5] crake, 'cry'.
[6] yeve, 'give'.

'Go to the helm! what, howe! no nere!'[1]
'Steward, felow, a pot of bere!'
'Ye shalle have, sir, with good chere,
  Anon alle of the best . . .'

Then cometh oone and seyth: 'Be mery,
Ye shall have a storme or a pery.'[2]
'Holde thow thy pese! thow canst no whery,[3]
  Thow medlyst wondyr sore.'
Thys menewhyle the pylgryms ly,
And have theyr bowlys fast theym by,
And cry aftyr hote malvesy:[4]
  Thow helpe[5] for to restore.

And som wold have a saltyd tost,
Ffor they myght ete neyther sode[6] ne rost;
A man myght sone pay for theyr cost,
  As for oo day or twayne.
Som layde theyr bookys on theyr kne,
And rad so long they myght nat se.
'Allas, myne hede wolle cleve on[7] thre!'
  Thus seyth another certayne . . .

A sak of strawe were there ryght good,
Ffor som must lyg theym in theyr hood:
I had as lefe be in the wood,
  Without mete or drynk.
For when that we shall go to bedde,
The pumpe is nygh oure beddes hede;
A man were as good to be dede
  As smell therof the stynk!

Works of 'Mirthe and solas' also claimed the attention of poets. Such writings were popularized in hall and market-place by a host of professional minstrels who had at their finger-tips a vast and highly variegated repertoire. They could tell a devout story, or narrate the affecting details of some saint's life, but they could also reel off coarse *fabliaux* or the more decorous romance. The fifteenth century still found people eager to listen to the romances which had been composed in earlier centuries, and also to hear any new ones which the minstrel could recite. Among such new works were *Sir*

[1] no nere! 'no nearer to the wind!'
[2] pery, 'squall'.
[3] whery, ?.
[4] malvesy, 'malmsey'.
[5] Thow helpe, 'their health'.
[6] sode, 'boiled'.
[7] cleve on, 'split in'.

Triamour, Sir Torrent of Portugal, The Squire of Low Degree, Parthenope of Blois.

We can sympathize with these fifteenth-century authors who came into the field so late in the day, and who must have felt that all the best material had been used. They could only take the French romances and give them a new English form, sometimes by cutting out much introspection and conversation (*Life of Ipomadon*), or by giving them a strongly didactic note (*Le Bone Florence, Parthenope*). Often, however, they took the easiest course, and piled incident upon incident without much thought of structure (*Generydes, Sir Triamour*), so that long, rambling narratives resulted which relied on picturesque incident or elaboration of detail for their main effects (*Le Bone Florence, Sir Cleges*, the *Squire of Low Degree*). In a few romances there is a good sense of narrative (*Le Bone Florence, Life of Ipomadon*) or of dialogue (*Sir Gawayne and Dame Ragnell, Sir Triamour*), but on the whole, the romance form was living on its past.[1]

All this body of verse has been preserved in a wealth of manuscripts, some of them handsome presentation copies, the work of highly trained scribes and illuminators, some of them good workmanlike 'shop' copies, varying in quality according to their price, and some of them cheaply made or amateur productions. All helped to make known the variety of contemporary verse, and to encourage the making of collections of favourite pieces in 'commonplace-books' by enthusiasts. These 'commonplace-books' or scrap-books are revealing evidence of personal likes and interests. The well-known British Museum MS. Egerton 1995 is a good example. This was written about 1470–80, and consists of some fifteen items of a very diverse nature. Romance is represented by the *Seven Sages of Rome*; history by Lydgate's *Chronicle of the Kings of England*, the *Siege of Rouen*, and the prose chronicle of a citizen of London, William Gregory. Advice on health is given in a number of little treatises like Lydgate's *Sapientia phisicorum* or 'directions for blood-letting'. Etiquette is dealt with in the *Book of Courtesy*, and hunting in two treatises setting out the names of hawks and the terms of venery. Miscellaneous information on the assize of bread, the names of the Bishops of England, and of the London churches, prognostications in Latin, and some gnomic verses *Erthe upon Erthe* complete the volume. Here in some 450 pages

[1] See Vol. I, Part II.

its owner had a 'library' *in parvo*, and many fifteenth-century lovers of letters had similar volumes, as for instance that now in the National Library of Scotland (Advocates, 19.3.1). This is a volume of 432 pages mostly written down by a John Hawghton. It contains much religious poetry: carols, Lydgate's *Life of Our Lady* (Books V–VII), the *Trental of St. Gregory*, Lydgate's *Stans Puer ad Mensam* and a prose *Life of St. Katharine*. Romance is represented by *Sir Gowther* and *Sir Isumbras*. There is much miscellaneous material: poems on 'marvels' and deceit; prognostics on thunder; medical and alchemical receipts; 'Proper terms' for game, &c.

7

To turn from English to Scottish poetry is not to move into a very different world. It has been asserted, with some justice, that there is no need to differentiate sharply between the two literatures before the mid-fifteenth century. In the first place, little is known about the Celtic influences on such few writings as have come down to us from before the early fourteenth century. Secondly, writings after that date follow lines familiar to the student of English medieval literature. The fourteenth century saw little Scottish literature save Barbour's *Bruce* and the works of Huchoun, and well into the fifteenth century the writing of poems and chronicles enshrining the adventures of national heroes and outlining the course of Scottish history occupied the attention of native poets. Andrew of Wyntoun's *Original Chronicle of Scotland* (*c.* 1424) is the link between the earlier work of this kind and the *Acts and Deeds of the Illustrious and Valiant Champion, Sir William Wallace* (*c.* 1482), by Henry the Minstrel, or Blind Harry, as he is sometimes called. This kind of poetry slowly gave place to a more sophisticated and literary genre which made use of the common stock which Chaucer in England and his contemporaries in France had made so popular. Scottish poetry in the fifteenth century slowly passes from the octosyllabics of heroic declamation and nationalistic fervour to enjoy the many forms and measures and the subject-matter which were available in the poetry of Chaucer, Machaut, Deschamps, and others. Only when this was accomplished towards the end of the fifteenth century could Scottish authors fully assert their individuality. To label them 'Scottish Chaucerians' is to single out one element only in their poetic equipment, and to disguise the fact that, like Chaucer, they look to France for much that gave form and style to their writings. In addition to this body of writers, there was also the alliterative variety of verse, steadily losing ground but not yet extinct,[1] and as we can see from the Bannatyne and Maitland collections lyric poetry was being written to edify, amuse, and instruct.[2] A few words about Barbour's *Bruce* are necessary, although the poem was finished by 1375, for it marks a decisive moment in Scottish literature.[3] The long struggle waged by Scotland for her independence made itself felt in literature for a long time, and here in the *Bruce* Scottish themes and personages are the life of the poem. Barbour writes more as an historian than as a teller of romance, and his object is to preserve for posterity the exploits and patriotism of Bruce and of those who fought with him for Scotland's freedom. The aggressive spirit of the English is contrasted with the defensive attitude which animates the Scots, and Barbour infuses into his poem the temper which went to the making of Bruce's Scotland. Thus it is that the poem is a strange amalgam of the old *chanson de geste* and the chivalric romance. The actions of the hero are often as bloody and violent as those of earlier warriors such as Gautier d'Arras or Raoul de Cambrai. The heroic element is stressed: Bruce is as sagacious in council as he is unmatched in the field, while Douglas exhibits even more of the primitive hero. He is harder and more determined than his leader, since his personal wrongs have inflamed him more fiercely against the English. It is the national cause, however, rather than individual wrongs that animates Bruce and most of his followers. A sense of responsibility controls their actions; loyalty to Scotland, not as in chivalric romance to a lady, or a king, or to a remote ideal.

Not that chivalry is absent. Throughout the poem much is done that would have been left undone but for the ideals which

[1] For alliterative poetry, see Vol. I, Part II.

[2] For lyric verse, see Vol. III, Chap. I.

[3] John Barbour (1316?–95) was probably born at Aberdeen. In 1357 he was Archdeacon of Aberdeen, and as such received a safe-conduct to travel to the schools at Oxford. Later he probably studied at Paris. In 1375 he composed the *Bruce*, and for the rest of his life he was a busy and prosperous ecclesiastic who was frequently called on by the king for various services of State. He received a pension from Robert II for his labours. A large collection of lives of the saints (Univ. Lib. Camb. Gg. ii. 6) and fragments of a Troy Book, attributed to Barbour by Henry Bradshaw, are not accepted by most critics as Barbour's work.

animated knights at their highest moments. There is no senseless denigration of the enemy's merits. The valour of the 'douchty lord Douglas' is equalled by the 'high prowess' of Sir Ingram de Umfraville, while Barbour stays to laud the action of Sir Giles de Argentine, who bade King Edward 'gud day' when he saw him turn to fly while he himself rode forward

> And in that place than slayne wes he.
> Of his ded wes rycht gret pite
> He wes the thrid best knycht, perfay,
> That men wist lyfand in his day.

These lines are characteristic of a chivalric temper which pervades the poem alongside a fiercer, more violent note, for much of the poem is taken up with violent action—single combats or the encounters of army with army are fully and vigorously described. The noise, excitement, and movement of fighting fill Barbour's pages, and culminate in the classic description of the fight between Bruce and De Bohun at Bannockburn. The fights are not described merely for the pleasure their hearing would give to an audience, but as part of the daring struggle against the English invader. Behind the whole poem is the feeling so memorably expressed by Barbour in his famous apostrophe:

> A! fredome is a noble thing!
> Fredome mayss[1] man to haiff liking;
> Fredome all solace to man giffis,
> He levys[2] at ess that frely levys!
> A noble hart may haiff nane ess,
> Na ellys nocht that may him pless,
> Gyff fredome failȝhe;[3] for fre liking
> Is ȝharnyt[4] our all other thing.

The *Original Chronicle of Scotland*, by Andrew of Wyntoun,[5] is a work of some merit as a chronicle-history, but it is poor poetry. Andrew is animated by the desire to make his listeners aware of their heritage, and although his chronicle is ostensibly a history of the world from its earliest (original) times, its main purpose is to emphasize the claims of Scotland to an independent existence. From the eighth century, therefore, he makes Scottish

[1] mayss (makes). [2] levys (lives).
[3] failȝhe (fail). [4] ȝharnyt, 'yearned for'.
[5] Andrew of Wyntoun (1350?–1420?) was a Canon Regular of St. Andrew's and afterwards Prior of St. Cerf's Inch in Lochleven from about 1395 to the time of his death. His patron was Sir John Wemyss.

history his main theme, and tells his story in detail. He relies on a variety of sources for his material up to the time of Bruce, and from then onwards his own account is a valuable authority.

Wyntoun's circumscribed life as a cleric did little to develop any poetic powers he may have had. He uses the octosyllabic couplet in a dull, mechanical fashion and little would have been lost could he have written in prose. His greatest importance, perhaps, is as an indication of how deep-felt was the patriotic feeling against the English. Wyntoun extols the bravery of the Scot and shows a bitter hatred of the English. He has no doubt as to King Edward's fate:

> The sawlys that he gert[1] to slay down thare
> He sent quhare his sawl nevyrmare
> Wes lyk to come, that is the blys
> Quhare alkyn[2] joy ay lestand[3] is.

This vigorous patriotic note is also sounded with great emphasis by the author of the *Wallace*. His identity has been the cause of much dispute. John Major, the author of *Historia Majoris Britanniae*, asserted that the work was written by 'Blind Harry' or Henry the Minstrel as he is sometimes called, and that it was composed during Major's infancy (*c.* 1460). Recently, however, it has been shown that the epithet *reyffar* (vi. 381), applied to King Edward I by Wallace, is an echo of words used in an Act of the Scottish Parliament of 1482 regarding Edward IV, and that therefore the year 1482 or 1483 is a more likely date. (The sole surviving manuscript was written by James Ramsay in 1488.) 'Blind Harry the Minstrel' has also come in for some heavy criticism, and it is hardly too much to say that we are now uncertain whether he was blind or called Harry or a minstrel. Major, however, spoke of him as blind from birth and existing by reciting in the halls of lords (*coram principibus*) as a wandering minstrel. From this critics have found it an easy step to think of him as going from hall to hall, picking up new items for his repertory the more readily because his blindness had accustomed him to rely on his ear. Thus, like Blind Homer, he recited the deeds of heroes and their descendants in the defence of their country. It is a charming story, but there is little to show that it is true. Indeed, much of the evidence points to a contrary conclusion. Henry, it is true,

[1] gert, 'made, caused'. [2] alkyn, 'every'. [3] lestand, 'lasting'.

proclaims himself 'a burel (ignorant) man', who writes 'a rurall dytt' (a rustic song), but this is but 'common form', as we have seen in English poets of this age. The metres he uses—the couplet and the nine-line stanza—do not bear out his depreciatory statements, nor do the descriptions of natural scenery, the many classical allusions, nor the 'aureate' terms. The author of the *Wallace*, whoever he was, cannot be thought of as ignorant or uncouth. To turn to the poem itself: it is a production in which everything is sacrificed on the altar of patriotism. The author does not allow himself to be hampered by considerations of historical accuracy. Fact and fiction are inextricably mingled as a glowing picture of Scotland's fight for freedom is created. The story is told so as to exalt Wallace as a national leader. No exploit is too daring for him, no odds too great. He kills armed men although himself unarmed; he is the equal of Hector and Achilles combined; 'Awful Edward durst nocht Wallace abid, In playn battaill for all England so wid'. Wallace is the avenger, the scourge of the English, so that 'It was his lyff, and maist part of his fude, To see thaim sched the brynand Southroun blude'. The tone of the whole work is suggested by the opening lines:

> Our ald ennemys cummyn of Saxonis blud,
> That neuyr ȝeit[1] to Scotland wald do gud,
> Bot euir on fors,[2] and contrar haile thair will,[3]
> Quhow gret kyndnes thar has beyne kyth[4] thaim till:
> It is weyle knawyne on many diuers syde,
> How thai haff wrocht in to thair mychty pryde,
> To hald Scotlande at wndyr[5] euirmair.

A strong hatred of England and of the English permeates the poem. There is a savage element in Wallace and his followers, and they burn and kill without mercy. Many descriptions are given of such scenes, of Wallace's superhuman strength, and of 'acts of prowess eminent'. It is the story of a barbarous chieftain of barbarous times, and we must accept this and all that flows from it, just as we must accept the grotesquely false historical background against which the action takes place. This falsification of history reaches its height in an episode in which romance and wish-fulfilment take the place of fact. Wallace is said to

[1] ȝeit (yet). [2] euir on fors, 'ever acted by force'.
[3] contrar haile thair will, 'entirely against their (the Scots) will'.
[4] kyth, 'shown'. [5] at wndyr, 'in an inferior position'.

have reached as far south as St. Albans, and an ultimatum sent by him to Edward, cowering in the Tower, is finally replied to, but 'No man was thar that durst to Wallace wend'. At this juncture the queen volunteers to take the message, and the poem goes on to describe her arrival at St. Albans and her reception by Wallace in terms more suitable to a romance than to an heroic chronicle. Despite the queen's blandishments ('Wallace', scho said, 'yhe war clepyt my luff') Wallace refuses to treat with her, and although he shows her every courtesy, insists on his country's demands. It is with a jolt that we remember that history tells us how Wallace never penetrated farther south than Newcastle and that Edward was known as *malleus Scotorum.*

In short, our pleasure in the poem comes not from its tone but from the skill with which the minstrel tells his tale. He is a facile artist, and moves easily in the decasyllabic couplet, well aware of its possibilities, and well instructed in the use of rhetorical figures. Thus he pictures Wallace lamenting the death of Sir John de Graham as follows:

> He lychtyt[1] doun, and hynt[2] him fra thaim aw
> In armys up; behaldand[3] his paill face,
> He kyssyt him, and cryt full oft; 'Allace!'
> My best brothir in warld that euir I had!
> My a fald[4] freynd quhen I was hardest stad!
> My hop, my heill,[5] thow was in maist honour!
> My faith, my help, strenthiast in stour![6]
> In the was wyt,[7] fredom, and hardines;
> In the was trewth, manheid, and nobilnes;
> In the was rewll, in the was gouernans;
> In the was wertu with outyn warians[8] . . .

The chronicle poets, however, belonged essentially to a fast dying state of society. While it was laudable to commemorate in song the exploits of past heroes, much that was of interest lay outside this field, and here the powerful influence of Chaucer and his disciples was of great moment. Both in matter and form English poets were laid under contribution, and outstanding among poems written in the 'Chaucerian' tradition is the

[1] lychtyt (lighted).
[2] hynt, 'held'.
[3] behaldand (beholding).
[4] a fald, 'truest'.
[5] heill, 'health'.
[6] strenthiast in stour, 'strongest in conflict'.
[7] wyt, 'knowledge'.
[8] warians, 'fickleness'.

Kingis Quair. That its author owes much to a study of Chaucer cannot be doubted. In places Chaucer's situations are closely copied, in others it is Chaucer's phrasing that is followed. The Chaucerian seven-line stanza (which takes its name 'rhyme royal' from this poem) is adopted, and the poem concludes with a recommendation of the work to 'my maisteris dere, Gowere and Chaucere'. Gower's influence is less marked, but that of Lydgate's *Temple of Glass* is clear enough at times. More important still, the whole work is an allegorical love poem, complete with dream, with interviews with Venus, Minerva, and Fortune, and tricked out with much well-known detail made familiar by the *Romance of the Rose*. In spite of all this it is an original work. In taking over all these stock elements the author has refused to be overcome by them. He uses them for his own purpose and often as freshly as if they had never been used before. The all-important moment of the first sight of the beloved has never been more admirably stated than in the poet's words:

> And therwith kest I doun myn eye ageyne,
> Quhare as I sawe, walking under the toure,
> Full secretly new cummyn hir to pleyne,
> The fairest or the freschest yong floure
> That ever I sawe, me thoght, before that houre,
> For quhich sodayn abate, anon astert
> The blude of all my body to my hert.

It is also an original work in its attitude to its subject-matter. Here the lover's suit to the lady finds its consummation in marriage, not in 'courtly love'. The lover is closely questioned by Minerva, who agrees to help him only when he has convinced her that 'in vertew [his] lufe is set with treuth', and that it is 'ground and set in Cristin wis'. Although the poet makes use of a well-worn literary form, he gives it a life of its own because he uses it to tell (or seem to tell) his own story. From the moment he sets out to obey the injunction 'Tell on, man, quhat the befel', the poem has a personal note, and the verses often have an intensity of feeling rarely met with in medieval poetry. The poet is an artist in words. He piles up his adjectives and nouns but makes them effective:

> With new fresche suete and tender grene,
> Oure lyf, oure lust,[1] oure governoure, oure quene.

[1] lust, 'pleasure'.

He uses the artifices of the rhetoricians with skill, as in the lines above, and as in:

> My wele in wo, my frendis all in fone,[1]
> My lyf in deth, my lyght into derkness,
> My hope in feer, in dout my sekirness,[2]
> Sen sche is gone: and God mote hir convoye,
> That me may gyde to turment and to joye!

At times he falls back on a cliché: 'the colde stone', 'the rokkes blak', but he is capable of 'a turtur quhite as calk',[3] or of speaking of the fish 'with bakkis blewe as lede', and comparing their bright scales to the glitter of a suit of armour ('That in the sonne on thair scalis bryght As gesserant[4] ay glitterit in my sight'). The management of the stanza and the lyrical quality of many passages denote the work of one who has studied his masters with attention and has gone on to strike out his own music.

Who wrote the *Kingis Quair*? The scribe who finished copying the unique manuscript now in the Bodleian (MS. Arch. Selden B. 24) wrote at the end of the poem 'Quod Jacobus Primus, Scotorum Rex Illustrissimus', while on a blank space opposite the third stanza of the poem a different hand from any in the manuscript has written: 'Heirefter followis the quair Maid be King James of Scotland ye firſt callit ye Kingis quair and maid q[n] his Ma. was In Ingland.' The writer of this second note gives us the title of the poem, which is not stated elsewhere, and also says that it was composed by James while in England.[5] James I of Scotland was a prisoner in England for many years, and the story of the poem parallels in many ways his wooing of Joan Beaufort and marriage. Although attempts have been

[1] fone, 'foes'.

[2] sekirness, 'security'.

[3] a turtur quhite as calk, 'a turtle-dove white as chalk'.

[4] gesserant, 'a coat of mail'.

[5] James I of Scotland (1394–1437) was the third son of Robert III and was captured by an English ship when *en route* to France in 1406. He remained a prisoner in England, first at the Tower and then at various other places, until late in 1423 negotiations for his release were successful. Among the stipulations he was required to take an English wife, and this he did on St. Valentine's Eve, 1424, when he married Joan Beaufort. He was in Scotland by April 1424, and began a reign of thirteen years. He instituted many reforms in Church and State, and lived a happy married life until he was murdered on 20 February 1437. James was a most accomplished king. He excelled in manly sports and loved all the arts. In addition to the *Kingis Quair*, he has been credited with various poems. Of these *Christis Kirk on the Grene* and *Peblis to the Play* are of importance, poems first found in the Bannatyne and Maitland MSS. respectively.

made to find an author for the poem other than James, these have not been generally accepted. The case for King James has recently been strengthened by Sir William Craigie, who has argued convincingly that the Scottish linguistic features were probably added by scribes, such as the writer of Selden B. 24, and that the poem was originally written in post-Chaucerian Southern English by an author in close touch with the language which he wrote and able to use it correctly. It is highly unlikely that this would have been possible to anyone whose connexions and training were purely Scottish. On the other hand, as Sir William says, 'accepting King James as the author, everything becomes normal and natural; eighteen years' residence in English surroundings, added to an acquaintance with the works of Gower and Chaucer, and no doubt of contemporary English poets, would be amply sufficient to qualify him as a competent maker of poetry after these models'.

The other outstanding 'Scottish Chaucerian' is Robert Henryson, generally identified with 'the scholemaister of Dunfermeling', one who deserves a high place among Scottish medieval poets.[1] His work is more insular than that of Chaucer or of his contemporary Dunbar, but it has an originality and ease of expression which give it distinction. Henryson is rooted in his Scottish world, for as Allan Ramsay observed of these early Scottish poets: 'Their Poetry is the Product of their own Country. . . . Their Images are native, and their Landskips domestick; copied from those Fields and Meadows we every day behold. The Morning rises . . . as she does in the Scottish Horizon. We are not carried to Greece or Italy for a Shade, a Stream or a Breeze . . . the Rivers flow from our own Fountains, and the Winds blow upon our own Hills.' So Henryson

[1] Robert Henryson (1429?–*c.* 1508). No material exists upon which to base a very firm biography of Henryson. A number of Robert Henrysons existing in Scotland in the second half of the fifteenth century have been discovered, but none of them clearly to be identified with the poet. His name was attached to a number of poems in early manuscripts and printed books, and he is mentioned in Dunbar's *Lament for the Makaris*:

> In Dunfermelyne he hes done roune
> With Maister Robert Henrisoun.

This poem was printed in 1508, so he must have been dead by then. The poet is generally identified with Robert Henryson, Master of the Grammar School attached to the Benedictine abbey of Dunfermline. It is not certain that he is the Henryson who incorporated in the University of Glasgow (1462) or the notary who witnessed certain deeds at Dunfermline.

draws his imagery from freshly observed every-day events and scenes. He observes the 'fronsyt[1] face', 'runclit[2] beik', 'hyngand[3] Browis, and hir voce so hace'[4] of the Frog with 'hir logrand[5] leggis, and hir harsky hyd'.[6] Here his observation is exact and detailed as compared with much of the stock material commonly used by English poets of this time. He sees the labourers

> Sum makand dyke, and sum the pleuch can wynd,
> Sum sawand sedis fast from place to place,
> The harrowis hoppand in the saweris trace.

He delights in homely phrases and in alliterative jingles drawing strength and colour from these popular elements. Similarly the humour of the folk plays throughout his work, especially in the *Fables*, while the movement of the verse with its frequent alliteration often emphasizes the movement of his narrative in the happiest fashion. Take for example the meeting of the town mouse with her sister the country mouse:

> The hartlie joy, God! geve ye had sene,
> Beis kith[7] quhen that thir Sisteris met;
> And grit kyndnes wes schawin thame betwene,
> For quhylis thay leuch[8], and quhylis for joy thay gret,[9]
> Quhyle(s) kissit sweit, quhylis in armis plet.[10]

A warm humanity infuses all his work. The cry of Orpheus 'Quhair art thow gane, my lufe Euridices?' and the superscription Troilus placed over the grave of Cresseid:

> Lo, fair Ladyis, Crisseid, of Troyis toun,
> Sumtyme countit the flour of Womanheid,
> Under this stane lait Lipper lyis deid.

express his graver emotions, but he could also delight in the antics and feelings of the animals in the *Fables*, as he sees their likeness to humans, and records their failings and their activities. Thus, gorged with the stolen kid, the Fox seeks a resting-place, and

> Unto ane derne[11] for dreid he him addrest,
> Under ane busk, quhare that the sone can beit,
> To beik his breist and bellie he thocht best;
> And rekleslie he said, quhair he did rest,

[1] fronsyt, 'frounced, wrinkled'. [2] runclit, 'wrinkled'.
[3] hyngand, 'overhanging'. [4] hace, 'hoarse'.
[5] logrand, 'loosely hanging'. [6] harsky hyd, 'rough skin'.
[7] kith, 'shown'. [8] leuch, 'laughed'. [9] gret, 'wept'.
[10] plet, 'folded'. [11] derne, 'secret place'.

Straikand[1] his wame[2] aganis the sonis heit,
'Upon this wame set wer ane bolt full meit.'[3]

Henryson's output was not large, but he essayed many forms. His shorter poems are unimportant, although the vigour of his alliterative verses in his extravagant *Sum Practysis of Medecyne* is worthy of remark. *Orpheus and Eurydice* tells of the quest of Orpheus as he proceeds 'by Watlingis Street' to seek out his lady in the realm of Pluto. The story is well told, and is interspersed with lyrical passages and some vivid descriptions as when Orpheus reaches Eurydice, and finds her

Lene and deidlyk, and peteouss paill of hew,
Rycht warsche and wane, and walluid[4] as the weid,
hir Lilly lyre wes lyk unto the leid.

In *Robene and Makyne* Henryson gives us one of the earliest forms of the *pastorelle* that was to have so great a vogue. This charming piece of rustic wooing, with its *moralitas*, 'The man that wilt nocht when he may Sall have nocht when he wald', is played out by Robene and Makyne on 'a gude green hill' amid the flocks feeding in 'a full fair dale', and ends with the solitary Robene left

In dolour and in care
Keepand his hird under a huche[5]
Amangis the holtis hair.[6]

Henryson manages the narrative with skill. The background, the characters, and the interplay of grave and gay are all expressed in brief but telling lines.

In the *Testament of Cresseid* the 'scholemaister' in Henryson is in the ascendant. He adds a pendant to Chaucer's poem which drives home with unrelenting emphasis what happened after the parting of 'fals Cresseid, and trew Knicht Troilus'. Henryson pictures Cresseid stricken down with leprosy, living out her life with 'cop and clapper' in the Spital House 'at the tounes end'. As she begs for alms one day Troilus and his company come her way

Than upon him scho kest up baith hir Ene,[7]
And with ane blenk[8] it come into his thocht,
That he sumtime hir face befoir had sene.
Bot scho was in sic plye[9] he knew hir nocht,
Yit than hir luik into his mynd it brocht

[1] straikand, 'stroking'. [2] wame, 'belly'.
[3] Upon . . . meit, 'How fitly were an arrow set (planted) in this belly'.
[4] warsche . . . walluid, 'withered . . . dried up'.
[5] huche, 'cliff', or 'steep bank'. [6] holtis hair, 'bare woods'.
[7] Ene, 'eyes'. [8] blenk, 'glance'. [9] plye (plight).

> The sweit visage and amorous blenking[1]
> Of fair Cresseid sumtyme his awin darling . . .
>
> Ane spark of lufe than till his hart culd spring
> And kendlit all his bodie in ane fyre

and he throws down to her a princely alms. Cresseid learns that it was Troilus who passed, whereupon she makes her testament and dies. A fellow leper takes her ruby ring to Troilus, who

> Siching full sadlie, said: 'I can no moir,
> Scho was untrew, and wo is me thairfoir.'

Henryson tells his story with dignity and poignancy. The pauses for the great 'set pieces', depicting Saturn, Jupiter, Mars, and others, or the 'Complaint of Cresseid' give richness and detail, but do not unduly delay the action. The versification has much of Chaucer's felicitous power of varying the stresses so that monotony is avoided, while a rich vocabulary is aptly but not extravagantly employed to give life and colour to the verse. The *Testament* forms a not unworthy pendant to Chaucer's poem.

The death of Henryson (*c.* 1508) came at a moment when his contemporary Dunbar (*c.* 1460–*c.* 1530) was pouring out his astonishing variety of poems. In him Scottish poetry finds a champion who can use all the forms, knows all the traditions, and can extoll or laugh at them as the mood takes him. Once his work has been read it is impossible to think of Scottish poetry as 'provincial' or 'Chaucerian': it stands on its own merits.[2]

[1] amorous blenking, 'loving glances'.
[2] For Dunbar, see Vol. III, Chap. I.

VII

FIFTEENTH-CENTURY PROSE

FIFTEENTH-CENTURY prose has not been well treated by literary historians. Indeed, much of it has scarcely received more than a bare mention in accounts which have lavished space upon Pecock, Fortescue, Malory, and Caxton. Pecock and Malory, in particular, have interested critics, yet neither of them had much influence on English prose. While attention has been thus diverted, the main movement of prose writing has been missed. If we wish to know what was done for prose in this century we shall find it best to give only limited attention to the four authors we have mentioned and to concentrate far more than has been the fashion on the many writers—known and unknown—who took over from the fourteenth century an inheritance which they fostered and developed with zeal and success.

I

The preliminary requisite for any successful development of an English prose style had been secured when English gained the upper hand over French or Latin as the normal vehicle for written communications between Englishmen. It was a difficult matter for those educated to write in French to accustom themselves to the use of English, and sometimes we find a letter in which both languages struggle for supremacy. Rose Mountefort writes to her 'cousin', probably in the early part of Richard II's reign, as follows:

Tresentere cosyn and tresbonement ame, ieo vous saluce, aucy tressouent cum ieo plus and mult desire de oyere bone nouvel de vos, and sy de myu voles oyere, ieo su passe malade enloe seyt nostre seyner. Treschere cosyn, ieo vous pry bryng a wryt of trespas en ver Richard forde of Sulyhul, Wyliam Noryng of yzerdeley, Wilyam Ducy of Northfield, the wheche trespas hu duden the waley of twenty mark Touching to me and my tenante. Myn owne dere cosyn, thenk on this enterelyche; make the coste and I shall wel quite. Adeu, le sente trinite vos comande, enscripte en hast en la manere de Codbarow a la fest sent Ambrose

vostre chere cosyn dam Rose Mountefort.[1]

[1] 'Fair cousin and gentle friend, I greet you as often as I can, and very much

This kind of macaronic prose, written naturally and without self-consciousness, would be difficult to find before 1375 or after 1425.

Once this linguistic struggle was over, the way was clear for the next development. Put in the broadest terms there were two schools of prose usage open to writers from Chaucer's time onwards. When a clerk found himself asked to write in English, the most obvious thing for him to do was to make use, as best he could, of the constructions, phrasing, and rhetorical figures to which he was accustomed in Latin. Similarly, the scholar was likely to write English in a way that approximated as closely as possible to the Latin which was his daily reading. There was, however, another way. Even as early as the latter part of the fourteenth century men had realized that there was something alien to the English of everyday speech in the form which prose was taking. In 1387 Usk says that he will ignore the 'queynt knitting coloures' (i.e. curious fine phrases, that 'knit' or join words together) and use 'rude wordes and boystrous, to maken the cacchers[1] ther ben the more redy to hente sentence'.[2] About the same time Wyclif was declaiming against the 'pomposam eloquenciam' of many preachers, advocating a plain, direct method of speaking, and an avoidance of the use of rhythmical ornament and other rhetorical devices. *Nude et apte* was his formula for good prose. Lastly, John of Trevisa had discussed a similar problem with his lord when, about 1387, he asked Sir Thomas of Berkeley whether he should write in verse or in prose. He was told: 'In prose, for comynlich prose is more clere than ryme, more esy, and more playn to knowe and understonde.' English prose during the fifteenth century had to decide between these issues.

It must be remembered that prose had an ever-widening field before it. All available knowledge was rapidly becoming its province; for much that hitherto had been written in Latin

wish to hear good news of you, and if you wish to hear news of me, I've got over my illness; God be praised. My dear cousin, I beg you to bring a writ of trespass against Richard Ford of Solihull, William Noring of Yardley, William Ducy of Northfield, the said trespass being done to the value of twenty marks against me and my tenant. My own dear cousin, think on this earnestly; pay the costs and I will requite you. Good-bye, I commend you to the Holy Trinity. Written in haste in the manor of Codbarow on S. Ambrose day.

Your dear cousin, Dame Rose Mountfort.'

[1] cacchers (catchers), 'hunters'.

[2] hente sentence, 'seize the meaning'.

began to take on English dress, while new opportunities for the use of the vernacular were arising. To some extent these varying matters required varying styles. 'Heigh stile, as when Kings endite' was evidently in the minds of the city of London, when, encouraged by the king's example, it began to write letters such as:

Right high, right myghty, and right honurable Prince, we recomaunde vs un-to your Lordly excellens in the most humble and seruisable maner that we can best ymagine and deuise, Thankyng lowly your noble grace of the gracious lettres in makyng gladsom in vndyrstandyng and passyng confortable in fauoring of our pouer degrees Whyche you liked late to send vs from Craille vpon case in Normandie . . . whyche hath made vs notable report and right comfortable exposicion of thestate and tidinges of that lond, blessed be god.

This is only an English version of the stock pattern to be found in the medieval books of *dictamen*. Its 'humble and serviceable', 'imagine and devise', 'notable report and right comfortable exposition', &c., follow a pattern, and are an attempt 'to embellish, ornate and make fair our English'—an attempt which had its dangers. It led to a prose analogous to that elaborate type of poetry practised by Lydgate and his followers, who developed an aureate use of language and an ability to 'cloke in subtle terms, with colour tenebrous' what little they had to say, to the detriment of both prose and verse.

The cultivation of the *florida verborum venustas*, as Professor E. F. Jacob has shown, flourished in the fifteenth century, and writers in Latin, such as John Whethamstede, favour the 'recondite and precious, or an impressive rotundity. The influence of Cicero is yet to come, and the medieval as opposed to the renaissance attitude still holds sway.' This may be seen both in poets and prose writers. Lydgate, Hawes, Dunbar, and Barclay follow the medieval tradition: Wyatt and Surrey, the humanist. Not until late in the fifteenth century does a new sense of the use of language begin to show itself. 'Enlarged and adorned' prose, therefore, had a powerful ally in some of its Latin models, and much official and clerical prose was composed in this fashion, as, for example, in the English letters of the University of Oxford, or those in collections, such as the Christ Church letters, or in the various documents in the Letter Books K and L of the city of London.

Latin was also, in varying degrees, at the back of much religious and homiletic prose. It may be allowed that this did not imply mere slavish imitation: the great fourteenth-century writers—Rolle, Hilton, and even Wyclif—had shown otherwise. Often when the writer had the advantage of a Latin version (or a French translation of the Latin) before him, his work achieved a tautness and coherence that was frequently lacking in contemporary original prose. An outstanding writer, such as Nicholas Love,[1] used his Latin originals so skilfully that he produced a translation of the *Meditationes Vitae Christi* which gives us some of the most beautiful prose of the century—a prose ordered and controlled by a clear grasp of its underlying sequences of thought and argument and by the use of many of the devices of the rhetoricians.[2]

It is prose of this kind (though not often of this quality) which gave grounds for R. W. Chambers's claim that the continuity of English prose is to be found in the sermon and in every kind of devotional treatise. While there is much truth in this, prose was also continuing to develop along simpler and more conversational lines. Men who owed little or nothing to French or Latin were constantly attempting to put down their thoughts in a clear and unornamented fashion. They have little to offer the seeker of 'fine prose'; their only endeavour was to state their ideas in a straightforward fashion, almost as simply as if they were talking. English was used in a thousand petty ways which helped to give men a better control of the medium. In civic affairs the London guilds make it serve their purpose: letters from the corporation, ordinances and proclamations, proceedings in the mayor's court are written in English. Men make wills, write letters, attempt little treatises on hawking or fishing, set down medical or herbal recipes, or note what seasons or days are fortunate—all in English.

Prose had almost everything to learn and there were no great writers whose influence was all-pervasive, so that prose in this century developed by much trial and error and owed much to 'unprofessional' as well as to professional writers.

To take the prose written by ordinary men first. Here we are

[1] Nicholas Love was prior of the Carthusian house of Mount Grace, at Ingleby, Yorkshire. His translation of the *Meditationes* was licensed by Archbishop Arundel, about 1410, for reading by the devout laity and to the confutation of heretics or Lollards.

[2] See also p. 216.

fortunate, for the fifteenth century is the century of the Pastons, the Celys, and the Stonors—to name only the three greatest known families of letter-writers of this period. Here, as perhaps nowhere else, can we see what powers of handling the language were possessed by all that variety of men and women who used the pen mainly or solely to state their own business or pleasures. Naturally no thought of publication was ever in the writers' minds—indeed they frequently exhort their correspondents to burn their letters when read—and their writings reveal the ability of many to write straightforward unaffected prose. Every kind of topic is dealt with: descriptions of riots, forays, and executions; requests for money, books, cooking materials, or wives; accounts of legal proceedings and unsuccessful bribery; of attempts to hold courts, execute distraints, engage servants; descriptions of possible brides, of weddings, of feasts, of illnesses—in short, everything that formed part of the fabric of medieval life. A correspondent, describing the execution of the Duke of Suffolk in a small boat at sea, apologizes for blurs in his letter because 'I am right sorry of that I shalle say, and have soo wesshe this litel bille with sorwfulle terys that on ethes[1] ye shalle reede it'. This personal, direct note marks the whole series of letters. To illustrate the straightforward, homely clarity of this way of writing we may turn to a vivid account given by an eyewitness of a manor court held by the Duke of Suffolk, at Hellesdon, in 1478.

He tells us that the duke was full of spleen against Sir John Paston, and at

hys beyng ther that daye ther was never no man that playd Herrod in Corpus Crysty play better and more agreable to hys pageaunt[2] then he dud. But ye schall understond that it was after none, and the weder hot, and he so feble for sekenes that hys legges wold not bere hyme, but ther was ij men had gret payn to kepe hym on hys fete; and ther ye were juged. Som sayd, 'Sley'; some sayd, 'Put hym in preson.' And forth com my lord, and he wold met you with a spere, and have none other mendes for the troble at ye have put hym to but your hart blod, and that will be gayt with hys owen handes.

One more example may be taken from a letter written from Calais in 1476 by Thomas Betson to Katherine Ryche, the eldest daughter of Elizabeth Stonor by her first husband, when Katherine was little more than a child. Betson writes a long

[1] on ethes, 'with difficulty'. [2] pageaunt, 'play'.

amusing letter to her, his bride to be, bidding her to overcome her dislike of meat, and 'evene as you loffe me to be mery and to eate your mete lyke a woman'; he tells her to 'grete well my horsse', and goes on:

I praye you, gentill Cossen, comaunde me to the Cloke,[1] and pray hym to amend his unthryffte maners: ffor he strykes ever in undew tyme, and he will be ever affore, and that is a shrewde condiscion. Tell hym with owte he amend his condiscion that he will cause strangers to advoide and come no more there. I trust to you that he shall amend agaynest myn commynge, the which shalbe shortely with all hanndes and all ffeete with Godes grace. . . . And Almyghty Jhesu make you a good woman, and send you many good yeres and longe to lyveffe in helth and vertu to his plesour. At greate Cales on this syde on the see, the ffyrst day off June, whanne every man was gone to his Dener, and the Cloke smote noynne, and all oure howsold cryed after me and badde me come down; come down to dener at ones! and what answer I gaveffe hem ye know it off old.

Letters like these are proof enough that before the end of the century a tradition of what constituted good prose had been created. The prose of Sir Thomas More descends from the wit and grace of this kind of writing as well as from the tradition of devout prose. These letter-writers are drawn from various stations of life, and the ease of a Thomas Betson in writing playfully to his little friend is matched by the dramatic description of the Duke of Suffolk's behaviour or by other passages which might be taken from fifteenth-century letters. Here we are dealing with writings put together with no thought of their literary quality: we could not have a better opportunity of assessing the ordinary person's ability to use his pen or of the plain style which he affected. Some of his fellows, however, while they would not have claimed more than an amateur status, undoubtedly wrote for a wider circle of readers, and we might well expect their work to show a greater control over their medium.

This is exactly what we find in the writings of William Thorpe,[2] the Lollard, and of Margery Kempe, the mystic.

[1] Cloke (clock).

[2] William Thorpe (d. 1460?) was born in the north of England in the mid-fourteenth century. He studied at Oxford and took priest's orders. He was tried for heresy in 1397 and imprisoned. On his release he became an itinerant preacher and was again arrested for heresy at Shrewsbury and brought before the Archbishop of Canterbury. The result of this examination and the date of his death are unknown.

Thorpe's writing is in the main an account, written down many years after the event (and slightly modernized by Tyndale), of his examination for heresy before the Archbishop of Canterbury in 1407. It gives a clear and vivid account of the interview, and sets out in dialogue form the thrust and parry of the disputants. Thorpe's command of prose is shown in the careful expositions of his theological position and belief. Here the utmost nicety of expression was essential if he was to save his life, and Thorpe's English comes out of the ordeal most successfully. For example:

And the Archbishoppe asked me, 'What was holye church'. And I said, 'Syr I told you before what was holye churche: but since ye aske me this demaunde: I call Christe and his sayntes holye church'. And the Archbishop saide vnto me, 'I wotte wel that Christ and his saintes are holy church in heauen, but what is holy church in earth'. And I said, 'Sir, though holy church be euery one in charity, yet it hath two partes. The first and principall part hathe ouercomen perfectly all the wretchednesse of this life, and raigneth ioyfully in heauen with Christe. And the other part is here yet in earth, besily and continually fighting day and night against temptacions of the fiend, forsaking and hatyng the prosperity of this world, despising and wythstanding their fleshly lustes, which only are the pilgrimes of Christ, wandering toward heauen by stedfast faithe, and grounded hope, and by perfect charity.'

Not only was his prose sufficient for this purpose, but it could also take a lively turn:

Sir I know well that wan diuers men and women wil go thus, after their own wils, and finedyng out one pilgrimage, they wil orden with them before to haue with them bothe men and women, that can well singe wanton songes, and some other Pilgrimes will haue wyth them bagge pipes, so that euerye towne that they come thorow, what with the noise of their singing, and with the sound of their piping, and wyth the iangling of their Canterbury bels, and with the barking out of dogs after them, that they make more noyse, than if the kynge came thereaway, wythall his clarions, and many other mynstrels. And if these men and women be a month out in their pilgrimage, many of them shalbe an half yere after great jangelers, tale-tellers and liers.

And the Archbishop said to me: leud losell thow seest not farre enough in this matter, for thou considerest not the great trauell of Pilgrims, therfore thou blamest that thinge that is praisable. I say to thee that it is right well done, that Pilgrimes haue with them bothe singers and also pipers, that whan one of them that goeth barefote striketh his too vppon a stone, and hurteth hym sore, and maketh hym to blede: it is wel done that he or his felow begin than a song, or els take out of his bosome a bagpipe for to drive away wyth such mirth the hurt of his felow. For with such solace the trauel and werines of pylgrymes is lightly and merily brought forth.

Margery Kempe of Lynn was illiterate herself, as far as we can tell, but there can be little doubt that her autobiography was taken down at her dictation and conveys her own way of expressing herself.[1] In common with those of her time and class, she used a homely, vivid style and made use of phrases such as 'that wicked worm, Wiclif', or proverbs such as 'many men spekyn of Robyn Hood, and shoote neuere his bowe', or in speaking of an opponent she tells him that 'thou wost no more what thou blaberest than Balamis asse'—all phrases and proverbs, as we have already seen, used by her contemporaries.[2] The following passage illustrates how close to actual speech her language could be, and how clearly her narrative reveals its teller:

Than went þis creatur forth to London wyth hir husbond vn-to Lambhyth, þer þe Erchebisshop lay at þat tyme. And, as þei comyn in-to þe halle at aftyr-noon, ther wer many of þe Erchebysshoppys clerkys & other rekles men boþe swyers & ȝemen[3] whech sworyn many gret oþis & spokyn many rekles wordys, & þis creatur boldly vndyrname[4] hem & seyd þei schuld ben dampnyd but þei left her sweryng & oþer synnes þat þei vsyd. & wyth þat cam forth a woman of þe same town in a pylche[5] & al for-schod[6] þis creatur, bannyd hir, & seyd ful cursydly to hir in þis maner, 'I wold þu wer in Smyth-feld, & I wold beryn a fagot to bren þe wyth; it is pety þat þow leuyst.' Þis creatur stod stylle & answeryd not, & hir husbond suffred wyth gret peyn & was ful sory to heryn hys wyfe so rebukyd.

[1] Margery Kempe (1373?–1440?) was the daughter of John Brenham, sometime Mayor of Lynn. She was married in 1393 to John Kempe, a burgess, and seems to have been in business herself as an unsuccessful brewer and miller. After bearing her husband fourteen children she made an agreement with him that they should live chaste thereafter (1413). Soon she began a series of pilgrimages to the Holy Land, Rome, and Santiago. These, and many religious experiences which were accompanied with 'boystous' spells of crying and religious mania, are vividly retold in her autobiography, which was set down in her old age with the aid of two clerks about 1432–6.

[2] See above, p. 156. [3] ȝemen, 'yeomen'. [4] vndyrname, 'reproved'.

[5] pylche, 'an outer garment of skin dressed with the hair'.

[6] for-schod, 'reviled'.

Than þe Erchbusshop sent for þis creatur in-to hys gardeyn. Whan sche cam to hys presens, sche salutyd hym as sche cowd, prayng hym of hys gracyows lordshyp to grawnt hir auctoryte of chesyng hyr confessowr & to be howselyd euery Sonday, ȝyf God wold dysposen hir þerto, vndyr hys lettyr and hys seel thorw al hys prouynce. & he grawnt it her ful benyngly all hir desyr wyth-owtyn any syluer er gold, ne he wold latyn hys clerkys takyn any-thyng for wrytyn ne for seelyng of þe lettyr.

Or again:

On þe next day be-tyme sche payd for hir lodgynge, speryng[1] at hir oostys yf þei knewe of any felaschep to-Akun-ward. Þei seyd, 'Nay'. Sche, takyng hir leue of hem, went to þe chirche for to felyn & preuyn[2] yf hir felyng wer trewe er not. Whan sche cam þer, sche saw a cumpany of powr folke. Þan went sche to on of hem, speryng whidyr þei wer purposyd to gon. He seyd, 'To Akun'[3]. Sche preyid hym þat he wolde suffyr hir to gon in her cumpany. 'Why, dame', he seyd, 'hast þu no man to gon wyth þe?' 'No', sche seyd, 'my man is gon fro me'. So sche was receyuyd in-to a cumpany of powr folke, &, when þei comyn to any towne, sche bowte hir mete & hir felaschep went on beggyng. Whan þei wer wyth-owtyn þe townys, hir felaschep dedyn of her clothys, &, sittyng nakyd, pykyd hem. Nede compellyd hir to abydyn hem & prolongyn hir jurne & ben at meche mor cost þan sche xulde ellys[4] a ben. Thys creatur was a-bauyd[5] to putte of hir cloþis as hyr felawys dedyn, & þerfor sche thorw hir comownyng[6] had part of her vermyn & was betyn & stongyn ful euyl boþe day & nyght tyl God sent hir oþer felaschep. Sche kept forth hir felaschep wyth gret angwisch & disese & meche lettyng[7] vn-to þe tyme þat þei comyn to Akun.

There were not many Thorpes or Kempes writing in the fifteenth century, it is true, but wills, civic records, books of the chase, of gardening, and the like, all show that English prose could express the everyday commonplaces, desires, and requirements of most people. Such prose reached out to no great heights, but was content with stating its matter in simple, but often vigorous and dramatic language. It knew little of cadence or of striking phrases, yet at times it achieved something of both by its unaffected use of homely speech rhythms which were native to fifteenth-century people of ordinary education and breeding.

[1] speryng, 'asking, inquiring'. [2] felyn & preuyn, 'feeling and proving'.
[3] Akun (Aachen). [4] ellys, 'otherwise'. [5] a-bauyd, 'afraid'.
[6] comownyng, 'association'. [7] lettyng, 'hindrance'.

3

But prose had to give expression to something more than these straightforward practical matters. It had to convey the religious, didactic, philosophical, and scientific ideas of the age. This was a heavy burden for a prose which was still far from fully developed, but a laudable attempt was made to meet these various demands. Religious and homiletic themes found expression in such works as Nicholas Love's *Mirror*, or Capgrave's *Life of S. Gilbert*, or in collections of pious tales and *exempla*, such as the *Gesta Romanorum*, or the *Golden Legend*, or the *Book of the Knight of La Tour Landry*, or *Jacob's Well*. Learned argument and exposition are to be found in the works of philosophical interest of Pecock: past and contemporary English history in the *Brut* and in Capgrave's *Chronicle*, while Fortescue's treatise on the *Governance of England* sets out a philosophy of political ideas. Scientific treatises, such as translations of Lanfranc's *Science of Cirurgie*, or John of Bordeaux's plague pamphlet, put new problems before the prose writer. Add to these, tractates on the *Craft of Numbering*, the keeping of horses, hawking, hunting, and fishing; on travel and pilgrimages; or huge tomes such as Trevisa's translation of Bartholomew's *De Proprietatibus Rerum*, and something of the volume of prose that the century produced will be evident.

These works bring us into contact with the 'professional' writers, who hoped that their work would have as widespread a circulation as medieval conditions made possible. A strong didactic purpose informs many of these, of which the *Gesta Romanorum* may serve as an excellent example. It was one of the most famous compilations of the Middle Ages. Originally compiled in Latin, probably in England late in the thirteenth century, this collection of tales was greatly in demand among preachers and moralists, and in the fifteenth century was given an English form. Three versions are known: one of about 1440, containing seventy stories; a second of about the same date, but only forty-six of its ninety-six stories belong properly to the *Gesta*, the remainder coming from the twelfth-century fabulist, Odo of Cheriton, and other sources. A third version was made late in the century: it contains only thirty-two stories, in a confused order, and without the allegorical expositions. These three independent translations made within some fifty years of one another are evidence enough of the continued popularity of the *Gesta*. This is not difficult to understand when we examine the ingredients which went to its making. The wide range of stories which it contains are all told in simple, straightforward language, and include all those elements dear to the medieval mind. Here are to be found 'nigromancers' and other workers of magic; dragons and loathly worms; beautiful princesses and gallant youths; tyrants and fiends. Deeds of daring are the results of wagers; prisons, pits, and fetters fail to hold men, despite magic rings and pursuit by unicorns. Yet much homely detail keeps these stories within bounds: men go by ways that are 'stony, thorny and scraggy', or watch the catchpoles dragging men at the tail of a string of horses; the watchmen disturb the silence of the night by their horns and the nightingales 'synge wondir swetly'. The ease and simplicity with which the several stories are told may be seen from the following extract:

Polemius was an Emperoure in the cetee of Rome, þe whiche hadde iij sonnes, that he moche lovid. So as þis Emperoure laye in a certeyne nyght in his bedde, he thowte to dispose his Empir, & he thought to yeve his kyngdome to the slowest of his sones. He called to him his sonnes, & saide, 'he that is the sloweste of yow, or most slewth is in, shall have my kyngdom after my discese'. 'Þenne shall I have hit', quod the Eldest sone, 'for I am so slowe, & swiche slewthe is in me, that me hadde lever late my fote brynne in the fyr, whenne I sitte þer by, than to withdrawe, & save hit'. 'Nay', quod the secounde, 'yet am I mor worthi thanne þow; for yf case that my necke wer in a rope to be hongid; & yf þat I hadde my two hondes at wille, and in on honde þe ende of þe rope, and in that oþer honde a sharpe swerde, I hadde levir dye and be hongid, þan I wolde styr myn arme, and kitte þe rope, whereby I myte be savid'. 'Hit is I', quod the thirde, 'that shalle regne after my syre, for I passe hem bothe in slewthe. Yf I lygge in my bedde wyde opyn, & þe reyne reyne vppon boþe myn yen, yee, me hadde leuer lete hit reyne hem oute of the hede, than I turnid me oþere to the right syde, or to the lyfte syde'. Þenne the Emperoure biquathe his Empir to the thirde sone, as for the slowist.

Even more popular than the *Gesta Romanorum* was the *Legenda Aurea*. This work, by Jacobus de Voragine, was translated into English about 1438 in a version of 179 items of the original cycle. These simply-told stories of the lives of the saints were immensely popular. They instructed and entertained at the same time, and were compounded of a mixture of the credible and incredible so dear to the medieval mind. Another good example of the way in which English was being used for homiletic purposes may be seen in Mirk's *Festial*. This was a collection of sermons with *exempla* attached, written for the aid of such priests as those who 'excuson hem by defaute of bokus and sympulnys of letture'. It contained sermons for various feast days throughout the year, and each of these made considerable use of *exempla* to drive home their points by means of homely, lively incident, or relation of some exciting story, or account of the supernatural. All this matter was conveyed in such a way that a simple priest, and a still simpler congregation, could understand it without difficulty, by the use of language such as the following:

> Then þe fende operyd yn syght of all þe pepull lyke a man of Inde, blak altogedyr as pich, wyth a sharpe nase and a lodely face, wyth a berde down to his fete, blake as soote, wyth een brennyng as doth yern yn þe fyre sparklyng on yche syde, and blowyng flamys of brennyng fure, wyth hys hondys bownden byhynde hym wyth chaynys brennyng.

Here is a prose admirably suited to its audience. The writer appeals to the sense of colour and of drama inherent in simple folk, and in his clear language pictures in their imaginations the Devil, as they had often seen him in the religious plays, black and beast-like as possible, and as the stage direction says, 'with gunpowder burning in pipes in his hands, and in his ears'. His comparisons have the air of being proverbial ('as black as pitch' or 'black as soot') and refer to homely, everyday things. A rather more secular note is struck in the *Alphabet of Tales* and in the *Book of the Knight of La Tour Landry*, both translated from the French. The *Alphabet* is a handy work of reference, for the preacher had but to turn to Abstinence, Accidia, Adulation, &c., for *exempla* upon these themes. The knight's book was written—with the aid of two priests and two clerks—for the edification of his daughters, and was translated into English first about 1450 by an author who for the most part kept closely to the original. The subject-matter conveyed instruction under the guise of a series of stories. The old knight, for example, instructs his daughters in the virtues of humility, courtesy, and goodly demeanour by telling of how the King of

England chose for wife the humblest and quietest of the three daughters of the King of Denmark, and by other similar tales. The knight's daughters are warned against disobedience, the wearing of strange fashions, the perils of indulging in gaiety at feasts, jousts, and plays, or of coming late to divine service. His two clerks and two priests ransacked Scriptures and many other writings for illustrative matter, and there resulted a book which was still sufficiently popular in 1484 for Caxton to re-edit it, and to make what was practically a new translation. As a source book of medieval life and thought this book takes a high place: wherever we open it we find stories—and conclusions drawn from them—which throw a flood of light on contemporary conditions. A few lines from the prologue show the translator at his best, for he is here translating into prose the verse prologue of the original.

As y was in a gardin, al heui and full of thought, in the shadow, about the ende of the monthe of Aprill, but a littell y rejoysed me of the melodie and song of the wilde briddes; thei sang there in her langages, as the thrustill, the thrusshe, the nytinggale, and other briddes, the which were full of mirthe and ioye; and thaire suete songe made my herte to lighten, and made me to thinke of the tyme that is passed of my youthe, how loue in gret distresse had holde me, and how y was in her seruice mani tymes full of sorugh and gladnesse, as mani lovers ben.

4

Prose was to be put to more severe trials, however, than were placed on it by the moralists and tellers of didactic stories. The growing ability to read in the vernacular was considerable enough by the second quarter of the century to compel attention from those who hitherto had confined their views and arguments to readers able to read and think in Latin. Now it was becoming necessary for scholars to step down into the arena where ordinary laymen, in such intervals of leisure as came to them, were demanding information and instruction in matters formerly only interpreted to them orally by priests and clerks. Hence, despite the fact that 'langagis ben not stabli and foundamentali writen', vernacular exposition of the Faith was growing, and a prose had to be formed which would convey the niceties of argument, illustration, and philosophical reasoning. This was attempted on a large scale by Reginald Pecock, Bishop of St. Asaph and later of Chichester.[1]

This scholarly and pugnacious man set himself to meet by argument the teaching of the Lollards and other 'Bible men'. Instead of invoking the powers of the statute *De Heretico Comburendo*, Pecock invoked those of reason—and of reason in the vernacular. He had a fanatical belief in 'the doom of reason' and in the use of the syllogistic method, for as he says:

'so stronge and so myȝti in al kindis of maters, that though al the aungels of hevene wolden seie his conclusions were not trewe, yitt we schulde leeve the aungels seiyng, and we schulden truste more to the proof of thilk sillogisme than to the contrarie seiyng of alle the aungels in hevene, for that alle Goddis creaturis musten nedis obei the doom of resoun, and such a sillogisme is not ellis than doom of resoun'.

In keeping with this view, Pecock proceeded to confute his opponents by argument, and to instruct them and all the faithful by a series of philosophical disquisitions on many matters of faith and doctrine. He writes in English, he tells us, to instruct and to inculcate the love of God, and uses 'the common peplis langage' for this purpose, just as the preachers use it for their sermons. But while Pecock could talk of writing in the ordinary man's language, he rapidly found that such a language had none of the resources of vocabulary or expression which would convey abstract philosophical ideas. Pecock, therefore, was forced to invent words. This he did with great energy, yoking together English and foreign elements, and often producing strange and uncouth results. Part of our difficulty in reading Pecock to-day arises from this. His pages are disfigured with such words as 'agenvnstondabilnes' (unchangeableness), 'knowyngal' (pertaining to knowledge), 'vntobethoughtvpon' (unconsidered), 'neperte' (inferiority), or 'outdroughte' (extract). Technical words new to English (tropology, anagogy) are used;

[1] Reginald Pecock (1390?–1461?) was born in Wales, went to Oxford early in the fifteenth century, and in due course graduated as a Doctor of Divinity. He was elected to a fellowship at Oriel College, Oxford, about 1417, took major orders in 1420 and was priested in 1421. He went to London as Rector of St. Michael Royal about this time, and in 1424 became Bishop of St. Asaph, and six years later was translated to Chichester. He was tried and convicted of heresy in 1457, and on 4 December recanted, and his offending works were burnt by the executioner. Pecock was condemned to pass the rest of his days at Thorney Abbey, where he died *c.* 1461. He was the author of many works, only five of which have survived (see Bibliography).

suffixes in *-al* or *-ioun* are tagged on to existing words; foreign words are anglicized or translated into their nearest equivalent, and so on. Pecock was determined to make the truth as he understood it known and if possible clear to all men, and if the language was not there to help him, he was prepared to help the language. It is this deep-felt anxiety to make himself clear which renders much of Pecock's writings nearly unreadable to-day. We are spared nothing. The schoolman's delight in distinctions almost for the sake of distinctions, the logical reduction of every aspect of the point at issue to its ultimate terms, the scrupulous effort to leave no loophole or ambiguity —all these habits of mind are seen in the laboured, over-elaborated prose of Pecock. His habit of inversion, of the use of synonym, of finishing his sentence with a verb, does not make it easier to know exactly where we are in any of his arguments, and although there is almost invariably a clear logical thread running throughout all that he writes, it is not always apparent on a first reading. The following is a fair specimen:

In proceding vpon þis mater forto schewe how bi strengþe and light of natural resoun men myghte come into knowing, lord, of þi lawe of kynde which þou askist to be kept of men, and into what treuþis of þilk lawe þey myght and schulde firste come forto hem knowe, and into what oþere trouþis next, and so in what ordre and processe þei myght and schulde, if þei wolde, fynde treuþe aftir treuþe into tyme þei schulde fynde out al þi lawe of kinde bi natural witt and natural light which þou lord god hast sett in her soulis, þus y bigynne: Right as þe bodily iȝen[1] of men if þei ben open, kunnen not be idel from aboute biholding and from geting of mych knowing such as longiþ to þe iȝen to gete, and þat bi proces of tyme vpon ful manye seable þingis fer and neer, certis so þe resoun of men, which is þe iȝe of þe soule and þe ynner iȝe of þe soule and þe ynner iȝe of men, can not be idil, but þat aftir men ben come into sufficient age of resonyng forto vse her resoun, wiþynne proces of tyme, if þei wolen, þei mowe and schulen bi quyknes or delyuernes and bisynes of her resoun falle into so manye fold consideraciouns bi occasioun of her v outward wittis and of her v inward wittis, þat as it were nedis þei muste come into knowing þat summe þingis ben oonli being wiþout lijf as stonys, watir and erþe, and þat summe þingis han a growing lijf oonly as herbis and treis, and summe þingis han þe seid growing lijf and þerwiþ also þei han a feeling or a sensitijf lijf as

[1] iȝen, 'eyes'.

beestis and briddis, and summe oþere þingis han þe seid growing lijf and feeling lijf as han beestis and þerwiþ þei han a resonyng lijf and free willing lijf ferþer and aboue beestis and whiche beestis han not, as men and wymmen; and to þe kunnyng of manye mo treuþis þan þese now rehercid, men schulen needis come in proces of tyme, and al for þe quyknes and delyuernes which her resoun haþ in enquering and concluding, prouyng and driving wiþ help of þe seid x sensitjf wittis, as open experience witnessiþ at þe fulle.

Passages like this are characteristic of his work and make it impossible to keep Pecock where it has been fashionable to place him since Babington's edition of the *Repressor* in 1860. He is not one of the glories of fifteenth-century prose, nor can we accept the implication that he is of great importance in the development of English prose style. Pecock remains a lonely phenomenon.

His insistence on the 'doom of reason' was the outstanding feature of his teaching. 'Reason' he declared to be 'more necessarie to Cristen men, and . . . more worthi than is the outward Bible and the kunnyng therof.' By reason man can guide his conduct and build his institutions, religious and temporal. Virtue, he argued, is dependent on the free will, and grace is given to assist the religious man. Virtuous deeds are necessary to fulfil man's potentialities and thus to fulfil God's purpose, and eventually to bring man to heaven. These virtuous deeds are necessarily based on reason: there is no virtue in unreasoning ignorance. Pecock's Four Tables, which are explained at length in the *Donet*, the *Follower to the Donet*, and the *Rule of Christian Religion*, all rest on reason and faith, with reason predominating. These Four Tables set out the 'menal virtues' which are the means leading to the 'eendal virtues', and Pecock constantly refers to them as the outline of his philosophical system.

For reason to have its fullest scope it was necessary that man's knowledge should be as accurate and all-embracing as possible. Hence Pecock was a strong advocate for the active testing of doctrine and historical writings by the light of reason. The authority of Aristotle or of the Fathers should be questioned if the matter was one that allowed of reason, for he declared that 'Aristotil made not philosofie' but was 'a laborer to knowe the trouthis of philosofie as othire men weren'. In holding such ideas he was clearly ahead of his time, and that immense confidence which marks all his writings at last carried him too far, and gave opportunities to his ecclesiastical enemies which led to his ruin. Although he says in the *Folewer* that 'y neuer bowid yit in wil neither in word, ond with goddis grace neither y schall in tyme comyng' in the maintenance of truth, yet the day was to come when he was forced to say: 'I am in a strait betwixt two, and hesitate in despair as to what I shall choose. If I defend my opinions and position, I must be burned to death; if I do not, I shall be a byeword and a reproach.' In the end he retracted, handed the executioner some fourteen of his works for public burning, and spent the rest of his days in close confinement in the remote Fenland Abbey of Thorney. He was allowed 'no books to look on, but only a portuous,[1] a mass-book, a psalter, a legend and a Bible: nothing to write with; no stuff to write upon'. The 'pestiferous virus' of his writings, of which Edward IV complained, had but little chance to spread after this, and the fifteenth century rapidly forgot him. It was not until the present century that any determined attempt was made to print his extant writings.

The death of Pecock, about 1461, came at a time when another thinker was beginning to put into writing the ideas which a lifetime of busy, anxious experience had engendered in him. Lawyer, negotiator, politician, administrator, Fortescue learnt political and constitutional wisdom by experience.[2] His legal *dicta*, however, are not remarkable, for it was not when he

[1] portuous, 'breviary'.

[2] Sir John Fortescue (*c.* 1394–*c.* 1476). Fortescue's birthplace is unknown, and so are the details of his youth and education prior to his admission to Lincoln's Inn *c.* 1420. He was a serjeant-at-law by 1430, and had been elected an M.P. eight times by 1437. After his appointment as a king's serjeant he became Chief Justice on 20 January 1442 and was knighted soon afterwards. In addition to his ordinary duties he acted as adviser to the Government in many ways, but maintained an independence of judgement in a number of important political decisions. By 1454 he was so identified with the Lancastrian cause as to incur the enmity of the Yorkists. His activities on behalf of the Lancastrians finally led to his supersession as Chief Justice, and he joined Queen Margaret at St. Albans and Towton Moor, and was attainted, 1461. He followed the deposed King Henry VI to Scotland, then to Flanders, where he remained for some seven years, and here he probably wrote the *De Laudibus Legum Angliae*. He returned to England in 1471, but was captured at Tewkesbury in the same year. His life was spared and he was pardoned in October 1471. After this he became a member of the Council of Edward IV, and on writing in favour of the king and refuting his own arguments against the king and title (*Declaration upon Certain Writings*), he was restored to his estates in 1475. The short remainder of his life—he is not heard of after 1476—was probably passed at his manor of Elrington, Gloucestershire.

was presiding in his court that he showed at his greatest or most original. His present reputation rests on his exposition of political theory; first in his Latin works, *De Natura Legis Naturae* and *De Laudibus Legum Angliae*, and his English work *On the Governance of England*. The first two of these works do not concern us deeply, but they set out in some detail Fortescue's ideas on the nature of the monarchy and on the conduct of princes. Many of these ideas are given an English form in the *Governance of England*, where for the last time Fortescue explains his political theory. There are two kinds of kingdom; the first the *dominium regale*—absolute monarchy—he rejects in favour of the *dominium politicum et regale*—a monarchy both politic and royal, for he argues that the absolute monarch possesses nothing which is denied to the politic king save the power to do wrong. He is concerned to show how a political monarch can best serve the State, and after a long discussion of the economic resources of the realm, the relation between the commons and their rulers, and the dangers of over-mighty subjects, he proceeds to discuss the appointment and composition of a body which will help the king to exercise his functions, always bearing in mind that the King of England has no power to alter the law, for a politic king can only change the law by the consent of his people expressed in Parliament. The Council, as Fortescue conceived it, was to be partly administrative, partly advisory—an executive which would put forward proposals for the consideration of Parliament. Such a scheme, Fortescue believed, would preserve parliamentary rights, while helping the day-to-day conduct of affairs, and would relieve the king of much dangerous responsibility. Fortescue's theory is based on experience: he is cautious, limited in his suggestions; and it must be admitted vague on important points such as the method by which the Council should be chosen, or the way in which the various estates should be represented in Parliament.

His treatment of his subject shows the man. He is strongly influenced by his studies: biblical references abound, while quotations from classical and ecclesiastical authors (whether of his own finding or from a convenient 'commonplace book') are frequent. There is much of the medieval scholar about his method. Yet he is capable of leaving his book learning and making use of what he has seen with his own eyes and learnt from his long sojourn in foreign countries, especially in France. Thus, in a famous passage, he contrasts the French commons with the English, and refers scornfully to the craven nature of the French, 'wherfore it is right selde that Ffrenchmen be hanged ffor robbery, ffor thai haue no hartes to do so terable an acte. Ther bith therfore mo men hanged in Englande in a yere ffor robbery and manslaughter, then ther be hanged in Ffraunce ffor such maner of crime in vij yeres'. He states his views in an admirably clear terse English. Where in Pecock we are struggling with the pattern of a long, complicated sentence of many words, Fortescue expresses his ideas with point and clarity. So he opens his work: 'Ther bith ij kyndes off kyngdomes, of the wich that on is a lordship callid in laten *dominium regale*, and that other is callid *dominium politicum et regale*. And thai diversen in that . . . .' His illustrations, as shown above, are clear and concrete, and of a homely nature. Thus the poverty of the French peasantry is vividly before us when he writes:

> Thai drinken water, thai eyten apples, with brede right browne made of rye; thai eyten no flesshe but yf it be right seldon a litle larde, or the entrales and heydes of bestes slayn for the nobles and marchauntes of the lande. Thai weren no wolen, but yf it be a pouere cote vndir thair vttermest garnement, made of grete caunuas, and callid a froke. Thair hausyn beth of lyke caunuas, and passyn nat thair kne, wher fore thai beth gartered and ther theis bare. Thair wyfes and childeren gone bare fote; thai mowe in non other wyse leve.

Fortescue writes clearly because his mind works within narrowly defined limits. He will speculate only so far as his experience as a lawyer and an administrator will serve to guide him, and will furnish him with materials. So he conducts us from one part of his argument to another by a series of closely related facts or ideas. Illustrations of these are allowed, but not abused, and each sentence is taut and forms an integral unit in the structure which he is building. In common with other fifteenth-century writers, Fortescue is not capable of writing a highly complex prose, but what straightforwardness, simplicity, and clear thinking could accomplish may be seen on almost any page of the *Governance of England*.

5

Apart from narrative and exposition, prose had much to accomplish in other fields. Scientific writings in the vernacular were wellnigh unknown before 1400, but throughout the fifteenth century they steadily increased in number and variety. Treatises dealing with special diseases abound. We have works on stone or gout, or on the diseases of women, as well as John of Bordeaux's *Tractatus de morbo epidemiae*—the most popular of plague pamphlets, of which over forty manuscripts have survived. Even more popular was the little manual sometimes entitled the *Judgment of Urines*. Nearly seventy manuscripts (mostly of the fifteenth century) still exist of this popular work. Writings of this kind are couched in simple direct English, generally for the use of laymen, as is clear from the heading of one of these tracts in the Cambridge University Library: 'Tractatus . . . composuit breviter in lingua materna magis plane ad intelligentiam laicorum.' Surgical works, both large and small, also appeared. John of Arderne was the most famous English surgeon of his day, and translations of various of his works appeared after 1400.[1] Vernacular renderings of other surgical works, like that of the great French surgeon, Guy de Chauliac, or those of William of Saliceto, or John of St. Paul, may also be noted. There are individual tracts on special topics, and it is clear that works in the vernacular on medicine and surgery of every description were in circulation in some numbers during the fifteenth century.

Allied to these were writings on plants, herbs, and herbal remedies. Such works begin to appear in a vernacular form

[1] John of Arderne (1307–1380(?)). Little is known of Arderne's early life. He was born in 1307 and may have studied medicine at Montpellier and probably served as a surgeon in the English Army in France. He practised for a time in Wiltshire, and from 1349 to 1370 at Newark, and finally came to London in 1370. By 1376 he had written his important monograph on Fistula, and probably his treatise on Clysters as well, while his *De Cura Oculorum* was composed in 1377. He also wrote on Phlebotomy and on Plants and their medical properties and compiled a book of recipes and notes of cases. His works were much sought after in his own time and later, and although originally composed in Latin, were soon translated. A manuscript in the library of Emmanuel College, Cambridge, for example, contains an English version of most of his works. Arderne was a man of wide experience and good judgement who preferred clinical experience to the teaching of the schools. His own statements concerning the qualities needed in a good surgeon show that he set himself high ideals, and at the same time had a strong belief that the labourer was worthy of his hire.

in the fourteenth century, but their number is trebled or quadrupled in the next century. Many set out 'the vertuys of Erbys aftyr Galyon, Ypocras and Socrates', while others are based on a translation of Aemilius Macer, *De virtutibus herbarum.* Others again treat of the virtues of a special herb, rosemary or betony or the like, or of the preparation of oils or medicinal waters from herbs. Not only medical but natural science flourished in this period. The most valuable indication of the knowledge of natural science at this time is afforded by the great encyclopaedia of Bartholomeus Anglicus. Trevisa's translation of his *De Proprietatibus Rerum* was completed on 6 February 1398, and for long remained a standard work. It circulated in its full form and in an abstract before an abridged edition was printed by Wynkyn de Worde in 1495 and by Berthelet in 1535. It was reissued with some additions by Stephen Batman, under the title of *Batman upon Bartholomew*, in 1582. Perhaps it was optimistic on Thomas East's part to think that his contemporaries would be satisfied with information first compiled over 300 years earlier, but there can be no doubt that it was still considered a trustworthy source in the fifteenth century. Caxton did not scruple to translate the French *Image du Monde* in 1480, and much that appears in his version also appears at greater length in Bartholomew. The pursuit of knowledge was a difficult matter in medieval times, and fifteenth-century inquirers were ready enough to read in Trevisa's version of how elephants could be captured by the singing of maidens in the Ethiopian desert, or of how cinnamon was shot from the phoenix's nest with leaden arrows. They learnt that the 'men of Ireland be singularly clothed and unseemly arrayed and scarcely fed; they be cruel of heart, fierce of cheer, angry of speech, and sharp'; that 'the bear bringeth forth a piece of flesh imperfect and evil shapen, and the mother licketh the lump, and shapeth the members with licking', and that 'by the spleen we are moved to laugh, by the gall we are wroth, by the heart we are wise, by the brain we feel, by the liver we love'.

Many of the topics in Bartholomew were taken up and developed by later writers. There are numerous tracts dealing with the nature and influence of the planets and with the signs of the zodiac and their effects on human bodies. There are also treatises on the significance of the months and days in the lives and fortunes of men, while the science of alchemy was popularized by tractates in English which were constantly being written and circulated. Many other little treatises dealt with more practical matters and made further demands on prose writers. A number of manuals of arithmetic appeared, while others dealt with the keeping of horses, hawks, fish, or doves. Hunting was one of the commonest of aristocratic recreations, and the second Duke of York's translation of Gaston de Foix's *Livre de Chasse* under the title of the *Master of Game* was very popular. Smaller treatises on hunting also appeared, and in particular works on hawking, in which information on the care and training of hawks is set out in a clear and workmanlike fashion. The subject was still of sufficient importance in 1486 to warrant the publication of the *Book of St. Albans*, reputed to be the work of Dame Juliana Berners, but much of it is taken from Twici's *L'art de venerie* (*c.* 1320) and from other treatises which have not been traced. The edition of 1496, by Wynkyn de Worde, was memorable for its inclusion of 'a treatise of fishing with an angle'. In this, we learn that if the fisherman fail of one fish,

he maye not faylle of a nother yf he dooth as this treatyse techyth: but yf there be nought in the water. And yet atte the leest he hath his holsom walke and mery at his ease, a swete ayre of the swete sauoure of the meede floures: that makyth hym hungry. He hereth the melodyous armony of fowles. He seeth the yonge swannes: heerons: duckes: cotes and many other foules wyth theyr brodes. Whyche me semyth better than alle the noyse of houndys: the blastes of hornys and the scrye of foulis that hunters: fawkeners & foulers can make.

The writer of this passage knows what he wants to say, and says it with some felicity of phrasing and a delight in outdoor sights and scenes rarely met with in medieval literature. The author of the *Anatomy of Melancholy* swept this passage with his drag-net to the confusion of those who quote it as an example of Burton's own style. Although Burton probably took the passage from an Elizabethan intermediary, his version differs hardly at all from the original.

For those who wished to be more venturesome than these sportsmen, and to embark upon real or imaginary journeys, instructive manuals were prepared. The outstanding work, of course, was the well-known *Travels of Sir John Mandeville*, the author of which need have been no traveller himself as his information has been traced to earlier sources. This purports to be a guide-book for travellers to Jerusalem, but is also an account of the wonders of the East in the realms of the Great Cham. It was in great demand and translated into many languages. At least four versions of the original (which scholars are now generally agreed was in French and written about 1356) were in circulation during the fifteenth century, and over thirty manuscripts in English have survived. It is written in a simple style, and the paragraph is built up of a series of loosely related sentences:

'And all be it þat men fynden gode dyamandes in Ynde, yit natheles men fynden hem mor comounly vpon the roches in the see, and vpon hilles where the myne of gold is. And þei growen many togedre, on lytill, another gret. And þer ben . . . And þei . . .'

The authorship of the work is still something of a mystery. The preface tells us that the *Travels* were composed by Sir John Mandeville, a native of St. Albans, but modern research identifies the author with one of two men, Jean de Bourgogne, a Liège physician, and Jean d'Outremeuse, a Liège chronicler. Both of them were literary figures of some importance, but it is not possible to be certain which of them wrote the travels, though modern opinion inclines to Jean de Bourgogne. These matters are relatively unimportant compared with the many interesting points raised by the work itself. That the writer gave the public something they wanted is clear from the several versions in English and the large number of existing manuscripts. The subject-matter, besides being intrinsically interesting, is treated in a way that cannot fail to hold the reader's attention. The author combines truth and fiction, and gives so many vouchers of time and place and numbers—or even more engagingly writes: 'Of Paradys can I noght speke properly, for I hafe noght bene thare'—that we are forced to believe what he says, and his simple way of writing only serves to reinforce the air of perfect honesty and good faith which it is his desire to create.

Other works of travel of a less ambitious and more practical nature were produced. There is an anonymous 'hand book' for travellers across Europe by the Lowlands to Venice and so to the eastern Mediterranean and home through the Straits of Gibraltar. This gives much advice on practical matters: guides and their habits, the choice of travelling impedimenta, hints as to weather and 'the usaunce of the hote lands', and how to conduct oneself, for our author tells us that 'englissh men have but little love in meny parties, but yet hit be for their money, or the better of gouernaunce'. Other accounts of the pilgrimages both to Rome and Jerusalem also survive as, for example, that of John Capgrave, whose work the *Solace of Pilgrims*, written about 1450, gives an account in great detail of the topography, legends, and buildings of the Holy City.

6

While the majority of writers of the fifteenth century were busy endeavouring to make use of prose for new ends, here and there we meet with a writer who holds firmly to the old ways. Such a one was Sir Thomas Malory. In one of the most fortunate moments for English literature he decided to make use of his tedious leisure as a prisoner of Edward IV by reading and reducing into English the vast compilation of stories about Arthur which he found, in the main, in his 'French book'. A full account of what this entailed and of Malory's turbulent career will be found elsewhere in this series,[1] but some appreciation of Malory's work is essential to any survey of fifteenth-century prose. As Sir E. K. Chambers has said, he came late to his high theme. By the fifteenth century whatever had existed of the chivalric life mirrored in the *Morte Darthur* had long since passed away. The age of Malory was no fruitful soil in which to replant the ideal of chivalry; his own experiences in the Wars of the Roses must have taught him that. Occasionally he exclaims against the times, but for the most part he retires into a world of long ago. It is a world of heroes—and one into which few but heroes are admitted. It is unconcerned with getting and spending. Kings and knights serve queens and ladies in court or in the field in an unending series of settings designed for the most part to show them to advantage. It is a world wherein the ordinary sordid affairs of business and politics are not allowed to intrude. Many battles are fought: many quests undertaken. Love and war are the twin poles of men's existence. In the course of relating much concerning these matters Malory also

[1] Vol. II, Part II, pp. 185 ff.

contrives to tell some of the greatest stories of the world, and in one of them—that of Lancelot and Guenevere—rises to the height of his great argument. Malory's conduct of the final books of the *Morte* has long been recognized as a masterpiece of story-telling. The movement is splendidly controlled and maintained, while the figures of Arthur, Lancelot, Gawaine, and Guenevere move in and out ineluctably pressing forward to the great final scenes and the break-up of the Round Table and of all Arthur's dreams.

This story is the more effective since it follows the Grail section of the *Morte Darthur*—a section in which Malory moves in a world whose values are other than those of the world of Mark and Arthur. The Cistercian writers who had given shape to this part of the French work used by Malory had thrown into sharp relief the quest for heavenly things as opposed to the quest for earthly rewards. Corbenic is set up against Camelot, and during the whole of the Grail story we are forced to adopt a scale of the highest values. Lancelot, the hero of much of the work, falls short when measured by these exacting standards, and the vision of the Grail is therefore withheld from him. So Lancelot 'falls to his love again', and the final books move on to the familiar conflict between human love and human loyalty. The Grail theme is all-important: it is not an excrescence or an interruption, but an integral part of the story.

In coming late to his subject Malory suffered under the difficulty which his text presented to him. His original was a 'jumble of stories about Arthur', lacking in structure and proportion and overladen with the accretions of time and oral tradition. Malory had no great skill in disentangling the various threads in this tangled skein. He took his good where he found it, and was not over-particular if a deal of secondary material got into his narrative. Much of the *Morte Darthur*, therefore, is best read for its individual scenes and not for its connected story. It is only in the great final books that Malory takes a firm hold of his materials and allows nothing to interfere between him and the telling of his tale.

Throughout his work he uses a prose that is simple and yet supple enough for his many needs. Most of his sentences are short and uninvolved, and he starts sentence after sentence with such words as 'and', 'then', 'when', &c. Few writers have been more successful than Malory in his use of dialogue and narrative, for he has the art of combining them in such proportion as always to seem right. Moreover, the dialogue is singularly terse and direct, so that Malory's prose is as capable of irony as Chaucer's verse. 'Kynge Pelham hym self aroos vp fyersly & sayd, "Knyght, hast thou slayn my broder; thow shalt dye therfor or thou departe." "Wel", said Balen, "Se it yourself".' Or again, ' "And thou be of the Table Round", sayd Turguyne, "I defy thee and alle thy felawship." "That is ouermoche sayd", sayd syre Launcelot.' Words are used with a nice sense of their value, now with the utmost precision, as 'and either smote other in middes of their sheeldes that the pastrellys, surcingles and cruppers brast', or so as to obtain the utmost emotional effect, as ' "That blast", said Balyn, "is blowen for me. For I am the pryse and yet I am not dede".'

The effectiveness of Malory's writing is increased by the life and colour which continuously animate his pages. Men give one another great strokes, 'tracynge and trauercynge, racynge and foynynge and hurtlyng to gyder', or ride 'brim as any boar'. Merlin comes before Arthur 'al be furred in black shepe skynnes . . . in a russet gowne', and a dreadful dragon comes flying out of the west, 'and his hede was enameled with asure, and his sholders shone as gold, his taylle ful of tatters, his feet ful of fine sable, and his clawes lyke fyne gold'.

But his prose can do more difficult things than this. When occasion demands, the dignity, solemnity, or sorrow of a scene is fully and subtly conveyed. This is clear from such famous passages as the Arthur and Sir Bedevere episode, or in the parting of Guenevere and Lancelot, or in Sir Ector's threnody over Sir Lancelot. A less familiar example will illustrate this power of Malory's to construct a cadenced passage worthy of its occasion:

> Allas said Sir Bors that euer Sir Launcelot's kynne sawe yow for now haue ye lost the best knyght of oure blood / and he that was alle oure leder and oure socour / and I dare saye and make it good that all kynges crysten nor hethen may not fynde suche a knyghte for to speke of his nobylnesse and curtosye with his beaute and his gentylnesse / Allas said sire Bors what shalle we doo that ben of his blood / Allas said Ector de marys / Allas said Lyonel.

Yet Malory's prose, though it could achieve effects like this, was not a prose for everyday purposes. The main stream of our prose had to seek other channels: Malory remains as a beautiful inland lake, cut off from the outer world, beside whose waters men have found rest and refreshment from his day to ours.

In the Prologue of his edition of 1485 Caxton wrote what is still the best tribute. He has printed the book, he says,

to the entente that noble men may see and lerne the noble actes of chyualrye / the Ientyl and vertuous dedes that somme knyghtes vsed in tho dayes / by whyche they came to honour / and how they that were vycious were punysshed and ofte put to shame and rebuke / humbly besechyng al noble lordes and ladyes wyth al other estates of what estate or degree they been of / that shal see and rede in this sayd book and werke / that they take the good and honest actes in their remembraunce / and to folowe the same / Wherein they shalle fynde many Ioyous and playsaunt hystoryes / and noble & renomed actes of humanyte / gentylnesse and chyualryes / For herein may be seen noble chiualrye / Curtosye / Humanyte / frendlynesse / hardynesse / loue / frendshyp / Cowardyse / Murdre / hate / vertue / and synne / Doo after the good and leue the euyl / and it shal brynge you to good fame and renommee.

Caxton printed the *Morte Darthur*, so he tells us, after he had 'accomplysshed and fynysshed dyuers hystoryes as wel of contemplacyon as of other hystoryal and worldly actes of grete conquerors & prynces / And also certeyn bookes of ensaumples and doctryne'. An account, therefore, of Caxton's life and works is a fitting and indispensable end to a history of fifteenth-century prose.

7

Caxton's life divides into two parts. For the first fifty years of it he was engaged in his calling as a merchant, while the last twenty were devoted to those activities which have made him famous in English history. If he had died at the end of the first period English literature might have remembered him for his version of the *Recuyell of the Histories of Troy* (translated in September 1471), but only students of the economic history of the period would have followed his career as he rose to the highest office obtainable by an Englishman trading in the Low Countries at that time. Caxton tells us that he was born in the Weald of Kent, and was sent to school, but where we are not told. In 1438, when about sixteen years old, he was apprenticed to Robert Lange, a prominent mercer of London. In 1441 we find him in Bruges—a great centre of the cloth trade—and there he remained after his apprenticeship ceased, presumably in business on his own account. In 1453 he was sufficiently established to be admitted to the Livery of the Mercers' Company, and ten years later he was Governor of the English Nation of Merchant Adventurers in the Low Countries—a position which allowed him to rule over his fellow merchants and their staffs with great authority, and to make rules and regulations concerning every side of their trade. In this capacity he moved about from place to place, returning to his headquarters at Bruges where he lived in the 'Domus Angliae' with the other merchant adventurers. It is not until 1469 that we have any record of his interests in literature, and about that time he relinquished his office as Governor and began to translate Raoul Le Fèvre's French account of the *History of Troy*.

No adequate explanation can be given of what caused a highly successful merchant, at the height of his powers, to relinquish his position for a life of books, nor can we account for the favour which he found in the eyes of Margaret, dowager Duchess of Burgundy, and sister of Edward IV. Caxton, like Chaucer, moved into new circles, to the infinite profit of our literature, and that must suffice. In March 1469 he tells us that he thought it would be 'a good besynes to translate hyt [the *Recuyell of the Histories of Troy*] in to oure englissh'; but he soon wearied of his work, and laid it aside, until 'on a tyme het fortuned' he showed it to Margaret, who advised him to improve the English and to continue with his translation. This he did, partly in Ghent, and finally in Cologne, where he finished his work in 'the holy city' on 19 September 1471.

He resided in Cologne from 1470 to December 1472, as recent researches into the city archives have established, and while there he studied the art of printing, and probably assisted in the production of an edition of Bartholomew the Englishman's *De Proprietatibus Rerum*, and of that *Dialogus de vera Nobilitate* which was later to be the source of the first English secular play, *Fulgens and Lucres*, and the translation of which Caxton was to publish at Westminster in 1481. He was still, however, engaged in negotiations concerning trade in the Low Countries and Burgundy until 1475, and his new-found interests prospered but slowly. During these years, however, he furnished himself with a press and two founts of type, probably supplied by the printer and type-founder John Veldener of Louvain. He also obtained the assistance of Colard Mansion, a well-known scrivener and illuminator of Bruges, and together they printed the first book in the English language—the *Recuyell of the Histories of Troy* (Bruges, 1475). Caxton tells us that he had promised various friends to let them have copies of his translation, but his eyes and hands were wearied by so much copying:

> Therfore I haue practysed & lerned at my grete charge and dispense to ordeyne this said book in prynte after the maner & forme as ye may here see, and is not wreton with penne and ynke as other bokes ben, to thende that euery man may haue them attones, for all the bookes of this storye named the recule of the historyes of troyes thus empryntid as ye here see were begonne in oon day, and also fynyshid in oon day.

This was followed in 1475 by the *Game and Play of the Chess*, Caxton's second attempt at translation, in which he used the two French versions of the Latin of Jacobus de Cessolis. Something will be said later of his abilities as a translator, but we may note that in producing the *Troy* and the *Chess* books Caxton early betrayed two of the main interests which were to govern his future publications—love of romance and a predilection for works of a moralizing nature. A third work in French, *Les quatre dernières choses*, was also printed at Bruges by Caxton; it marked the end of his life abroad, for in 1476 he returned to England, and by September had set up his sign 'At the Red Pale' over a shop in Westminster which he rented from the Abbey of Westminster for 15 shillings per annum. From this time until his death in 1491 Caxton made a contribution to English literature that it would be hard to over-estimate. It is important, however, that the nature of this contribution should not be misunderstood or confused. We have to distinguish between Caxton the printer and Caxton the man of letters.

As our first printer Caxton is worthy of our undying regard. The sneers of Gibbon and Disraeli, and any modern attempts to write down his services to English literature, must be regarded as ignorant and unworthy. Except that he omitted to print *Piers Plowman*, Caxton showed a real understanding of what was best in the available literature of his time. The printer of the first editions of the *Canterbury Tales*, *Troilus and Criseyde*, *Confessio Amantis*, *Morte Darthur*, to say nothing of various smaller works of Chaucer and Lydgate, deserves our warmest praise. But Caxton's services to literature were not confined to one class of writing. He showed an admirable catholicity of taste, while retaining a preference for certain kinds of books. The works of the great writers of antiquity he did not attempt to print in their original languages. That was being done by countless continental presses, and Caxton preferred to translate afresh, or use the translations of others. Prose romance was represented by *Godfrey of Boulogne*, *Charles the Great*, *Paris and Vienne*, *Blanchardyn and Eglantine*, *The Four Sons of Aymon*, and *Morte Darthur*. The *Recuyell of the Histories of Troy*, *The History of Jason*, and *Eneydos* contained much classical myth and story, while the favourite beast fable was represented by *Reynard the Fox* and *The Fables of Aesop*. Other instructive works of a more austere nature were to be found in the translations of Boethius and Cicero. Morality and piety were the informing qualities of another large group of which the work wrongly attributed to St. Bonaventura and translated into English by Nicholas Love as *The Mirror of the blessed life of Jesu Christ*, the *Dicts or Sayings of the Philosophers*, and the *Golden Legend* are outstanding examples. *The Book of Good Manners*, *The Moral Proverbs* of Christine de Pisan, *The Curial* of Alain Chartier, *The Book of the Knight of the Tower* were among works published by Caxton which have a didactic purpose, and so, in a different fashion, has *The Governal of Health*. Books of a more informative nature were not neglected: Trevisa's translation of Higden's *Polychronicon*, as well as a *Description of Britain*, *The Chronicles of England*, and an encyclopaedic work, *The Mirror of the World*; books on chivalry and war, *The Order of Chivalry* and *The Book of the Feats of Arms and Chivalry*; and books of elementary grammar and vocabularies. In addition to works in these categories Caxton also published service books, indulgences, statutes of the Realm, and other minor pieces.

This was an impressive body of work for a pioneer printer to have accomplished between 1475 and 1491. We may well discount any denigration of Caxton's services to literature so far as quantity, range, and quality of his output is concerned. Nor is it fair to say that he 'purveyed to his aristocratic English public a selection of the books, French or English, from a former generation, when time and public preference had winnowed them from the mass'. He certainly had an aristocratic public, but equally certainly he had (and knew he had) a more general public. The size, variety, and literacy of this public is only slowly becoming clear, but sufficient is known about it for us to be able to say that Caxton was doubly lucky in the moment of his commencing to print. He found a considerable reading public available, and he found that the public had been accustomed for half a century at least to reading matter of every possible kind. Caxton had only to reap what others had sown.

This is not to deny that he followed custom centuries old by which authors sought for recognition and recompense by dedicating their work to some rich patron. Caxton had many such: Edward IV, Richard III, Henry VII, Margaret of Burgundy, Mary Beaufort, and Elizabeth of York, are all mentioned by him, as are the Earls of Warwick, Rivers, Oxford, and Arundel. To these he was indebted for encouragement when the burden of translation or publishing seemed overwhelming. Thus the Earl of Arundel promised to take 'a good quantity' of copies of the *Golden Legend* at a time when Caxton found himself 'halfe desparate to have accomplished it', and it was Margaret of Burgundy's 'dredefull commandment' which set him to work again on the *Recuyell*. But in addition to these aristocratic patrons, Caxton looked to a wider public, and was quick to respond to their needs. William Pratt, mercer, and 'my synguler frende and of olde knowlege', brought him a French *Book of Good Manners* and begged him to translate and publish it. Similar requests were made by other London friends and merchants: William Daubeny, a royal treasurer, asked Caxton to translate the romance of *Charles the Great*, while the popular encyclopaedia *The Mirror of the World* was the outcome of 'the request, desire, coste and dispense of the honourable and worshipful man Hugh Bryce, Alderman & Cytezeyn of London' who wanted to make a present to the Lord President Hastings.

In response to commands and requests such as these Caxton could reasonably expect a good sale for his works. One of the secrets of his success was the skill with which he judged the nature of his potential patrons. He knew that some of his books would have only a limited appeal, while others were of a general interest. This is clear from many of his invaluable prologues. In them he indicates the nature of the book and the kind of audience to whom it should appeal. *Tully of Old Age* or *Eneydos*, for instance, are not for every 'rude and vnconnynge man to see, but to clerkys and very gentylmen that vnderstande gentilnes and scyence'. Others are for 'ladies and gentilwymen', others for 'every gentilman born to arms, and all manere of men of werre, captains, souldiours, vytallers'. Some of his books, however, he hoped would have a wider public: 'All men' or 'every man livyng' are invited to read such works as the *Recuyell* or *Boethius*; and the *Golden Legend* he hopes will profit all those who read, or hear it read. Again, he says that he has 'translated and reduced out of ffrensshe in to englysshe *Godfroy of Bologne* to thende that euery cristen man may be the better encoraged tenterprise warre for the defense of Cristendom'.

The truth seems to be that Caxton satisfied a special and a general demand. He undoubtedly gratified his own tastes, and at the same time satisfied those of a growing public whose eagerness for literature had been steadily increasing through the earlier years of the century. For long they had been forced to accept what chance brought their way. Only the most energetic and well-to-do could hope to collect what they wanted. Even so ardent a collector as Sir John Paston was sometimes defeated as his unsuccessful attempts to get the books of Sir James Gloys, the family chaplain, witness. The Pastons were rich enough to employ a copyist, W. Ebesham, to satisfy their needs, and we may note that among other works which remained in quires as they were written were Cicero's *De Senectute* and *De Amicitia*. If they had waited a few years they could have purchased in Caxton's edition the Earl of Worcester's translation of these two works. We know that within ten years of Caxton's starting to print in England they had a copy of the *Game and Play of the Chess*, and there can be no doubt that many others were ready to respond to the advertisement which Caxton issued telling anyone who wanted his wares to 'come to Westmonester in to the almonesry at the reed pale and he shall have them good chepe'.

From the time that he first began to translate the *Recuyell* Caxton was constantly at work turning into English books in French, Dutch, or Latin. Within some twenty-three years no less than twenty-four books had to be translated by him before they could be printed. This involved a very considerable intellectual and physical effort, and the results of this part of his work fill some 5,600 pages of print. Caxton is very modest about his abilities, both as a translator and as a writer of English. With regard to the first, we need not take his protestations too seriously. His school and commercial education had given him a sound working knowledge of the languages which he used, and while he was not a finished scholar, the imperfection in his translations may often be ascribed to haste rather than to ignorance. His knowledge of French, in practice, was good: in the *Mirror* we are told that there are only ten mistakes in translation, and editors of other works of his make similar statements. He worked quickly—the *Mirror*, a work of 200 folio printed pages, was translated in ten weeks, and *Godfrey of Boulogne*, which ran to 288 folio pages, took twelve weeks—often turning his French into English with little attempt at making a good English sentence of it, and at times transferring French words bodily where no English equivalent was to hand. As might be expected, he improved as he went on. His sentences in the *Recuyell* are those of an amateur, and we must not judge him on his earliest efforts. Yet it must be admitted that he rendered his original in too piecemeal a fashion, with the result that his sentences are often very unEnglish in their flow, and complicated in structure. Thus he allows himself to write sentences such as 'a moche meruyllous dragon and ferdful', or 'the whyche thynges for example to be conformed to theym yf they seme good ben for to be herde propyce and expedyent'.

Any discussion, however, of his merits as a translator must involve the wider consideration of his merits as a writer of English. In forming a judgement we have, in addition to his translations, the invaluable prologues and epilogues which he attached to some of his works, and these give many precious indications of his hopes and fears as a writer. 'Rude and simple' is his favourite way of describing his powers of writing English, and almost every piece of original work by him harps upon his ignorance, inexperience, and lack of skill. To some extent these protestations were common form, but Caxton was genuinely concerned about his limitations as a writer. To begin with he lacked any training in the use of 'the art of rhetoric or of gay terms'. Eloquence he regarded as 'soo precious and noble that amooste noo thyng can be founden more precious than it'. In common with most people of his time, he sincerely believed in the 'polysshed and ornate termes' for which he praised Skelton, and made attempts to follow what he thought to be the most elegant current English. But innumerable difficulties beset him, for he could get no one to advise him where the best English was to be found. Almost at the end of his life we find him still uncertain. In the preface to *Eneydos* (1490) he tells us how he wrote a few pages, but when he came to look it over he saw that it was full of 'fair and strange terms'—the very thing that recently he had been told to avoid, since such terms, it was said, perplexed the common reader. On the other hand, the old and homely terms he was asked to use instead were difficult to employ, and when he sought the advice of the Abbot of Westminster, and was shown a book written in Old English, he found it 'more like Dutch [i.e. German] than English'. He comes to the heart of the matter when he says that 'comyn Englysshe that is spoken in one shyre varyeth from a nother', and he illustrates this by his story of the merchant who asked for *egges* and not for *eyren*, and was thought to speak in French.[1] He finally decides to use 'Englysshe not ouer rude, ne curyous, but in suche termes as shall be vnderstanden by goddys grace'. The whole of his writings prior to this, however, show them generally erring on the side of 'fair and strange terms'. Here he followed a tradition nearly a century old which held it necessary to augment the language in a variety of ways. An earlier chapter has discussed this matter, and the examples given there will be found to have an affinity to Caxton's works in this respect. The practice of using pairs of synonymous words was especially cultivated by Caxton. This was no new practice, and may even be seen in Old English prose, but in Caxton it has become a stylistic trick. No doubt it enabled him to use both an English and a French word, 'so that if he missed his reader's understanding with one barrel he might hit with another', but for modern readers this is merely tiresome. Another common feature of Caxton's style is his tendency to make use of a French word such as *occision* without bothering to translate it. (When he was called on to use the word again in another book he realized the weakness of this practice and wrote 'slaughter or occision'.) Similarly we get 'spider or spyncop'; 'worldy or terryen'; 'sourded or rose up', but frequently we are left with the French word only—'consomme' (complete), 'corrempe' (break), 'escimuz' (prickly), 'excusacion' (excuse), or 'musarde' (vagabond).

[1] See above, p. 106.

In addition to this uncertainty about diction, Caxton was even more uncertain about his writing of prose. The major part of his life had been spent out of England, and the Duchess of Burgundy, no doubt, had good reason to find 'defaut in myn englysshe'. Much reading of French literature had accustomed Caxton's ear to the long, involved sentences, but had failed to instruct him in their grammatical and logical construction. Caxton, therefore, attempted throughout his literary work to use the long sentence, without success. His average sentence length is between two and three times that of modern prose, and is full of faults. The excessive length is made the more unpleasing by the number and variety of subordinate clauses and phrases employed. Relative and substantival clauses are the most frequently used—running to great lengths, as may be seen in one sentence of 136 words in the prologue to the *Golden Legend* where 'and' and 'that' are each used *six* times. This lack of variety is constant in Caxton's prose; connectives such as 'which', 'wherefore', 'and', 'but', 'while', and 'that' are continuously overworked and give a monotonous and clockwork effect. Other constantly recurring stylistic features are the free use of anacoluthon, of the pleonastic pronoun, of the omission of the subject or verb, and the careless use of connecting words.

Writers upon Caxton's prose have taken these and other characteristics into account, and have given widely differing verdicts as to its merits. Most, it is true, have based their views on one particular volume of his works, and have looked no farther. Thus Oscar Sommer finds little that is pleasing from his study of the *Recuyell*, while Kellner ranks Caxton as a great writer of prose on the evidence of *Blanchardyn and Eglantine*. Craik says that he has a style of 'admirable clearness', but Krapp declares that 'he has only one device for elevating his style, and that is in the multiplication of words. . . . For form and structure his feeling is rudimentary.' We must allow that Caxton lacked any sensitive feeling for prose, and only stumbled on a good sentence by accident. The reader of Caxton is fortunate if he does not find himself in difficulties on every page, difficulties which arise from an inability to see how the sentence is planned. It is not that his prose has an archaic flavour which is unpleasing, but rather that it is often involved and confused in sentence structure. Malory can use archaisms, but his cadence and movement carry us successfully through his sentences. The great seventeenth-century users of the long sentence had a fundamental logical control of their periods: however majestic and laden with image and reference, all was at the service of the main idea.

Caxton humbly followed his original for the most part: if it was a good French prose that he was translating something of its merits came out in his versions, and vice versa. When he departed from his original it was seldom for the better. His own prologues and epilogues show how limited were his powers as a writer of prose, although those written in his later years show an increasing mastery of the art of prose composition. Their value is for the insight they give us into the problems which beset Caxton as a translator and printer, for their many personal touches, or for occasional scenes like the meeting of the pluralist Dean and the Country Vicar:

There were duellynge in Oxenford two prestes bothe maystres of arte / of whome that one was quyck and coude putte hym self forth / And that other was a good symple preest / And soo it happed that the mayster that was perte and quyck was anone promoted to a benefyce or tweyne / and after to prebendys / and for to be a Dene of a grete pryncès chappel / supposynge and wenynge that his felaw the symple preest shold neuer haue be promoted but be alwey an Annuel / or at the most a parysshe preest / So after longe tyme that this worshipful man this dene came rydynge in to a good paryssh with a x or xij horses / lyke a prelate / and came in to the chirche of the sayd parysshe / and fond there this good symple man somtyme his felawe / whiche cam and welcomed hym lowely / And that other badde hym good morowe mayster Johan / and toke hym sleyghtly by the hand and axyd hym where he dwellyd / And the good man sayd / in this paryssh / how sayd he / are ye here a sowle preest or a paryssh preste / nay syr said he / for lack of a better though I be not able ne worthy J am parson and curate of this parysshe / and thenne that other aualed his bonet and said mayster parson I praye you to be not displeasyd / J had supposed ye had not be benefyced / But mayster sayd he / J pray you what is this benefyce worth to yow a yere / Forsothe sayd the good symple man / I wote neuer / for I make neuer accomptes therof / how wel J haue had hit four or fyue yere / And knowe ye not said he what it is worth / it shold seme a good benefyce / No forsothe sayd he / but J wote wel what it shalle be worth to me / why sayd he / what shalle hit be worth / Forsothe sayd he / yf J doo my trewe dylygence in the cure of my parysshens in prechyng and techynge / and doo my parte longynge to my cure /

I shalle haue heuen therfore / And yf theyre sowles ben lost or ony of them by my defawte / J shall be punysshed therfore / And herof am J sure / And with that word the ryche dene was abasshed And thought he shold be the better / and take more hede to his cures and benefyces than he had done.

The history of printing in England before 1500 is so much the history of Caxton's press that we are apt to forget his companions in the art. The earliest press set up during his lifetime was one at Oxford in 1478, while another commenced to print at St. Albans in 1479. Both were mainly concerned in the publication of works in Latin for scholastic use. At Oxford only one book was published in English, Mirk's *Festial* (1486). At St. Albans two vernacular works came from the press, but both of considerable interest. *The Chronicles of England* (1485) was not a mere reprint, but in addition to Caxton's text (1480: 1482) included a history of the popes and other ecclesiastical information. The other was the so-called 'Book of St. Albans', *The Book of Hawking, Hunting, and Blasing of Arms* (1486).[1]

Apart from these two presses which published nothing after 1486, the only other press of note was that of John Lettou, founded in 1480, and merged into a joint venture by Lettou and William de Machlinia in 1482. This press was mainly engaged in the publication of works in Latin on ecclesiastical matters, or in legal texts and year-books up to 1483, when de Machlinia became the sole proprietor. After this date and before 1491 he issued some twenty volumes, but only six of them were in English, and none of outstanding importance.

The death of Caxton in 1491 left only two printers at work—Wynkyn de Worde, who succeeded Caxton at Westminster, and Richard Pynson at London. Wynkyn de Worde published very little for the first few years after Caxton's death, contenting himself almost entirely with reprints. In 1495 he issued the *Vitas Patrum*, a translation by Caxton, finished according to de Worde on the last day of Caxton's life. The same year saw the publication of another large new work, Trevisa's translation of Bartholomew's *De Proprietatibus Rerum*. The next year was a notable one, for de Worde published seven new works, seven reprints, and the *Statutes of the Realm* for five separate years. The most interesting of the new works was the treatise on fishing[2] attached to his edition of the 'Book of St. Albans'.

[1] See above, p. 198.

[2] See above, p. 198.

He continued to publish new books and reprints until the end of the century. Many of them are of little interest now, but we owe to him the first editions of such famous works as *Robin Hood* (1500), *Bevis of Hampton* (1500), *Sir Eglamour* (1500), Lydgate's *The Assembly of the Gods* (1498) and *The Siege of Thebes* (1500?) and the first published work of Skelton, *The Bowge of Court* (1499?).

Richard Pynson, a graduate of Paris, early in his printing career published an edition of the *Canterbury Tales* (1490); on the whole he was content to publish reprints, and has to his credit a bare dozen books hitherto unprinted in his first ten years as a printer (1490–1500). Most of these are of small moment, but we are indebted to him for the first editions of Mandeville's *Travels* (1496) and *Guy of Warwick* (1500).

A survey of the work of the printers between 1477 and 1500 reveals the strength of the demand for religious and didactic works. Caxton, de Worde, and Pynson all devoted something like half their output to meeting this demand. Once that was satisfied, they turned to other needs. Literature of information and instruction received about the same attention from Caxton as did the romances and poems. Both de Worde and Pynson, however, apparently found the former a better market, for de Worde published some 28 works of information and instruction to 18 of a more literary nature, while Pynson increased this disparity still further by publishing 41 of the former to 18 of the latter. In all this, as might be expected, prose works predominated, but much of Chaucer and Lydgate, as well as some verse romances got into print. Further, some 80 per cent. of the prose was translation, much of it dating from about 1470 onwards.

8

As we look back at the prose of the fifteenth century we see (as did Caxton) that a variety of styles were practised. There were writings in 'ouer curyous termes', and writings in 'old and homely termes', while others were more readable since they were 'not over rude ne curyous but in suche termes as shal be vnderstanden'. Gradually a prose was being formed which had not surrendered its native characteristics in order to acquire greater flexibility and power. It remained an English prose, just as the Anglo-Saxon Chronicle, or the *Ancren Riwle*, or the writings of Wiclif were English prose, and it assimilated foreign words and constructions by adapting them to English patterns and rhythms. Thus, despite the overwhelming importance attached by Latin writers to the ordering of the sentence and the nice use of the *cursus*, little of this can be seen in English prose of the period. The insistence on throwing the accent on the penultimate syllable, and of avoiding the accented monosyllable which was so important to Latin writers, failed to secure acceptance. What Professor Saintsbury calls the 'trochaic hum' prevailed, and prose had to wait until the sixteenth century, and until the Ciceronian influence was stronger, before the effects familiar to us in the cadences of the Collects and the Book of Common Prayer became naturalized.

Prose written under the influence of medieval Latin in the fifteenth century, such as that of Lydgate, Pecock, the City Fathers, or the University of Oxford, made but limited headway. The majority of writers did not accept this way of writing, and what this meant may be seen by comparing the two following passages, each of them translations of the *De Imitatione Christi*. The first, dated about 1460, is by an anonymous writer and runs:

Trouþe is to be sought in holy writings, & not in eloquence. Euery holy writing owiþ to be radde with þe same spirit wherewiþ it was made. We owin in scriptures raþer to seke profitabilnes þan highnes of langage. We owe as gladly to rede simple and deuote bokes as hye bokes and profounde sentences.

This is rendered by William Atkynson about 1504:

The principall thynge that we shall inquyre in scripture is charite & nat elygance in speche, & we shuld endeuoure our selfe to rede the scripture with as great fervour of spryte as it was receyued firste. And wisdome wolde we shude folowe these auctors and bokes where we may haue moste swete & profitable fedyng for owre soule. The fame of sotell phylosophers, the knowlege of poetes & retoricke, as a smoke or fume vanissheth awey: but the trouthe of god abydeth without ende.

Atkynson's version of the passage, especially of the third sentence, with its 'phylosophers, . . . poetes & retoricke', together with its image of 'smoke or fume', is a movement towards a richer, more cadenced prose, it is true, but also towards a prose more verbose and pretentious in manner, and one which was to lead to the excesses of Tudor prose. The 'aureate' language, the over-latinization, the constant use of Latin or French constructions, the flamboyance accompanying an enthusiastic use of rhetorical 'colours'—all these, on the whole, are kept at bay by most writers, and prose acquired a certain flexibility, and within limits pursued a straightforward path. A more skilful use of Latin was made by many writers who, following St. Jerome and current tradition, had endeavoured 'non verbum e verbo, sed sensum exprimere de sensu'. One such writer, a Carthusian monk of Beauvale, in Nottinghamshire, wrote in 1411: 'Ne I translate not þe wordes as þei bene wrytene, one for a noþere, þat is to seye þe englische worde for þe latyne worde', for he says that many Latin words are not understandable in English, and so he will put the matter in such a way that it will be clearly understood without serious alteration of his original. This he does, keeping pretty closely to the Latin for the most part in thought, but using a variety of English constructions which are syntactical equivalents of the Latin. By so doing he gives a clear exposition of Suso's *Horologium Sapientiae*, and a lively and realistic account of the lives of St. Elizabeth of Spalbeck and St. Mary of Oignies. Another translator from the Latin, Nicholas Love, while less faithful to the original in his *Mirror of the Blessed Life of Jesu Christ*, at the same time composed what was perhaps the most popular book of the century. His prose is so singularly easy and natural that Professor R. W. Chambers may well have been right when he claimed that Love did more than Hereford or Purvey's rendering of the Scriptures in providing a model for future writers of English prose. For example:

Thus standen they to gidre, etyng and spekyng, with grete ioye to hem of the blessed presence of hir lorde: but neuertheles with grete drede and turbulance of his aweie passyng: and no wonder, for thei louede hym so tenderly that they myghte not with esy herte bere the wordes of his bodily departyng from hem, and namely oure lady, his blessed moder, that louede him passynge all othere. We mowe wel suppose that sche, touchede and stired souereynly with the swetnesse of moder loue, as she satte nexte hym at the mete, leyde doun her hede swetely, and restede vpon his blessid breste, as seynt John dide bifore in that forseide and moste worthy sopere.

And so with swete teres sighynge, sche spak to hym in this manere preienge: My dere sone, if thou wilt alway go to thy fader, I preie the lede me with the. And oure lorde confortynge her seide: I pray the, dere moder, take not heavily my goynge fro the, for I goo to the fader for thy beste, and it is spedeful that thou dwelle her yit awhile to conferme him that schulle trewely byleue in me: and after I schal come and take the with me into euerlastyng blisse. And then sche seide: My swete sone, thy wille be done.

Translation indeed played a most important part in the development of our prose. Translations from the Latin and the French form a considerable section of the prose literature of the century, and the form and coherence of the English sentence was often largely dependent on the quality of the original. As time went on, 'an increased recognition of both the mechanical and the logical processes of structure, if not in many cases a capable control over them' was manifested, and readers were encouraged to expect and welcome technical accomplishment and the production of a prose 'clear, easy and plain'. This was not brought about in a day, nor everywhere at the same time, but throughout the century writers were slowly learning to write sentences in which the parts were grammatically combined: the old enemies of anacoluthon, pleonasms, synthetic verbs, and the like were in retreat. A wide variety of constructions begins to give life and variety to prose, and an effort is made to achieve a structural coherence of sentence and paragraph. The way forward to a more developed and cadenced prose has been attained.

CHRONOLOGICAL TABLES AND BIBLIOGRAPHY

The dates of many fifteenth-century works are disputed, and a question-mark necessarily appears after many titles. The dates even of works to which no question-mark is attached are often conjectural and should be understood as merely approximate. For the dating of Chaucer's works, see Chapter III above and the chronological table in Vol. I, Part II.

The author's name (if known) is followed by the title of the work. The letters tr. are added if it is a translation, and the name of the translator (if known), the printer, and the date of publication follow.

Date	Public Events	Literary and Cultural History
1400	Murder of Richard II. Rising of Owen Glendower.	G. Chaucer d. (?).
1401	Statute *de heretico comburendo* enacted.	
1402	Henry IV marries Joan of Navarre. Battle of Homildon Hill.	John Trevisa d.
1403	Glendower conquers South Wales. Battle of Shrewsbury. War with France.	Stationers' guild incorporated.
1405	Archbishop Scrope's revolt and execution. French landing in Wales to aid Glendower.	..
1406	James I of Scotland captured. Henry accepts the 'thirty-one articles'. The French invade Guienne. Siege of Aberystwyth.	Statute of Apprentices.
1407	Parliament at Gloucester. Truce with France. H. Bowat becomes Archbishop of York.	William Wey b. (?).
1408	Battle of Bramham Moor. Surrender of Harlech Castle.	John Gower d.
1409	Henry IV ill. Contest for power between Prince Henry and Archbishop Arundel. University of Oxford ordered by the Pope to condemn the Wyclifite doctrines.	..

Verse	*Prose*
1400–50. Anon., *Alexius. Avowing of Arthur. Awntyrs of Arthur. Tale of Beryn. Le Bone Florence. The Cuckoo and the Nightingale. Duke Rowland and Sir Otuel. Emaré. The Erle of Toulouse. Generydes. Ipomadon. Laud Troy-Book. Morte Arthur* (stanzaic). *Pride of Life* (morality play). *Roberd of Sicily. Siege of Melayne. Sir Amadace. Sir Cleges. Sir Gawayne and the Carle of Carlile. Sir Gowther. Sir Torrent. Sir Triamor. Song of Roland. Sowdon of Babylon. Urbanitatis.* Mirk, *Instructions for Parish Priests* (*c.* 1400).	1400–50. Anon., *Alexander. King Ponthus and the Fair Sidone.* *c.* 1400. Anon., *The Chastising of God's Children*, tr. (W. de Worde 1492). *The Craft of Dying*, tr. Ps.-Aristotle, *The Governance of Lordships* (*Secreta Secretorum*), tr. Peter of Blois, *The Twelve Profits of Tribulation*, tr. (W. de Worde, 1499). J. de Hildesheim, *The Three Kings of Cologne*, tr. (W. de Worde *c.* 1496(?)). Lanfrank, *Antidotarie and Cirurgie*, tr. L. d'Orléans, *Book of Vices and Virtues*, tr., and see 1440 and *Royal Book*, tr. Caxton 1484 (?). J. Mandeville, *Travels*, tr. (Pynson 1496). J. Mirk, *Festial* (Caxton 1483).
..	..
C. de Pisan, *Letter to Cupid*, tr. Hoccleve. Lydgate, *Complaint of the Black Knight* (1400–2). J. (?) Quixley, Translations of Gower's *Ballades.*	..
Anon., *Mum and the Soothsayer* (1403–6).	*Dives and Pauper* (1403–10. i. Pynson 1493, ii. W. de Worde 1496).
..	..
Hoccleve, *La Male Regle* (?).	Gaston III (Phébus) de Foix, *The Master of Game* (1406–13), tr. Edward, Duke of York.
Scogan, *Moral Balade.*	..
Lydgate, *The Churl and the Bird* (i. Caxton 1477 (?), ii. n.d., iii. W. de Worde, n.d. etc.). *Reason and Sensuality* (?).	Vegetius, *Knighthood and Battle* (?), tr.
..	Anon., *Lantern of Light. Mirror of the Life of Christ*, tr. Love (i. Caxton 1486 (?), ii. 1490, iii. W. de Worde 1494).

Date	Public Events	Literary and Cultural History
1410	The Lollard Badby burnt.	..
1411	Alliance with John of Burgundy, and expedition to France. Oxford purged of Lollardy.	..
1412	Alliance with Orleanists and second expedition to France.	..
1413	Accession of Henry V. Arrest and escape of Oldcastle.	Benedict Burgh b. St. Andrews recognized as a *studium generale.*
1414	Oldcastle's insurrection. Preparations for attack in France. Alien priories suppressed. H. Chichele becomes Archbishop of Canterbury.	..
1415	Battle of Agincourt. Council of Constance condemns Wyclifite heresies.	Edward, second Duke of York, d. Thomas Norton b. William Worcester (*or* Botoner) b. Fifty-one plays of the *Ordo paginarum* entered in the York *Liber Memorandorum* (the 'York Plays'). Charles d'Orléans becomes a prisoner in England.
1416	King Sigismund in England.	..
1417	End of the Great Schism. Invasion of Normandy. Capture and execution of Oldcastle.	R. Pecock elected Fellow of Oriel College, Oxford (?).
1418	Siege of Rouen.	..
1419	Murder of John of Burgundy by the Dauphin. Surrender of Rouen.	..
1420	Treaty of Troyes. Siege of Melun. Marriage of Henry V to Catherine of Valois, daughter of Charles VI of France.	Andrew of Wyntoun d. (?). Towneley cycle (the Wakefield Plays) practically complete by this date.
1421	Battle of Bougé. Henry VI b.	..

Verse	*Prose*
Boethius, *Consolation of Philosophy*, tr. Walton (Caxton 1478). Lydgate, *Temple of Glass* (?).	..
Hoccleve, *Regement of Princes.*	..
Lydgate, *Troy Book* (1412–20).	..
..	Deguilleville, *Pilgrimage of the Soul* (?), tr. (Caxton 1483).
Brampton, *Seven Penitential Psalms* (?). Lydgate, *Departure of T. Chaucer for France* (1414–20).	Anon., *English Chronicles of London* (?).
Anon., *The Crowned King* (?). Hoccleve, *Address to Oldcastle. Legend of St. Margaret*, tr. Lydgate (1415–26).	..
..	..
..	..
Page, *Siege of Rouen* (?).	..
Anon., *Friar Daw's reply* (to *Jack Upland c.* 1390)(?), and see 1450.	..
Lovelich, *History of the Holy Grail* (?). Lydgate, *Siege of Thebes* (1420–2. W. de Worde, *c.* 1500).	Anon., *Alphabet of Tales* (?), tr. *Life of St. Katherine of Siena*, tr. (W. de Worde 1490). *Miracles of Mary* (?), tr. Ps.-Aristotle, *Governance of Princes* (*Secreta Secretorum*), tr. J. Yonge. Giraldus Cambrensis, *The Conquest of Ireland* (?), tr.
Lydgate, *Life of Our Lady* begun (?).	..

Date	Public Events	Literary and Cultural History
1422	Accession of Henry VI. Bedford regent.	William Caxton b. (?). Thomas Littleton b. Higham Ferrers School founded.
1423	..	..
1424	Battle of Verneuil. Release of James I of Scotland and his marriage to Joan Beaufort.	R. Pecock made Bishop of St. Asaph. R. Holme gives 16 vols. to Cambridge University.
1425	Conflict between Gloucester and Cardinal Beaufort. J. Kemp becomes Archbishop of York.	..
1426	Beaufort as Cardinal retains his See of Winchester.	Thomas Hoccleve d.
1427	..	John Tiptoft b. First record of the Newcastle-upon-Tyne craft play of Noah (?).
1428	Siege of Orleans.	..
1429	Joan of Arc at Chinon. Joan raises siege of Orleans. Battle of Patay. Charles VII crowned at Reims.	R. Henryson b. (?). Sir Richard Ros b. Lincoln College, Oxford, founded by R. Fleming, Bishop of Lincoln.
1430	Joan of Arc captured. Henry VI in France (1430–2). James II of Scotland b.	R. Pecock translated to Bishopric of Chichester.
1431	Joan of Arc condemned and burnt. Waning of English fortunes in France.	..
1432	..	Ewelme School founded by Michael de la Pole. Sevenoaks School founded by William Sevenoaks, grocer. Wye College, Kent, founded by John Kemp, Archbishop of York.

Verse	*Prose*
Lydgate, *Epithalamium to the Duke of Gloucester* (1422–3).	Capgrave, *Sermon on the Orders under the Rule of St. Augustine* (written down 1451). Lydgate, *The Serpent of Division* (?).
James I of Scotland, *The Kingis Quair*. Anon., *Guy of Warwick*, tr. Lydgate (1423–6).	..
Lydgate, *Danse Macabre* (1424–33).	..
Anon., *Avowynge of Arthur* (?). *Castle of Perseverance* (?) (morality play). *Ipomydon* (?). *Merlin*, tr. Lovelich.	Anon., *Siege of Troy*, tr. *Life of St. Dorothea* (?), tr. (1425–50).
Audelay, *Salutation of St. Bridget* (?). Lydgate, *Mummings at London* (1424–30). G. de Deguilleville, *Pilgrimage of the Life of Man*, tr. Lydgate (1426–8).	..
Lydgate, *Pedigree of Henry VI*.	..
..	..
Lydgate, *Coronation Address to Henry VI*; *Mummings* for (i) Mercers, (ii) Goldsmiths.	..
Anon., Manuscript of York Plays (1430–40). Ps.-Aristotle, *An ABC*, tr. Lydgate, *Mumming at Hertford*. Wyntoun, *Chronicle*.	Anon., *Life of Alexander* (?), tr. *Life of St. Katherine of Siena*, tr. (W. de Worde 1491–3). *Life of St. Elizabeth of Spaldeck*, tr. *Life of Mary of Oegines*, tr. *Chronicles of London*—first important recension. Continuation of *Brut*. *Gesta Romanorum* (?), tr. G. de Deguilleville, *Pilgrimage of the Life of Man* (?), tr. Suso, *The Seven Points of True Love*, tr. J. de Voragine, *Golden Legend*, and see 1438.
Lydgate, *Fall of Princes* (1431–8. Pynson 1494).	..
Lydgate, *Henry VI's Triumphal Entry into London* (?).	M. Kempe, *The Book of Margery Kempe* (rev. and enlarged, 1436–8).

Date	Public Events	Literary and Cultural History
1433	..	..
1434	..	..
1435	Conference of Arras. Death of Bedford. York in command in Normandy.	St. Bernard's College, Oxford, founded on the site of St. John's College. First gift of Humphrey, Duke of Gloucester, of books to Oxford University.
1436	Paris recovered by the French. Scotland at war with England.	..
1437	James I of Scotland murdered. James II succeeds.	..
1438	..	All Souls College, Oxford, founded by Henry Chichele, Archbishop of Canterbury.
1439	..	Godshouse (afterwards Christ's College), Cambridge, founded by William Byngham, rector of St. John Zachary, London. Tattershall College, Lincs., founded by Sir Ralph Cromwell. Gift of 129 volumes by Humphrey, Duke of Gloucester, to Oxford University.
1440	Siege of Harfleur.	Margery Kempe d. (?). Gilbert Banester b. (?). Eton College founded by Henry VI. Charles d'Orléans released. R. Wyche, the Lollard, burnt.
1441	Trial and condemnation of Duchess of Gloucester.	King's College, Cambridge, founded by Henry VI. St. Anthony's School, London, founded by Henry VI.
1442	Duke of Somerset's campaign in France.	Anthony Woodville, Earl Rivers, b. (?). Sir John Fortescue appointed Chief Justice.

Verse	*Prose*
Burgh, *Letter to Lydgate* (1433–40). Lydgate, *Lives of Saints Edmund and Fremund.*	..
..	Rolle, *Mending of Life*, tr. Misyn.
..	Anon., version of *Brut.* Rolle, *The Fire of Love*, tr. Misyn.
Anon., *The Libel of English Policy* (1436–7?).	..
Lydgate, *The Horse, the Goose, and the Sheep* (1437–40. Caxton *c.* 1477).	..
Anon., *Scottish Alexander Buik.*	J. de Voragine, *Golden Legend* (?), tr.
Lydgate, *Lives of Saints Albon and Amphabell.*	Capgrave, *Commentary upon Genesis.*
Anon., *Ballet of the Nine Nobles*, tr. Longuyon. Capgrave, *Life of St. Norbert.* C. d'Orléans, *Poems.* Palladius, *On Husbandry*, tr. Harding, *Chronicle* (early recension). Russell, *Book of Carving and Nurture* (?).	Anon., *Jacob's Well* (?). Ps.-Aristotle, *Government of Princes* (*Secreta Secretorum*), tr. Banester, *Guiscardo and Ghismonda* (1440–5). Geoffrey the Grammarian, *Promptorium Parvulorum.* La Tour Landry, *Book of the Knight of the Tower* (tr. by Caxton 1484). Legrand, *Book of Good Manners*, tr. Shirley. L. d'Orléans, *Book of Vices and Virtues*, tr. *c.* 1440. Anon., *Life of St. Jerome*, tr.
..	..
..	..

Date	*Public Events*	*Literary and Cultural History*
1443	John Stafford appointed Archbishop of Canterbury.	..
1444	Peace negotiations with France.	John Plummer, Master of Song of the Chapel Royal (1444–55). Gift of 134 volumes by H. Duke of Gloucester to Oxford University.
1445	Marriage of Margaret of Anjou and Henry VI.	..
1446	..	..
1447	Arrest and death of Humphrey, Duke of Gloucester.	William Lychefelde d.
1448	..	Magdalen College, Oxford, founded by William of Waynflete. Queens' College, Cambridge, founded by Margaret of Anjou (re-founded by Elizabeth Woodville, 1465).
1449	Renewal of war with France. Loss of Rouen and eastern Normandy.	..
1450	Jack Cade's rebellion. Impeachment and execution of Duke of Suffolk. Murder of Bishops Ayscough and Moleyns.	John Lydgate d. *English Register of Godstow Nunnery* compiled (?). The Bible printed at Mainz. Glasgow recognized as a *studium generale.*
1451	..	..
1452	Richard III b. James III of Scotland b. John Kemp translated as Archbishop of Canterbury and William Booth as Archbishop of York.	..

Verse	*Prose*
Bokenham, *Lives of Holy Women* (1443–6).	Pecock, *Rule of Christian Religion*; *The Donet* (1443–9).
Lydgate, *Miracles of St. Edmund.*	..
Ps.-Aristotle, *Secrets of Old Philosophers* (*Secreta Secretorum*), tr. Lydgate and Burgh. Idley, *Instructions to his Son* (1445–50?). Lydgate, *Testament* (?); *Queen Margaret's Entry into London.*	..
Hoccleve, *Poem to the Duke of York* (1446–8). Lydgate, *Poem on the Nightingale* (1446–8).	..
Lychefelde, *Complaint of God* (?).	..
Anon., *Craft of Lovers* (1448–9). Metham, *Amoryus and Cleopes.*	..
..	..
c. 1450. Chartier, *La Belle Dame sans Merci*, tr. Sir R. Ros. *Eger and Grime. Generydes* (?). Harding, *Chronicle. J. Upland's Rejoinder* (to Daw Topias). *Ratis Raving* (?). *Wedding of Sir Gawayne and Dame Ragnell.* 1450–75, *Assembly of Gods*, tr.	*c.* 1450. *Life of St. Augustine*, tr. Capgrave. *Revelations of St. Birgitte*, tr. *Merlin. Siege of Thebes*, tr. T. à Kempis, *Imitation of Christ*, tr. Capgrave, *Solace of Pilgrims.* C. de Pisan, *Epistle of Othea*, tr. Scrope (?). G. de Tignonville, *Dicts and Sayings of the Philosophers*, tr. Scrope.
..	Roger of Sempringham, *Life of St. Gilbert*, tr. Capgrave.
..	..

Date	Public Events	Literary and Cultural History
1453	Edward, Prince of Wales, b. Henry VI becomes insane. The Duke of York appointed as Regent. Constantinople captured by the Turks. End of the Hundred Years War.	John Dunstable, musician, d.
1454	Henry VI resumes power. Thomas Bourchier becomes Archbishop of Canterbury.	..
1455	Wars of the Roses begin. First battle of St. Albans. Second regency of York.	Henry Abyngdon, Master of Song of the Chapel Royal (1455–78).
1456	York dismissed from office.	John Shirley d.
1457	..	Pecock recants and is confined in Thorney Abbey.
1458	..	..
1459	Battle of Blore Heath.	John Fisher b.
1460	James II of Scotland d. James III succeeds. Warwick enters London. Battle of Northampton. York claims the Crown. Battle of Wakefield.	Reginald Pecock d. (?). Walter Kennedy b. (?). John Skelton b. (?). *English Register of Osney Abbey* compiled (?).
1461	Second battle of St. Albans. Edward IV proclaimed king and Henry VI deposed. Battle of Towton.	..
1462	Margaret of Anjou invades Northumberland with French troops.	Richard Misyn d. (?).
1463	Flight of Margaret to Flanders.	..
1464	Battles of Hedgeley Moor and Hexham. Marriage of Edward IV to Elizabeth Woodville.	John Capgrave d. Osbern Bokenham d. not before this year.
1465	G. Neville becomes Archbishop of York. Coronation of Queen Elizabeth.	John Hardyng d. W. Dunbar b. (?). H. Boece b. (?). Queens' College, Cambridge, re-founded by Elizabeth Woodville.

Verse	*Prose*
..	..
..	Pecock, *The Follower* (1454–6).
..	Pecock, *The Repressor* (?). Ps.-Aristotle, *Book of the Government of Princes* (*Secreta Secretorum*), tr. Hay. Bonet, *Book of the Law of Arms*, tr. Hay. Lull, *Book of the Order of Knighthood*, tr. Hay. Pecock, *Book of Faith* (?).
..	..
..	..
..	Wey, *Itineraries to Jerusalem.*
..	..
Anon., *Book of Courtesy.* Manuscript of the Wakefield cycle (Towneley Plays). Henryson, *The Testament of Cresseid.*	Anon., *The Book of Quinte Essence* (?). *Ipomedon.* Rolle, *Amendment of Life*, tr., and see 1434. First version of Worcester, *Book of Noblesse*, by this date.
Ostensible date of events dramatized in the Croxton Play. Ashby, *Poems* (1461–3).	..
Adam of Cobsam, *The Wright's Chaste Wife.*	Wey, *Itineraries to St. James.*
..	Capgrave, *Chronicle* (1463–4).
Harding, *Chronicle* (revised version).	Anon., second continuation of *Brut* (1464–70).
Anon., *Rauf Coilyear* (1465–1500). *Wisdom* (morality play) (?).	B. de Pistoja, *Declamation of Noblesse*, tr. J. Tiptoft (Caxton 1481). Cicero, *Tullius of Friendship*, tr. J. Tiptoft (Caxton 1481).

Date	*Public Events*	*Literary and Cultural History*
1466	Henry VI captured and imprisoned in the Tower. Elizabeth of York b.	..
1467	..	John Colet b. (?).
1468	Warwick disgraced.	..
1469	Warwick's conspiracy and return to power. James III of Scotland marries Margaret of Denmark. Battle of Edgecote.	..
1470	Warwick expelled and is reconciled with Margaret. Warwick again master of England. Henry VI reinstated. Edward V b.	John Tiptoft d. Cambridge University Library completed (?).
1471	Edward IV lands at Ravenspur and captures London. Battle of Barnet. Warwick slain. Battle of Tewkesbury. Henry VI deposed. Murder of Henry VI.	William Caxton translates the *Recuyell of the Histories of Troy* (printed 1475).
1472	Richard, Duke of Gloucester, marries Anne Neville.	..
1473	Treaty signed with the Hanseatic League. James IV of Scotland b.	St. Catharine's College, Cambridge, founded by R. Wodelarke, Provost of King's College. John Warkworth made Master of Peterhouse, Cambridge.
1474	Treaty with Burgundy.	Stephen Hawes b. (?).
1475	Edward IV invades France. Treaty of Picquigny.	Alexander Barclay b. (?). Gavin Douglas b. (?). George Ashby d.
1476	Lawrence Booth becomes Archbishop of York.	Sir John Fortescue d. (?). William Wey d. William Caxton sets up his press at Westminster.

Verse	*Prose*
..	..
Chester 'banns' composed (?).	..
Part of *Ludus Coventriae* manuscript.	Anon., *Catholicon Anglicum*. Fortescue, *De Laudibus Legum Angliae* (1468–70). Gregory, *Chronicle* (1468–70).
..	Malory, *Morte Darthur* (1469–70. i. Caxton 1485, ii. W. de Worde 1498). Warkworth, *Chronicle*.
Anon., Brome play of *Abraham and Isaac* (1470–80). *Court of Sapience* (Caxton, 1481(?)).	Anon., *Croyland Chronicle* (continuation). C. de Pisan, *The Body of Policy* (?), tr.
Ripley, *Compend of Alchemy*.	Anon., *History of the Arrival of Edward IV*. Fortescue, *Governance of England*.
..	G. de Tignonville, revision by Worcester of *Dicts and Sayings of the Philosophers*, tr., see 1450. Cicero, *Tullius of Old Age*, tr. Worcester, and see 1481.
..	Anon., *Recuyell of the Histories of Troye*, tr. Caxton (i. Caxton, Bruges 1473–4, ii. French version by R. Lefèvre, Bruges 1475–6).
..	Littleton, *Tenures* (?).
Anon., *Assembly of Ladies* (1475–1500). *The Flower and the Leaf* (1475–1500). *Mankind* (morality play).	J. de Cessolis, *The Game and Play of the Chess*, tr. Caxton (i. Caxton, Bruges 1476, ii. Caxton 1483). R. Lefèvre, *Jason* (Caxton, Bruges 1475–6). J. Mielot, *Les Quatre Choses derrenieres* (Caxton, Bruges 1475–6), and see 1478. C. de Pisan, *Epistle to Othea*, tr. Babington (*c.* 1475).
	..

Date	*Public Events*	*Literary and Cultural History*
1477	Duke of Clarence arrested.	The 'Makcullock manuscript' of Scottish poetry compiled after this date (1477–88).
1478	Clarence executed. Anne Mowbray marries Richard, Duke of York.	Sir T. More b. First book printed at Oxford (?). G. Banester Master of Song of the Chapel Royal (1478–86).
1479	Plague rampant in England.	First book printed at St. Albans. W. Cornish, Master of the Song-School at Westminster Abbey.
1480	T. Rotherham becomes Archbishop of York.	First book published by J. Lettou.
1481	War with Scotland.	T. Littleton d.
1482	Treaty of Edinburgh.	William Worcester (*or* Botoner) d. (?).

Verse	*Prose*
Cato, *Parvus Cato et Magnus*, tr. Burgh (i. Caxton 1477, ii. 1477 (?), iii. 1481 (?)). Chaucer, *Anelida* (Caxton 1477 (?)). *The Temple of Brass*, i.e. *Parliament of Fowls* (Caxton 1477 (?)). Lydgate, *The Churl and the Bird* (i. Caxton 1477 (?), ii. Pynson 1493, etc.); *The Horse, the Goose, and the Sheep* (i. Caxton 1477 (?), ii. W. de Worde, n.d.); *Stans Puer ad Mensam* (Caxton 1477 (?)); *Temple of Glass* (i. Caxton 1477 (?), ii. W. de Worde 1495 (?), iii. 1500). Anon., *Book of Courtesy* (i. Caxton 1477, ii. W. de Worde 1492). Norton, *Ordinal of Alchemy*.	R. Lefèvre, *History of Jason*, tr. Caxton (i. Caxton 1477, ii. G. Leeu, Antwerp 1492). G. de Tignonville, *Dicts or Sayings of the Philosophers*, tr. A. Woodville, Lord Rivers (i. Caxton 1477, ii. 1479 (?), iii. 1489 (?)).
Chaucer, *Canterbury Tales* (i. Caxton 1478, ii. 1484, iii. Pynson 1492, iv. W. de Worde 1498). C. de Pisan, *Moral Proverbs*, tr. Lord Rivers (Caxton 1478).	Anon., *Liber Niger of Henry VI* (?). Boethius, *De consolatione philosophiae*, tr. Chaucer (Caxton 1478 (?)). J. Mielot, *The four last things*, i.e. *The Cordial*, tr. Lord Rivers (Caxton 1479), and see 1475.
••	••
••	Anon., *Vocabulary in French and English* (i. Caxton 1480, ii. W. de Worde 1497). Chronicles of England, i.e. the *Brut* (i. Caxton 1480, ii. 1482, iii. St. Albans 1486, iv. Machlinia 1486, v. G. Leeu, Antwerp 1493). Higden, *Polychronicon*, tr. Trevisa and Caxton (i. Caxton 1482, ii. W. de Worde 1498). *Description of Britain* [an extract from *Polychronicon*] (Caxton 1480). Ovid, *Metamorphoses*, tr. Caxton.
Anon., *Court of Sapience* (Caxton 1481 (?)).	Anon., *Godfrey of Boulogne*, tr. (Caxton 1481). *Reynard the Fox*, tr. Caxton (i. 1481, ii. 1489, iii. Pynson 1494). *Mirror of the World*, tr. (i. Caxton 1481, ii. 1490). Cicero, *Tullius of Friendship*, tr. (Caxton 1481); *Tullius of Old Age*, tr. Worcester (Caxton 1481).
Henry the Minstrel, *Sir W. Wallace*. Anon., *Lancelot of the Laik* (1482–1500).	Caorsin, *Siege of Rhodes*, tr. Kay (Lettou and Machlinia (?)).

Date	*Public Events*	*Literary and Cultural History*
1483	Death of Edward IV. Edward V succeeds and is placed in the Tower. Gloucester proclaimed Protector. Execution of Hastings. Usurpation of Gloucester as Richard III. Murder of the princes. Buckingham's conspiracy and death.	Benedict Burgh d. Anthony Woodville, Earl Rivers d. Rotherham College, Yorks., founded by Thomas Rotherham, Archbishop of York.
1484	Edward, Prince of Wales d.	..
1485	Henry Richmond (Henry VII) lands in Wales. Battle of Bosworth Field. Death of Richard III and accession of Henry VII.	..
1486	Henry VII married to Elizabeth of York. Arthur, Prince of Wales b. J. Morton becomes Archbishop of Canterbury.	L. Squier, Master of Song of the Chapel Royal (1486–93).
1487	..	..
1488	James III of Scotland d. James IV of Scotland succeeds.	Miles Coverdale b. Duke Humphrey's Library opened at Oxford.
1489	Margaret, d. of Henry VII, b.	Thomas Cranmer b.

Verse	*Prose*
Gower, *Confessio Amantis* (Caxton 1483 (?)).	Anon., *Book called Cathon*, tr. (Caxton 1483). Deguilleville, *Pilgrimage of the Soul*, tr. (Caxton 1483). Mirk, *Festial* and *Sermons* (Caxton, i. 1483, ii. 1491 (?), iii. Pynson 1493 (?)). De Voragine, *Golden Legend*, tr. Caxton (i. 1483 (?), ii. 1487 (?), iii. W. de Worde 1493).
Chaucer, *House of Fame* (Caxton 1484 (?)); *Troilus and Criseyde* (Caxton 1484). Lydgate, *Life of Our Lady* (Caxton 1484 (?)).	Aesop, *Fables*, tr. Caxton (i. Caxton 1484, ii. Pynson 1497 (?)). A. Chartier, *The Curial*, tr. Caxton (Caxton 1484 (?)). La Tour Landry, *The Knight of the Tower*, tr. Caxton (Caxton, 1484), and see 1440. R. Lull, *Order of Chivalry*, tr. Caxton (Caxton 1484 (?)). L. d'Orléans, *Royal Book*, tr. Caxton (Caxton 1484 (?)), and see 1400.
..	Anon., *Chronicles of England* (i. St. Albans 1485, ii. W. de Worde 1497). *Charles the Great*, tr. Caxton (Caxton 1485). *Morte Darthur*, tr. Malory (i. Caxton 1485, ii. W. de Worde 1498. *Paris and Vienne*, tr. Caxton (i. Caxton 1485, ii. G. Leeu 1492). *Revelation of Evesham* (Machlinia 1485). *Life of St. Winifred*, tr. Caxton (Caxton 1485).
H. Medwall, *Interlude of Nature* (1486–1500. J. Rastell 1525 (?)).	*Mirror of the Life of Christ*, tr. Love (i. Caxton 1486 (?), ii. 1490 (?), iii. W. de Worde 1494), and see *c.* 1409. *Book of St. Albans* (i. St. Albans 1486, ii. W. de Worde 1496).
..	J. Legrand, *Book of Good Manners*, tr. Caxton (i. Caxton 1487, ii. Pynson 1494, iii. 1500).
..	..
Skelton, *On the Dolorous Death of the Earl of Northumberland.*	Anon., *Blanchardine and Eglantine*, tr. Caxton (Caxton 1489 (?)). *Doctrinal of Sapience*, tr. Caxton (Caxton 1489 (?)). *Governal of Health*, tr. (Caxton 1489 (?)). C. de Pisan, *Feats of Arms and of Chivalry*, tr. Caxton (Caxton 1489 (?)). H. de Villeneuve, *The Four Sons of Aymon*, tr. Caxton (1489 (?)).

Date	*Public Events*	*Literary and Cultural History*
1490	..	Sir Thomas Elyot b. (?). Sir David Lindsay b. George Ripley d. (?).
1491	Henry VIII b.	W. Caxton d.
1492	Columbus discovers the West Indies.	..
1493	..	William Newark Master of Song of the Chapel Royal (1493–1509).
1494	..	The Aldus Press (Venice) established. Aberdeen University founded by W. Elphinstone, Bp. of Aberdeen.
1495	..	John Bale b.
1496	..	Jesus College, Cambridge, founded by William Alcock, Bp. of Ely.

Verse	*Prose*
..	Anon., *Treatise of the Art and Craft to know well to die*, tr. Caxton (i. Caxton 1490 (?), ii. Pynson 1495 (?)). John of Ireland, *Treatise on Political Wisdom.* Virgil, *Eneydos* (Fr. version of the *Aeneid*), tr. Caxton (Caxton 1490 (?)).
..	Anon., *Ars Moriendi*, tr. Caxton (i. Caxton 1491 (?), ii. W. de Worde 1497 (?)). *Book of Diverse Ghostly Matters*, tr. Caxton 1491 (?). *Life of St. Katherine of Siena*, tr. (W. de Worde 1491–3). *Life of St. Elizabeth of Hungary*, tr. (W. de Worde 1491–3). Jerome, *Vitas Patrum*, tr. (W. de Worde 1495).
G. de Alet, *The Ghost of Guy*, tr. (Pynson 1492).	Anon., *Chastising of God's Children*, tr. (W. de Worde 1492 (?)). *Dialogue of Solomon and Marcolphus*, tr. (G. Leeu, Antwerp 1492).
Anon., *Life of St. Margaret* (Pynson 1493).	Anon., *The Seven Wise Masters of Rome*, tr. (i. Pynson 1493, ii. W. de Worde 1505). *This Treatise is of Love*, tr. (W. de Worde 1493 (?)). *Dives and Pauper* (i. Pynson 1493, ii. W. de Worde 1496), and see 1403.
Boccaccio, *Fall of Princes*, tr. Lydgate (Pynson 1494).	W. Hilton, *Scale of Perfection* (W. de Worde 1494).
..	Bartholomeus Anglicus, *De Proprietatibus Rerum*, tr. Trevisa (W. de Worde). R. Fitzjames, *Sermon* (i. W. de Worde 1495 (?), ii. 1499 (?)).
Anon., *Epitaph on the Duke of Bedford* (Pynson 1496 (?)). *Life of Petronilla* (Pynson 1496 (?)).	Anon., *The Abbey of the Holy Ghost* (i. W. de Worde 1496, ii. 1500). *Meditations of St. Bernard*, tr. (i. W. de Worde 1496, ii. 1499). *Miracles of Our Lady* (W. de Worde 1496 (?)). *Parvula* (i. W. de Worde 1496, ii. 1497). *Rote of Consolation* (i. W. de Worde 1496, ii. 1499). Alcock, *Mons Perfectionis* (i. W. de Worde 1496, ii. 1497, iii. 1498 (?)). *Spousage of a Virgin* (i. W. de Worde 1496, ii. 1497 (?), iii. 1498 (?)). Mandeville, *Travels*, tr. (i. Pynson 1496, ii. W. de Worde 1499). J. de Hildesheim, *Three Kings of Cologne*, tr. (i. W. de Worde 1496 (?), ii. 1499 (?)), and see *c.* 1400.

Date	*Public Events*	*Literary and Cultural History*
1497	Cabot discovers the American mainland.	Gilbert Banester d. John Heywood b.
1498	..	Erasmus comes to Oxford.
1499	..	..
1500	..	John Warkworth d. King's College, Aberdeen, completed. The 'Gray Manuscript' of Scottish poetry compiled (?).

Verse	*Prose*
H. Medwall, *Fulgens and Lucres* (interlude) (printed J. Rastell before 1520).	Alcock, *Sermon on Luke viii* (W. de Worde 1497).
Anon., *Assembly of the Gods* (i. W. de Worde 1498, ii. n.d., iii. n.d.), and see 1450.	Anon., *Doctrinal of Death* (W. de Worde 1498). *Information for Pilgrims to the Holy Land* (W. de Worde).
Skelton, *Bowge of Court* (W. de Worde n.d.).	Anon., *Contemplation of Sinners* (W. de Worde 1499). Peter of Blois, *The Twelve Profits of Tribulation* (W. de Worde 1499 (?)), and see *c.* 1400.
Anon., *Bevis of Hampton* (W. de Worde 1500 (?)). *Sir Eglamour* (W. de Worde 1500). *Golagros and Gawayne* (?) (Edinburgh 1508). *The Green Knight* (?). *Guy of Warwick* (Pynson n.d., W. de Worde 1500). *Romance of Partenay* (*Lusignan*), 1500 (?). *Robin Hood* (i. W. de Worde 1500, ii. Pynson 1500). *Squire of Low Degree* (1500 (?)). Chaucer, *Complaint of Mars* (J. Notary 1500 (?)).	Anon., *Book of Cookery* (Pynson 1500 (?)). *Melusine*, tr. (W. de Worde 1510). *A Profitable Treatise*, tr. T. Betson (W. de Worde). *The Three Kings' Sons*, tr.

BIBLIOGRAPHY

This bibliography is arranged in seven sections:

I. General Bibliographies and Works of Reference.
II. General Collections and Anthologies.
III. General Literary History and Criticism (general literary history and criticism (*a*) English, (*b*) Scottish; metre and versification; rhetorical theory and prose style).
IV. Special Literary Studies and Literary Forms (language; scribes and scriptoria; libraries; printers and printing; historical literature; correspondence).
V. The Background of Literature (constitutional, political, and legal history; biographies of statesmen; religion and religious thought; science and scientific thought; education and culture; architecture and allied arts: painting, sculpture, and stained glass; manuscripts; music; social life; chivalry).
VI. Individual Authors.
VII. Anonymous Writings (works in verse or prose, original or translations; romances composed between 1400 and 1500).

Since the bibliography is to be 'selective and directive', a great deal of less important matter is necessarily omitted, and a general reference to the *Cambridge Bibliography of English Literature* must suffice.

The following abbreviations are used in the citing of works of reference and current periodicals:

Archiv	*Archiv für das Studium der neueren Sprachen* (various places)
BS	The Bibliographical Society
CBEL	*Cambridge Bibliography of English Literature*
CHEL	*Cambridge History of English Literature*
EETS OS	Early English Text Society. Original Series
EETS ES	,, ,, ,, ,, Extra Series
EETS SS	,, ,, ,, ,, Supplementary Series
EHR	*English Historical Review*

ES	*Englische Studien* (Leipzig)
JEGP	*Journal of English and Germanic Philology* (Bloomington and Urbana)
JRLB	*John Rylands Library Bulletin*
MLN	*Modern Language Notes* (Baltimore)
MLR	*Modern Language Review*
MP	*Modern Philology* (Chicago)
PBSA	*Papers of the Bibliographical Society of America* (New York)
PMLA	*Publications of the Modern Language Association of America* (New York)
PQ	*Philological Quarterly* (Iowa City)
RES	*Review of English Studies*
SP	*Studies in Philology* (Chapel Hill, N. Carolina)
STS	Scottish Text Society
VCH	*Victoria County History*

The place of publication may be assumed to be Great Britain unless it is otherwise stated. The date of the first edition is followed by that of the most recent edition.

I. GENERAL BIBLIOGRAPHIES AND WORKS OF REFERENCE

All students of this period will find indispensable the work of J. E. Wells, *A Manual of the Writings in Middle English, 1050–1400* (New Haven, 1916) with its nine supplements (1919–51). This work not only covers the period up to 1400 with an admirable section on Chaucer, but gives many references to fifteenth-century literature. An expansion and rewriting of Wells, to include the fifteenth century, is in active preparation and the first two fascicules, dealing with the Romances, the *Pearl* poet, and religious writings, have been published under the general editorship of J. Burke Severs—*A Manual of the Writings in Middle English, 1050–1500* (New Haven, 1967, 1970). Until this work is completed a useful short guide is provided by L. L. Tucker and A. R. Benham, *A Bibliography of Fifteenth Century Literature* (Seattle, Washington, 1928). The introduction and critical apparatus provided by E. P. Hammond in her *English Verse between Chaucer and Surrey* (Durham, North Carolina, 1927) are of first-rate importance. The *CBEL* (vol. i, 1940,

Supplement, vol. v, 1957) affords a wealth of information, and a new and revised edition is in preparation. For current work see *The Annual Bibliography of English Language and Literature* (1920 onwards), published by the Modern Humanities Research Association. *The Year's Work in English Studies* (1919 onwards) is published by the English Association and provides a serviceable guide to the most important work of each year, while *Speculum* from vol. xiv (1934) onwards has a quarterly 'Bibliography of American Periodical Literature'. *Abstracts of English Studies*, issued frequently (now ten times a year) at Boulder, Colorado, since 1958, usefully summarizes recent work. A valuable conspectus of research will be found in L. F. McNamee's *Dissertations in English and American Literature accepted by American, British and German Universities, 1865–1964* (1968). *The Index of Middle English Verse* by Carleton Brown and R. H. Robbins (New York, 1943) is indispensable for information about manuscript and printed sources of medieval poetry, and this has been amplified by a *Supplement . . . to the Index*, edited by R. H. Robbins and J. L. Cutler (Lexington, 1965). These two volumes completely supersede the work of Carleton Brown, *A Register of Middle English Religious and Didactic Verse*, BS (2 vols., 1916–20). Help may also be found by consulting 'A Bibliographical and First Line Index of English Verse printed through 1500', *PBSA* xlix (1955), 153–80. For the study of the literary origins of many works see S. Thompson, *Motif Index of Folk Literature* (6 vols., 1932–6; new and enlarged edn., Copenhagen, 1955–8), supplemented by G. Bordman, *Motif-Index of the English Metrical Romances* (Helsinki, 1963). W. L. Renwick and H. Orton provide a useful introduction and bibliography in *The Beginnings of English Literature to Skelton* (1939, 1962) and W. Matthews a bibliography in *Old and Middle English Literature* (New York, 1968). *A Census of Medieval and Renaissance Manuscripts in the United States and Canada*, edited by S. de Ricci and W. J. Wilson (3 vols., New York, 1935–40), deals fully with this topic. The various volumes of the *VCH* contain detailed information on the life, culture, education, &c. of the period. For translations see the *Bibliography of English Translations from Medieval Sources*, by C. P. Farrar and A. P. Evans (New York, 1946). A wider field is surveyed in *The Medieval Literature of Western Europe. A Review of Research, mainly 1930–1960*, ed. J. H. Fisher (New York, 1966).

II. GENERAL COLLECTIONS AND ANTHOLOGIES

This section comprises: (1) collections of verse; (2) of prose; (3) of verse and prose; (4) anthologies of translations; (5) readers.

1. Collections of Verse

From the many collections of varying merit the following may be consulted: J. Ritson and W. C. Hazlitt, *Ancient Songs and Ballads from the Reign of Henry the Second to the Revolution* (1790, 1877); T. Wright, *Political Poems and Songs* (Rolls Series, 2 vols., 1859, 1861); W. C. Hazlitt, *Remains of the Early Popular Poetry of England* (4 vols., 1864–6) reprints a large number of pieces not easily available elsewhere; F. J. Furnivall, *Political, Religious and Love Poems*, EETS os 15 (1866, 1903); G. G. Perry, *Religious Pieces in Prose and Verse*, EETS os 26 (1867, rev. 1913); F. J. Child, *The English and Scottish Popular Ballads* (1882–98); J. Kail, *Twenty-six Political and other Poems from Digby MS. 102*, EETS os 124 (1904); E. K. Chambers and F. Sidgwick, *Early English Lyrics* (1907); R. Dyboski, *Songs, Carols, and other Miscellaneous Poems*, EETS ES 101 (1908); R. L. Greene, *Early English Carols* (1935); G. H. McKnight, *Middle English Humourous Tales in Verse* (Boston, 1913); E. P. Hammond, *English Verse between Chaucer and Surrey* (1927); F. M. M. Comper, *Spiritual Songs* (1936); C. Brown, *Religious Lyrics of the Fifteenth Century* (1939); R. H. Robbins, *Secular Lyrics of the Fourteenth and Fifteenth Centuries* (1952, 1955); R. H. Robbins, *Historical Poems of the Fourteenth and Fifteenth Centuries* (1959); R. T. Davies, *Medieval English Lyrics* (1963); C. and K. Sisam, *The Oxford Book of Medieval English Verse* (1970).

Scottish poetry is also admirably dealt with by G. Gregory Smith in his *Specimens of Middle Scots* (1902), which gives a concise linguistic survey as well as a full account of the early sources. A more recent work with a select bibliography is that of A. M. Kinghorn, *The Middle Scots Poets* (1970). A large selection of verse will be found in *Scottish Poetry from Barbour to James VI*, edited by M. M. Gray (1935), in which the extracts have been slightly normalized for the general reader. Many medieval poems are given in *The Oxford Book of Scottish Verse*, chosen by J. MacQueen and T. Scott (1966), and in *Ballattis of Luve*, ed. J. MacQueen (1970).

There are also the sixteenth-century collections known as the Asloan, Bannatyne, and Maitland Folio and Quarto MSS. These have all been edited for the STS, the first, third, and fourth by Sir William Craigie and the second by W. Tod Ritchie. They are briefly described by G. Gregory Smith in the introduction to his book of *Specimens* (see above).

2. Collections of Prose

English Prose, edited by H. Craik (vol. i, 1893), has short extracts from authors of this period, each prefaced by a brief biographical and critical notice, but this has been replaced by W. Matthews, *Later Medieval English Prose* (1963), which gives a wide selection of passages dealing with many sides of medieval life and thought. Spelling and punctuation have been modernized.

3. Collections of Verse and Prose

One of the most valuable of collections is still that of T. Wright and J. O. Halliwell, *Reliquiae Antiquae* (2 vols., 1841–3, 1845), which contains many rare and important extracts from manuscript sources. Its texts, however, need careful checking before they are used for scholarly purposes. A series of extracts dealing with the life of the period will be found in the present writer's *England from Chaucer to Caxton* (1928). An unusually interesting collection of pieces, with a valuable introduction, will be found in A. W. Pollard's *Fifteenth Century Prose and Verse* (1903), presented in a modernized spelling.

4. Anthologies of Translations

Translations of medieval texts into modern English are numerous but not very satisfactory. *The Dunbar Anthology*, one of the earliest, edited by E. Arber (1901), has been superseded by W. A. Neilson and K. G. T. Webster's *Chief British Poets of the Fourteenth and Fifteenth Centuries* (Boston, 1916). This work has for its companions two volumes by J. L. Weston dealing largely with fourteenth-century poetry: *Romance, Vision and Satire, English Alliterative Poems of the Fourteenth Century* (Boston, 1912), and *The Chief Middle English Poets* (Boston, 1914). Other works which may be consulted are E. Rickert, *Early English Romances in Verse* (2 vols., 1908); M. H. Shackford, *Legends and Satires from Medieval Literature* (Boston, 1913); M. Schlauch,

Medieval Narrative, a Book of Translations (New York, 1928); M. R. Adamson, *A Treasury of Middle English Verse, Selected and Rendered into Modern English* (1930); *Medieval English Verse and Prose in Modernised Versions*, compiled by R. S. Loomis and R. Willard (New York, 1945). Much more than translation will be found in A. R. Benham's *English Literature from Widsith to the Death of Chaucer* (New Haven, 1916) which gives a valuable survey of the literature, life, and thought of this period with long translations from relevant sources.

5. Readers

Two well-known books of extracts, with notes and apparatus, are those of O. F. Emerson, *A Middle English Reader* (New York, 1905, 1915), and A. S. Cook, *A Literary Middle English Reader* (Boston, 1915). The standard German publications of this kind are F. Kluge, *Mittelenglisches Lesebuch* (Halle, 1904, 1912); A. Brandl and O. Zippel, *Mittelenglische Sprach- und Literaturproben* (Berlin, 1917, 1927; English translation 1949); R. Kaiser, *Medieval English* (Berlin, 1954, 1958). The requirements of modern scholarship are fully satisfied by several outstanding works: *Fourteenth Century Verse and Prose*, edited by K. Sisam (1921), also with a Vocabulary by J. R. R. Tolkien (1922); E. P. Hammond's *English Verse between Chaucer and Surrey* (1927); F. Mossé's *Manuel de l'anglais du Moyen Age*, ii (2 vols., Paris, 1945), translated by J. A. Walker as *A Handbook of Middle English* (Baltimore, 1952).

Although they deal with works falling outside this period, much help will be found from the following: B. Dickins and R. M. Wilson, *Early Middle English Texts* (1951, 1956), and J. A. W. Bennett and G. V. Smithers, *Early Middle English Verse and Prose* (1966, 1968).

III. GENERAL LITERARY HISTORY AND CRITICISM

This section comprises: (1) general literary history and criticism, (*a*) English, (*b*) Scottish; (2) metre and versification; (3) rhetorical theory and prose style.

1. General Literary History and Criticism

(*a*) *English Literature*

A great deal of information (which, however, requires using with care) will be found in T. Warton's *History of English Poetry*

(3 vols., 1774–81; Index, 1806), edited by W. C. Hazlitt (4 vols., 1871). Vols. iv–vi of H. Morley's *English Writers* (1889–91) give a useful account with running commentary and paraphrase of literature between Chaucer and Caxton. A most readable account will be found in J. J. Jusserand's *Histoire littéraire du peuple anglais des origines à la Renaissance* (Paris, 1894–1904; trans., 3 vols., 1895–1909), while vol. i of W. J. Courthope's *History of English Poetry* (6 vols., 1895–1910) gives special attention to questions of the development of literary forms and of origins. A wider view of European literature, showing the place of English literature therein, is given in G. Saintsbury's *The Flourishing of Romance and the Rise of Allegory* (1897, 1907), and in G. Gregory Smith's *The Transition Period* (1900). W. H. Schofield, *English Literature from the Norman Conquest to Chaucer* (1906), gives an exhaustive survey of its subject, while W. P. Ker's *Medieval English Literature* (1912; reissued with new bibliography 1969) is invaluable, both for its comprehensive survey and for its stimulating comments. There are some excellent passages in E. Legouis's contributions to the *Histoire de la littérature anglaise* (Paris, 1924; trans. 1926–7, rev. 1930), while O. Elton in *The English Muse* (1933) writes attractively, although in outline only, on this period in his early chapters. In addition there are the standard outline histories, which give some account of medieval literature, such as G. Saintsbury, *A Short History of English Literature* (1898), G. Sampson's digest, *The Concise Cambridge History of English Literature* (1941, rev. 1969), or A. C. Baugh and others, *A Literary History of England* (New York, 1948, 1967). Vol. ii (1908) of the *CHEL* is wholly devoted to Chaucer and the fifteenth century as is the present volume.

Apart from works of literary history, a few volumes of general literary criticism may be mentioned. W. P. Ker throws much light on a number of authors and on medieval authorship in his *Essays on Medieval Literature* (1905), while his *Form and Style in Poetry* (1928) is full of suggestive observations. J. M. Berdan's *Early Tudor Poetry, 1485–1547* (New York, 1920) deals at length with the cultural background of the fifteenth century, while the introduction to E. P. Hammond's *English Verse between Chaucer and Surrey* (1927) is the best short account of the poetical developments during the same period. *The Allegory of Love* (1936), by C. S. Lewis, deals brilliantly with one side of

'Chaucerian' poetry and its origins. On the history of the lyric, see A. K. Moore, *The Secular Lyric in Middle English* (Lexington, Kentucky, 1951) and R. Woolf, *The English Religious Lyric in the Middle Ages* (1968), and 'Later Poetry: The Popular Tradition', in *History of Literature in the English Language*, vol. i, ed. W. F. Bolton (1970).

(*b*) *Scottish Literature*

This section covers general literary history and criticism; foreign influences. For language see Section IV (1) and for selections and collections see Section II.

There are a number of general literary histories of Scotland which have something to say of the earlier periods. Of these the works of G. Gregory Smith are outstanding, both for their scholarship and for their understanding of the nature of this literature. In chapter ii of *The Transition Period* (1900), and more fully in chapters iv, x, and xi of vol. ii of the *CHEL*, will be found invaluable material. The same writer's *Scottish Literature, Character and Influence* (1919) deals mainly with later periods, but is good on Henryson and the continuity of Scottish literature. The next best work is that of T. F. Henderson, *Scottish Vernacular Literature* (1898, rev. edn. 1910). This is a rather leisurely production, but will be found useful. A highly personal and lively account is given by Agnes Muir Mackenzie in *An Historical Survey of Scottish Literature to 1714* (1933), while K. Wittig considers *The Scottish Tradition in Literature* (Edinburgh, 1958). Finally, there is the admirable survey of the chronicle-histories by F. Brie, *Die nationale Literatur Schottlands von den Anfängen bis zur Renaissance* (Halle, 1937).

The French influence is best discussed by Janet M. Smith in *The French Background of Middle Scots Literature* (1934). This corrects and supplants Francisque Michel's *Critical Inquiry into the Scottish Language* (1882), and also contains a good bibliography.

2. Works on Metre and Versification

Of the innumerable works on metre useful contributions in various ways are made by J. Schipper, *Englische Metrik in historischer und systematischer Entwicklung* (Bonn, 1881–8) and *Grundriß der englischen Metrik* (Vienna, 1895; trans. as *A History of English Versification*, 1910); M. Kaluza, *Englische Metrik in historischer Entwicklung dargestellt* (Berlin, 1909; trans. 1911). By far the most useful work in English is G. Saintsbury, *A History of English Prosody* (3 vols., 1906–10); a shorter work is his *Historical Manual of English Prosody* (1910). There are some excellent critical observations in C. Patmore's 'English Metrical Law', *Amelia* (1878), and from a more recent standpoint in W. K. Wimsatt and M. C. Beardsley, 'The Concept of Metre', in *Hateful Contraries* (Lexington, 1965), pp. 108–45, with useful references. In his two volumes, *Verses of Cadence* (1954) and *The Prosody of Chaucer and his Followers* (1962), J. G. Southworth attempts to reassess the rhythmical character of Chaucer's poetry; but he has not won much support, though I. Robinson in *Chaucer's Prosody* (1971) accepts part of his thesis. The traditional view is expounded by P. F. Baum, *Chaucer's Verse* (Durham, N.C., 1961). For help on problems of 'alliterative' metres see first the appendix in *Sir Gawain and the Green Knight*, ed. J. R. R. Tolkien and E. V. Gordon (1925; 2nd edn. rev. N. Davis, 1967), and M. Borroff, *Sir Gawain and the Green Knight: A Stylistic and Metrical Study* (New Haven, 1962). This may be supplemented by vol. i of J. P. Oakden's *Alliterative Poetry in Middle English* (2 vols., 1930–5), while M. M. R. Stobie's 'Influence of Morphology on Middle English Alliterative Poetry', *JEGP* xxxix (1940), 319–36, is a useful discussion of the development of this metre and carries it into the fifteenth century. For problems of metre in fifteenth-century rhymed verse see especially J. Schick in his edition of Lydgate's *Temple of Glass*, EETS ES 60 (1891); C. S. Lewis, 'The Fifteenth-Century Heroic Line', *Essays and Studies*, xxiv (1938); D. A. Pearsall's introduction to his edition of *The Floure and the Leafe* (1962).

3. Rhetorical Theory and Prose Style

The work of the medieval rhetoricians is conveniently summarized and discussed by C. S. Baldwin, *Medieval Rhetoric and Poetic* (New York, 1928), and by J. W. H. Atkins, *English Literary Criticism: The Medieval Phase* (1943). There is an important discussion by J. M. Manly in his Warton Lecture 'Chaucer and the Rhetoricians' in the *Proceedings of the British Academy*, xii (1926), 95–113, while an excellent summary of research on this subject will be found in D. Everett, 'Some Reflections on Chaucer's "Art poetical"' in *Essays on Medieval*

English Literature (1955). J. J. Murphy in 'A New Look at Chaucer and the Rhetoricians', *RES* NS xv (1964), 1–20 raises interesting questions, and the references on page 6, note 9 of J. M. Steadman's 'Courtly Love as a Problem of Style', in *Chaucer und seine Zeit*, ed. A. Esch (Tübingen, 1968), continue the discussion. For a number of texts of the rhetoricians, see E. Faral, *Les Arts poétiques du XIIe et du XIIIe siècle* (Paris, 1924).

There has been some discussion of the prose style of this period, but much remains to be done. G. Saintsbury, in his *History of English Prose Rhythm* (1912), pp. 56–101, devotes some attention to the general problem, as well as to the characteristics of the several authors. G. P. Krapp, *The Rise of English Literary Prose* (New York, 1915), is mainly concerned with prose of later periods. For a more recent view and some extended analysis of passages, see M. Schlauch, 'Chaucer's Prose Rhythms', *PMLA* lxv (1950), 568–89, and the same writer's 'Chaucer's Colloquial English', *PMLA* lxvii (1952), 1103–16.

The influence of the Latin books of *dictamen* is illustrated by J. C. Mendenhall, *Aureate Terms: a Study in the Literary Diction of the Fifteenth Century* (Lancaster, Pennsylvania, 1919), and also by E. F. Jacob in a valuable article 'Florida verborum venustas', *JRLB* xvii (1933), 264–90, while A. C. Clark's articles on the Latin *cursus* may be found in *The Cursus in Medieval and Vulgar Latin* (1910) and in his *Prose Rhythm in English* (1915). For references to letter-writing manuals and their influence see N. Davis, 'The *Litera Troili* and English Letters', *RES* NS xvi (1965), 233–44.

On the use of the *cursus* in England, see the article by N. Denholm-Young in *Oxford Essays in Medieval History presented to H. E. Salter* (1934), 68–103, and one by H. G. Richardson, 'An Oxford Teacher of the Fifteenth Century', *JRLB* xxiii (1939), 436–57. Much information on this matter is scattered about the pages of two learned works: W. F. Schirmer, *Der englische Frühhumanismus* (Leipzig, 1931), and R. Weiss, *Humanism in England during the Fifteenth Century* (1941, 1957).

A good deal of information on the prose style of this period will be found in vol. ii of the *CHEL*, where Miss A. D. Greenwood writes on 'The Beginnings of English Prose' and 'English Prose in the Fifteenth Century', and E. Gordon Duff on 'The Introduction of Printing into England'. A. W. Pollard's *Fifteenth Century Prose and Verse* (1903) prints some useful texts.

R. W. Chambers and M. Daunt's *London English, 1384–1425* (1931) will be found invaluable, both for its texts and for its references. The most stimulating single discussion of prose style and its development is by R. W. Chambers, *On the Continuity of English Prose* (1932), extracted from the preface to *Harpsfield's Life of More*, EETS 186 (1932). An article by the present writer, 'Fifteenth Century Secular Prose', *RES* xxi (1945), 257–63, attempts to emphasize an aspect of prose insufficiently noticed by Chambers, and the discussion has been carried on by R. M. Wilson, 'On the Continuity of English Prose', *Mélanges Mossé* (Paris, 1959), 486–94, by N. Davis, 'Styles in English Prose of the Late Middle and Early Modern Period', *Langue et Littérature* (Université de Liège, 1961), 165–81, and in a wider context by I. A. Gordon, *The Movement of English Prose* (1966).

S. K. Workman's *Fifteenth Century Translation as an Influence on English Prose* (Princeton, 1940) has much of value, while E. Zeeman explores the methods of one writer in 'Nicholas Love: a Fifteenth-Century Translator', *RES* NS vi (1955).

IV. SPECIAL LITERARY STUDIES AND LITERARY FORMS

This section comprises: (1) language; (2) scribes and scriptoria; (3) libraries; (4) printers and printing; (5) historical literature; (6) correspondence.

1. The Language

Among many works dealing with the history of the language the following may be consulted. The whole of the material is being charted by R. C. Alston's *Bibliography of the English Language from the Invention of Printing to the Year 1800*. This work is projected in 20 volumes and is now in progress (1965–). Other standard works are O. F. Emerson, *The History of the English Language* (New York, 1894, 1924); O. Jespersen, *Growth and Structure of the English Language* (1906; 9th edn., 1945) and *A Modern English Grammar*, parts i–vii (1909–49); K. Luick, *Historische Grammatik der englischen Sprache* (Leipzig, 1914–40, 1964); S. Moore, *Historical Outlines of English Phonology and Middle English Grammar* (Michigan, 1919, rev. 1951); R. Huchon, *Histoire de la langue anglaise* (Paris, 2 vols., 1923–30), of which vol. ii deals with this period; H. C. Wyld, *A Short*

History of English (1913, rev. 1927) and *A History of Modern Colloquial English* (1920, 1936); R. Jordan, *Handbuch der mittelenglischen Grammatik* (Heidelberg, 1925, 1934); K. Brunner, *Die englische Sprache* (Halle, 2 vols., 1950–1, rev. edn. Tübingen, 1960–2); B. M. H. Strang, *A History of English* (1970). More specialized studies are R. E. Zachrisson, *The Pronunciation of English Vowels, 1400–1700* (Gothenburg, 1913), and A. Kihlbom, *A Contribution to the Study of Fifteenth Century English* (Uppsala, 1926). Much important information is in E. J. Dobson's *English Pronunciation 1500–1700* (1957, 1968), especially vol. ii on Middle English and later phonology.

For syntax, see E. Einenkel, *Streifzüge durch die mittelenglische Syntax* (Münster, 1887); L. Kellner, *Historical Outlines of English Syntax* (1892); vols. ii–iv of O. Jespersen's *Modern English Grammar*; T. F. Mustanoja, *A Middle English Syntax*, part i (Helsinki, 1960); F. Th. Visser, *An Historical Syntax of the English Language* (Leiden, 1963–). A good deal of work has been done on the syntax and diction of individual authors, qq.v.

The Oxford English Dictionary, ed. J. A. H. Murray et al. (1884–1928; corrected reissue, 13 vols., 1933), is the best authority on diction and usage at present, but will eventually be superseded for the early period by the *Middle English Dictionary* (Ann Arbor, 1952–), which is in process of production. In a separate part (1954) entitled *Plan and Bibliography* will be found an exhaustive list of documents covering this period.

2. Scribes and Scriptoria

For all matters concerning scribes and the medieval scriptorium the indispensable book is W. Wattenbach, *Das Schriftwesen im Mittelalter* (Leipzig, 1896). G. H. Putnam, *Books and their Makers during the Middle Ages* (2 vols., New York, 1896–7), F. A. Gasquet, *The Old English Bible* (1908), and J. W. Thompson, *The Medieval Library* (Chicago, 1939), contain a good deal of miscellaneous information; see especially the chapters on 'The Scriptorium' and on 'Paper, the Book Trade, and Book Prices' in Thompson's volume. See also chapter xvii on 'Printed Books, the Book Trade, and Libraries' in vol. ii of *Medieval England*, ed. A. L. Poole (1958). *The Care of Books* (1901, 2nd edn., 1902) by J. W. Clark is useful, while an article which enlarges our knowledge of scribal habits was contributed by J. Taylor,

'The Monastic Scriptorium', *Library*, 1st ser. ii (1890), 237–44, 282–91. The working of the famous scriptorium at St. Albans is discussed by H. B. Luard in his introduction to the *Chronica Majora* of Matthew Paris (Rolls Series, 7 vols., 1872–83), C. Jenkins, *The Monastic Chronicler* (1922), and R. Vaughan, *Matthew Paris* (1958). For references to the scriptorium of John Shirley see below. Much new information about scribes and scribal habits will be found in articles by N. Davis. See *English and Germanic Studies*, iv (1951); *RES* NS iii (1952); *Neophilologus*, xxxviii (1953); *Proc. Brit. Acad.*, xl (1955); *Mélanges Mossé* (Paris, 1959); *Medieval Literature and Civilization*, ed. D. A. Pearsall and R. A. Waldron (1969). H. J. Chaytor's *From Script to Print* (1945) provides a valuable introduction to problems arising from scribal methods and practice.

The materials used by scribes are very fully listed in an article by D. V. Thompson, 'Trial Index for Medieval Craftsmanship', *Speculum*, x (1935), 410–31, and the same author deals with an important subject in 'Medieval Parchment Making', *Library*, 4th ser. xvi (1936), 113–17. Prices of manuscripts and the cost of copying are well dealt with by H. E. Bell, 'The Price of Books in Medieval England', *Library*, 4th ser. xvii (1937), 312–32. The method of regulating the prices of university textbooks is admirably studied by J. Destrez, *La 'Pecia' dans les manuscrits universitaires du* XIII*e et du* XIV*e siècle* (Paris, 1935) and by R. Steele in his article 'The Pecia', in *Library*, 4th ser. xi (1931), 230–4. The present writer's 'The Production and Dissemination of Vernacular Manuscripts in the Fifteenth Century', *Library*, 5th ser. i (1947), 167–78, deals with a topic that requires much more study.

3. Medieval Libraries

Medieval libraries have been fully discussed from many points of view. The classic work on the arrangement and equipment of the library is that of J. W. Clark, *The Care of Books* (1901, 1902). This may be supplemented by the valuable work of B. H. Streeter, *The Chained Library* (1931). For good general accounts of medieval libraries see E. Edwards, *Memoirs of Libraries* (2 vols., 1859); E. A. Savage, *Old English Libraries* (1911); J. W. Thompson, *The Medieval Library* (1939); *The English Library before 1700*, ed. F. Wormald and C. E. Wright (1958). Fuller accounts will often be found in various places, e.g. the library of Merton College, Oxford, is admirably dealt with in P. S. Allen's 'Early Documents connected with the Library of Merton College', *Library*, 4th ser. iv (1924), 249–76, H. W. Garrod, 'The Library Regulations of a Medieval College', ibid. viii (1927), 312–35, and F. M. Powicke, *The Medieval Books of Merton College* (1931). The contents of many monastic libraries have been investigated, pre-eminently by M. R. James, and the results of much of this work are gathered together in *Medieval Libraries of Great Britain*, edited by N. R. Ker (1941, rev. 1964). The libraries of great private collectors, such as Duke Humphrey or Tiptoft or Edward IV, are dealt with in the standard biographies. Those of lesser collectors are not so easily surveyed. Specimens of various types of collections may be found in two articles by E. Rickert, 'Chaucer at School', *MP* xxix (1932), 257–74, and 'King Richard II's Books', *Library*, xiii (1933), 144–7, and in *Paston Letters and Papers*, edited by N. Davis (1971), no. 316.

4. Printers and Printing

For information concerning printers and printing in the latter part of the fifteenth century the foundation work is that of A. W. Pollard and G. R. Redgrave, *A Short Title Catalogue of Books printed in England, Scotland and Ireland, and of English Books printed abroad, 1475–1640*, BS (1926, 1946; revised edn. in preparation). This has been rearranged by Paul G. Morison so as to show what books were printed by individual printers: *An Index of Printers, Publishers and Booksellers* (Charlottesville, 1950). Another valuable aid is C. E. Sayle's *Early English Printed Books in the University Library* [Cambridge] (4 vols., 1900–7). For incunabula, the standard work is that of E. G. Duff, *Fifteenth Century English Books*, BS (1917). Reference may also be made to 'Early Printed Books' by V. Scholderer in *The Bibliographical Society, 1892–1942. Studies in Retrospect*, BS (1945), 32–41. Much valuable information on the printing of medieval works at the opening of the printing era will be found in E. Ph. Goldschmidt's *Medieval Texts and their First Appearance in Print*, BS (1943), and in C. F. Bühler's *The Fifteenth Century Book* (Philadelphia, 1960). For paper, see R. H. Clapperton's *Paper: An Historical Account of its Making by Hand* (1934), and an informative article on the making of paper in England by A. Stevenson, 'Tudor Roses from John Tate', *Studies in*

Bibliography, xx (1967), 15–34. And see E. Heawood, 'Sources of Early English Paper Supply', *Library*, 4th ser. x (1930), 288–307.

For printers the writings of E. G. Duff are invaluable. See *A Century of the English Book Trade*, BS (1905), and *Printers, Stationers and Bookbinders of Westminster and London from 1476 to 1535* (1906). For Caxton see below. W. de Worde is considered by H. R. Plomer in his *Wynkyn de Worde and his Contemporaries from the Death of Caxton to 1535* (1925), while the present writer's handlist of publications by W. de Worde in *Books and Readers 1475 to 1557* (1951, 1969) gives the fullest list at present of de Worde's publications. A full list of articles on all aspects of the subject is given by W. L. Heilbronner, *Printing and the Book in Fifteenth-Century England* (Charlottesville, 1967).

5. Historical Literature

This section comprises historical writings of both national and local importance.

The outstanding work is by C. L. Kingsford, *English Historical Literature in the Fifteenth Century* (1913). This may be supplemented by his *Prejudice and Promise in Fifteenth-Century England* (1925) and by F. J. Starke, *Populäre englische Chroniken des 15. Jahrhunderts* (Berlin, 1935).

The chief chronicles in English dealing with the century are: *The Brut*, ed. by F. Brie, EETS os 131, 136 (1906–8); J. Capgrave, *The Chronicle of England*, ed. by F. C. Hingeston, Rolls Series (1858); R. Fabyan, *The New Chronicles of England and France* [1516?], ed. by Sir H. Ellis (1811); *Historical Collections of a Citizen of London in the Fifteenth Century*, ed. by J. Gairdner, Camden Soc. (1876); *Three Fifteenth Century Chronicles*, ed. by J. Gairdner, Camden Soc. (1880).

Other chronicles of national or local interest are: *An English Chronicle*, ed. by J. S. Davies, Camden Soc. (1856); *Chronicle of the Rebellion in Lincolnshire in 1470*, ed. by J. G. Nichols, *Camden Miscellany*, i (1847); *Warkworth's Chronicle*, ed. by J. O. Halliwell [-Phillipps], Camden Soc. (1839). Two verse chronicles should be noted: *Hardyng's Chronicle*, ed. by Sir H. Ellis (1812), and J. Page's 'Siege of Rouen', for which see *The Brut* (above).

For town chronicles see *Chronicles of London*, ed. by C. L. Kingsford (1905), *A Chronicle of London*, ed. by Sir N. H. Nicolas and E. Tyrrell (1827), while a sumptuous edition of *The Great Chronicle of London* has been made by A. H. Thomas and I. D.

Thornley (1938). For other town chronicles see R. Flenley, *Six Town Chronicles of England* (1911).

6. Correspondence

The correspondence of the fifteenth century is admirably summarized and discussed by C. L. Kingsford in his *English Historical Literature in the Fifteenth Century* (1913), and more fully in *Prejudice and Promise in Fifteenth-Century England* (1925).

Collections of letters have been edited as follows: *The Paston Letters* were first edited by Sir J. Fenn under the title *Original Letters, written during the Reigns of Henry VI, Edward IV, and Richard III* . . . (5 vols., 1787–1823), and subsequently by J. Gairdner (3 vols., 1872–5; 4 vols., 1901; 6 vols., 1904). Gairdner's introduction is of the highest value. A selection of the letters, from previous editions, was made by Alice D. Greenwood (1920), since when other selections have been made, notably from the manuscripts by N. Davis (1958). He also prepared a selection in modern spelling (1963) and has under preparation a new edition of the whole correspondence, *Paston Letters and Papers of the Fifteenth Century*, the first volume of which appeared in 1971. It contains thirteen facsimiles. The letters and their background were surveyed by the present writer in *The Pastons and their England* (1922, 1968). Facsimiles of some letters were given in Sotheby's catalogue of 1 April 1931, when a number of letters were offered for sale and were bought by the British Museum. For the present whereabouts of all the letters, see *The Pastons and their England* (1968), 265–76, and for their history see Davis's edition.

The Stonor Letters were admirably edited, with a valuable introduction, by C. L. Kingsford, Camden Soc. (2 vols., 1919). A few supplementary letters, edited by the same hand, will be found in the *Camden Miscellany*, xiii (1923). The Camden Society has also published three other collections of considerable interest: *The Plumpton Correspondence* (1839), ed. by T. Stapleton; *The Letters and Papers of John Shillingford, Mayor of Exeter, 1447–50* (1871), ed. by S. A. Moore; and *The Cely Papers, 1475–88* (1900), ed. by H. E. Malden. The last is incomplete, and a new edition by Alison Hanham is being prepared for the Early English Text Society.

There are also a number of letters in English scattered about various works as, for instance, in *The Official Correspondence of*

Thomas Bekynton, Archbishop of Canterbury, ed. by G. Williams, Rolls Series (2 vols., 1872), and in the three series of *Original Letters*, ed. by Sir Henry Ellis (11 vols., 1824–46). The first volume of J. O. Halliwell[-Phillipps's] *Letters of the Kings of England* (1846) is useful, but its value is decreased by the modernized spelling. Many official letters preserved in the Guildhall archives are printed in R. R. Sharpe's *London and the Kingdom* (3 vols., 1894–5), iii. 359–92; in H. T. Riley's *Memorials of London in the 13th, 14th and 15th Centuries* (2 vols., 1868); in J. Delpit's *Collection des documents français en Angleterre* (Paris, 1847), and in Chambers and Daunt, *London English 1384–1425* (1931). A number of royal letters appear in R. R. Sharpe's *Calendar of Letter Book K of the City of London* (1911).

A few letters in English will be found in *Litterae Cantuarienses*, ed. by J. B. Sheppard, Rolls Series (3 vols., 1887–9), and in the same editor's *Christ Church Letters*, Camden Soc. (1877), 6–67. The University of Oxford occasionally wrote letters in English, which are to be found in *Epistolae Academicae*, ed. by H. Anstey, Oxford Hist. Soc. (2 vols., 1898).

Other letters of interest are: *The Letters of Margaret of Anjou*, ed. C. Munro, Camden Soc. (1863), which contain, in addition to the queen's letters, some seventeen by T. Bekynton, not to be found in his *Official Correspondence* (above); *The Memorials of St. Edmund's Abbey*, ed. by T. Arnold, Rolls Series (3 vols., 1890–6), iii. 241–79; R. T. Davies, *Extracts from the Municipal Records of the City of York* (1843), 150–8; R. C. Anderson, *Letters of the Fifteenth and Sixteenth Centuries from the Archives of Southampton* (1901), 1–29; E. Rickert, 'Some English Personal Letters of 1402', *RES* viii (1932), 257–63. A selection of letters entitled *A Medieval Post Bag* (1934), chosen and edited by L. Lyell, contains a large number of letters from many fifteenth-century collections.

V. THE BACKGROUND OF LITERATURE

This section comprises: (1) constitutional, political, and legal history; (2) biographies of statesmen; (3) religion and religious thought; (4) science and scientific thought; (5) education and culture; (6) architecture and allied arts: painting, sculpture, stained glass; (7) manuscripts; (8) music; (9) social life; (10) chivalry.

For some of these sections much help will be obtained by consulting the appropriate chapter in *Medieval England*, a new edition of F. P. Barnard's *Companion to English History* (1902), which was revised by H. W. C. Davis (1924), and was again rewritten and revised by A. L. Poole (2 vols., 1958); or the appropriate volume in the *Oxford History of England*: M. McKisack, *The Fourteenth Century 1307–99* (1959), E. F. Jacob, *The Fifteenth Century 1399–1485* (1961). For more detailed information the reader is referred to *English Historical Documents*, iv, *1327–1485*, edited by A. R. Myers (1969). All these have valuable bibliographies.

1. Constitutional, Political, and Legal History

The constitutional and political history may first be studied in the pioneer work of W. Stubbs, *A Constitutional History of England* (3 vols., 1880) and in his *Historical Introductions to the Rolls Series* (1902). More modern works are those of Sir Charles Oman, *History of England 1377–1485* (1906); Sir J. H. Ramsay, *The Genesis of Lancaster, 1307–99* (2 vols., 1913) and his *Lancaster and York* (2 vols., 1892); K. H. Vickers, *England in the Later Middle Ages* (1913); S. B. Chrimes, *English Constitutional Ideas in the Fifteenth Century* (1936); *Lancastrians, Yorkists and Henry VII* (1964); J. E. A. Jolliffe, *The Constitutional History of Medieval England* (1937), and G. O. Sayles, *The Medieval Foundations of England* (1948; rev. 1950). A masterly survey of this and preceding periods will be found in Sir Maurice Powicke's *Medieval England 1066–1485* (1931).

Much can be learnt from the special studies of kings. For Edward III the work of W. Longman, *The Life and Times of Edward III* (2 vols., 1869), is still useful. *Richard II* by A. B. Steel (1941) embodies much original research and is particularly valuable concerning the Peasants' Revolt. More recent works of value are *The Hollow Crown: a Life of Richard II*, by H. F. Hutchinson (1961), and *The Court of Richard II* by G. Mathew (1968). J. H. Wylie's work (despite his curious style) still remains our best authority on the *History of England under Henry the Fourth* (4 vols., 1884–98). This he continued in three volumes on *The Reign of Henry the Fifth* (1914–29), the third volume being completed by W. T. Waugh. For other accounts of the life of Henry V see the works of R. B. Mowat (1919) and H. F. Hutchinson (1967). The introduction by C. L. Kingsford to his edition of *The First English Life of Henry V* (1911) contains much of value.

For Henry VI see the monograph of M. Christie (1922), while C. L. Scofield's *The Life and Reign of Edward the Fourth* (2 vols., 1923) is full of information on all phases of the reign. J. Gairdner's *The Life and Reign of Richard III* (1898) gives a judicious account of this disputed monarch's activities. Two more recent surveys are those of P. M. Kendall, *Richard III* (1955) and V. B. Lamb, *The Betrayal of Richard III* (1959, 1968).

Those interested in legal history should turn to the classic volumes by F. Pollock and F. W. Maitland, *The History of English Law before the Time of Edward I* (2 vols., 1895, rev. 1968), in which the foundations are admirably displayed. To this, Sir W. Holdsworth's second volume in his *History of English Law* (12 vols., 1922–38, with later revisions) will be found the proper sequel. Much valuable material will be found in the introductions and documents published from 1889 by the Selden Society.

2. Biographies of Statesmen

The lives of individual statesmen which yield valuable information are many and will be found conveniently listed in the bibliographies to the *Cambridge Medieval History*, vol. vii (1932), 894–5; vol. viii (1936), 905–7. A few of the most important are S. Armitage-Smith, *John of Gaunt* (1904); J. E. Lloyd, *Owen Glendower* (1931); H. B. Workman, *John Wyclif* (2 vols., 1926); K. H. Vickers, *Humphrey, Duke of Gloucester* (1907); R. J. Mitchell, *John Tiptoft* (1938), and P. M. Kendall, *Warwick the Kingmaker* (1957).

3. Religion and Religious Thought

This section covers (*a*) general works; (*b*) the secular clergy; (*c*) the regular clergy.

(*a*) *General works*. Hastings's *Encyclopaedia of Religion and Ethics* (13 vols., 1908–27) is an invaluable work of reference, while J. P. Whitney's *Bibliography of Church History* (Historical Association Leaflet lv, 1923) is helpful.

A highly selected list of references is all that can be given concerning the Church in the fourteenth and fifteenth centuries. A good general sketch will be found in *The English Church in the XIV and XV Centuries (1272–1486)*, by W. W. Capes (1900). This may be supplemented on the constitutional side by the work of H. M. Gwatkin, *Church and State to the Death of Queen Anne* (1917). Conditions in the fourteenth century are examined by W. A. Pantin in *The English Church in the Fourteenth Century* (1955), in the classic study by G. M. Trevelyan, *England in the Age of Wycliffe* (1899), in H. B. Workman, *John Wyclif* (2 vols., 1926), and in K. B. McFarlane, *John Wycliffe and the Beginnings of English Nonconformity* (1952). Fifteenth-century developments are treated in J. A. F. Thomson, *The Later Lollards, 1414–1520* (1965), and in G. A. Leff, *Heresy in the Later Middle Ages* (1967).

(*b*) *The secular clergy*. For much information, not always well arranged, see E. L. Cutts, *Parish Priests and their People* (1898). To this may be added F. A. Gasquet, *Parish Life in Mediaeval England* (1906), which is corrected and supplemented by a number of articles by G. G. Coulton, conveniently collected in *Ten Medieval Studies* (1930), and in *Medieval Studies: First Series* (2nd edn., rev. with three appendixes, 1915). The economic position of the clergy is admirably discussed by H. G. Richardson in 'The Parish Clergy of the Thirteenth and Fourteenth Centuries', *Trans. Royal Hist. Soc.*, xi (1912), 89–128. The relation between priest and people is the subject of B. L. Manning's study, *The People's Faith in the Time of Wyclif* (1919). A wide range of material is surveyed by G. G. Coulton in his *Medieval Panorama* (1938), 137–206. The two volumes by G. R. Owst, *Preaching in Medieval England* (1926) and *Literature and Pulpit in Medieval England* (1933, 1961) are invaluable.

(*c*) *The regular clergy: monks and monasticism*. The best introduction to this subject is a small monograph by A. H. Thompson in the 'Cambridge Manuals of Science and Literature' entitled *English Monasteries* (1913). After this the various works by D. Knowles are invaluable, viz. *The Religious Orders in England*, vol. ii: *The End of the Middle Ages* (1955); *Medieval Religious Houses, England and Wales* (with R. N. Hadcock, 1953, 1972), and a catalogue of *Religious Houses of Medieval England* (1940). Although it does not deal with this period, the same writer's *The Monastic Order in England* (1940, 1963) is most valuable, especially for its section on the 'Work and Influence of the Monks', pp. 448–560. For a detailed and fascinating study of women in religion see E. Power, *Medieval English Nunneries* (1922). The architectural history of the monasteries is discussed by A. H. Thompson (above), by D. H. S. Cranage, *The Home of the Monk* (1926), and by R. L. Palmer, *English Monasteries in the Middle Ages* (1930).

For more detailed information reference may be made to the various Bishops' Registers, many of which have been printed by the Canterbury and York Society; to the many Visitation Records such as those edited by A. H. Thompson, *Visitations of Religious Houses in the Diocese of Lincoln, 1420–1436* (1914), or to the monastic chronicles such as may be found in the Rolls Series. For a picture of the day-to-day administration of ecclesiastical affairs, see for example *The Register of Henry Chichele, Archbishop of Canterbury*, ed. by E. F. Jacob, 4 vols. (1938–47) or *Canterbury Administration*, ed. by Irene J. Churchill, 2 vols. (1933).

For the friars much may be learned from *The Early English Friars Preachers* by Father W. A. Hinnebusch (Rome, 1951). There are also many authoritative works on the friars by A. G. Little, and more recently J. R. H. Moorman has studied *The Grey Friars in Cambridge 1225–1538* (1952) and produced a full-scale work on the *History of the Franciscan Order to 1517* (1968). For the Augustinian order, see A. Gwynn, *The English Austin Friars in the Time of Wyclif* (1940), H. E. Salter, *Chapters of the Augustinian Canons*, Oxford Hist. Soc. 74 (1920), and F. Roth, *The English Austin Friars, 1249–1538*, ii (New York, 1961).

4. Science and Scientific Thought

The history of English science in this period remains to be written. The following works may be consulted, but the information they give about English conditions is very meagre. The fullest outline is L. Thorndike, *A History of Magic and Experimental Science* (6 vols., New York, 1923–58), and this may be supplemented by his *Science and Thought in the Fifteenth Century* (New York, 1929). The best popular account is that of W. C. D. Dampier-Whetham (later Sir William Dampier), *History of Science and its Relations with Philosophy and Religion* (1929, rev. 1942), or his *Shorter History of Science* (1944). Some evidence of the wealth of fifteenth-century manuscript material awaiting investigation will be found in H. S. Bennett's article on 'Science and Information in English Writings of the Fifteenth Century', *MLR* xxxix (1944), 1–8, while Mrs. D. W. Singer has made an exhaustive survey of alchemical material in her *Catalogue of Latin and Vernacular Alchemical Manuscripts in Great Britain and*

Ireland dating from before the XVI Century (3 vols., Brussels, 1928–31). A list of alchemical poems will be found in Carleton Brown and R. H. Robbins, *The Index of Middle English Verse* (1943) and its *Supplement*, by Robbins and J. L. Cutler (1965). The beginner will find excellent material on the subject of alchemy in J. Read, *Prelude to Chemistry: An Outline of Alchemy, its Literature and Relationships* (1936), and in F. S. Taylor, *The Alchemists* (New York, 1949).

The art and practice of medicine are dealt with in the following: J. J. Walsh, *Medieval Medicine* (1920); H. P. Cholmeley, *John of Gaddesden and the Rosa Medicinae* (1912); G. Henslow, *Medical Works of the Fourteenth Century* (1894); C. Singer, *A Short History of Medicine* (1928); M. J. Hughes, *Woman Healers in Medieval Life and Literature* (New York, 1943), and D. Guthrie, *A History of Medicine* (1945, 1958).

Fifteenth-century translations of medical works have been published by the EETS: *Lanfranc's Cirurgie*, edited from the texts of 1396 and 1420 by R. von Fleischhacker (OS 102, 1894), John of Arderne's *Fistula in Ano*, edited with an introduction by Sir D'Arcy Power (OS 139, 1910) and *The Cyrurgie of Guy de Chauliac*, i, edited by M. S. Ogden (265, 1971). A full account by Power of Arderne's other works will be found in the *Seventeenth Annual International Congress of Medicine*, 1913, Section 23, pp. 107–33. The history of the Black Death and other outbreaks of plague in England is admirably dealt with in great detail by J. F. D. Shrewsbury in his *History of Bubonic Plague in the British Isles* (1970). Plague pamphlets by a number of medieval writers are listed and evaluated by K. Sudhoff, *Archiv für Geschichte der Medizin*, iii (1910), 58–80. The English manuscripts are described on pp. 297–303. A further treatment with valuable references will be found in Mrs. D. W. Singer's article, 'Some Plague Tractates (Fourteenth and Fifteenth Centuries)', *Proceedings of the Royal Society of Medicine* (Section of the History of Medicine), ix (1916), 159–212.

The knowledge of the world and its phenomena at this time is best seen from Trevisa's translation of Bartholomew the Englishman's *De Proprietatibus Rerum*. This work was finished in 1398, and first printed by W. de Worde (*c*. 1495). A 'newly corrected, enlarged and amended' edition by Stephen Batman was published by T. East in 1582 under the title of *Batman upon Bartholomew*. A facsimile reprint of these two editions has been made (Ann Arbor, 1933). A modern edition of Trevisa's work is in preparation under the general editorship of M. C. Seymour. A selection, together with a useful introduction, has been made by R. Steele, *Medieval Lore* (1905). This and other encyclopedias are well discussed by C.-V. Langlois, *La Connaissance de la nature et du monde au moyen âge* (Paris, 1911), where a full bibliography will also be found.

5. Education and Culture

All study of medieval education of a pre-university stage must begin with the works of A. F. Leach. *The Schools of Medieval England* (2nd edn., 1916) is the best single volume, although it is not conveniently arranged. His *Educational Charters and Documents, 598 to 1909* (1911) contains much essential matter. His final conclusions will be found in 'Some Results of Research in the History of Education in England' in *Proceedings of the British Academy*, vi (1915), 433–80. In addition, many valuable contributions were made by him to the *VCH*, while *English Schools at the Reformation, 1546–8* (1896) carries forward his researches outside this period. His work and historical method have frequently been criticized, but are defended by W. N. Chaplin in *The Journal of Educational Studies*, ii (1962–3).

Much confusion on medieval education is dispelled by the studies of G. G. Coulton, 'Monastic Schools in the Middle Ages', *Medieval Studies*, x (1913), and 'Religious Education before the Reformation' in *Ten Medieval Studies* (1930), 108–22. F. Watson's *The English Grammar Schools to 1660* (1908) outlines the late medieval curriculum, and D. Gardiner's *English Girlhood at School* (1929) has a pleasant chapter on women's education, while that available to the laity is dealt with by R. B. Hepple, *Medieval Education in England* (1932). There is an informative article by L. Thorndyke in *Speculum*, xv (1940), 400–8, entitled 'Elementary and Secondary Education in the Middle Ages'. The most extended treatment of the curriculum is provided by T. W. Baldwin in a small volume, *William Shakspere's Petty School* (Urbana, 1943), and in two massive volumes, *William Shakspere's Small Latine and Lesse Greek* (Urbana, 1944). Baldwin is dealing with sixteenth-century conditions, but much concerning earlier practice emerges from his tomes. For a judicious survey see G. R. Potter, 'Education in the

Fourteenth and Fifteenth Centuries', *Cambridge Medieval History*, vii (1936), 688–717, and an article by J. W. Adamson on 'The Extent of Literacy in the Fourteenth and Fifteenth Centuries', *Library*, 4th ser. x (1930), 162–93.

The standard history of the medieval university is by H. Rashdall, *The Universities of Europe in the Middle Ages* (2 vols. in 3, 1895; rev. edn. by F. M. Powicke and A. B. Emden, 1936). A good brief treatment will be found in R. S. Rait's *Life in the Medieval University* (1912), in C. P. McMahon's *Education in Fifteenth Century England* (1947), or in Rashdall's chapter 'The Medieval Universities' in *Cambridge Medieval History*, vi (1929), 539–61. Many valuable collections of documents dealing with the history of Oxford and Cambridge have been published. Among them are H. Anstey, *Munimenta Academica*, Rolls Series (2 vols., 1868), Anthony à Wood, *The History and Antiquities of the University of Oxford*, ed. by J. Gutch (2 vols. in 3, 1792–6), and H. E. Salter, *Medieval Oxford* (1936), relating to Oxford; and C. H. Cooper, *Annals of Cambridge* (3 vols., 1842), *Grace Book A*, ed. S. M. Leathes (1897), and the recent discovery of early constitutional documents by Father M. B. Hackett, *The Original Statutes of Cambridge University* (1970), relating to Cambridge. Reference should also be made to the publications of the Oxford Historical Society (1885 onwards) and the Cambridge Antiquarian Society (1859 onwards). The standard histories are those of C. E. Mallet, *A History of the University of Oxford* (3 vols., 1924–7), and J. B. Mullinger, *The University of Cambridge from the Earliest Times to the Royal Injunctions of 1535* (1873).

For the early history of the Scottish universities, see R. S. Rait, *The Universities of Aberdeen* (Aberdeen, 1895); R. G. Cant, *A Short History of the University of St. Andrews* (Edinburgh, 1926); J. D. Mackie, *The University of Glasgow* (1954).

6. Architecture and Allied Arts

Architecture

The best work for the reader wishing to study the art and architecture of this period is G. G. Coulton, *Art and the Reformation* (1928). For admirable studies of Gothic architecture and the internal fittings and decoration of churches, the works of F. Bond should be consulted, especially *Gothic Architecture in*

England (1905, 1912) and *An Introduction to English Church Architecture from the Eleventh to the Sixteenth Century* (2 vols., 1913). An original and stimulating view is provided by J. Harvey in his *Gothic England: A Survey of National Culture* (1947). For military architecture see A. H. Thompson, *Military Architecture in England during the Middle Ages* (1912). For domestic architecture see *Domestic Architecture in England from Richard II to Henry VIII* (2 parts, 1859) by J. H. Parker and T. H. Turner. There are valuable chapters on Domestic Architecture and on Military Architecture in A. L. Poole's *Medieval England* (1958), i. 37–47, 98–127.

Painting

Medieval painting and decoration are authoritatively treated by T. Borenius, 'English Primitives', *Proceedings of the British Academy*, xi (1925), 75–88, and by the same writer and E. W. Tristram in *English Medieval Painting* (Florence and Paris, 1927). Professor Tristram has also compiled an exhaustive history of wall paintings for this and earlier periods, *English Medieval Wall Painting* (3 vols., 1944–55). To these may be added A. Caiger-Smith, *English Medieval Mural Paintings* (1963) and M. D. Anderson, *Drama and Imagery in English Medieval Churches* (1963). A useful survey, with bibliographies, will be found in O. E. Saunders, *A History of English Art in the Middle Ages* (1932). See also J. Evans, *English Art 1307–1461* (1949) and M. Rickert, *Painting in Britain: the Middle Ages* (1954, 1965).

Sculpture

Medieval sculpture is fully dealt with by E. S. Prior and A. Gardner in *An Account of Medieval Figure-Sculpture in England* (1912); a convenient smaller work, fully illustrated, is by A. Gardner: *A Handbook of English Medieval Sculpture* (1935). Some light on the medieval craftsman will be found in M. D. Anderson, *The Medieval Carver* (1935), D. Knoop and G. P. Jones, *The Medieval Mason* (1933), and R. E. Swartout, *The Monastic Craftsman* (1932).

Stained Glass

For this consult the works of J. D. Le Couteur, *English Medieval Painted Glass* (1926), the well-illustrated work of Sir H. E. Read, *English Stained Glass* (1926), and C. Woodforde,

English Stained and Painted Glass (1954). For more detailed studies see other works by C. Woodforde, and those of F. Harrison, *The Painted Glass of York Minster* (1928), K. Harrison on that of King's College, Cambridge (1952), and an elaborate volume with magnificent illustrations of the windows of King's College by H. Wayment (1971). Another useful volume is the work of G. M. Rushforth, *Medieval Christian Imagery as illustrated by the Painted Windows of Great Malvern Priory Church* (1936).

7. Manuscripts

Medieval manuscripts comprise every kind of production from priceless illuminated folios down to wretchedly scribbled notes or *opuscula*. If an ability to read manuscripts is required the student should read F. Madan's article in *Medieval England*, ed. by H. W. C. Davis (1924), and practise by reading the examples provided by W. W. Skeat, *Twelve Facsimiles of Old English MSS.* (1892), C. Johnson and H. Jenkinson, *English Court Hand* (2 vols., 1915), C. E. Wright, *English Vernacular Hands from the Twelfth to the Fifteenth Centuries* (1960), or M. B. Parkes, *English Cursive Book Hands 1250–1500* (1969). For Latin texts the indispensable work is that of S. H. Thomson, *Latin Bookhands of the Later Middle Ages* (1970) which provides a wealth of facsimiles with transcriptions and notes. For help with abbreviations consult C. T. Martin, *The Record Interpreter* (1890, 1910) or A. Cappelli, *Dizionario di abbreviature* (Milan, 1899, 1912).

There is an admirable introduction to the study of illuminated manuscripts by Margaret Rickert in vol. i, pp. 561–605, of *The Text of the Canterbury Tales*, ed. by J. M. Manly and E. Rickert (Chicago, 8 vols., 1940). Other useful works are J. H. Middleton, *Illuminated Manuscripts* (1892); J. A. Herbert, *Illuminated Manuscripts* (1892); O. E. Saunders, *English Illumination* (Paris, 1928); C. R. Dodwell, *The Canterbury School of Illumination* (1954). One of the most beautiful is by E. G. Millar, *English Illuminated Manuscripts of the Fourteenth and Fifteenth Centuries* (Paris and Brussels, 1928). A survey of illuminated manuscripts in the Bodleian Library, by O. Pächt and J. J. G. Alexander, is in process of publication (vols. i–iii, 1966–72).

A number of facsimiles with coloured and collotype reproductions have been issued, such as *Queen Mary's Psalter*, ed. by

Sir G. F. Warner (1912); *The Luttrell Psalter*, ed. by E. G. Millar (1932); *The Romance of Alexander*, ed. by M. R. James (1933). Many volumes of the Roxburghe Club give complete or partial reproductions of famous illuminated manuscripts, while single pages have been reproduced from the collections in the British Museum and the Bodleian and are available in postcard or booklet form, or as colour transparencies.

8. Music

An approach to the study of medieval English music may best be made through F. Ll. Harrison, *Music in Medieval Britain* (1958), which is essentially a study of music and liturgy; and also through the relevant chapters of *The New Oxford History of Music*, ii and iii (1954, 1960). These works contain specialized bibliographies. The forthcoming second edition of G. Reese, *Music in the Middle Ages* should contain an authoritative account of the subject, as do the early chapters of Reese, *Music in the Renaissance* (New York, 1954). The only book which centres upon a single composer is S. W. Kenney, *Walter Frye and the Contenance Angloise* (Yale Studies in the History of Music, iii, New Haven, 1964). Secular music has been poorly served, but the following articles will provide a starting-point for further study: C. C. Olson, 'Chaucer and the Music of the Fourteenth Century', *Speculum*, xiv (1941), 64–92, and 'The Minstrels at the Court of Edward III', *PMLA* lvi (1941), 601–12. Outstanding for the latter part of the fifteenth century is J. Stevens, *Music and Poetry in the Early Tudor Court* (1961).

For editions of English music in the fifteenth century, five volumes of the series *Musica Britannica* are relevant: vol. iv, *Mediaeval Carols*, ed. J. Stevens (2nd edn., 1958); vol. viii, *John Dunstable: Complete Works*, ed. M. F. Bukofzer (2nd edn., 1970); vols. x–xii, *The Eton Choirbook*, ed. F. Ll. Harrison (1956–61). In the series Early English Church Music, vol. viii is the first of a group of volumes entitled *Fifteenth-Century Liturgical Music*, ed. A. Hughes. The Old Hall Manuscript is newly edited by A. Hughes and Margaret Bent, in the series *Corpus Mensurabilis Musicae*, vol. xlvi (1969), and the works of Walter Frye are edited in vol. xix of the same series by S. W. Kenney, and those of Robert Fayrfax in vol. xvii, by E. B. Warren. Valuable material will be found in the three volumes of Sir John Stainer, *Early Bodleian Music* (1901), and the two volumes of *Early*

English Harmony, ed. Dom Anselm Hughes and H. E. Wooldridge (vols. xvii and xxxv of the *Publications of the Plainsong and Mediaeval Music Society*, 1897, 1912).

9. Social Life

(a) General

The social history of these centuries is admirably summarized by G. M. Trevelyan in his *English Social History* (1944). His *England in the Age of Wycliffe* (1899, 1909) should also be consulted. The best introduction to the Chaucerian period is the brilliant survey of G. G. Coulton, *Chaucer and his England* (1908, 1965). A new bibliography was provided by T. W. Craik (1963). For the fifteenth century W. Denton's *England in the Fifteenth Century* (1888) is still useful, as is also J. E. T. Rogers's *Six Centuries of Work and Wages* (2 vols., 1884, 1886). Miss A. Abram's two volumes, *English Life and Manners in the Later Middle Ages* (1913) and *Social England in the Fifteenth Century* (1909), are full of information. V. Redstone's article in the *Transactions of the Royal Historical Society*, xvi (1902), 159–200, C. L. Kingsford's *Prejudice and Promise in Fifteenth-Century England* (1925), and the present writer's *The Pastons and their England* (1922, 1968) will give the necessary background for much of the century. Conditions in Wales are conveniently summarized by W. Rees, *South Wales and the March, 1284–1415* (1924).

There is much to be gleaned from the appropriate chapters of vol. ii of H. D. Traill's *Social England* (rev. edn., 6 vols., 1901–4), a well-illustrated work. A more scholarly account of general conditions is *Medieval England*, edited by A. L. Poole, for which see p. 259 above. *Wayfaring Life in the Middle Ages* (trans. 1889; 3rd edn. rev. and enlarged, 1925) by J. J. Jusserand provides in an attractive way more than its title would suggest, while much good desultory reading can be had in T. Wright's *A History of Domestic Manners and Sentiments in England* (1862), and the same author's *Womankind in Western Europe* (1869). The present writer's *Life on the English Manor: A Study of Peasant Conditions, 1150–1400* (1937, 1947) will be found useful for an account of conditions only slowly changing in this period.

Contemporary material of various kinds, illustrating the life and times of the period, will be found in G. G. Coulton, *Social Life in Britain from the Conquest to the Reformation* (1918); E. Rickert,

Chaucer's World, ed. C. C. Olson and M. M. Crow (New York, 1948); *English Historical Documents*, iv, *1327–1485*, ed. A. R. Myers (1969). For illustrations from manuscripts, see R. S. Loomis, *A Mirror of Chaucer's World* (Princeton, 1965); M. Hussey, *Chaucer's World* (1967); D. Hartley and M. M. Elliott, *Life and Work of the People of England: The Fourteenth Century; The Fifteenth Century* (2 vols., 1925, 1928).

(*b*) *Towns and Town Life*

A. S. Green's *Town Life in the Fifteenth Century* (2 vols., 1894) remains the best general work on the rise, growth, and organization of the English towns. Her work may be supplemented by that of M. Dormer Harris, *Town Life in an Old English Town* (1898) and by her edition of *The Coventry Leet Book*, EETS os 134, 135, 138, 146 (1907–13). Other good collections of local records which help to create the contemporary scene are: W. Hudson and J. C. Tingey, *Records of the City of Norwich* (2 vols., 1906–10); Hudson's *Leet Jurisdiction in Norwich*, Selden Soc., v (1892); M. Sellers, *York Memorandum Book*, Surtees Soc. (2 vols., 1912–15). Much help in understanding the medieval town will be gained from F. W. Maitland's illuminating study, *Township and Borough* (1898), and from the two volumes of M. Bateson's *Borough Customs*, Selden Soc. (1904–6).

Both Sir W. Besant, *Medieval London* (2 vols., 1906), and W. J. Loftie, *A History of London* (1884), give interesting accounts of medieval conditions and organizations. Much more detail is given in H. T. Riley's *Memorials of London and London Life*, A.D. *1276–1419* (2 vols., 1868), R. R. Sharpe's *London and the Kingdom* (3 vols., 1894–5), and the same author's series of *Calendars of Letter Books of the City of London* (1889–1912), of which Letter Books I, K, and L deal with this period, and should be consulted with his invaluable *Calendar of Wills proved . . . in the Court of Husting, London, 1258–1688* (2 vols., 1889–90). Further information will be found in the works of A. H. Thomas, *A Calendar of Select Pleas and Memoranda of the City of London, 1381–1412* (1932), *1413–1437* (1943), and of P. E. Jones, *1437–1482* (1954, 1961).

There is a valuable study of one aspect of town organization to be found in S. Thrupp, *The Merchant Class of Medieval London* (Chicago, 1948), and another in E. M. Carus-Wilson's *Medieval Merchant Adventurers* (1954). Chapter viii on 'Towns and Trade' in *Medieval England* (above, p. 259), i. 209–63, will be found useful, and *Street Life in Medieval England* by G. T. Jones, afterwards Salusbury (1939, 1948), has much to attract.

For the guilds of London the indispensable guide is G. Unwin, *The Gilds and Companies of London* (1908, 1938). Much information may be gained from *English Gilds*, ed. by J. Toulmin Smith and Lucy T. Smith, with an essay on guilds by L. Brentano, EETS os 40 (1870). For further details reference should be made to the individual histories of the several guilds, most of which are well furnished with documents and extracts from early records. See, for example, F. Consitt, *The London Weavers' Company* (1933); S. Thrupp, *The Bakers of London* (1933); M. Sellers, *The York Mercers and Merchant Adventurers* (Surtees Soc., 1918).

10. Chivalry

For a general account of chivalry the most convenient summary will be found in the article on 'Knighthood and Chivalry' in the *Encyclopaedia Britannica*, xv (1911 edn.) which corrects the earlier standard work of C. Mills, *History of Chivalry* (2 vols., 1826). Good short surveys will also be found in F. W. Cornish, *Chivalry* (1901), and in the chapter on chivalry by Miss A. Abram in the *Cambridge Medieval History*, vi (1929), 799–814. A collection of useful and learned essays on chivalry in various countries was edited by E. Prestage, *Chivalry* (1928), and was accompanied by a good bibliography. A comprehensive treatment, with up-to-date bibliography, is R. Barber, *The Knight and Chivalry* (1970).

Two outstanding French works are C.-V. Langlois, *La Société française au* XIIIe *siècle d'après dix romans d'aventure* (Paris, 1904), and the full-dress study by L. Gautier, *La Chevalerie* (Paris, 1884; new edn. 1900; trans. 1890). This work, based on a close acquaintance with the French romances, is the most detailed account of chivalry that has been written; and, despite certain stylistic peculiarities and its reliance almost entirely on French source material, is an indispensable book on this subject. A masterly account is given in S. Painter's *French Chivalry* (Baltimore, 1940), and some useful material will be found in *The Indian Summer of English Chivalry* (Durham, North Carolina, 1960) by A. B. Ferguson. Much information can also be had from reading such first-hand material as can be found in the

French and English romances, or in works such as those of Froissart and Malory. With these should be read *The Medieval Society Romances* (New York, 1924) by S. F. Barrow.

For the vexed problems of Courtly Love and the Courts of Love the early standard works are the originating study by G. Paris in *Romania*, xii (Paris, 1883) followed by W. A. Neilson's *Origins and Sources of the 'Court of Love'* (Harvard Studies in Philology 6, 1899), and J. F. Rowbotham, *The Troubadors and the Courts of Love* (1895). More recently, however, the whole concept of Courtly Love has come under fire, and use should be made of the series of studies by A. J. Denomy reviewing the position in *Medieval Studies*, vi (1944), 175–260; vii (1945), 107–49; and finally in *The Heresy of Courtly Love* (New York, 1947). E. Talbot Donaldson has an illuminating chapter on 'The Myth of Courtly Love' in *Speaking of Chaucer* (1970); and both this and an article by G. R. Coffman, 'Chaucer and Courtly Love once more', in *Speculum*, xx (1945) have useful bibliographies. There is also an informative article by J. F. Benton on 'The Court of Champagne as a Literary Centre' in *Speculum*, xxxvi (1961), as well as much on the subject in general in D. W. Robertson, *A Preface to Chaucer* (Princeton, 1963), 391–505, and P. Dronke, *Medieval Latin and the Rise of European Love-Lyric* (2 vols., 1965, 1966).

VI. INDIVIDUAL AUTHORS

John of Arderne, 1307–1380?

The life and works of this celebrated surgeon have been studied by Sir D'Arcy Power, who edited Arderne's *Treatises of Fistula in Ano*, EETS os 139 (1910). A full account of Arderne's other works is given by the same author in the *Reports of the Seventeenth Annual International Congress of Medicine*, 1913, Section 23, pp. 107–33.

George Ashby, *c.* 1390–1475

His works were first edited by Mary Bateson, EETS ES 76 (1899). Corrections of this edition by F. Holthausen will be found in *Anglia*, xlv (1921), 77–104, together with Ashby's 'Prisoner's Reflections'. In 'The *Liber de dictis philosophorum antiquorum* and Common Proverbs', C. F. Bühler discusses the use made of proverbs in Ashby's poems: see *PMLA* lxv (1950), 282–9.

WILLIAM ATKYNSON, d. 1509

The *De Imitatione Christi* of Thomas à Kempis was translated by Atkynson (books i–iii) and by Margaret, Countess of Richmond and Derby (book iv). Books i–iii were printed by de Worde, *c.* 1502; by R. Pynson in 1503; and all four books by Pynson in 1504. The whole was edited by J. K. Ingram, EETS ES 63 (1893).

JOHN AUDELAY, *fl.* 1426

E. K. Whiting's edition of the *Poems of John Audelay*, EETS 184 (1931) supersedes that of J. O. Halliwell-Phillipps, edited for the Percy Society, xiv (1844). There is an article on 'Der Dichter John Audeley und sein werk' by J. E. Wülfing in *Anglia*, xviii (1896), 175–217. The carols were edited and annotated by E. K. Chambers and F. Sidgwick (1911), while W. F. Storck and R. Jordan edited the text of 'De Tribus Regibus Mortuis' with a brief introduction in *ES* xliii (1910), 177–88.

ANTHONY BABYNTON, d. 1537

A translation (of about 1475) was made by Babynton of Christine de Pisan's *Epistle of Othéa to Hector*. The only manuscript is in the British Museum, Harleian 838. It was identified and described by H. N. MacCracken in *MLN* xxiv (1909), 122–3. The work was also translated earlier by Stephen Scrope (q.v.).

GILBERT BANESTER, *c.* 1420–87

His *Tale of Guiscardo and Ghismonda* (*c.* 1440–5) has been edited by H. G. Wright in *Tales from the Decameron*, EETS 205 (1937). An early edition of 1597, *Certaine Worthye Manuscript Poems*, was reprinted in Edinburgh (1812). A short carol of his is printed by R. L. Greene, *The Early English Carols* (1935). For the life of Banester, Master of the Children of the Chapel

Royal, see W. H. Grattan Flood, *Early Tudor Composers* (1925), 13–16.

John Barbour, 1316?–95

The Actes and Life of the most Victorious Conqueror, Robert Bruce King of Scotland has survived in two late-fifteenth-century manuscripts, and was first printed in Edinburgh in 1571 and again in 1616 and 1620. The best modern edition is that of W. W. Skeat, EETS ES 11, 21, 29, 55 (1870–89). A revision of this edition was made by Skeat for the STS in 1893–4 (2 vols., nos. 31, 32). Another modern edition, with good bibliography, was edited by W. M. MacKenzie (1909). The poem has been translated by G. Eyre-Todd (1907), and by M. Macmillan (1914).

Studies of Barbour will be found in B. ten Brink and Schofield, *CHEL*, vol. ii, as well as in T. F. Henderson, *Scottish Vernacular Literature* (rev. edn. 1910), G. J. Neilson, *Barbour* (1900), and K. Wittig, *The Scottish Tradition in Literature* (Edinburgh, 1958), 11–32. An excellent comparison of Barbour and Henry the Minstrel will be found in W. A. Craigie, 'Barbour and Blind Harry', *Scottish Review*, xxii (1893), 173–90.

Juliana Berners *or* Barnes, *fl.* 1400–50?

The Book of Hawking, Hunting and Blasing of Arms (known as the Book of St. Albans) was first printed at St. Albans (1486) and again with the addition of the *Treatyse of Fysshynge* (W. de Worde, 1496). The hunting section is attributed to 'Dam Julyans Barnes'; but who she was, and even the correct form of the name, are unknown. A facsimile of the 1486 edition was issued by W. Blades (1881; reprinted 1905), and of the *Treatyse of Fysshynge*, edited by M. G. Watkins (1880). An important article on the book by E. F. Jacob appeared in *JRLB* xxviii (1944), 99–118. The hunting section was separately edited by G. Tilander (Karlshamn, 1964). A translation was made by W. van Wyck (New York, 1933), in which he traced the source material of the *Treatyse of Fysshynge*; A. L. Binns has pointed out sources of the earlier treatises, *JRLB* xxxiii (1950), 15–25, while E. Pafort has investigated the early editions by de Worde, *SP* v (1952). The best discussion of sources and authorship is by Rachel Hands in *RES* NS xviii (1967), 373–86.

BENET OF NORWICH, *fl.* 1340

A translation of the pseudo-Aristotelian *ABC* (commonly attributed to Burgh) has been shown to be by Benet. See M. Förster, *Archiv*, ci (1898), 29–64.

THOMAS BETSON, *fl.* 1500

In 1500 W. de Worde printed 'a ryght profytable treatyse compendiously drawen out of many & dyvers wrytynges of holy men' by T. Betson. It consists of the catechism, occasional prayers, excerpts from St. Bernard, &c. It has been reprinted in facsimile (Cambridge, 1905).

HECTOR BOECE, 1465?–1536

His work on Scottish history was translated into Scottish prose by John Bellenden (1490?–1550) about 1530–3 and published (1540?) under the title *Chroniklis of Scotland*. Later it was rendered into English prose for Holinshed's *Chronicle* by W. Harrison (1577). For comments on Boece's work see F. Brie, *Die nationale Literatur Schottlands* (Halle, 1937). The *Chroniklis* have been edited for the STS in 2 vols., vol. i by R. W. Chambers and E. C. Batho, 3rd ser. 10 (1938), and vol. ii by E. C. Batho and H. W. Husbands, 15 (1941).

OSBERN BOKENHAM, *c.* 1392–*c.* 1464

His lives of saintly women were first edited by Lord Clive in a black-letter reprint for the Roxburghe Club (1835) together with an introduction. They were also collected by C. Horstmann in vol. 1 of Kölbing's Altenglische Bibliothek (Heilbronn, 1883), and more recently in a definitive text, with a long introduction, by M. S. Serjeantson, EETS 206 (1938). This edition has a facsimile of a page of the unique manuscript. Bokenham also wrote a geographical account of England in a prose translation of Higden's *Polychronicon*, entitled *Mappula Angliae*. This was edited with a brief introduction by C. Horstmann, *ES* x (1887), 1–40.

The sources of Bokenham's legends are briefly discussed by G. Willenberg, *ES* xii (1889), 1–37. S. Moore has two interesting articles on Bokenham and others, 'Patrons of Letters in Norfolk and Suffolk, *c.* 1450', *PMLA* xxvii (1912), 188–207, xxviii (1913), 79–105. Further remarks on Bokenham will be found in the present writer's 'The Author and his Public in the Fourteenth and Fifteenth Centuries', *Essays and Studies by Members of the English Association*, xxiii (1938), 7–24 and in a note by M. B. Hackett, O.S.A., in *Notes and Queries*, ccvi (1961), 246–7.

THOMAS BRAMPTON, *fl.* 1414

The paraphrase of the *Seven Penitential Psalms in English* attributed to Brampton (about 1414) was edited with an introduction and notes by W. H. Black, Percy Soc., no. 7 (1842).

BENEDICT BURGH, *c.* 1413–83

Burgh's best-known works are his translations, known as the *Magnus Cato* and the *Parvus Cato*. These have been admirably edited by M. Förster, who published a text with a critical discussion and a bibliography of the manuscripts in *Archiv*, cxv (1905), 298–323 and cxvi (1906), 25–34. A more recent edition is that of P. Wilson (1924). The earliest printed edition (containing both works) was published by Caxton (1477). Facsimiles of these were issued in 1906.

Burgh's other effusions are: *A Christmasse Game*, first edited by T. Wright, *Specimens of Old English Carols*, Percy Soc. (1841), 28–31, and again by E. Flügel in *Anglia*, xiv (1892), 463–6; his *Praise of Lydgate* appears in R. Steele's edition of *Secrees of Old Philisoffres* (below) and E. P. Hammond's *English Verse between Chaucer and Surrey* (1927), 189–90. Together with Lydgate he made a verse translation of the pseudo-Aristotelian *Secreta Secretorum*, known as *Secrees of Old Philisoffres*, edited with introduction by R. Steele, EETS ES 66 (1894). This edition has a facsimile page from Sloane MS. 2464.

JOHN CAPGRAVE, 1393–1464

Capgrave's verse translation of the life of St. Katharine of Alexandria was edited by C. Horstmann for the EETS, OS 100 (1893). An account of Capgrave's life was contributed to this volume by F. J. Furnivall, who added some characteristically pungent comments on Horstmann's editorial shortcomings.

The best known of Capgrave's prose works, *The Chronicle of England*, was edited by F. C. Hingeston (Rolls Series, 1858). It has a long introduction and a valuable bibliography of Capgrave's works, pp. xxi–ix. A full and critical account of this text and of the verse life of St. Katharine (above) was given by W. Dibelius in *Anglia*, xxiii (1900), 153–94, 323–75, 427–72, and xxiv (1901), 211–63, 269–308. *The Lives of St. Augustine and St. Gilbert of Sempringham* have been edited by J. Munro in EETS os 140 (1910), while Capgrave's description of Rome, under the title of *Ye Solace of Pilgrimes*, has been edited by C. A. Mills (1911). It has a valuable introduction by H. M. Bannister on Capgrave's manuscripts. Knowledge of these has been greatly increased by an article in the *Transactions of the Cambridge Bibliographical Society*, v (1969–70), 1–35, by P. J. Lucas entitled 'John Capgrave, O.S.A. (1393–1464), Scribe and Publisher'. A fifteenth-century collection of legends, translated by Capgrave and others under the title of *Nova Legenda Angliae*, was printed with additions by W. de Worde (1516). They were re-edited by C. Horstmann (2 vols., 1901). A new examination of the *Nova Legenda* by P. J. Lucas is to be issued in *The Library*.

Facsimile pages of Capgrave's manuscripts form the frontispieces of the editions of *The Chronicle of England* and of *The Lives of St. Augustine and St. Gilbert* mentioned above.

W. Caxton, *c.* 1422–1491

This entry comprises: (1) fifteenth-century editions of works translated by Caxton; (2) fifteenth-century editions of other works printed by Caxton; (3) facsimiles; (4) modern editions of Caxton's translations; (5) Caxton's life and works; (6) general criticism; (7) Caxton's language and style.

1. *Works translated by Caxton*

The early editions of Caxton's own works are given in alphabetical order of the principal word of each title: *Ars Moriendi* (*c.* 1491; W. de Worde, *c.* 1497); *The Arte and Crafte to knowe well to dye* (*c.* 1490); *Blanchardyn and Eglantine* (*c.* 1489); *The Book callid Cathon* (*c.* 1483); *Charles the Grete* (1485); *The Curial* (*c.* 1484); *The Doctrinal of Sapyence* (*c.* 1489); *Eneydos* *c*). 1490); *The Boke of the Fayttes of Armes and of Chyualrye* (*c.* 1489–90); *Fables of Esope* (1484; Pynson, 1497, 1500); *The Four Sonnes of Aymon* (*c.* 1489; W. de Worde 1504); *The Game and Playe of the Chesse* (Bruges, *c.* 1475; Westminster, *c.* 1483); *The Golden Legend* (*c.* 1483, *c.* 1487); *The Book of Good Maners* (1487; Pynson, 1494, 1500); *The Recuyell of the Historyes of Troye* (Bruges, 1473–4); *The History of Jason* (*c.* 1477); *The Knyght of the Toure* (1484); *The Lyf of Saynt Wenefryde* (1485); *The Mirrour of the World* (*c.* 1481, *c.* 1490); *Le Morte Darthur*, Malory, adapted by Caxton (1485); *The Book of the Ordre of Chyvalry or Knyghthode* (*c.* 1484); *Parys and Vyenne* (1485; Antwerp, 1492); *Polychronicon*, Trevisa's translation with Caxton's continuation (*c.* 1482); *Reynard the Foxe* (1481, 1489; Pynson, 1494; W. de Worde, 1525?); *The Book Ryal* (*c.* 1487); *The Siege and Conquest of Jherusalem* or *Godefroy of Boloyne* (1481). In addition, Caxton's translation of the *Vitas Patrum* of St. Jerome was printed after his death by W. de Worde (1495), while his translation of *Ovyde hys Book of Methamorphose* (trans. 1480) was not printed in full until 1968, when it was issued in a facsimile of the unique manuscript; the latter part had been printed in 1924.

2. *Other Works printed by Caxton*

Anelida, *The Compleynt of Anelida* and other Chaucerian short poems (*c.* 1477); Boethius, *De consolatione philosophie* (*c.* 1478); *The Book of Curtesye* (*c.* 1477–8); *Canterbury Tales* (*c.* 1478, 1484); *Parvus Catho* with *Magnus Catho* (*c.* 1477, 1481); *Chronicles of Englond* (1480, 1482); Lydgate, *The Chorle and the Birde* (*c.* 1477); *Commemoratio Lamentationis . . . Beate Marie* (*c.* 1487); Gower, *Confessio Amantis* (1483); *The Court of Sapience* (*c.* 1480); *Les quatre derrenieres choses* [i.e. *The four last things*] (Bruges, 1475–6; Westminster, 1479); *The Dictes or Sayengis of the Philosophres* (1477, *c.* 1479, *c.* 1487); *Directorium Sacerdotum* (*c.* 1487, *c.* 1489); Mirk, *The Festial* (1483, *c.* 1491); *The Fifteen Oes*, prayers in English and Latin (*c.* 1491); *The Governayle of Helthe* (*c.* 1489); *Le Recueil des histoires de Troyes* (Bruges, 1475–6); *Hore beate Virginis Marie* (*c.* 1477, *c.* 1480, *c.* 1489, *c.* 1490); *Horologium Sapientie* (*c.* 1491); Lydgate, *The Hors, the Shepe, and the Ghoos*, (*c.* 1477); *The Book of Fame*, i.e. Chaucer's *House of Fame* (*c.* 1484); *Infancia Saluatoris* (*c.* 1477); Lydgate, *The Lyf of our Lady* (*c.* 1484); *The Moral Proverbes of Cristyne* [de Pisan] (1478); *The Temple of Bras* [Chaucer's *Parlement of Foules*] (*c.* 1477); *Septenuaire des pseaulmes de penitence* (Bruges, 1475–6); *The Pylgremage of the Sowle* (1483); *Quattuor Sermones* (*c.* 1483); *Speculum vite Cristi, the Myrroure of the Blessyd Lyf of Jhesu Cryste* (*c.* 1486); Lydgate, *Stans puer ad mensam*, &c. (*c.* 1477); *Statutes of Henry VII* (*c.* 1480); Lydgate, *The Temple of Glas* (*c.* 1477); Chaucer, *Troylus and Cresede* (*c.* 1484); *Tullius of Olde Age, &c.* (1481); *Vocabulary in French and English* (*c.* 1480).

3. *Facsimiles*

Ars Moriendi, ed. E. W. B. Nicholson (1891); *The Arte and Crafte to knowe well to dye*, ed. E. Lumley (1875); *The Book of Curtesye*, ed. F. Jenkinson (1907); *Parvus Cato* with *Magnus Cato*, ed. F. Jenkinson (1906); Lydgate, *The Churl and the Bird*, ed. F. Jenkinson (1906); *The Dictes and Sayings of the Philosophers*, ed. W. Blades (1877); *The Game of the Chesse*, ed. V. Figgins (1855); *The Recuyell of the Historyes of Troye*, ed. H. O. Sommer (1894); *Le Morte Darthur*, ed. H. O. Sommer (1889–91); Lydgate, *The Temple of Glass*, ed. F. Jenkinson (1905); *Vocabulary*, ed. J. C. T. Oates and L. Harmer (1964).

4. *Modern Editions of Caxton's Translations*

Aesop, *Fables*, ed. R. T. Lenaghan (1967); *Blanchardyn and Eglantine*, ed. L. Kellner, EETS ES 58 (1890); *Charles the Grete*, ed. S. J. H. Herrtage, EETS ES 36–7 (1880–1); *The Curial*, ed. P. Meyer and F. J. Furnivall, EETS ES 54 (1888); *Eneydos*, ed. W. T. Culley and F. J. Furnivall, EETS ES 57 (1890); *The Book of Fayttes of Armes and of Chyualrye*, ed. A. T. P. Byles, EETS 189 (1932); *The Foure Sonnes of Aymon*, ed. O. Richardson, EETS ES 44–5 (1884–5); *The Game of Chess*, ed. W. E. A. Axon (1883); *The Golden Legend*, ed. F. S. Ellis (Kelmscott Press, 3 vols., 1892); *The Recuyell of the Historyes of Troye*, ed. H. O. Sommer (1894); *The History of Jason*, ed. J. Munro, EETS ES 111 (1913); *Le Morte Darthur*, ed. H. O. Sommer (1889–90); *The Knight of the Tower*, ed. M. Y. Offord, EETS SS 2 (1971); *The Mirrour of the World*, ed. O. H. Prior, EETS ES 110 (1913); *The Book of the Ordre of Chyualry*, ed. A. T. P. Byles, EETS 168 (1926); *Ovyde his Methamorphose*, six books, ed. S. Gaselee and M. T. B. Brett-Smith (1924); *Paris and Vienne*, ed. MacEdward Leach, EETS 234 (1957); *Polychronicon*, ed. C. Babington and J. R. Lumby, Rolls Series (1865–86); *Reynard the Fox*, ed. N. F. Blake, EETS 263 (1970); *Life of St. Winifred*, ed. C. Horstmann (1880); *Godeffroy of Boloyne*, or *The Siege and Conqueste of Jerusalem*, ed. M. N. Colvin, EETS ES 64 (1893).

5. *Caxton's Life and Works*

The indispensable works for the study of Caxton as a typographer are W. Blades, *The Life and Typography of William Caxton* (2 vols., 1861–3; rev. edn. in one volume, 1882); S. de

Ricci, *A Census of Caxtons* (BS, 1909); E. G. Duff, *William Caxton* (1905) and *Fifteenth Century English Books* (BS, 1917); and N. F. Blake, *Caxton and his World* (1969). A full list with details of all Caxton's publications will be found in the above volumes. Of less importance are H. R. Plomer, *Caxton* (1925) and G. P. Winship, *William Caxton* (1909, rev. edn. Berkeley, 1937). W. J. B. Crotch published Caxton's *Prologues and Epilogues*, together with a valuable biographical article on Caxton, in EETS 176 (1928) and he also printed some new documents in *Library*, 4th ser. vii (1927), 387–401; viii (1928), 426–55; ix (1928), 48–52. The work of N. S. Aurner, *Caxton, a Study of the Literature of the First English Press* (1926) is still valuable, but has been superseded by N. F. Blake, who in *Caxton and his World* (above), together with a number of articles published during 1962–9, has greatly increased our knowledge.

6. *General Criticism*

A good deal of critical comment will be found in the works of N. S. Aurner and N. F. Blake mentioned above. In addition two important articles are those of H. B. Lathrop, 'The First English Printers and their Patrons', *Library*, 4th ser. iii (1922), 69–96, and A. T. P. Byles's 'William Caxton as a Man of Letters', *Library*, 4th ser. xv (1934), 1–25. More recently D. B. Sands has discussed 'Caxton as a Literary Critic', *PBSA* li (1957), 312–18, while C. F. Bühler considers the problem of *Caxton and his Critics* (Syracuse University Press, 1960). The present writer's article 'Caxton and his Public', *RES* xix (1943), 113–19, discusses the nature and education of the reading public of Caxton's day. A full list of writers on this topic will be found in N. F. Blake's 'Select Bibliography' on pp. 241–9 of *Caxton and his World* (1969).

7. *Caxton's Language and Style*

Caxton's language and style have been studied notably by L. Kellner in an exhaustive introduction to *Blanchardyn and Eglantine*, EETS ES 58 (1890). P. de Reul in his *Language of Caxton's Reynard* (1901) deals with problems of syntax, and E. Flügel discusses 'Caxton's Old English Words', *MP* i (1903), 343. R. R. Aurner studies *Caxton and the English Sentence*, University of Wisconsin Studies in Language and Literature 18 (1923), 23–59. A. T. P. Byles has some interesting remarks on

'Caxton's Method and Style as a Translator' in his EETS edition of *The Book of the Ordre of Chyualry* (above). H. Wiencke, *Die Sprache Caxtons* (Leipzig, 1930), may also be consulted. In *Caxton and his World* (1969), N. F. Blake makes a valuable study of Caxton's language and style, and this, together with the references he gives there, is the best starting point for this part of Caxton's work. His introduction to his edition of *Reynard* (above) is important for the influence of Dutch on Caxton's vocabulary.

Geoffrey Chaucer, *c.* 1340–*c.* 1400

This entry comprises: (1) early editions of (*a*) Chaucer's works, (*b*) Chaucerian 'Apocrypha'; (2) manuscripts; (3) facsimiles; (4) editions of complete works; (5) editions of particular works; (6) biography; (7) general criticism; (8) books and articles on special aspects: (*a*) canon and chronology, (*b*) indebtedness to other authors, (*c*) prose writings, (*d*) diction, (*e*) metre; (9) bibliographies and concordances.

1. *Early Editions*

(*a*) *Chaucer's Works*

The early editions of Chaucer's works are as follows: *The Canterbury Tales*, first printed by Caxton in 1478 and 1484, by W. de Worde in 1498, and by Pynson in 1492 and 1526. The relations of these prints one to the other and to the manuscripts have been discussed by W. W. Greg in *PMLA* xxxix (1924), 737–61.

The earliest editions of other works (in alphabetical order) are as follows: *Chaucer's ABC* (Speght, 1602); *Anelida and Arcite* (Caxton, 1477?; Thynne, 1532); *Astrolabe* (Thynne, 1532); Boethius, *De Consolatione philosophie* (Caxton, 1478; Thynne, 1532); *The Book of the Duchesse* (Thynne, 1532); *Chaucer's Words to Adam* (Stow, 1561); *The Compleynt of Venus* (J. Notary, 1500?; Thynne, 1532); *Compleint to his Lady* (Stow, 1561); *Compleint to his Purs* (Caxton, 1477?; Thynne, 1532); *Compleynt unto Pite* (Thynne, 1532); *The Former Age* (Morris, Aldine Chaucer, 1866); *Fortune* (Caxton, 1477?; W. de Worde, 1515; Thynne, 1532); *Gentilesse* (Caxton, 1477?; Thynne, 1532); *Hous of Fame* (Caxton, 1484?; Pynson, 1526; Thynne, 1532); *Lak of Stedfastnesse* (Thynne, 1532); *Legend of Good Women* (Thynne, 1532);

Lenvoy à Buxton (J. Notary, 1500?; Thynne, 1532); *Lenvoy à Scogan* (Caxton, 1477?; Thynne, 1532); *Parlement of Foules* (Caxton, 1477?; Rastell, 1525?; Pynson, 1526); *Rosemounde* (*Athenæum*, i (1891), 440); *Truth* (Caxton, 1477?; W. de Worde, before 1519); *Troilus and Criseyde* (Caxton, 1484?; W. de Worde, 1517; Pynson, 1526; Thynne, 1532); *Womanly Noblesse* (*Athenæum*, i (1891), 742).

Poems partially written by Chaucer or of doubtful authorship are: *The Romaunt of the Rose* (Thynne, 1532); *Against Women Inconstant* (Stow, 1561); *Complaynt d'Amours* (*Academy*, i (1888), 307), and *Merciles Beaute* (Percy, *Reliques* (1767), ii. 11).

(*b*) *Chaucerian 'Apocrypha'*

The most important poems of the Chaucer 'Apocrypha' are as follows: *The Assembly of Ladies* (Thynne, 1532); *The Tale of Beryn* (Urry, 1721); *The Court of Love* (Stow, 1561); *The Craft of Lovers* (Stow, 1561); *The Cuckoo and the Nightingale* (Thynne, 1532); *The Flower and the Leaf* (Speght, 1598); *The Isle of Ladies* or *Chaucer's Dream* (Speght, 1598); *La Belle Dame sans Merci* (Pynson, 1526); *The Plowman's Tale* (Thynne, 1532).

2. *Manuscripts*

Many manuscripts of Chaucer's writings have survived, especially of the *Canterbury Tales*. Of these, Professor J. M. Manly traced some eighty-three, and a full account of them is given in the first two volumes of *The Text of the Canterbury Tales*, ed. by J. M. Manly and E. Rickert (Chicago, 8 vols., 1940). Valuable criticisms and appreciations of their work may be found in *The Year's Work in English Studies*, xxi (1940), 46–50, and in *RES* xviii (1942), 93–109, both by D. Everett, while R. K. Root's article in *SP* xxxviii (1941), 1–13, and that of G. Dempster, *PMLA* lxi (1946), 379–415, are both of importance. Use may also be made of the many publications of the Chaucer Society, e.g. *The Eight-Text Edition of the Canterbury Tales, with Remarks on . . . the Manuscripts* by W. W. Skeat (1909). For further help there is A. Brusendorff, *The Chaucer Tradition* (1925), and *The Manuscripts of Chaucer's Canterbury Tales* by W. S. McCormick and J. E. Heseltine (1933).

For *Troilus and Criseyde* at least seventeen manuscripts and some fragments survive. Three works published by the Chaucer

Society, two by R. K. Root, *The Manuscripts of Troilus and Criseyde* (1915) and *The Textual Tradition of Chaucer's Troilus* (1916), and one by J. S. P. Tatlock, *The Development and Chronology of Chaucer's Works* (1907), will be found useful. Single texts of various manuscripts were published by the Chaucer Society, nos. 63, 64, 79, 87, 88 (1881–95), and also some *Specimen Extracts*, ed. by W. S. McCormick and R. K. Root (1914).

Of Chaucer's other poems, manuscripts exist in varying numbers. There are at least twelve manuscripts of *The Legend of Good Women*, fifteen of *The Parlement of Foules*, three of *The Book of the Duchess*, three of *The Hous of Fame*, while the minor poems have been preserved reasonably freely. Ten manuscripts of the prose *Boethius* and twenty-two of *A Treatise of the Astrolabe* remain. Details will be found in F. N. Robinson's edition (below), but those for the verse texts should be verified from the Robbins–Cutler *Supplement to the Index*.

3. *Facsimiles*

There is a facsimile of *The Works of Geffray Chaucer* (Thynne, 1532) with introduction by W. W. Skeat (1905). Another facsimile of Thynne, supplemented by facsimiles of the works attributed to, or associated with, Chaucer that were published as additions to the complete works in 1542, 1561, 1598, and 1602, was published by the Scolar Press in 1969, with an introduction by D. S. Brewer. The Chaucer Society published *Autotype Specimens of the Chief Chaucer MSS.* in four parts (nos. 48, 56, 62, and 74, 1876–85) and the last of these parts, containing the Ellesmere MS., has since been published in a collotype facsimile (2 vols., 1911). *To Rosemounde* was reproduced in facsimile by W. W. Skeat, *Twelve Facsimiles of Old English Manuscripts* (1892). A photogravure facsimile of Caxton's edn. of *Anelida and Arcite* (1477?) was published in 1905. *The MSS. of Chaucer's Troilus and Criseyde with 23 Collotype Facsimiles of all the MSS.*, ed. by R. K. Root, was published by the Chaucer Society, no. 98 (1914). For collotype reproductions of pages of various manuscripts of the *Canterbury Tales* see C. F. E. Spurgeon, *Five Hundred Years of Chaucer Criticism and Allusion* (3 vols., 1925), i. 26, 33, ii, frontispiece; and also J. M. Manly and E. Rickert, *The Text of the Canterbury Tales* (8 vols., 1940), i, frontispiece, and pp. 565, 567, 571, 573, 577, and frontispieces to vols. ii, iii, and iv. Miss Spurgeon reproduces pages from

Caxton's edition of the *Canterbury Tales* (1484) in vol. i, pp. 61, 62, and 64, and from Pynson's edition of Chaucer (1526) in vol. i, p. 75, while *The Education of Chaucer* by G. A. Plimpton (1935) reproduces many pages of various types of Chaucerian manuscripts, including a complete copy of the Primer.

4. *Editions of Complete Works*

The earliest edition of Chaucer's complete works (and of poems not by him) was published without a general title-page by Pynson in 1526. This was followed by Thynne's edition of 1532, *The Workes of Geffray Chaucer* (above); both contained much spurious matter. Stow published *The Workes of Geffrey Chaucer* (1561) and added a large number of non-Chaucerian pieces. *The Workes of our Antient and Learned English Poet, Geffrey Chaucer, newly Printed*, were published by T. Speght in 1598. This edition called forth the interesting 'Animadversions upon the Annotations and Corrections of some imperfections of impressions of Chaucer's works, . . . set down by Francis Thynne' (son of the editor of 1532; printed in EETS os 9 (1865, 1875)) which led to Speght's corrected edition of 1602 (repr. 1687). The next edition was by J. Urry, *The Works of Geoffrey Chaucer* (1721), which was severely censured for the editor's treatment of the text. A number of collected editions of no outstanding interest followed, until a new definition was given to Chaucerian studies by the publication of *The Complete Works of Geoffrey Chaucer* (Oxford, 6 vols., 1894) by W. W. Skeat, followed by a supplementary volume vii, *Chaucerian and Other Pieces* (1897). This may be used with F. W. Bonner's 'The Genesis of the Chaucer Apocrypha', *SP* xlviii (1951), 461–91. The history of the various editions, with a number of facsimiles, is admirably told in *The Book of Geoffrey Chaucer* by C. Muscatine, printed for the Book Club of California (San Francisco, 1963).

Of editions of the poems and prose in one volume the long-established editions by W. W. Skeat, *The Student's Chaucer* (1895) and *The Globe Chaucer*, by A. W. Pollard and others (1898, 1913) have now been completely replaced by the authoritative work of F. N. Robinson, *The Complete Works of Geoffrey Chaucer* (Boston, 1933; 2nd edn. 1957). Good editions of important poems are A. C. Baugh, *Chaucer's Major Poetry* (New York, 1963) and E. T. Donaldson, *Chaucer's Poetry: an Anthology for the Modern Reader* (New York, 1958).

5. *Editions of Particular Works*

Among editions of particular works there are of special note: *The Canterbury Tales of Chaucer*, by T. Tyrwhitt (5 vols., 1775–8). This edition was outstanding in its day (although little recognized at the time), and remained of unrivalled authority for over a century as the first serious attempt to restore the genuine text. It was accompanied by a valuable 'Essay on Chaucer's Language and Versification', and an Introductory Discourse. Skeat's text in his six-volume edition (1894) naturally improved on that of Tyrwhitt; and valuable contributions were made by J. Koch in *Chaucers Canterbury Tales nach dem Ellesmere MS.* (Heidelberg, 1915) and by W. S. McCormick, *The Manuscripts of Chaucer's Canterbury Tales. A Critical Description of their Contents* (1933); but it was not until J. M. Manly and Edith Rickert made a close inspection of all the surviving manuscripts that a really critical text was established. This is now available in vols. iii and iv of their work: *The Text of the Canterbury Tales* (Chicago, 8 vols., 1940). Much help in using these volumes will be found in Germaine Dempster's article 'Manly's Conception of the Early History of the Canterbury Tales', *PMLA* lxi (1946), 379–415. Manly's *The Canterbury Tales* (New York, 1928) contains a long and valuable introduction, but the *Tales* have been cut in places for general use. A. C. Cawley has edited the *Tales* from the Ellesmere MS. (Everyman's Library, 1958). Innumerable editions of separate *Tales* have been produced.

The Book of Troilus and Criseyde (Princeton, 1926), ed. by R. K. Root, gives a full study of the manuscripts, and source material, with introduction and notes. *The Minor Poems* of Chaucer were edited by Skeat (1888) and a second and enlarged edition was published in 1896. J. Koch has re-edited all the poems except *The Canterbury Tales* and *Troilus and Criseyde* under the title *Geoffrey Chaucers kleinere Dichtungen* (Heidelberg, 1928). D. S. Brewer has edited *The Parlement of Foulys* with introduction and apparatus (1960).

6. *Biography*

'The study of Chaucer's life may be divided into two periods, that of the Legend, and that of the Appeal to Fact.' The legend may be found in its fullest and most absurd form in *A Life of Geoffrey Chaucer* by W. Godwin (2 vols., 1803; 4 vols., 1804).

A modern attempt at an imaginative biography is that of M. Chute, *Geoffrey Chaucer of England* (New York, 1946, 1962), which includes a useful bibliography. More sober accounts began with *The Life of Chaucer*, by Sir Harris Nicolas, prefixed to the Aldine Chaucer (1845), and the survey and discussion by T. R. Lounsbury in vol. i of *Studies in Chaucer* (New York, 3 vols., 1892). The documents themselves were collected by the Chaucer Society, and issued as *Life Records of Chaucer*, Second Series, nos. 12, 14, 21, and 32 (1875–1900). There is a good summary by R. E. G. Kirk prefaced to no. 32, and an index to the whole by E. P. Kuhl, *MP* x (1913), 527–52. Reference also should be made to J. R. Hulbert, *Chaucer's Official Life* (Menasha, 1912), and to new material provided in J. M. Manly, *Some New Light on Chaucer* (New York, 1926), or in the same author's edition of *The Canterbury Tales* (1928). All previous work, however, has been superseded by *Chaucer Life Records*, ed. M. M. Crow and C. C. Olson (1966). Chaucer iconography is discussed by M. H. Spielmann, *The Portraits of Chaucer* (Chaucer Society, 2nd ser. no. 31, 1900), by A. Brusendorff, *The Chaucer Tradition* (1925), 13–27, and by G. L. Law and W. H. Smith in 'George Vertue's Contributions to Chaucerian Iconography', *MLQ* v (1944), 303–22, while the portrait of Chaucer painted by order of Hoccleve in his *Regement of Princes* is reproduced as the frontispiece to vol. i of C. F. E. Spurgeon's *Five Hundred Years of Chaucer Criticism and Allusion* (1925). Chaucer's ancestry has been investigated by the following, among others: A. A. Kern, *The Ancestry of Chaucer* (Baltimore, 1906); M. B. Ruud, *Thomas Chaucer* (Minneapolis, 1926); A. C. Baugh, 'Kirk's Life Records of Thomas Chaucer', *PMLA* xlvii (1932), 461–515; R. Krauss in 'Chaucerian Problems: Especially the Petherton Forestership and the Question of T. Chaucer', *Three Chaucer Studies* (ed. Carleton Brown, New York, 1932).

For the political and cultural background of Chaucer's lifetime, see above, pp. 258–72. A useful volume of contemporary documents will be found in *Chaucer's World*, compiled by E. Rickert and edited by C. C. Olson and M. M. Crow (New York, 1948). An illustrated account is given by R. S. Loomis in his *Mirror of Chaucer's World* (Princeton, 1965) and by M. Hussey, *Chaucer's World* (1967).

7. *General Criticism*

For elementary students of Chaucer, A. W. Pollard's *Chaucer* (1893, rev. 1903) will be found useful. For a more modern and fuller treatment see R. D. French, *A Chaucer Handbook* (New York, 1927, 1947), while G. H. Cowling, *Chaucer* (1927), and P. van Dyke Shelley, *The Living Chaucer* (Pennsylvania, 1940), are worth consulting at early stages. Further help will be found in the pioneer work of B. ten Brink, *Chaucer Studien* (Münster, 3 vols., 1870); in the stimulating essay on Chaucer by J. R. Lowell, reprinted in *My Study Windows* (Boston, 1871); and in T. R. Lounsbury's *Studies in Chaucer* (New York, 3 vols., 1892). For more recent general studies see R. K. Root, *The Poetry of Chaucer* (Boston, 1906, rev. 1922); E. Legouis, *Chaucer* (Paris, 1910, trans. 1913, 1957); G. L. Kittredge, *Chaucer and his Poetry* (Boston, 1915, 1946); A. Brusendorff, *The Chaucer Tradition* (1925); G. K. Chesterton, *Chaucer* (1932); J. L. Lowes, *Geoffrey Chaucer* (1934, 1958); N. Coghill, *The Poet Chaucer* (1949); J. S. P. Tatlock, *The Mind and Art of Chaucer* (Syracuse, 1950); G. H. Gerould, *Chaucerian Essays* (Princeton, 1952); D. S. Brewer, *Chaucer* (1953, 1960); J. Speirs, *Chaucer the Maker* (1951, 1960); K. Malone, *Chapters on Chaucer* (1951); R. Preston, *Chaucer* (1952); C. Muscatine, *Chaucer and the French Tradition* (Berkeley, 1957); P. F. Baum, *Chaucer: a Critical Appreciation* (Durham, N.C., 1958); B. H. Bronson, *In Search of Chaucer* (Toronto, 1960, 1963); W. Clemen, *Chaucers frühe Dichtung* (Göttingen, 1963), trans. C. A. M. Sym (London, 1963); D. W. Robertson, *A Preface to Chaucer* (Princeton, 1963); M. Bowden, *A Reader's Guide to Geoffrey Chaucer* (New York, 1964); P. G. Ruggiers, *The Art of the Canterbury Tales* (Madison, 1965); R. M. Jordan, *Chaucer and the Shape of Creation* (Cambridge, Mass., 1967); S. S. Hussey, *Chaucer: An Introduction* (1971).

Chapters taken from a number of the above works will be found in the following collected volumes of criticism: E. Wagenknecht, *Chaucer: Modern Essays in Criticism* (New York, 1950, 1959); R. J. Schoeck and J. Taylor, *Chaucer Criticism* (2 vols., Notre Dame, 1960, 1961); C. A. Owen, *Discussions of the Canterbury Tales* (Boston, 1968); H. Newstead, *Chaucer and his Contemporaries* (New York, 1968). There are numerous other composite volumes such as *Chaucer and Chaucerians*, ed.

D. S. Brewer (1960); *Companion to Chaucer Studies*, ed. B. Rowland (Toronto, 1968); *Chaucer's Mind and Art*, ed. A. C. Cawley (1969). Full-length critical works on individual poems are J. A. W. Bennett, *The Parlement of Foules: An Interpretation* (1957) and *Chaucer's Book of Fame* (1968); and Ida L. Gordon, *The Double Sorrow of Troilus* (1970).

8. *Books and Articles on Special Aspects*

(*a*) *Canon and Chronology*

Some of the most useful books and articles on special aspects are as follows. The canon and chronology of Chaucer's works are studied in J. Koch, *The Chronology of Chaucer's Writings*, Chaucer Soc. (1890); W. W. Skeat, *The Chaucer Canon* (1900); J. S. P. Tatlock, *The Development and Chronology of Chaucer's Works*, Chaucer Soc. (1907); E. P. Hammond, *Chaucer: a Bibliographical Manual* (New York, 1908), 51–72; A. Brusendorff, *The Chaucer Tradition* (1925); J. Koch, *Geoffrey Chaucers kleinere Dichtungen* (Heidelberg, 1928).

The following articles are of outstanding importance: J. L. Lowes, 'The Prologue to the *Legend of Good Women* as related to the French Marguerite Poems and to the *Filostrato*', *PMLA* xix (1904), 593–683; 'The Prologue to the *Legend of Good Women* considered in its Chronological Relations', *PMLA* xx (1905), 749–864. (This second study should be read with that of M. Lossing, 'The Prologue to the *Legend of Good Women* and the *Lai de Franchise*', *SP* xxxix (1942), 15–35, which challenges some of its conclusions.) A third study by Lowes is entitled 'The Date of Chaucer's *Troilus and Criseyde*', *PMLA* xxiii (1908), 285–306. Other important articles are G. L. Kittredge, *The Date of Chaucer's Troilus*, Chaucer Soc. (1909); F. Tupper, 'Chaucer's Tale of Ireland', *PMLA* xxxvi (1921), 186–222; J. S. P. Tatlock's 'Chaucer's Retractions', *PMLA* xxviii (1913), 521–9; J. Koch, 'Alte Chaucerprobleme und neue Lösungsversuche', *ES* lv (1921), 161–225, and 'Chaucers Boethiusübersetzung', *Anglia*, xlvi (1922), 35–51; V. Langhans, 'Die Datierung der Prosastücke Chaucers', *Anglia*, liii (1929), 235–68. An attempt to use astronomical data for chronology more precisely than has hitherto been done is made by J. D. North, 'Kalenderes enlumyned ben they', *RES* NS xx (1969), 129–54, 257–83, 418–44.

(*b*) *Indebtedness to Other Authors*

Chaucer's indebtedness to various authors and the sources and analogues of his writings have been widely investigated. Miss Hammond gives a good critical survey of these in her *Chaucer: a Bibliographical Manual* (New York, 1908), 73–105, and so do T. R. Lounsbury, *Studies in Chaucer* (3 vols., 1892, 1962), ii. 167–426, and W. W. Skeat, *The Works of Geoffrey Chaucer* (6 vols., 1894), iii. 370–504. See also 'Chaucer as a Literary Critic', by W. H. Wells, *MLN* xxxix (1924), 255–68. *The Sources and Analogues of Chaucer's Canterbury Tales*, ed. by W. F. Bryan and G. Dempster (1941, 1958), is the authoritative work on the *Tales*.

Chaucer's use of ancient literature is studied in the following: G. W. Landrum, 'Chaucer's Use of the Vulgate', *PMLA* xxxix (1924), 75–100, in which she summarizes her unpublished Radcliffe College thesis. The classical writers who influenced Chaucer are dealt with by E. F. Shannon, *Chaucer and the Roman Poets* (Cambridge, Mass., 1929), and J. Koch, 'Chaucers Belesenheit in den römischen Klassikern', *ES* lvii (1923), 8–84; B. L. Jefferson, *Chaucer and the Consolation of Philosophy of Boethius* (Princeton, 1917); B. A. Wise, *The Influence of Statius upon Chaucer* (Baltimore, 1911); E. K. Rand, *Ovid and his Influence* (1925), 145–9; R. L. Hoffman, *Ovid and the Canterbury Tales* (1966); H. R. Patch, *The Tradition of Boethius* (New York, 1935); R. A. Pratt, 'Chaucer's Claudian', *Speculum*, xxii (1947), 419–29.

For the influence on Chaucer of medieval ideas and of medieval authors see as follows:

(i) *French*: The general literary background is sketched by a master hand in W. P. Ker, *Epic and Romance* (1896), and in his *Medieval English Literature* (1912, 1969), also by E. R. Curtius, *European Literature and the Latin Middle Ages*, tr. W. B. Trask (New York, 1953), and W. H. Schofield, *Chivalry in English Literature* (Gloucester, Mass., 1912), 11–72. A more limited but important side of medieval life is discussed in W. G. Dodd's *Courtly Love in Chaucer and Gower* (Boston, 1913), in T. A. Kirby, *Chaucer's 'Troilus': A Study in Courtly Love* (Baton Rouge, Louisiana, 1940, 1959), in C. S. Lewis, *The Allegory of Love* (1936), and in D. Everett, *Essays on Middle English Literature* (1955), 125–30. The more direct influence of French poetry on Chaucer was stressed in a pioneer (and exaggerated) study by E. C. Sandras, *Étude sur Chaucer considéré comme imitateur des trouvères* (Paris, 1859). Lisi Cipriani's 'Studies in the Influence of the *Romance of the Rose* on Chaucer', *PMLA* xxii (1907), 552–95, was followed by a full-length study by D. S. Fansler, *Chaucer and the Roman de la Rose* (New York, 1914). One of the most important of recent books is C. Muscatine, *Chaucer and the French Tradition* (Berkeley, 1957), while H. Braddy has re-examined Chaucer's relations with a single author in *Chaucer and the French Poet, Granson* (Baton Rouge, Louisiana, 1947). A number of outstanding papers have been written by J. L. Lowes on Chaucer and his use of French poetry. Among them are 'The Prologue to the *Legend of Good Women* . . .' (p. 288 above); 'Chaucer and the *Miroir de Mariage*', *MP* viii (1910–11), 165–86, 305–34; 'Illustrations of Chaucer Drawn Chiefly from Deschamps', *Romanic Review*, ii (1911), 113–28. A brilliant summary of his conclusions is presented in his chapter 'The World of Books' in *Geoffrey Chaucer* (1934). Other valuable articles on the love-vision are W. O. Sypherd, *Studies in Chaucer's Hous of Fame*, Chaucer Soc. (1907); G. L. Kittredge, 'Guillaume de Machaut and the *Book of the Duchess*', *PMLA* xxx (1915), 1–24; B. H. Bronson, 'The Book of the Duchess Re-opened', *PMLA* lxvii (1952), 863–81; W. H. French, 'The Man in Black's Lyric', *JEGP* lvi (1957), 231–41. In '*Le Songe Verte* and Chaucer's Dream Poems', *MLN* xxiv (1909), 46–7, W. O. Sypherd briefly discusses these poems.

(ii) *Medieval Latin authors*: Among the many authors known to Chaucer mention may be made of Alanus de Insulis (Aleyn), two of whose works were used by Chaucer, the *De Planctu Naturae* and the *Anticlaudianus*. Texts of these will be found in Migne, *Patrologia Latina*, ccx (1855), 431 ff., and *Anticlaudianus* has been edited by P. Bossuat (Paris, 1955). Arnoldus Villanova (Arnold of the Newe Toun) wrote a treatise on alchemy, the *Rosarium Philosophorum*, which was printed by Ashmole in his *Theatrum Chemicum* (1652): Chaucer mentions it in the *Canon's Yeoman's Tale*. Macrobius, the author of a commentary on the *Somnium Scipionis* of Cicero, furnished the model for much medieval dream-literature, and was drawn on by Chaucer on several occasions. For the text of Macrobius see that of L. von Jan (2 vols., Leipzig, 1852). The *Commentary on the Dream of Scipio* has been translated with an introduction by W. H. Stahl (New York, 1952). The influence and work of both Arnold and

Macrobius are examined by W. C. Curry in his *Chaucer and the Medieval Sciences* (New York, 1926, rev. 1960). The *De Consolatione Philosophiae* of Boethius has already been mentioned, and also the work of the medieval rhetoricians such as Geoffrey de Vinsauf (above, Section III. 3), but the article of K. Young, 'Chaucer and Geoffrey of Vinsauf', *MP* xlii (1944), 178–82, is also of interest. Lastly, the work of Vincent of Beauvais has been very thoroughly examined by P. Aiken, who in a series of articles has shown how extensive was Chaucer's knowledge of Vincent's encyclopedia the *Speculum Majus* (Venice, 1494), consisting of the *Speculum Naturale*, *Speculum Doctrinale*, and *Speculum Historiale*. For her work see *PMLA* li (1936), 361 ff.; *Speculum*, x (1935), 281 ff.; xiii (1938), 232 ff.; xvii (1942), 56 ff.; and *SP* xxxiii (1936), 40 ff.; xxxv (1938), 1 ff.; xli (1944), 371 ff.; liii (1956), 22–4.

(iii) *Italian*: The best works on this subject are H. M. Cummings, *The Indebtedness of Chaucer's Works to the Italian Works of Boccaccio*, Univ. of Cincinnati Studies, 10 (1916, 1967), and M. Praz, 'Chaucer and the Great Italian Writers of the Trecento', *Monthly Criterion*, vi (1927), 18–39, 131–57, 238–42. The translation of *Il Filostrato* by N. E. Griffin and A. B. Myrick (Philadelphia, 1929) or that in prose by R. K. Gordon in *The Story of Troilus* (1934) may be found useful. Other important studies of a more limited nature are to be found in K. Young's 'Chaucer's Use of Boccaccio's *Filocolo*', *MP* iv (1906–7), 169–77; 'Aspects of the Story of Troilus and Criseyde', *Wisconsin Studies in Language and Literature*, ii (1918), 67–94; 'Troilus and Criseyde as Romance', *PMLA* liii (1938), 38–63; also R. A. Pratt, 'Chaucer's Use of the *Teseida*', *PMLA* lxii (1947), 598–621, and 'Chaucer and the Roman de Troyle et de Criseida', *SP* liii (1956), 509–39. See also S. B. Meech, *Design in Chaucer's Troilus* (Syracuse, N.Y., 1959) and E. Salter, 'Troilus and Criseyde: a Reconsideration', *Patterns of Love and Courtesy*, ed. J. Lawlor (1966), 86–106. W. C. Curry in 'Destiny in Chaucer's *Troilus*', *PMLA* xlv (1930), 129–68, relates the idea of destiny in Boethius to that in Chaucer, while C. S. Lewis makes a valuable contribution with his 'What Chaucer really did to "Il Filostrato"' in *Essays and Studies of the English Association*, xvii (1932), 56–75, a view which is considered by R. Sharrock in 'Second Thoughts: C. S. Lewis on Chaucer's *Troilus*', *Essays in Criticism*, viii (1958), 123–37. A much disputed problem is discussed in G. L. Kittredge's 'Chaucer's Lollius', *Harvard Studies in Classical Philology*, xxviii (1917), 47–134, in H. Lange, *Anglia*, xlii (1918), 345–51, R. Imelmann, *ES* xlv (1912), 406, L. H. Hornstein, *PMLA* lxiii (1948), 64–84, and in R. K. Root's edition of *Troilus and Criseyde* (Princeton, 1926), xxxvi–xl.

For Dante, see J. L. Lowes, 'Chaucer and Dante', *MP* xiv (1917), 705–35; C. Looten, 'Chaucer and Dante', *Rev. de litt. comp.* v (1925), 545–71, and J. A. W. Bennett, 'Chaucer, Dante and Boccaccio', *Medium Ævum*, xxii (1953), 114–15.

(iv) *English authors*: Chaucer's indebtedness to English authors has not yet been very fully investigated. There is a good introductory article by D. S. Brewer, 'The Relationship of Chaucer to the English and European Traditions' in *Chaucer and Chaucerians* (1966). In connection with Chaucer's knowledge of romance reference should be made to the work of L. H. Loomis, particularly her articles 'Chaucer and the Auchinleck MS.: "Thopas" and "Guy of Warwick"' in *Studies in Honor of Carleton Brown* (New York, 1940), 111–28, and 'Chaucer and the Breton Lays of the Auchinleck MS.', *SP* xxxviii (1941), 14–33, reprinted with other articles by her in *Adventures in the Middle Ages* (New York, 1962), 111–87. See also her fully documented study of *Sir Thopas* in *Sources and Analogues* (above, p. 289), 486–559. See also the interesting note of R. M. Smith, 'Three Notes on the Knight's Tale', *MLN* li (1936), 318–22. 'Chaucer's Debt to Langland' is discussed by N. K. Coghill in *Medium Ævum*, iv (1935), 90–4, while M. Schlauch in *Chaucer's Constance and Accused Queens* (New York, 1927) and in her chapter on *The Man of Law's Tale* in *Sources and Analogues* deals with the interconnections between Chaucer's work and that of Gower. These are further considered (with other matters) in Carleton Brown's article, 'The Man of Law's Head-Link and the Prologue of the *Canterbury Tales*', *SP* xxxiv (1937), 8–35. In his *Literature and Pulpit in Medieval England* (1933, 1961), 229–30, G. R. Owst draws attention to the similarities between the work of the sermon-writers, 'these past-masters in the art of vivid Realism and incisive portraiture', and that of Chaucer. Later authors' allusions to Chaucer's work are gathered together by C. F. E. Spurgeon, *Five Hundred Years of Chaucer Criticism and Allusion 1357–1900* (3 vols., 1925). See also W. L. Alderson's 'A Check List of Supplements to Spurgeon's Chaucer Allusions', *PQ* xxxii (1953), 418–27.

(c) Prose Writings

For a general discussion of prose see V. Langhans, 'Die Datierung der Prosastücke Chaucers', *Anglia*, liii (1929), 235–68. For 'The Art of Chaucer's Prose' see M. Schlauch, in *Chaucer and Chaucerians*, ed. D. S. Brewer (1966), 140–63, and the same writer's 'Chaucer's Prose Rhythms', *PMLA* lxv (1950), 568–89, and P. F. Baum, *JEGP* xlv (1947), 38–42. Chaucer's authorship of the *Parson's Tale* has been much disputed. See H. Simon, 'Chaucer a Wicliffite', *Chaucer Society Essays*, Part III (1876), for the most important attack. This was answered by Koch in *Anglia*, ii (1897), 540–4, while the question was reviewed afresh by H. Spies, *Chaucers religiöse Grundstimmung und die Echtheit der Parson's Tale*, Studien zur englischen Philologie, I (Halle, 1913), 626–721, who gives a summary of the whole discussion. The sources of the *Parson's Tale* are admirably studied by Germaine Dempster in *Sources and Analogues* (above, p. 289), 723–60, a work which supersedes Kate O. Petersen's *The Sources of the Parson's Tale* (Boston, 1901).

Boethius: The outstanding work on this prose version by Chaucer is that of B. L. Jefferson, *Chaucer and the Consolation of Philosophy of Boethius* (Princeton, 1917). For general information on Boethius and his work see H. F. Stewart, *Boethius* (1891); E. K. Rand in *Harvard Studies in Classical Philology*, xv (1904); and H. M. Barrett, *Boethius* (1940). The text of the *Consolatio*, together with a translation, was edited by H. F. Stewart and E. K. Rand for the Loeb Classics (1918).

Treatise on the Astrolabe: This was first printed in Thynne's edition of 1532. Little work has been done on this treatise. There is an article by G. L. Kittredge in *MP* xiv (1917), 513–18 discussing whether the work was written for Lewis Chaucer or Lewis Clifford, and letters on this point appear in *The Times Literary Supplement*, by J. M. Manly (7 June 1928), by W. Rye (28 June 1928), and by H. W. Garrod (11 Oct. 1928). The date of the work has been discussed by S. Moore in *MP* x (1912), 203–5, and by G. L. Kittredge in *MP* xiv (1917), 513–18. *Chaucer and Messahalla on the Astrolabe*, by R. T. Gunther (1929), deals with the scientific aspects of the work. The possibility that another astronomical work is by Chaucer is discussed by D. J. Price in *The Equatorie of the Planetis*, with a linguistic analysis by R. M. Wilson (1955). For an astronomer's views on these two works, see J. D. North, 'Kalenderes enlumyned ben they', *RES* NS xx (1969), 432–7.

(d) Diction

The modern study of Chaucer's language dates from the classic essay of F. J. Child, 'Observations on the Language of Chaucer', *Memoirs of the American Academy of Arts and Sciences*, viii (1861–3), 445–502. His work was condensed and reprinted by A. J. Ellis in vol. i of his *On Early English Pronunciation*, Chaucer Soc. (5 vols., 1868–88), to which Ellis added much of importance in vols. i and iii. Child's disciples, J. M. Manly, in 'Observations on the Language of Chaucer's *Legend of Good Women*', *Harvard Studies and Notes in Philology and Literature*, ii (1893), 1–120, and G. L. Kittredge, in *Observations on the Language of Chaucer's Troilus*, Chaucer Soc. (1894), carried on Child's work. More recently F. Wild, in his *Die sprachlichen Eigentümlichkeiten der wichtigeren Chaucer-Handschriften*, Wiener Beiträge, 44 (1915), has provided useful help for studying the language of Chaucer's manuscripts.

Chaucer's grammar was first systematically treated by B. ten Brink, *Chaucers Sprache und Verskunst* (Strassburg, 1884; rev. edn. Leipzig, 1920). A translation by M. Bentinck Smith was published in 1901, but the book is now antiquated. Beginners will be helped by Skeat's summary treatment in vol. vi of his edition of Chaucer; by R. D. French, *A Chaucer Handbook* (1927, 1947), 339–67; and by K. Sisam, *The Clerkes Tale* (1923), or Carleton Brown, *The Pardoner's Tale* (1935). For more general grammatical help see the works listed in Section IV. 1.

Other special topics of interest to the student of Chaucer's diction are: W. Haeckel, *Das Sprichwort bei Chaucer* (Leipzig, 1890), which has been followed by the fuller treatment of the subject by B. J. Whiting, *Chaucer's Use of Proverbs* (Cambridge, Mass., 1934). His puns are considered by P. F. Baum in *PMLA* lxxi (1956), 225–46, while M. Masui examines *The Structure of Chaucer's Rime Words* (Tokio, 1964). Chaucer's imagery has been investigated by F. Klaeber, *Das Bild bei Chaucer* (Berlin, 1893), while his ethical conceptions are studied at length in W. Héraucourt's *Die Wertwelt Chaucers* (Heidelberg, 1939). The rhetorical models followed by Chaucer were well discussed and illustrated by J. M. Manly, 'Chaucer and the Rhetoricians', *Proceedings of the British Academy*, xii (1926), and further useful work has been done by T. Naunin, *Der Einfluß der mittelalterlichen Rhetorik auf Chaucers Dichtung* (Bonn, 1929). J. Mersand's *Chaucer's Romance Vocabulary* (New York, 1937, 1959) is a useful study of Chaucer's diction, but is often inaccurate in detail. With it should be read J. R. Hulbert's 'Chaucer's Romance Vocabulary', *PQ* xxvi (1947), 302–6. *A Guide to Chaucer's Pronunciation* by H. Kökeritz (New Haven, 1954) may be consulted as an elaboration on the brief treatment of this subject in the standard editions of Chaucer. Many characteristic features of Chaucer's syntax are collected and classified by J. Kerkhof, *Studies in the Language of Geoffrey Chaucer* (Leiden, 1966).

(*e*) *Metre*

Chaucer's metres are discussed by many of the above writers and were exhaustively examined by J. Schipper, *Englische Metrik in historischer und systematischer Entwicklung dargestellt* (3 vols., Bonn, 1881–8). His treatment is a very mechanical one. For the opposite attitude see G. Saintsbury, *A History of English Prosody* (3 vols., 1906–10), i. 143–78. The most helpful remarks on metre are to be found in E. P. Hammond, *Chaucer: a Bibliographical Manual* (1908), 475–500, and the same writer's *English Verse between Chaucer and Surrey* (1927), 17–26. Reference may also usefully be made to J. M. Manly, *Canterbury Tales* (1928), 122–32; A. H. Licklider, *Chapters on the Metric of the Chaucer Tradition* (Baltimore, 1910); H. Reger, *Die epische Cäsur in der Chaucerschule* (Bayreuth, 1910); C. F. Babcock, 'The Metrical Use of Inflectional *-e* in Middle English with Particular Reference to Chaucer and Lydgate', *PMLA* xxix (1914), 50–92. J. G. Southworth's 'Chaucer's Final *-e* in Rhyme', *PMLA* lxii (1947), 910–35, was answered by E. T. Donaldson in the same journal, lxiii (1948), 1101–24, and the controversy continued in lxiv (1949), 601–10. For more recent studies, see P. F. Baum, *Chaucer's Verse* (Durham, N.C., 1961) and the books by J. G. Southworth and I. Robinson mentioned above, p. 250.

9. *Bibliographies and Concordances*

The most useful general bibliographical handbook is that of E. P. Hammond, *Chaucer: a Bibliographical Manual* (1908). Her work has been carried on by D. D. Griffith, *Bibliography of Chaucer, 1908–53* (Seattle, 1955), by W. K. Crawford, *Bibliography of Chaucer, 1954–63* (Seattle, 1967), and by A. C. Baugh,

Chaucer ('Goldentree Bibliographies', New York, 1968). The three latter volumes are mainly lists of books and references to the relevant reviews, but Miss Hammond's work is full of invaluable comment, discussion, and suggestion. J. E. Wells, *A Manual of the Writings in Middle English, 1050–1400* (New Haven, 1916, with supplements to 1951), chapter xiv, is a most useful compendium of facts concerning Chaucer's life, canon, chronology, synopses of individual works, &c., with a general bibliography up to 1945. Another valuable aid will be found in *The Cambridge Bibliography of English Literature*, vol. i (1941) and vol. v (1966) which cover the subject to the beginning of 1955. New editions of both these works are in preparation.

The most recent work can be conveniently surveyed in *The Chaucer Review: a Journal of Medieval Studies and Literary Criticism* (Pennsylvania State University Press, 1966–), and in *The Annual Bibliography of English Language and Literature*, published by the Modern Humanities Research Association since 1920. There is also a section on Chaucer in the May issues of *PMLA* since 1922, and another in *The Year's Work in English Studies* since 1921.

Three useful guides through this dense mass of material will be found in 'Fifty Years of Chaucer Scholarship' by A. C. Baugh, *Speculum*, xxvi (1951), 659–72; in R. R. Purdy, 'Chaucer Scholarship in England and America', *Anglia*, lxx (1952), 345–81; and in R. W. Ackerman's section on Chaucer in *The Medieval Literature of Western Europe: a Review of Research, mainly 1930–60*, ed. by J. H. Fisher (1966).

There is a concordance by J. S. P. Tatlock and A. G. Kennedy, *A Concordance to the Complete Works of Geoffrey Chaucer and to the Romaunt of the Rose* (Washington, D.C., 1927), while the glossary to vol. vi of Skeat's collected edition will be found helpful. For other aids, see H. Corson, *An Index of Proper Names and Subjects to Chaucer's Canterbury Tales* (New York, 1911) and *A Chaucer Gazetteer* by F. P. Magoun, Jr. (Stockholm, 1961).

Sir T. Clanvowe, *fl.* 1400

The reputed author of *The Cuckoo and the Nightingale* or *The Book of Cupid*. See Section VII.

Edward, Second Duke of York, 1373–1415

The translation made by the duke (*c.* 1406) of the *Livre de la chasse* of Gaston III (Phébus) Comte de Foix, known as *The*

Master of Game, was one of the most popular hunting manuals of the period. Edward's translation added a few chapters to the original, and his work has been reproduced in a magnificent edition by W. A. and F. Baillie-Grohman (1904). This edition has for introduction the most complete account of medieval hunting and of the contemporary writings thereon, as well as an excellent bibliography and a series of illustrations from manuscript sources. An edition containing the text only in a modernized version was published by the same editors in 1909.

SIR JOHN FORTESCUE, *c.* 1394–*c.* 1476

Fortescue's works, both English and Latin, have been brought together and carefully edited by his kinsman, Thomas Fortescue, Lord Clermont (2 vols., 1869). His English works have been published as follows: *The Governaunce of England* was first published by Sir John Fortescue-Aland (1714) and it appeared in Lord Clermont's edition (i. 449–74). The definitive edition, with a valuable introduction, is by Charles Plummer (1885). For Fortescue's minor works—*An Example that Good Counsel Helpeth, &c., The Commodytes of England, The Twenty-Two Rightwisnesses belongyng to a Kynge, Advice to Purchasers of Land, Of the Title of the House of York*, &c.—see the edition of Clermont, i. 475–554.

Translations of Fortescue's principal Latin work, *De Laudibus Legum Angliae*, began with R. Mulcaster's edition of the Latin and English, published by Tottel (1567). Selden's edition appeared in 1616; F. Gregor's in 1737; Lord Clermont's in 1869, and one by S. B. Chrimes in 1942. This latest edition contains a useful introduction on 'Fortescue's Life and Works' by the editor, and an important study of Fortescue's significance in English Law by H. D. Hazeltine.

'The Influence of the Writings of Sir John Fortescue', by C. A. J. Skeel, *Trans. Royal Hist. Soc.* x (1916), 77–114, a chapter by A. E. Levett in *The Social and Political Ideas of some Great Thinkers of the Renaissance and the Reformation*, ed. F. J. C. Hearnshaw (1925), 61–86, together with an interesting article on 'Sir John Fortescue on the Education of Rulers', by C. F. Arrowood, *Speculum*, x (1935), 404–10, and another by E. F. Jacob, 'Sir J. Fortescue and the Law of Nature', *JRLB* xviii (1934), 359–76, are the best modern articles on this writer.

JON GARDENER, *fl.* 1440

The author—whose name is probably fictional—of the earliest known vernacular treatise on gardening is said to have written, or more probably translated, his work *c.* 1440. It was first printed with notes by Lady Alicia Amherst (Mrs. Evelyn Cecil) in *Archaeologia*, liv (1894–5), 157–72. A facsimile of a page of the manuscript will be found in the same writer's *History of Gardening in England* (1895; 3rd rev. edn., 1910), 63–6. A new annotated edition is in A. G. Rigg, *A Glastonbury Miscellany of the Fifteenth Century* (1968), 103–16. See also Sir F. Crisp, *Medieval Gardens* (2 vols., 1924), i. 42.

SIR GILBERT HAY *or* GILBERT OF THE HAYE, *fl.* 1456

His prose manuscript (1456) was edited first for the Abbotsford Club in 1847 by D. Laing and then for the STS 44, 62 (2 vols., 1901–14) by J. H. Stevenson. The work contains *The Buke of the Law of Armys or Buke of Battaillis* translated from the French *Arbre des batailles* (*c.* 1385); *The Buke of the Governaunce of Princis*—a translation of a French version of the *Secreta Secretorum*; and *The Buke of the Ordre of Knychthede* from the French version of Ramon Lull's *Libre de cavayleria.* In addition, he translated from the French *The Buke of the Conqueror Alexaunder the Great*, from which long extracts were printed for the Bannatyne Club (1834) and by A. Hermann in *The Forraye of Gadderis, The Vowis* (Berlin, 1900).

JOHN HARDING, 1378–*c.* 1465?

The *Metrical Chronicle* of John Harding, together with Richard Grafton's continuation, was first published by Grafton in 1543, and was edited by Sir H. Ellis (1812). It survives in fifteen manuscripts (not all complete), and is fully described by C. L. Kingsford, *English Historical Literature in the Fifteenth Century* (1913), 140–9. Harding's own history and the three versions of his Chronicle are discussed at length by the same writer in *EHR* xxvii (1912), 462–82, and some extracts follow, ibid. 740–53.

HENRY THE MINSTREL (*or* BLIND HARRY), *fl.* 1470–92

The work of 'Blind Harry' entitled *The Actis and Deidis of the Illuster and Vailzeand Campioun, Schir William Wallace, Knicht of Ellerslie* survives in a manuscript of 1488, written by John

Ramsay. It was first printed about 1508, again in 1570 (repr. 1594, 1600, &c.). The standard edition was edited for the STS 6, 7, 16 (1885–9) by J. Moir, and a facsimile of the 1570 edition by Sir W. A. Craigie, STS 3rd ser. 12 (1940).

A number of modernized versions obtained wide circulation, commencing with that of an anonymous writer in 1701. The most famous of these versions was a free paraphrase by W. Hamilton of Gilbertfield, published at Glasgow (1722).

In addition to the standard histories of literature (see above, Section III. 1 (*b*)) reference may be made to W. H. Schofield, *Mythical Bards and the Life of William Wallace* (Boston, 1910); G. Neilson, 'Blind Harry's *Wallace*', *Essays and Studies of the English Association*, i (1910); and H. Heyne, *Die Sprache in Henry the Minstrel's 'Wallace'* (Kiel, 1910).

ROBERT HENRYSON, 1429?–1508?

The earliest printed editions of his principal works are as follows: *The Morall Fabillis of Esope the Phrygian* (1570, 1577); *The Testament of Cresseid* (Thynne, 1532; 1593); *Orpheus and Eurydice* (Chepman and Myllar, 1508); *Robene and Makyne* (1765); *The Abbay Walk* (1686).

For collected editions see those of D. Laing (1865); G. Gregory Smith (the standard work), STS 45–7 (1906–14), of which vol. i is a particularly valuable introduction; H. H. Wood (1933, 1958), which has some judicious introductory material to the various poems. For other modern editions, see C. Elliott, *Robert Henryson: Poems* (1963); D. Fox, *The Testament of Cresseid* (1968).

Henryson's work is critically surveyed by H. H. Wood, *Edinburgh Essays in Scots Literature* (1933), by M. W. Stearns, *Robert Henryson* (1949), and by J. MacQueen, *Robert Henryson: a Study of the Major Narrative Poems* (1967).

THOMAS HOCCLEVE, *c.* 1368–1426

A full account of the manuscripts of Hoccleve will be found in E. P. Hammond, *English Verse between Chaucer and Surrey* (1927), 57–8. The poems are grouped by her as follows: shorter poems *en masse*; single shorter poems; 'series' of linked poems; *The Regement of Princes* alone, and with other works not by Hoccleve. A few additional manuscripts are enumerated in *The Index of Middle English Verse* by Carleton Brown and R. H. Robbins (1943) and its *Supplement* (1965).

Facsimiles of pages of various Hoccleve manuscripts will be found in R. Garnett and E. Gosse, *English Literature* (4 vols., 1903), i. 190; R. K. Root, *The Manuscripts of Chaucer's Troilus and Criseyde*, Chaucer Soc., 1st ser. no. 98 (1914), 12; F. J. Furnivall and I. Gollancz, *Hoccleve's Minor Poems*, EETS ES 61 (1892), 73 (1897), 242; C. F. E. Spurgeon, *Five Hundred Years of Chaucer Criticism and Allusion* (3 vols., 1925), frontispiece to vol. i and i. 82; and H. C. Schulz, 'Thomas Hoccleve, Scribe', *Speculum*, xii (1937), 80–1.

Three of Hoccleve's minor poems, *The Letter of Cupid*, *The Mother of God*, and *To the King*, were all first printed in Thynne's 1532 edition of Chaucer. *The Tale of Jonathas* was incorporated (in a modernized and abridged version) by W. Browne in one of his eclogues printed in *The Shepherds Pipe* (1614; repr. 1869, 1894). Other works were first published as follows: *The Regement of Princes*, ed. by T. Wright for the Roxburghe Club (1860); 'Poem to Oldcastle', ed. by Grosart with *Poems of Richard James* (1880); 'The Story of the Virgin and her Sleeveless Garment', ed. by A. Beatty, Chaucer Soc., 2nd ser. no. 34 (1902).

The collected edition of Hoccleve's works, edited by F. J. Furnivall and I. Gollancz, will be found in EETS ES 61 and 73 (1892, 1897), containing the *Minor Poems*, and 72 containing *The Regement of Princes* and fourteen other poems (1897). A life of Hoccleve, by F. J. Furnivall, forms the introduction to no. 61. A new edition of the *Minor Poems*, revised by J. Mitchell and A. I. Doyle, appeared in 1971. Accounts of Hoccleve's life and work will be found in H. S. Bennett, *Six Medieval Men and Women* (1955), 69–99; J. Mitchell, *Thomas Hoccleve* (Durham, N.C., 1965) and *Thomas Hoccleve* (Urbana, 1968). 'The autobiographical element in Hoccleve' is discussed by J. Mitchell, *MLQ* xxviii (1967), 269–84 and in E. M. Thornley, *The Middle English Penitential Lyric* (1967). A. L. Brown has produced evidence that Hoccleve died in 1426 (*RES* NS viii (1957), 218).

Hoccleve's prosody is discussed by F. Bock, *Metrische Studien zu Hoccleves Versen* (Weilheim, 1900), and G. Saintsbury, *A History of English Prosody* (3 vols., 1906–10), i. 231–4. Various aspects of Hoccleve's diction and text are discussed by E. Vollmer, 'Sprache und Reime des Londoners Hoccleve',

Anglia, xxi (1898), 201–21; W. H. Williams, '*De Regimine Principum*, 299, 621', *MLR* iv (1909), 235–6; J. H. Kern, 'Zum Texte einiger Dichtungen Thomas Hoccleve's', *Anglia*, xxxix (1916), 389–494; and B. P. Kurtz, who has three articles on *Lerne to Die* in *MLN* xxxviii (1923), 337–40, xxxix (1924), 56–7, and *PMLA* xl (1925), 252–75.

There are critical estimates of Hoccleve's work by B. ten Brink, Jusserand, Courthope, Saintsbury, Hammond, and in vol. ii of the *CHEL*.

Sir Richard Holland, *fl.* 1450

The Buke of the Howlat was included in both the Bannatyne and Asloan manuscript collections and one leaf of an edition of *c.* 1503 exists. *The Buke* was edited by D. Laing for the Bannatyne Club (1823), and again for the STS by F. J. Amours, 27 (1897), 47–81, from the Asloan text; and by A. Diebler (Leipzig, 1893) and W. T. Ritchie, STS 2nd ser. 26 (1930), 128–58, from the Bannatyne text.

Peter Idley, *fl.* 1450

His *Instructions to his Son* have now been well edited with a full introduction by C. D'Evelyn (Boston, 1935). Earlier investigators were F. Miessner, *P. Idley's Instructions to his Son* (Greifswald, 1903) and M. Förster in *Archiv*, civ (1909), 293–6, who briefly discussed the sources of Book I. Seven manuscripts survive.

James I of Scotland, 1394–1437

James's most important work, *The Kingis Quair*, was first printed by W. Tytler in his *Poetical Remains of James the First, King of Scotland* (Edinburgh, 1783). Tytler used an imperfect transcript of the unique manuscript (Bodleian, Arch. Selden, B. 24) and was followed by later editors, until W. W. Skeat produced a reliable text for the STS 1 (1884; revised, 2nd ser. 1, 1911). It was also edited by A. Lawson (1910), who included in his edition *The Quare of Jelusy*. W. M. Mackenzie re-edited the text (1939) from the manuscript and prefaced his work with a useful and compact account of the various problems associated with James I and *The Kingis Quair*. A new edition by J. Norton-Smith appeared in 1971.

For James's life see the imaginative and vivid account of J. J. Jusserand, *Le Roman d'un roi d'Écosse* (Paris, 1895; tr. 1896), and for a more exact account the scholarly work of E. M. W. Balfour-Melville, *James I, King of Scots* (1936). The dispute as to the authorship was begun by J. T. T. Brown in his *The Authorship of the Kingis Quair* (1896). He was strongly opposed by J. J. Jusserand, *Jacques Ier d'Écosse fut-il poète?* (Paris, 1897). The problem is considered afresh, with full references, in W. M. Mackenzie's edition, pp. 16–26.

An important article by Sir William Craigie on 'The Language of *The Kingis Quair*' will be found in *Essays and Studies of the English Association*, xxv (1939), 22–38. Mackenzie also deals with the relation between *The Kingis Quair* and *The Court of Love* (q.v.), pp. 26–41, as does W. A. Neilson, 'The Origins and Sources of the "Court of Love"', *Harvard Studies and Notes in Philology and Literature*, vi (1899), 146–68, 233–6. Modern critics have devoted most of their attention to the literary merits of James's works, notably J. Preston, 'Fortunys Exiltree: a Study of *The Kingis Quair*', *RES* NS vii (1956), 339–47; M. F. Markland, 'The Structure of *The Kingis Quair*', *Research Studies of the State College of Washington*, xxv (1957), 273–86; J. MacQueen, 'Tradition and the Interpretation of the *Kingis Quair*', *RES* NS xii (1961), 117–31; J. R. Simon, *Le Livre du Roi* (Paris, 1967).

A number of other poems have been attributed to James. A poem entitled by Skeat *A Ballad of Good Counsel* first appeared in *Ane Compendious Buik of Godly and Spirituall Songis* (1578), and was included by J. R. Lumby in his edition of *Ratis Raving and other Moral and Religious Pieces in Prose and Verse*, EETS OS 43 (1870), and by W. W. Skeat in his edition of *The Kingis Quair* for the STS (above). Two other poems, *Peblis to the Play* and *Christis Kirk on the Grene*, have been attributed to James with less confidence. *Peblis to the Play* was first published by Pinkerton in his *Select Scottish Ballads* (1783), and *Christis Kirk on the Grene* first appeared as a broadside, printed by Patrick Wilson (1643).

John Kay

The Latin *Rhodie obsidionis descriptio* (Rome, 1478) by W. Caorsin was the source of Kay's work, printed by Lettou and Machlinia (1482?) under the title *The Siege . . . of Rhodes*. It has never been reprinted.

MARGERY KEMPE, *c.* 1373–*c.* 1440

The work of this 'writer' was known till recently only by a *Shorte Treatyse of Contemplacyon, taken out of the Boke of Margarie Kempe*, and published by W. de Worde in 1501. The researches of Miss H. E. Allen brought to light the whole book, and a modernized version of this, edited by the owner, Col. W. Butler-Bowdon, was published in 1936. An edition of the original text was undertaken by the EETS, and Part I, containing the text, facsimiles, and voluminous notes, was published in 1940 (no. 212). The text is by S. B. Meech, while the notes are contributed jointly by him and H. E. Allen. Part II by Miss Allen was to have contained a study of the women mystics of the Middle Ages in England, but she died before completing it.

WALTER KENNEDY, *c.* 1460–*c.* 1508

The *Poems of Walter Kennedy* have been collected and edited by J. Schipper with an introduction and notes in his edition published in Vienna (1901).

GEOFFREY DE LA TOUR-LANDRY, *fl.* 1360–1400

The Book of the Knight of La Tour-Landry, composed for the instruction of his daughters, was first printed by Caxton, in his own translation, in 1484. An earlier translation from Harleian MS. 1764 (*c.* 1440) was edited by T. Wright, EETS OS 33 (1868), and a revised edition of this by J. J. Munro was published for the Society in 1906. Selections from Caxton's text were printed by G. B. Rawlings, with notes and glossary (1902), and G. S. Taylor edited a modernized but unemasculated version in 1930. A complete edition of Caxton's text, edited by M. Y. Offord with full apparatus, was published by EETS in 1971 (SS 2).

Geoffrey's story of *King Ponthus and the Fair Sidoine* was translated anonymously about 1450, and has been edited by F. J. Mather in *PMLA* xii (1897), 1–150. The work is prefaced by an exhaustive introduction, ibid. i–lxvii, and follows the text of Bodleian MS. Digby 185.

NICHOLAS LOVE, *fl.* 1400

Love's translation of the *Meditationes Vitæ Christi*, wrongly attributed to St. Bonaventure, was written early in the fifteenth century under the title of *The Mirrour of the Blessed Lyf of Jesu Christ.* It was first published by Caxton (1486; ii, 1490; iii, W. de Worde 1494), and was edited in 1908 for the Roxburghe Club by L. F. Powell. An ordinary edition was issued at the same time. There is a valuable article by E. Zeeman on 'Nicholas Love: a Fifteenth-Century Translator', *RES* NS vi (1953), 113–27.

HENRY LOVELICH, *fl.* 1450

The complete text of Lovelich's *Merlin* was edited by E. A. Kock. The first two volumes were issued as EETS ES 93 (1904) and 112 (1913), while the third volume appeared as no. 185 (1930).

The History of the Holy Graal was edited for the Roxburghe Club, with a long introduction and notes, by F. J. Furnivall (2 vols., 1861–3). He also edited the four volumes of the text for the EETS ES 20, 24, 28, 30 (1874–8), the fifth volume, containing a study of the Legend of the Holy Grail, its sources, character, and development, being contributed by Dorothy Kempe, EETS ES 95 (1905).

The uncertainty as to this author's name was resolved by R. W. Ackerman, *MLN* lxvii (1952), 531–3.

WILLIAM LYCHEFELDE, d. 1447

Lychefelde's poem, *The Complaint of God*, was first edited by J. O. Halliwell, Percy Soc. 14 (1844), 87–8, and also by E. Borgström, with an historical and critical introduction, *Anglia*, xxxiv (1911), 508–25. A list of known manuscripts will be found in Brown and Robbins, *The Index of Middle English Verse* (1943). Although Lychefelde is reported to have left behind him 3,083 sermons 'written in English with his own hand', they seem to have perished, save for a little tract on the Five Senses. See G. R. Owst, *Preaching in Medieval England* (1926), 24.

JOHN LYDGATE, *c.* 1370–*c.* 1448–9

This entry comprises: (1) early editions of Lydgate; (2) manuscripts; (3) facsimiles; (4) editions of individual longer works; (5) editions of minor poems; (6) edition of prose work; (7) works attributed to Lydgate; (8) general criticism;

(9) books and articles on special topics: (*a*) versification, (*b*) prose, (*c*) sources.

1. *Early Editions*

The early editions of the more important of Lydgate's works are: *The Chorle and the Birde* (Caxton, 1477?; Pynson, 1493); *The Complaint of the Black Knight* (W. de Worde, n.d.); *The Danse Macabre* (in *The Falle of Princis*) (Tottel, 1554); *The Falle of Princis* (Pynson, 1494); *The Hystorye, Sege and Dystruccyon of Troye* (Pynson, 1513); *The Hors, the Shepe and the Ghoos* (Caxton, 1477?; W. de Worde, n.d., 1500); *The Lyf of Our Lady* (Caxton, 1484); *The Prouerbes of Lydgate* (W. de Worde, 1510?); *The Governaunce of Kynges and Prynces* (Pynson, 1511); *The Serpent of Division* (Rogers, 1559); *The Siege of Thebes* (W. de Worde, 1500?); *The Temple of Glas* (Caxton, 1477; W. de Worde, 1495?, 1500); *The Testament of J. Lydgate* (Pynson, 1515?); *The Vertues of the Masse* (W. de Worde, 1520?).

2. *Manuscripts*

Many manuscripts of Lydgate's various works have survived. We still have at least fifty-five manuscripts of the *Dietary*, forty-three of the *Life of Our Lady*, thirty-four of the lengthy *Fall of Princes*, thirty of *The Siege of Thebes*, twenty-three of the Troy Book, twenty of *Secrets of Old Philosophers*, fifteen of *The Churl and the Bird*, fifteen of *The Danse Macabre*, &c. Many of these are very handsome copies and were evidently executed for presentation to patrons. See, for example, Cottonian MS. Augustus A. IV, where Lydgate is shown kneeling before Henry V and presenting a copy of his Troy Book, or Harleian MS. 1766, where Lydgate and another are shown presenting the *Fall of Princes* to a seated figure. For further information about the practice of presenting copies of works to patrons, see K. J. Holtzknecht, *Literary Patronage in the Middle Ages* (Philadelphia, 1923), 478–9. The list of Lydgate's manuscripts in *The Index of Middle English Verse* by Brown and Robbins (1943), augmented in the *Supplement* by Robbins and Cutler (1965), supplants all the earlier lists, including that in the *DNB* and elsewhere. More detailed information concerning many of these manuscripts will be found in E. P. Hammond, *English Verse between Chaucer and Surrey* (1927), and by reference to the articles listed there.

3. *Facsimiles*

Several facsimiles of early editions of Lydgate's works were issued at Cambridge under the supervision of F. Jenkinson as follows: *The Chorle and the Birde* from Caxton's first edition of 1477? (1906); *The Horse, the Sheep and the Ghoos* from the 1500 edition of W. de Worde (1906); *The Temple of Glas* from Caxton's first edition of 1477 (1905).

4. *Editions of Longer Works*

There is no complete modern edition of Lydgate's works. Even the unflagging efforts of F. J. Furnivall to found a Lydgate Society to print everything Lydgate wrote were unsuccessful. His works are slowly being edited, mainly by the EETS. Among modern editions (which usually contain full introductions, notes, and apparatus) may be noted the following EETS volumes: *The Dance of Death*, ed. by F. Warren and B. White, 181 (1931); *The Fall of Princes*, ed. by H. Bergen, ES 121–4 (1918–19); *The History . . . of Troy*, ed. by H. Bergen, ES 97, 103, 106, 126 (1906–35); *The Pilgrimage of the Life of Man*, ed. by F. J. Furnivall and K. B. Locock, ES 77, 83, 92 (1899–1904); *Reason and Sensuality*, ed. by E. Sieper, ES 84, 89 (1901–3); *Secrets of Old Philosophers* (*The Governance of Princes*), ed. by R. Steele, ES 66 (1894); *The Siege of Thebes*, ed. by A. Erdmann and E. Ekwall, ES 108, 125 (1911–30); *The Temple of Glass*, ed. by J. Schick, ES 60 (1891). A critical edition of *The Life of Our Lady* has been made by J. A. Lauritis, R. A. Klinefelter, and V. F. Gallagher (Duquesne Studies, Louvain, 1961).

5. *Editions of Minor Poems*

The most important collections of the minor poems are to be found in the pioneer edition of J. O. Halliwell[-Phillipps], *The Minor Poems of Lydgate* (Percy Soc., 1840). This has been replaced by the definitive edition of the EETS in two volumes. The first of these has a long introductory essay on 'The Lydgate Canon', by the editor, H. N. MacCracken, and contains sixty-nine religious poems, EETS ES 107 (1911), while the second, edited by MacCracken and M. Sherwood, contains seventy-seven secular poems, EETS 192 (1934). A third part which was to contain essays on the canon and a commentary has not appeared.

6. *Edition of Prose Work*

For a discussion of Lydgate's prose work, *The Serpent of Division*, reference should be made to H. N. MacCracken's edition (1911) and to a note by the same author, *MLR* viii (1913), 103–4.

7. *Works attributed to Lydgate*

Many poems attributed to Lydgate by early editors have been shown not to be his. The classic work on the subject is that of H. N. MacCracken in 'The Lydgate Canon' (see above), to which should now be added the exhaustive appendix on the canon by W. F. Schirmer, *John Lydgate* (1961), 264–86.

8. *General Criticism*

The best critical work on Lydgate is that of Miss E. P. Hammond in her *English Verse between Chaucer and Surrey* (1927), 77, 101, and in her introductions and notes on the extracts from Lydgate which she prints in the same volume. A more favourable view of Lydgate has recently been advocated by W. F. Schirmer, *John Lydgate*, (first published in German 1952, tr. 1961), J. Norton-Smith, *John Lydgate: Poems* (1966), A. Renoir, *The Poetry of John Lydgate* (1967), and D. Pearsall, *John Lydgate* (1970). J. Schick's introduction to his edition of *The Temple of Glass* and that of E. Sieper to *Reason and Sensuality* are also valuable for the study of Lydgate's life and works. Thomas Gray made some study of Lydgate which is of interest, and may be found reprinted in E. Gosse's edition of Gray (1884), i. 387–409. Some further information and comment is given by W. J. Courthope, *History of English Poetry* (1895), i. 321–33; G. Saintsbury, *CHEL* ii (1908), 197–205; while an unduly laudatory account of Lydgate is given by Churton Collins in *Ephemera Critica* (1901), 99, 115, 198–9.

9. *Books and Articles on Special Topics*

Special topics are dealt with as follows:

(*a*) *Versification.* Much work has been done in an attempt to deal with Lydgate's unusual versification. In addition to the studies of Schick and Sieper mentioned above, the curious may consult A. H. Licklider, *Chapters on the Metric of the Chaucer Tradition* (Baltimore, 1910); H. Reger, *Die epische Cäsur in der*

Chaucerschule (Bayreuth, 1910); C. F. Babcock, 'The Metrical Use of Inflectional *-e* in Middle English, with Particular Reference to Chaucer and Lydgate', *PMLA* xxix (1914), 59–92; E. P. Hammond, 'The Nine-Syllabled Pentameter Line in some Post-Chaucerian MSS.', *MP* xxiii (1925), 129–52. G. Saintsbury in his *History of English Prosody*, i (1906), 219–31 discusses Lydgate's prosodic characteristics, and protests against the 'touching up' of the texts by his editors in the interest of 'smoothness'. C. S. Lewis attempted to make Lydgate's lines more readable by reading them as half-lines, each half-line containing not less than two or more than three stresses. His article, entitled 'The Fifteenth-Century Heroic Line', is printed in *Essays and Studies of the English Association*, xxiv (1938), 28–41.

(*b*) *Prose*. M. Schlauch has discussed 'Stylistic Attributes of John Lydgate's Prose' in *To Honor Roman Jakobson* (Paris, 1967), 1757–68.

(*c*) *Sources*. Lydgate's source material has been investigated by E. Koeppel, *Lydgate's Story of Thebes, eine Quellenuntersuchung* (Munich, 1884) and *Laurents de Premierfait und John Lydgate's Bearbeitung von Boccaccio's De Casibus Virorum Illustrium* (Munich, 1885), while extracts from the Latin and French texts are given in vol. iv of H. Bergen's edition of *The Fall of Princes* (above). The source material of *Reason and Sensuality* is carefully dealt with by J. Schick, *Kleine Lydgate-Studien* (*Anglia Beiblatt*, viii (1898), 134–54), and by E. Sieper, *Les Échecs amoureux und ihre englische Übertragung* (Weimar, 1898). Most of the introductions to the EETS editions have some remarks on the sources.

SIR THOMAS MALORY, *fl.* 1470

A bibliography to the date of publication will be found in Sir E. K. Chambers, *English Literature at the Close of the Middle Ages* (1946), which forms vol. ii, part ii, of this series. To this must now be added *The Works of Sir T. Malory*, edited by E. Vinaver (3 vols., 1947; 2nd edn., with up-to-date bibliography, 1967).

'SIR JOHN MANDEVILLE'

There are a number of English versions of the *Travels*, for details of which see J. W. Bennett's *The Rediscovery of Sir John Mandeville* (New York, 1954). The most important versions are: (1) Some thirty-three manuscripts of what is known as the

'Defective Version', which is an abridged version of the French text, and was printed by Pynson (1496) and by W. de Worde (1499, *c.* 1503, *c.* 1510). Thomas East reprinted it in 1568, and a limited edition of this, with the addition of the passage first published in 1725 from the Cottonian MS. Titus C. XVI (*c.* 1400), was reprinted at Oxford in 1932 with facsimiles of the woodcuts. (2) The Cottonian MS. was most recently reprinted by P. Hamelius for the EETS, OS 153–4 (1919, 1923) and by M. C. Seymour, *Mandeville's Travels* (1967). A facsimile of folio 60v appears in C. E. Wright's *English Vernacular Hands* (1960), 17. (3) British Museum MS. Egerton 1932, together with a French version, were printed for the Roxburghe Club by G. F. Warner (1889). This edition was enhanced by a long introduction which discusses the vexed questions of authorship, sources, and versions. The text has been modernized by M. Letts, *Mandeville's Travels: Texts and Translations*, in his edition for the Hakluyt Society, 2nd ser. 102 (1953). (4) The Bodley Version (MS. Rawl. D 99) is printed by Letts, and another Bodley Manuscript (MS. e Museo 116) is printed by M. C. Seymour, EETS 253 (1963), *The Bodley Version of Mandeville's Travels.*

The relation of the various groups of manuscripts is discussed by J. Vogels, *Handschriftliche Untersuchungen über die englische Version Mandeville's* (Crefeld, 1891). A brief but masterly account of the questions at issue will be found in K. Sisam, *Fourteenth Century Verse and Prose* (1921), 94–6, 238–42; a more recent account in M. C. Seymour's 1967 edition, pp. 272–6; and a full list of the manuscripts in his edition of the metrical version, *The Boke of Mawndevile*, EETS 269 (1973).

There is a good appreciation of Mandeville by A. D. Greenwood in *CHEL* ii (1908), 78–87, and full-length studies by M. Letts, *Sir John Mandeville; the Man and his Book* (1949), and by J. W. Bennett (above).

'Who was Sir John Mandeville?' has been treated by the above authors and also by D. Murray in *John de Berdens otherwise Sir John Mandeville and the Pestilence* (1891) and by I. Jackson, 'Who was Sir John Mandeville?', *MLR* xxiii (1928), 466–8, and also by P. Hamelius in his edition for the EETS (above).

A. Steiner, *Speculum*, ix (1934), 144–7 thinks the French original was written between 1365 and 1371, while M. C. Seymour, *Mandeville's Travels* (1967), p. xiii, suggests about 1357.

JOHN METHAM, *fl.* 1448

His *Amoryus and Cleopes* was first edited by H. Craig, EETS OS 132 (1916), 1–81, while in the same volume also appeared his 'Treatises on Palmistry and Physiognomy, Prognostications, etc.', 84–158. The unique manuscript is now deposited at Princeton University (Garrett, 141).

JOHN MIRK, *fl.* 1403

Liber festiualis or *The Festyuall* was first printed by Caxton in 1483, and it was so popular that there were twelve editions by Caxton, Pynson, de Worde, and others before 1500. The text was edited, under the title *Mirk's Festial*, with a glossary by T. Erbe for the EETS ES 96 (1905). Part II, which was to contain a full commentary, has not been published. His *Instructions for Parish Priests*, a work in couplets, was edited by E. Peacock, EETS OS 31 (1868, rev. 1902). It survives in seven manuscripts. An interpolated tract giving advice to village priests on how to answer ignorant but conceited laymen is printed by K. Young in *Speculum*, xi (1936), 224–31.

See also C. Horstmann, *Altenglische Legenden*, neue Folge (Heilbronn, 1881), cix–xxvii for a general account of the manuscripts and contents of the *Festial*, and *SP* xxxiv (1936), 36–48, for an analysis by L. L. Steckman of the Harleian MS. (2247, 1483) which is a collection of sermons drawn from the *Golden Legend* by Mirk.

For much interesting comment on Mirk, see the two works of G. R. Owst, *Preaching in Medieval England* (1926) and *Literature and Pulpit in Medieval England* (1933), *passim*, and that of J. A. Mosher, *The Exemplum in the Early Religious and Didactic Literature of England* (New York, 1911), 107–13.

RICHARD MISYN, d. 1462?

Misyn's translation of Rolle's *Incendium Amoris* (1435–6) was first edited by R. Harvey, EETS OS 106 (1896). It was also put into modern English by F. M. M. Comper with a valuable introduction by E. Underhill (1914, 1920). Misyn also translated Rolle's *De Emendatione Vitæ* under the title *Mendynge of Lyfe* (1434), and this is also included in Harvey's edition. A second translation, by an anonymous hand, entitled *Of the Amendment of Mannes Lif* (*c.* 1460), was edited by W. H. Hulme, Western Reserve Studies (Cleveland, 1919).

T. NORTON, 1415–?

The Ordinall of Alchemy has survived in thirty manuscripts and was first printed with an introduction by Elias Ashmole in his *Theatrum Chemicum* (1652), 1–106. There is a facsimile reproduction of this by E. J. Holmyard (1928). Further information about Norton will be found in an 'Enquiry into the Authorship of the *Ordinal*' by M. Nierenstein and P. F. Chapman, *Isis* (1922–3), 290–321. A new edition by J. Reidy is in preparation for EETS.

JOHN PAGE, *fl.* 1418

The unpolished verses of Page upon the Siege of Rouen (1418) intercalated in the *Brut* were edited by F. Madden and published in *Archaeologia*, xxii (1829), 350–98, by J. Gairdner in *Historical Collections of a Citizen of London*, Camden Soc. (1872), and by H. Huscher (Leipzig, 1927).

REGINALD PECOCK, *c.* 1390–*c.* 1461

Pecock's voluminous works have not survived in great numbers. A full list of his extant and lost writings will be found in V. H. H. Green's *Reginald Pecock* (1945), 238–45. This volume contains the most complete account of Pecock and his work, and supersedes E. A. Hannick's *Reginald Pecock* (Washington, 1922).

Contemporary accounts of Pecock will be found in *Three Fifteenth-Century Chronicles*, ed. by J. Gairdner, Camden Soc. (1880), 167 ff., and in *Monumenta Franciscana*, Rolls Series, 2 vols. (1858–82), ii. 174–5. Violently antagonistic accounts of Pecock are given by his contemporaries, Thomas Gascoigne, *Loci e Libro Veritatum*, ed. by J. E. T. Rogers (1881), and John Whethamstede, *Registrum*, Rolls Series, 2 vols. (1872–3), i. 279–88, ed. by H. T. Riley. Further information concerning Pecock may be found in *The Life of Dr. Pecock* by J. Lewis (1744, 1820), and in *Studies in English History* by J. Gairdner and J. Spedding (1881), 19–51. E. M. Blackie discusses Pecock's views and character in *EHR* xxvi (1911), 448–68, while further valuable studies are those of E. F. Jacob, 'Reginald Pecock, Bishop of Chichester', in the *Proceedings of the British Academy*, xxxvii (1953), 121–54, and E. E. Emerson, 'Reginald Pecock, Christian Rationalist', *Speculum*, xxxi (1956), 235–42.

Apart from the publication of *The Book of Faith* (see below),

Pecock's works remained in manuscript until 1860, when his most important work, *The Repressor of Overmuch Blaming of the Clergy*, Rolls Series, 2 vols. (1860), was edited by C. Babington. In addition to the text, vol. ii contains Pecock's vindication of his famous sermon at Paul's Cross, entitled 'Abbreviatio Reginaldi Pecock', and also extracts from John of Bury's answer to *The Repressor* (ii. 567–613). Babington's general introduction to Pecock's life and works, although superseded in some ways by more recent work, is still of great value. *The Repressor* was followed some fifty years later by *The Book of Faith*, ed. by J. L. Morison (1909). An earlier edition of this work was edited by H. Wharton in 1688, but this contained a summary only of Part I, although Part II was printed in full. The EETS has published three more works, two edited by E. V. Hitchcock: *The Donet*, OS 156 (1921) and *The Folewer to the Donet*, 164 (1924), both of which contain valuable introductions. *The Reule of Crysten Religioun* was edited by W. C. Greet, 171 (1927), while a description of this work had previously been made by J. Gairdner for Messrs. J. Pearson & Co.'s sale catalogue of 1911. Facsimiles of pages of these three works will be found as frontispieces to the EETS editions.

Pecock's language has been studied by C. Wager, 'The Language of Pecock', *MLN* ix (1894), 97–9; F. Schmidt, *Studies in the Language of Pecock* (Upsala, 1900); R. Huchon, *Histoire de la langue anglaise* (Paris, 2 vols., 1923–30), ii. 358–62. For his syntax, see B. Zickner, *Syntax und Stil in 'The Repressour'* (Berlin, 1900), and Miss Hitchcock's edition of *The Folewer*.

Estimates of Pecock as a writer of prose will be found in *CHEL* ii (1908), 287–96; G. P. Krapp, *The Rise of English Literary Prose* (1915), 64–75; R. W. Chambers, *On the Continuity of English Prose* (1932), 135–7.

J.? Quixley

A number of Gower's *Ballades Royal* were translated from the French into a Northern English dialect about 1402 by J.? Quixley. They will be found, edited by H. N. MacCracken, in the *Yorkshire Archaeological Journal*, xx (1909), 35–50.

George Ripley, d. 1490?

The Compende of Alkemye (or *The Twelve Gates*) survives in at least twenty-four manuscripts. It was first edited by Ralph

Rabbards (1591) and again by Cassel (1649). Elias Ashmole included it with most of Ripley's other works, both Latin and English, in his *Theatrum Chemicum* (1652), 117–93. Full information concerning the Latin and English manuscripts of his work will be found in D. W. Singer, *A Catalogue of Latin and Vernacular Alchemical Manuscripts in Great Britain and Ireland dating from before the XVI Century* (3 vols., Brussels, 1928–31).

SIR RICHARD ROS, 1429–?

His translation of Alain Chartier's *La Belle Dame sans Merci* has survived in seven manuscripts, and was first printed as Chaucer's by Pynson (1526) and in subsequent editions, until rejected by Tyrwhitt (1775). Skeat reprinted it from Thynne's 1532 edn. in *The Complete Works of Chaucer* (7 vols., 1884–7), vii. 299–326. There is an interesting series of articles on 'La Belle Dame sans Merci et ses imitations' by A. Piaget in *Romania*, xxx (1901), 22–48, 317–51; xxxi (1902), 315–49; xxxiii (1904), 179–208; xxxiv (1905), 375–428, 559–602. In *Sir Richard Roos, Lancastrian Poet* (1961) Miss E. Seaton made endeavours to show that Ros was responsible for much fifteenth-century poetry generally attributed to others. Her critical methods have been widely discredited.

JOHN RUSSELL, *fl.* 1450

His *Boke of Kervyng & Nortur* in rhyming quatrains has been edited by F. J. Furnivall in his *Early English Meals and Manners*, EETS OS 32 (1868, 1931), 1–83.

STEPHEN SCROPE, 1397?–1472

His *Dicts and Sayings of the Philosophers* has been twice edited in recent years. Miss M. E. Schofield published her privately printed edition of Scrope's text (Philadelphia, 1936) and Dr. Curt F. Bühler edited this text and others for his edition for the EETS, 211 (1941). Scrope's translation of Christine de Pisan's *Epistle of Othea to Hector or the Boke of Knyghthode*, made about 1440, was edited by Sir G. Warner for the Roxburghe Club (1904). In his introduction to this edition Sir George gives the fullest account of Scrope that we have, but both G. Poulett Scrope's *History of Castle Combe* (1852) and Gairdner's introduction to the *Paston Letters* (1904 edn., i. 153–6) will be found useful. Dr. Bühler has made a new critical edition of *The Epistle of Othea*, with full notes on sources, in EETS 264 (1970).

JOHN SHIRLEY, *c.* 1366–1456

The 'commonplace books' consisting of selections made by Shirley from Chaucer, Lydgate, and others are exhaustively discussed by E. P. Hammond in an important series of articles in *Anglia* and other periodicals. Details of these will be found in E. P. Hammond, *English Verse between Chaucer and Surrey* (1927), 191–7. On the general subject of Shirley's work, see also A. Brusendorff, *The Chaucer Tradition* (1926), 207–85, 453–73; E. P. Hammond, *Chaucer: a Bibliographical Manual* (1908), 515–17. The out-of-date work of O. Gaertner, *John Shirley, sein Leben und Wirken* (Halle, 1904) is replaced by the above and by an article by A. I. Doyle, 'More Light on John Shirley', *Medium Ævum*, xxx (1961), 93–101, which corrects the work of previous writers. Facsimile pages of Shirley's manuscripts may be seen in F. N. Robinson, *Harvard Studies and Notes in Philology and Literature*, v (1896), 178; the Chaucer Society's *Autotype Specimens of the Chief Chaucer MSS.* (1876), Part I, plate iv; and A. Brusendorff (above), 280.

A translation by Shirley of Legrand's *The Boke cleaped 'les bones meurs'* (*c.* 1440) exists in B.M. Additional MS. 5467 (cf. *The Book of Good Maners*, translated by Caxton, and published by him in 1487). Shirley's *Cronycle of the Dethe and False Murdure of James Stewarde* (*c.* 1440) was printed by J. Stevenson, *The Life and Death of King James the First of Scotland*, Maitland Club (1837).

WILLIAM THORPE, d. 1460?

The Examination of William Thorpe before Archbishop Arundel was probably first printed at Antwerp (*c.* 1530). There was a second edition in J. Foxe's *Actes and Monuments* and there were subsequent editions. It was reprinted in modern spelling by A. W. Pollard in his *Fifteenth Century Prose and Verse* (1903), 97–174.

JOHN TIPTOFT, EARL OF WORCESTER, *c.* 1427–70

His translation of Buonaccorso de Pistoia's *Controversia de Nobilitate*, entitled *The Declamacion of Noblesse*, was made about

1465 and was published by Caxton in 1481. It will be found reprinted by R. J. Mitchell in her study *John Tiptoft* (1938). Tiptoft also drew up the 'Ordinances for Joustes and Triumphes' (1466) printed as Appendix iv by F. H. Cripps-Day in *The History of the Tournament in England and France* (1918). What else Tiptoft translated is a matter of controversy. See H. B. Lathrop's article in *MLN* xli (1926), 496–501 and C. Clark in *TLS*, 22 Aug. 1952, p. 549; R. J. Mitchell (above), p. 242; K. B. McFarlane, 'William Worcester: a Preliminary Survey', in *Studies presented to Sir Hilary Jenkinson*, ed. J. C. Davies (1957), 215–16; and N. Davis in the paper mentioned below under William Worcester, pp. 251–3.

JOHN TREVISA, 1326–1402

A number of translations were made by Trevisa at the end of the fourteenth century. Higden's *Polychronicon*, translated by him about 1380, was first published by Caxton (1482); the edition by C. Babington and J. R. Lumby for the Rolls Series is in nine volumes (1865–86). This edition also contains the text of a later anonymous translation (*c.* 1450) which continues Higden's narrative to 1401. A useful selection will be found in K. Sisam, *Fourteenth Century Verse and Prose* (1921). For fuller information concerning the translations see B. L. Kinkade, *The English Translations of Higden's Polychronicon* (Urbana, 1934). Trevisa's possible participation in the Wycliffite translation of the Bible is dealt with by D. C. Fowler in 'John Trevisa and the English Bible', *MP* lviii (1960), 81–98.

Trevisa's translation of the great encyclopedia of Bartholomeus Anglicus, *De Proprietatibus Rerum*, was printed by W. de Worde (*c.* 1495), and a selection from this was edited by R. Steele under the title of *Medieval Lore* (1905). For further information see pp. 263–4 above. Trevisa's *Dialogue between Master and Clerk* was mentioned by J. Maclean in *J. Smyth's Lives of the Berkeleys* (3 vols., 1883), i. 343. It was printed by A. W. Pollard in his *Fifteenth Century Prose and Verse* (1903), 203–8, and by A. J. Perry, EETS 167 (1925).

Trevisa's life and work are dealt with in the introduction to the Rolls Series edition, and in H. J. Wilkins, *Was John Wycliffe a Negligent Pluralist? also John de Trevisa, his Life and Work* (New York, 1915; with an Appendix, 1916).

WILLIAM TWITI, *fl.* 1328

The *Treatise on Hunting*, by Twiti, Court Huntsman of Edward II, survives in an English translation of *c.* 1420. It was originally written about 1328 in Anglo-Norman, and was first printed in an edition of 25 copies by Sir Thomas Phillipps at his private press at Mildenhall. An edition of 40 copies was printed at Daventry by Sir Henry Dryden and was accompanied by an introduction and notes by the editor. A revised edition by the same author made in 1844 was printed at Northampton in 1908. The tract was also published by T. Wright and J. O. Halliwell in their *Reliquiae Antiquae* (1845), i. 149–54. An edition of both French and English texts, with important discussions, was published by G. Tilander as *La Vénerie de Twiti* (Uppsala, 1956).

THOMAS USK, d. 1388

The Testament of Love first appeared in print in Thynne's *Chaucer* (1532), and is included in W. W. Skeat's facsimile of Thynne's text (1905). It was printed in Skeat's *Complete Works of Chaucer*, vii (Oxford, 1897), 1–145, with an introductory note on p. xviii, while C. Schaar has contributed a helpful exegesis in his *Notes on Thomas Usk's Testament of Love* (Lund, 1950). There is an excellent appreciation of the work by C. S. Lewis in *The Allegory of Love* (1936), 222–31. One aspect of it is studied by S. H. Heninger in his article 'The Margarite–Pearl Allegory in *The Testament of Love*', *Speculum*, xxxii (1957), 92–8. Its date has been exhaustively considered by Ramona Bressie, *MP* xxvi (1928), 17–29. For the identification of the author's name, see *The Athenæum*, i (1897), 184, 215; Skeat, *Complete Works of Chaucer*, vii (1897), pp. xix–xxii; and H. Bradley, 'Thomas Usk and "The Testament of Love"', in *Collected Papers* (1928).

JOHN WALTON, *fl.* 1410

Walton's verse translation of Boethius, *De Consolatione Philosophiae*, survives in twenty-three manuscripts. The work was first printed in 1525 as *The Book of Comfort* by T. Rychard at Tavistock Monastery. It has been edited by M. Science, EETS 170 (1927) with a facsimile page of f. 62*a* of the Lincoln Cathedral MS. 108. A useful introduction and bibliography for further study of Walton will be found in E. P. Hammond, *English Verse between Chaucer and Surrey* (1927), 39–42.

WILLIAM WEY, *c.* 1407–76

The Itineraries of William Wey, Fellow of Eton College, to Jerusalem in 1458 and 1462, and to St. James of Compostella, are full of interesting information. They were printed for the Roxburghe Club (1857). A facsimile of the contemporary map to illustrate his journeys in the Holy Land will be found in the Roxburghe Club Publication 88 (1867).

ANTHONY WOODVILLE, EARL RIVERS, *c.* 1442–83

J. Mielot's translation of a Latin Cordiale, *Quatuor Novissima*, was probably the source from which Woodville made his English version, which was published by Caxton in 1479, under the title *Memorare nouissima*. It has never been edited in a modern edition. Woodville also translated from the French *The Dicts or Sayings of the Philosophers* which was published by Caxton (1477). A facsimile of this edition was issued by W. Blades (1877). For his 'balet' on fickle fortune see Ritson's *Ancient Songs*, ed. W. C. Hazlitt (1877), 149.

WILLIAM WORCESTER (*or* BOTONER), 1415–82?

An account of Worcester's career and writings will be found in the *DNB*. Much new light is given by K. B. McFarlane in 'William Worcester: a Preliminary Survey', in *Studies presented to Sir Hilary Jenkinson*, ed. J. C. Davies (1957), 196–221. His *Itinerarium* was edited by J. Nasmith in 1778, and by J. H. Harvey as *William Worcestre: Itineraries* in 1969, while the *Annales Rerum Anglicarum, 1324–1491* (now not thought to be his) was edited by T. Hearne (1728, 1774) and by J. Stevenson, *Letters and Papers Illustrative of the Wars in France*, Rolls Series (1861–4), vol. ii, pt. 2. The most recent account of the present state of knowledge about Worcester is that of N. Davis on pp. 249–53 of *Medieval Literature and Civilization*, ed. D. A. Pearsall and R. A. Waldron (1969).

ANDREW OF WYNTOUN, 1350?–1420?

The Orygynale Cronykil of Scotland, Wyntoun's only work, survives in at least nine manuscripts. It was first edited by J. Macpherson (1795), who published extracts only. In 1872–9 his work was revised by D. Laing and published in the 'Historians of Scotland' series. The definitive edition is by

F. J. Amours, STS 50, 53–4, 56–7, 63 (6 vols., 1902–14), of which vol. i contains full introductory matter. The standard literary histories of Scotland (see above, Section III. 1 (*b*)) treat of Wyntoun's value as an historical source and as literature. See also Sir H. Maxwell, *The Early Chronicles relating to Scotland* (1912).

James Yonge, *fl.* 1420

His translation of the *Secreta Secretorum*, attributed to Aristotle, was written in Ireland *c.* 1420, and was edited by R. Steele for the EETS ES 74 (1898), 119–248.

VII. ANONYMOUS WRITINGS

This section comprises (1) works in verse or prose, whether original or translations, whose authors are unknown; (2) romances that were probably *first written and composed* (not merely written down) in the fifteenth century. A number of romances are edited by W. H. French and C. B. Hale, *Middle English Metrical Romances* (1930), referred to below as 'French and Hale'.

1. Works in Verse or Prose

Alphabet of Tales

A translation of the *Alphabetum Narrationum*, entitled *An Alphabet of Tales*, was edited by M. M. Banks for the EETS OS 126–7 (1904–5). This edition lacks notes and introduction. The problem of the authorship of *Alphabetum* is excellently discussed by J. A. Herbert, *Library*, vi (1905), 94–101, who gives good reasons for rejecting Étienne de Besançon in favour of Arnold of Liège as the author.

Pseudo-Aristotle

Prose translations deriving from the *Secreta Secretorum* attributed to Aristotle were made during the fifteenth century in some numbers. The earliest, entitled *The Governance of Lordschippes*, dates from *c.* 1400 and was edited by R. Steele for the EETS ES 74 (1898), 41–118. About 1420 James Yonge (q.v.) translated it from a French version of Joffroi de Waterford, under the title of *The Gouernaunce of Prynces*, printed by Steele in the same volume, pp. 119–248. Two other anonymous translations were made in the earlier part of the century which have not yet been edited (MS. Bodl. Ashmole 396, and MS. Univ. Coll. Oxford, 85 § 2). About 1440 John Shirley the scrivener (q.v.) made a version entitled *The Gouernaunce of Prynces, seyd the Secrete of Secretes*, which will be found in B.M. Additional MS. 5467. The next translation was from an unidentified 'fraunch buke' and was made in 1456 by Gilbert Haye, *The Buke of the Governaunce of Princis*. This has been edited by J. H. Stevenson for the STS 62 (1914). An anonymous translation of *c.* 1460, entitled *The Secrete of Secretes*, was edited by R. Steele, also in EETS ES 74, 1–39.

Ars Moriendi

Early in the fifteenth century an anonymous translation from the Latin (perhaps of Gerson's *Ars Moriendi*) was made entitled *Of the Crafte of Dyinge*. It has been printed by C. Horstmann in his *Yorkshire Writers* (2 vols., 1895), ii. 406–20. A shorter version of much the same period, and also anonymous, entitled *The Craft of Deyng*, was edited for the EETS by Lumby in OS 43 (1870), 1–8. Caxton may have made the translation from the Latin which he printed about 1491, and he translated and abridged a French version which was printed after 15 June 1490. For an account of the work see F. M. M. Comper, *The Book of the Craft of Dying* (1917) and M. C. O'Connor, *The Art of Dying Well* (New York, 1942).

The Assembly of (the) Gods

The text was first printed by W. de Worde in 1498 in his edition of Chaucer. He attributed it to Lydgate, but on grounds of style this is not now accepted: see Schirmer, *Lydgate* (1961), 277. It was edited by O. L. Triggs, EETS ES 69 (1896).

The Assembly of Ladies

Three manuscripts have survived. The text was first printed by Thynne in his edition of *Chaucer* (1532) under the title *The Boke called Assemble de Damys*. It thus appears in Skeat's facsimile edition of Thynne (1905), and was also printed by Skeat in *The Complete Works of Chaucer* (7 vols., 1894–7), vii. 380–404. It was printed by Stow (1561) and in later editions, but was removed from the canon by Chalmers (1810). It has been re-edited with an introduction, notes, &c. by D. A. Pearsall (1962), who also discusses it in relation to *Generydes* in *RES* NS xii (1961), 229–37.

Ane Ballet of the Nine Nobles

This is a translation of Longuyon's *Vœux du Paon* and will be found in *Anglia*, xxi (1899), 360–3, edited with notes by W. A. Craigie, or as appendix x to I. Gollancz's edition of *The Parlement of the Thre Ages* (1915). The poem was first printed by Law, *Scotichronicon* (1521).

The Body of Policy

The Body of Polecye dates from about 1470 and is an anonymous prose translation of Christine de Pisan's *Le Livre du corps de policie* (*c.* 1405). The only manuscript is in the University Library, Cambridge (Kk. i. 5). The work published by J. Skot, *The Body of Polycye* (1521), appears to be a separate version.

The Book of Vices and Virtues

The French work of Lorens d'Orléans, known as *La Somme des vices et des vertus* or *Somme le roi*, was translated into English in a number of versions at intervals during the fifteenth century. Three manuscripts remain of 'the boc of Vices and Vertues', and these have been edited by W. N. Francis, EETS 217 (1942). Another version, which contains all or part of the French text, survives in five manuscripts, while a fragment of yet another version, known as the *Toure of All Toures*, remains in two manuscripts only. Finally, in 1487(?), Caxton published his own translation, *The Book Ryal or the Book for a King*, and this was reprinted by W. de Worde (1507). The multiplication of translations is explained by the limited circulation of medieval texts. (Compare the eight versions of portions of St. Birgitta's Revelations, seven of the *Secreta Secretorum*, &c.) Francis gives a useful introduction, with a facsimile of f. 1*a* of the Huntington Library MS. (HM 147) of *The Book of Vices and Virtues*.

The Conquest of Ireland

An anonymous translation of the *Expugnatio Hibernica* of Giraldus Cambrensis (*c.* 1188) was made about 1420 and is printed by F. J. Furnivall for the EETS OS 107 (1896). The work also exists in at least three recensions. See J. F. Dimock, Rolls Series, no. 21 (1867), v, and Furnivall, op. cit. ix–xii.

The Court of Love

The unique manuscript (Trinity College, Cambridge, R. 3. 19) was first printed in Stow's *Chaucer* (1561), and subsequently, until repudiated by W. W. Skeat in his 1878 revision of Bell's edition of Chaucer, where it is printed in vol. iv with other spurious works. It was edited again by Skeat for *The Complete Works of Chaucer* (7 vols., 1894–7), vii. 409–47. The best study is by W. A. Neilson, 'Origins and Sources of the "Court of Love"', *Harvard Studies in Philology*, vi (1899), 146–68. For the relation between *The Court of Love* and James I's *The Kingis Quair*, see W. M. Mackenzie, *The Kingis Quair* (1939), 32–7.

The Court of Sapience

Three manuscripts survive of this work, which was first printed by Caxton (1481?) and by W. de Worde (1510). There is a good modern edition by R. Spindler (Leipzig, 1927) and a useful series of extracts and an introduction to the poem in E. P. Hammond, *English Verse between Chaucer and Surrey* (1927).

The Craft of Lovers

This was first printed by Stow (1561) and in many subsequent editions of Chaucer. It was rejected from the canon by Tyrwhitt in his 'Account of the Works of Chaucer' which forms the introduction to vol. v of his *The Canterbury Tales of Chaucer* (1775–8). The poem is also fully discussed in *The Chaucer Canon* (1900), 120–2, by W. W. Skeat. Despite Tyrwhitt's view, the poem continued to be printed as Chaucer's until A. Chalmers's edition of 1810. Three manuscripts have survived.

The Craft of Venery

The Craft of Venery is to be found in B.M. Lansdowne MS. 285—a manuscript of the early sixteenth century. It was first printed by W. A. and F. Baillie Grohman in *The Master of Game* (1904), 247–8 and is included in G. Tilander's edition of Twiti (q.v.).

THE CUCKOO AND THE NIGHTINGALE

In two of the six extant manuscripts the poem is entitled 'The boke of Cupid god of loue'. First printed by Thynne in his edition of Chaucer's *Works* (1532), it was relegated to 'Poems attributed to Chaucer' in Skeat's revision of Bell's *Chaucer* (1878). A text based on Thynne is provided by Skeat, *The Complete Works of Chaucer*, vii (1897), 347–58, and a critical edition was produced by E. Vollmer, *Das mittelenglische Gedicht The Boke of Cupids* (Berlin, 1898). For the ascription of the poem to Sir Thomas Clanvowe (*fl.* 1400) by Skeat, see pp. lvii–xi of his *Works of Chaucer*, vol. vii. Brusendorff, *The Chaucer Tradition* (1926), 441–4, agrees that Clanvowe is the author and dates the poem as early as 1392. This view is supported by C. E. Ward's 'The Authorship of *The Cuckoo and the Nightingale*', *MLN* xliv (1929), 217–26, but is rejected by R. H. Robbins in an article on 'The Findern Anthology', *PMLA* lxix (1954), 630. See also K. B. McFarlane in *Lancastrian Kings and Lollard Knights* (1972), 183–4.

THE DANCE OF DEATH *or* DANSE MACABRE

The text edited for the EETS 181 (1931) by F. Warren and B. White contains an introduction, notes, and extracts. A text and a good bibliography will be found in E. P. Hammond, *English Verse between Chaucer and Surrey*, 124–42, who provides a French text on pp. 426–35. Chapter ix of R. Woolf's *The English Religious Lyric in the Middle Ages* (1968) is useful, while the subject is fully discussed by J. M. Clark, *The Dance of Death in the Middle Ages and the Renaissance* (1950), which includes a good bibliography.

DIVES AND PAUPER

Dives and Pauper (1403–10) was first printed by Pynson (1493) and afterwards by W. de Worde (1496). An important article by H. G. Pfander in *Library*, 4th ser. xiv (1933), 299–312, showed that it was not written by Henry Parker, the Carmelite, as was formerly supposed, and a further article in the same periodical by H. G. Richardson, xv (1934), 31–7, gave additional information, and a list of known extant manuscripts.

THE FLOWER AND THE LEAF

First printed by Speght in his edition of *Chaucer* (1598), it was relegated to 'Poems attributed to Chaucer' in Skeat's revised edition of Bell (1878). Skeat printed it in his *Complete Works of Chaucer*, vii (1897), 361–79, and it was edited by F. S. Ellis for the Kelmscott Press (1896) and by D. A. Pearsall (1962). It was modernized by Dryden and printed in his *Fables* (1700).

The authorship of the poem has been much disputed: see Skeat's edition vol. vii, p. lxii, and the references in E. P. Hammond's *Chaucer: a Bibliographical Manual* (1908), 423–4. G. L. Marsh adds to the discussion in *JEGP* vi (1906–7), 373–94, as does D. A. Pearsall in his edition of the poem, 3–20, where he argues against the view of Skeat that the author was a woman; and see R. H. Robbins, 'The Findern Anthology', *PMLA* lxix (1954), 630. For full discussions of possible sources see the articles by G. L. Kittredge, 'The Flower and the Leaf', *MP* i (1903), 1–17, and by G. L. Marsh, 'Sources and Analogues of *The Flower and the Leaf*', *MP* iv (1906), 121–67, 281–327. No manuscript has survived; a text formerly in the Marquis of Bath's library (Longleat 258) is missing.

Gesta Romanorum

The Latin *Gesta Romanorum* was translated into English by three independent authors in the fifteenth century, about 1430(?), 1430(?), and 1490(?) respectively. The Harleian MS. 7333 was edited for the Roxburghe Club in 1838 by F. Madden, and by S. J. H. Herrtage for the EETS ES 33 (1879). Herrtage also gives the text of the translation preserved in B.M. Additional MS. 9066 and Cambridge University Library, Kk. 1. 6. The third translation was published by W. de Worde (*c.* 1510), while short extracts appear in Madden, pp. 486–503, and Herrtage, pp. 429–44, together with information concerning the text. Extracts will be found in H. Morley's *Mediaeval Tales* (1886), and an exhaustive study of the original compilation was made by H. Oesterley (Berlin, 1872).

The Golden Legend

A translation from the *Legenda Aurea*, or the *Légende dorée*, was made about 1438, and is described by Pierce Butler in his *Study of the Legenda Aurea—Légende Dorée—Golden Legend* (Baltimore, 1899). The relation of this earliest translation to that of Caxton (1483?) is here discussed, and a useful bibliography is attached. A partial reproduction of Caxton's text was issued by the Holbein

Society (1878) and the work was published in three superb volumes by the Kelmscott Press (1892), ed. by F. S. Ellis. The same editor was also responsible for the publication of Caxton's text in the Temple Classics (7 vols., 1900). A review of the 'Fifteenth Century Editions of the *Legenda Aurea*' by R. F. Seybolt will be found in *Speculum*, xxi (1946), 327–38, while Sister Mary Jeremy has contributed a number of articles on Caxton's use of his source material in *Medieval Studies*, viii (1946), 97–106; *Speculum*, xxi (1946), 212–21; *MLN* lxiv (1949), 259–61; lxvii (1952), 313–17. Some of the material of the *Legenda* was also incorporated into other works. See C. Horstmann, *The Early South-English Legendary*, EETS os 87 (1887), and the same editor's *Nova Legenda Angliae* (2 vols., 1901). The Scottish Collection of Legends in metrical form dates from the late fourteenth century, and is mainly compiled from the *Golden Legend*. See W. M. Metcalfe, *Legends of the Saints*, STS (6 vols., 1888–96).

How the Good Wife Taught her Daughter

This and related texts were printed by F. J. Furnivall in *Early English Meals and Manners*, EETS os 32 (1868, 1931). There is a good modern edition with full bibliography and apparatus by T. F. Mustanoja (Helsinki, 1948).

The Imitation of Christ

The *De Imitatione Christi* exists in two versions of *c.* 1450, both of them apparently independent transcripts of another manuscript not very closely followed. The Dublin text was edited by J. K. Ingram for the EETS ES 63 (1893, 1905), 1–150; while the Cambridge text was edited by P. B. M. Allan (1923), and has been slightly modernized. The late-fifteenth-century translation of books i–iii by W. Atkinson and of book iv by Margaret, Countess of Richmond and Derby, was printed by R. Pynson (1504) and reprinted by J. K. Ingram (above), 151–283.

Informacion for Pylgrymes vnto the Holy Londe

The first three-quarters of the original Latin of this little guide was translated into English by an unknown hand. The remaining part was left in Latin. The guide was printed by W. de Worde (1498?) and reproduced in facsimile by E. G. Duff (1893).

THE ISLE OF LADIES

Under the title of 'Chaucer's Dream', this poem appeared in print for the first time in Speght's *Chaucer* (1598) and was included in subsequent editions until Skeat relegated it to 'Poems attributed to Chaucer' in his edition of Bell's *Chaucer* (1878). It was edited from the two surviving manuscripts by Jane B. Sherzer (Berlin, 1905).

JACOB'S WELL

Jacob's Well (*c.* 1440) is in process of being edited. A. Brandeis edited Part I for the EETS OS 115 (1900), but Part II has not yet appeared. A brief discussion of the treatise by F. J. Furnivall will be found in the *Academy* (1892), 171, and it is constantly quoted by G. R. Owst in his *Preaching in Medieval England* (1926) and *Literature and Pulpit in Medieval England* (1933).

KNYGHTHODE AND BATAILE

The *De Re Militari* of Vegetius was turned into 3,023 lines of rhyme royal (1457–60) by an anonymous writer. It has been edited by R. Dyboski and Z. M. Arend for the EETS 201 (1935). It was also put into prose for Thomas, Lord Berkeley early in the fifteenth century, and into Scottish prose about 1500. On all these see H. N. MacCracken, *Kittredge Anniversary Papers* (Boston, 1913), 389–403.

THE LANTERNE OF LIGHT

The Lanterne of Light, a Lollard tract of about 1409, was first published by R. Redman (1530?) and edited for the EETS OS 151 (1917) by L. M. Swinburn.

THE LIBEL OF ENGLISH POLICY

The Lybelle of Englyshe Polycye (*c.* 1436–7) was first printed in Hakluyt's *Voyages* (1598), i. 187–208. A text from a slightly different manuscript was edited by T. Wright in his *Political Poems and Songs*, Rolls Series (2 vols., 1861), ii. 157–205. In 1926 a definitive text based on a study of nine manuscripts was published by Sir G. Warner. The introduction to this edition gives all possible information, including the evidence for Sir George's belief that the poem may have been written by Adam

Moleyns. Sixteen manuscripts have been identified. See 'Some Manuscripts of *The Lybelle of Englyshe Polycye*', by F. Taylor, *JRLB* xxiv (1940).

Meditations of St. Bernard

An anonymous translation from the Latin, under the title of *Medytacions of Saynt Bernarde*, made 'by a devoute Student of the vnyuersitie of Cambrydge', was printed by W. de Worde (1496, 1499).

The Mirror of Man's Salvation

The *Speculum Humanae Salvationis*, the work of an unknown author, was translated under the title *The Miroure of Mans Saluacionne*. It was edited by A. H. Huth for the Roxburghe Club (1888), and this edition has for frontispiece a facsimile of a page of the unique manuscript. Reference may be made to O. Brix, *Über die mittelenglische Übersetzung des Speculum Humanae Salvationis*, Palaestra, 7 (Leipzig, 1900).

Palladius, *On Husbandry*

The mid-fifteenth-century verse translation of *Palladius on Husbondrie* was first edited for EETS, Part I by Barton Lodge, os 52 (1873), Part II by S. J. H. Herrtage, os 72 (1879). A better text was later edited by M. H. Liddell (Berlin, 1896), but a promised volume of notes and discussion has never appeared. For Latin texts see D. W. Singer, *Catalogue of Latin and Vernacular Alchemical Manuscripts* (1928–31), ii. 649–51.

The Pilgrimage of the Life of Man

G. de Deguilleville's *Pèlerinage de la vie humaine* was translated into prose under the title *The Pilgrimage of the Lyf of the Manhode* about 1430, and the one existing manuscript of this version was edited for the Roxburghe Club (1869) by W. A. Wright. A number of other manuscripts also contain prose versions, but their exact relationships to the above and to one another have not yet been determined.

Lydgate's verse rendering was edited from three manuscripts by F. J. Furnivall and K. B. Locock, EETS ES 77, 83, 92 (1899–1904). The same edition was also issued by the Roxburghe Club (1905).

The Pilgrimage of the Soul

A prose version of Deguilleville's *Pèlerinage de l'âme* was made about 1413, and was printed by Caxton (1483). A selection from this edition, omitting parts which the editor felt 'could neither be of advantage nor interest to the general reader', was edited by Katherine I. Cust in 1859 under the title of *The Boke of the Pylgremage of the Sowle.* This contains coloured illustrations from the British Museum Egerton MS. 615, and others from the prose French edition printed by Verard (Paris, 1499). Facsimiles of some pages of Caxton's print appear in *Apollo*, xiv (1931), 205–13.

Ratis Raving

Ratis Raving, composed in Scotland after 1450, is a moralizing work in couplets, containing the advice of a father to his son. It was first edited by J. R. Lumby, EETS os 43 (1870), but has been re-edited by R. Girvan, STS 3rd ser. 11 (1939) with an exhaustive introduction.

Saints' Lives

A considerable number of prose translations (usually from Latin) were made in this period. Among them may be noted *The Revelations of St. Birgitta*, ed. by W. P. Cumming for the EETS 178 (1928). A number of versions of the Revelations were made at different times in the fifteenth century, and they are fully described and some of them printed in this edition. The life of St. Catharine of Siena is to be found in *Anglia*, viii (1885), 184–96, ed. by C. Horstmann, '*A letter touchynge þe lyfe of seint Kateryn of Senys*' (*c.* 1430). The same editor is also responsible for '*Þe life of seint cristyn þe meruelous*' (*c.* 1430) in *Anglia*, viii (1885), 119–34. Horstmann also printed a prose life of Dorothea (*c.* 1425) in *Anglia*, iii (1880), 325–8. For further information concerning this saint, see J. M. Peterson, *The Dorothea Legend . . . Middle English Versions* (Heidelberg, 1910). '*The Lyfe of seint Elizabeth of Spalbeck*' (*c.* 1430) will be found in *Anglia*, viii (1885), 107–18. *The reuelations of Saynt Elysabeth, the Kynges doughter of hungarye* were first printed by W. de Worde (1493?). A modern text, ed. by C. Horstmann, will be found in *Archiv*, lxxvi (1886), 392–400. The same editor also published '*Þe lyfe of Seint Mary of Oegines*' (*c.* 1430) in *Anglia*, viii (1885), 134–84. Caxton first printed *The lyf of the holy and blessid vyrgyn saynt Wenefryde* (1485). For a modern text see *Anglia*, iii (1880), 293–319. Some particulars of the fifteenth-century *Life of St. Catharine of Alexandria* are given by A. Kurvinen in *English and Medieval Studies presented to J. R. R. Tolkien* (1962), 272–3.

THE SEVEN WISE MASTERS OF ROME

The Seven Wise Masters of Rome, first printed by Pynson in 1493, is a prose translation of the Latin *Historia Septem Sapientium*. It was reprinted by W. de Worde (1520), and this edition was used by G. L. Gomme, who edited the work for the Villon Society (1885). This popular selection of stories has survived in several versions, one of which was edited by K. Campbell (Boston, 1907), while an imperfect version was edited by K. Brunner for the EETS 191 (1933).

THE TALE OF GAMELYN

This poem was composed in the mid fourteenth century, and was included in some manuscripts of Chaucer's works as 'The Cook's Tale'. It was first printed by Urry (1721), and constantly thereafter. The Chaucer Society issued it as part of its Six Text edition of the *Tales*, nos. 8–10 and 13 (1869), and it was edited by F. J. Furnivall from another text in 1885 (no. 73). W. W. Skeat printed it as an appendix to vol. iv of his *Chaucer*, and issued it in a separate edition (1884; rev. 1893). It is included in French and Hale, 209–35, and in *Middle English Verse Romances*, ed. D. B. Sands (1966).

THE TWELVE PROFITS OF TRIBULATION

The Twelve Profits of Tribulation, an early-fifteenth-century prose tract, was printed by Caxton (1491(?); de Worde 1499). It is a translation of the Latin *Duodecim utilitates tribulationis*, sometimes attributed to Peter of Blois. An early version of this treatise is printed by C. Horstmann, *Yorkshire Writers* (2 vols., 1895), ii. 45–60.

Among minor anonymous works of this period the following are of interest: M. Förster, 'Eine nordenglische Cato-Version', *ES* xxxvi (1906), 1–55; G. H. Campbell, 'The Middle English *Evangelie*', *PMLA* xxx (1915), 529–613, 851–3; E. P. Hammond, 'The Eye and the Heart', *Anglia*, xxxiv (1911), 235–65, with text corrections by F. Holthausen, *Anglia*, xliv (1920), 85–93; R. W. Chambers and W. W. Seaton, *A Fifteenth-Century Courtesy Book* and *Two Fifteenth-Century Franciscan Rules*, EETS OS 148 (1914); W. H. Hulme, *Gospel of Nicodemus*, EETS ES 100 (1907); J. H. Blunt, *The Myroure of Oure Ladye*, EETS ES 19 (1873). A translation of Suso's *Horologium Sapientiae* was edited by C. Horstmann: '*The seuene poyntes of trewe loue and euerlastynge wisdame*', *Anglia*, x (1888), 323–89; an account of the existing manuscripts will be found in *Archiv*, clxix (1936), 76–81.

2. Romances Probably Composed in the Fifteenth Century

Full information and extensive bibliographies will be found in the new edition of J. E. Wells, *A Manual of the Writings in Middle English 1050–1500*, edited by J. Burke Severs (New Haven, 1967), fascicule i.

The Avowynge of King Arthur

This romance, of 1146 lines in tail-rhyme stanzas, is preserved only in the Ireland MS., written in the north-west Midlands in the second half of the fifteenth century. It has been edited by J. Robson in *Three Metrical Romances*, Camden Soc. (1842), by French and Hale, pp. 607–46, and by C. Brookhouse (Copenhagen, 1968).

The Awntyrs off Arthure at the Terne Wathelyne

This romance, in 55 thirteen-line stanzas using both rhyme and alliteration, exists in four manuscripts. It was first edited, from Bodleian MS. Douce 324, by J. Pinkerton in *Scotish Poems* (1792). There are several later editions, notably those by F. J. Amours in *Scottish Alliterative Poems*, STS 27 (1897) and by R. J. Gates (Philadelphia, 1969).

Blanchardyn and Eglantine

The original French verse romance was reduced into prose under the title *Blancadin et l'orgueilleuse d'amor*, and was translated by Caxton and printed by him in 1489(?). A modern edition has been produced for the EETS ES 58 (1890) by L. Kellner.

Le Bone Florence

This romance is in a north-Midland dialect and was composed about 1400. It consists of 2,187 lines in twelve-line stanzas. The unique manuscript (Camb. Univ. Libr., MS. Ff. ii. 38) has been printed in J. Ritson's *Ancient English Metrical Romanceës* (3 vols., 1802), iii. 1–92, and was edited by W. Viëtor and W. A. Knobbe (Marburg, Text, 1893; Intro., 1899).

Charles the Grete

This romance was translated and printed by Caxton (1485) from a French prose text entitled *Fierabras*. It was edited by S. J. H. Herrtage for the EETS ES 36–7 (1880–1).

Duke Rowlande and Sir Ottuell of Spayne

This romance was composed about 1400 and survives in one manuscript (B.M. Add. 31042). It consists of 1,596 lines in a northern dialect. It was edited by S. J. H. Herrtage for the EETS ES 35 (1880).

Eger and Grime

Composed in the mid fifteenth century near Linlithgow on the Firth of Forth, this romance survives in two versions. The shorter text is printed by French and Hale, 671–717, and by J. W. Hales and F. J. Furnivall, *Bishop Percy's Folio Manuscript* (1867–9), i. 354–400. The longer version of 2,860 lines, together with the shorter, has been edited by J. R. Caldwell, *Eger and Grime* (Cambridge, Mass., 1933), and more recently has been fully discussed by M. Van Duzee in *A Medieval Romance of Friendship: Eger and Grime* (New York, 1968).

Emaré

This romance was written about 1400 in the north-east, and consists of 1,035 lines in twelve-line stanzas. It has been edited by E. Rickert, EETS ES 99 (1906), and also by French and Hale. It is considered by M. Schlauch in *Chaucer's Constance and Accused Queens* (New York, 1929).

Eneydos

The French prose redaction of the *Aeneid*, entitled *Livre des eneydes* (Lyons, 1483), was used by Caxton. He printed his translation in 1490, and it was edited by W. T. Culley and F. J. Furnivall for the EETS ES 57 (1890).

The Erle of Toulous

The poem comes from the north-east Midlands and dates from the early fifteenth century. Four manuscripts survive, and a modern edition has been prepared by French and Hale, 383–419.

The Four Sons of Aymon

Originally in French verse, a prose redaction under the title *Les Quatre Filz Aymon* was printed at Lyons (1480). The English version was first printed by Caxton (1489), and this has been edited for the EETS ES 44–5 (1884–5) by O. Richardson.

Generydes

Generydes (*c.* 1450) exists in two independent versions of a French original. One of these (MS. Helmingham Hall: now Pierpont Morgan MS. 876) consists of 10,086 lines in couplets and was edited by F. J. Furnivall for the Roxburghe Club (1865). The other version (Trinity College, Cambridge, MS. 1283, *c.* 1450) is in 6,995 lines in rhyme royal. This was edited by W. A. Wright for the EETS OS 55, 70 (1873–8). See also D. A. Pearsall, 'Notes on the Manuscript of "Generydes"', *Library*, 5th ser. xvi (1961), 205–10, and '*The Assembly of Ladies* and *Generydes*', *RES* NS xii (1961), 229–37.

Godefroy of Bologne

This romance is a translation from the French *Livre d'Éracle*—a redaction of the *Historia rerum in partibus transmarinis gestarum* of William, Archbishop of Tyre. It was translated and printed by Caxton (1481), and edited by M. N. Colvin for EETS ES 64 (1893).

Golagrus and Gawain

This interesting poem was written in Scotland not long before 1500, and is in stanza form with much alliteration. It is based on the French *Perceval* and was first printed by Chepman and Myllar (1508). Since then it has been many times reprinted and was definitively edited by G. Stevenson for the STS 65 (1918), 67–110.

THE GRENE KNIGHT

Composed in the south Midlands about 1500 this poem is preserved in the Percy Folio (B.M. Add. MS. 27879) and was edited by Sir F. Madden, *Syr Gawayne* (1839). It has been considered by G. L. Kittredge in his study of *Gawain and the Green Knight* (Cambridge, Mass., 1916).

GUY OF WARWICK

The second version of this romance was made in the mid fifteenth century. It consists of 11,976 lines in couplets, and was edited for the EETS, ES 25–6 (1875–6), by J. Zupitza. R. S. Crane discusses the vogue of the romance from the fifteenth century onwards in *PMLA* xxx (1915), 125–94.

THE HISTORY OF THE HOLY GRAIL

For Henry Lovelich's version, see LOVELICH, above.

THE HISTORY OF JASON

The French *Les Fais et prouesses du noble et vaillant cheualier Jason*, by R. le Fèvre, was the source of the translation made by Caxton in 1477(?). It has been edited by J. Munro for the EETS, ES 111 (1913) (text only—the projected Part II never appeared). There is a late-fifteenth-century manuscript in the Hunterian Library, Glasgow University.

THE JEASTE OF SYR GAWAYNE

A south-Midland work of the mid fifteenth century, consisting of 541 lines in six-line stanzas. It is imperfect and survives in a transcript of *c.* 1564 in the Bodleian Library (MS. Douce 261). It was edited by Sir F. Madden in his edition of *Syr Gawayne* (1839), 207–23. The sources of the romance are studied by R. E. Bennett in *JEGP* xxxiii (1934), 57–63.

KING PONTHUS AND THE FAIR SIDONE

This prose work was composed about 1450 and is a translation from the French *Ponthus et Sidoine* by Geoffrey de la Tour-Landry (see above under LA TOUR). It has been edited by F. J. Mather, *PMLA* xii (1897), 1–150, who prints the only complete text (Bodleian MS. Digby 185).

Lancelot of the Laik

Lancelot of the Laik (Camb. Univ. Libr., MS. Kk. i. 5), composed between 1482 and 1500 in Lowland Scotch, is a dull work in couplets. It was first edited by J. Stevenson for the Maitland Club (1839), and then by W. W. Skeat for the EETS, os 6 (1865). This edition contains a good introduction and notes. More recently it has been edited by M. M. Gray for the STS, 2nd ser. 2 (1912).

The Laud Troy-Book

This work was composed about 1400 and is in 18,664 lines of four-stressed rhymed couplets. It is based on Guido's *Historia Destructionis Troiae*, though some use was probably made of Benoit de Sainte-Maure's *Roman de Troie* (*c.* 1184). It is preserved in one manuscript only, Bodleian Laud Misc. 595, and was edited by J. E. Wülfing for the EETS, os 121–2 (1902–4). D. Kempe's in *ES* xxix (1901) is the best introduction to the romance.

Lyfe of Alexander

A prose version in northern English, translated from the Latin *Historia de Preliis*, is to be found in the Lincoln Cathedral (Thornton) Manuscript of *c.* 1430. This was printed by J. S. Westlake for the EETS os 143 (1913). A valuable article on this and other versions of the Alexander story was contributed by G. L. Hamilton to *Speculum*, ii (1927), 113–31. See also F. P. Magoun, Jr., *The Gests of King Alexander* (Cambridge, Mass., 1929), and G. Cary, *The Medieval Alexander* (1956).

Lyfe of Ipomydon

Written in 2,346 lines in rhyming couplets, and composed in the east Midlands before 1425, this romance survives in one manuscript, B.M. Harley 2252. It was edited by H. Weber in his *Metrical Romances* (3 vols., 1810), ii. 281–365. Another version in tail-rhyme stanzas (*Ipomadon*), extending to 8,890 lines, is in MS. Chetham 8009 (*c.* 1500). There is also a prose version of *c.* 1460 (Longleat 257). All three were edited by E. Kölbing, *Ipomedon in drei englischen Bearbeitungen* (Breslau, 1889). French and Hale print selections from MS. Chetham.

MELUSINE

Originally composed in Latin by Jean d'Arras about 1382–94, the romance was printed at Geneva in 1478. It was translated into English prose about 1500 and survives in the unique manuscript B.M. Royal 18 B. ii. The text was edited for the EETS ES 68 (1895) by A. K. Donald.

MERLIN

The French *Roman de Merlin* was translated into English prose about 1450, and this was edited by H. B. Wheatley and W. E. Mead for the EETS OS 10, 21, 36, 112 (1865–99). Both this and Lovelich's *Merlin* (q.v.) were apparently derived from one French original. In no. 36 will be found an article on 'Arthurian Localities' by J. S. Stuart Glennie, and in no. 112 'Outlines of the Legend of Merlin' by W. E. Mead.

LE MORTE ARTHUR

This romance, preserved in a single manuscript (B.M. Harleian 2252) was composed in the north-west Midlands about 1400. It derives from a version of the prose *Morte Artu* and has been several times edited, e.g. by J. D. Bruce, EETS ES 88 (1903). Its sources and relation to Malory's work are debated by J. D. Bruce and H. O. Sommer in *Anglia*, xxiii (1900), 67, xxix (1906), 429, and xxx (1907), 209.

OCTAVIAN

There are three manuscripts of the mid fifteenth century, two in a northern dialect, Lincoln Cathedral MS. 91 (Thornton), and Camb. Univ. Libr., Ff. 2. 3. 8 in twelve-line tail rhyme, and a third independent manuscript in a south-eastern dialect in six-line stanzas (B.M. Cotton Caligula A. II). The romance derives from a French original. It may be found in H. Weber, *Metrical Romances* (3 vols., 1810), J. O. Halliwell[-Phillipps], *The Romance of the Emperor Octavian*, Percy Soc. 14 (1848), or G. Sarrazin, *Octavian: zwei me. Bearbeitungen der Sage* (Heilbronn, 1885).

PARIS AND VIENNE

Paris et Vienne, first printed by G. Leeu (Antwerp, 1487) was the source from which Caxton translated this romance and printed it on 10 December 1485. It has been edited by W. C. Hazlitt for the Roxburghe Club (1868) and by MacEdward Leach for the EETS 234 (1957).

PARTHENOPE OF BLOIS

This romance survives in two versions—five manuscripts in couplet and one in stanza form. The first is in a southern dialect and was edited for the Roxburghe Club in 1862 by W. E. Buckley, and by A. T. Bödtker for the EETS ES 109 (1912). Another version has come down only as a fragment of 308 lines in quatrains (MS. Penrose 10, Delamere), and was edited by R. C. Nichols for the Roxburghe Club (1873) and also appears on pp. 481–4 of Bödtker's edition.

THE RECUYELL OF THE HISTORIES OF TROYE

This was the first book translated by Caxton, and was printed at his press in Bruges in 1473–4. It is translated from the French of R. le Fèvre, *Le Recueil des histoires de Troyes*, written in 1464. Caxton's text has been reprinted by H. O. Sommer (2 vols., 1894).

THE ROMAUNS OF PARTENAY (LUSIGNAN)

Translated *c.* 1500 in the north-east Midlands in 6,615 lines of rhyme royal, the romance exists only in the Trinity College, Cambridge MS. 597 (R. 3. 17). It is a translation of a French version by Jean d'Arras and was edited by W. W. Skeat for the EETS OS 22 (1866, rev. 1899) with an introduction, notes, and glossary.

ROSWALL AND LILLIAN

No manuscript survives of this late-fifteenth-century piece, written in southern Scotland. There are fourteen leaves in rhyming couplets printed in Edinburgh in 1663 and a later print of 1775. It was edited by O. Lengert, 'Die schottische Romanze Roswall and Lillian', *ES* xvi (1892), 321 ff. from both versions, with commentary and notes in vol. xvii. 341 ff.

THE SCOTTISH ALEXANDER BUIK

No manuscript remains of this work, which survives in the unique copy of the text printed by A. Arbuthnet (1580). The poem is written in couplets and is in three parts, the first, 'Forray of Gadderis', being a translation of the *Roman d'Alixandre*, while the 'Avowis of Alexander' and the 'Great Battell of Effesoun' come from Longuyon's *Vœux du Paon.* The poem was edited for the Bannatyne Club (1831) by D. Laing, and again by R. L. G. Ritchie for the STS 2nd ser. 12, 17, 21, 25 (1921–9). The epilogue dates the work 1438. The possibility of J. Barbour's authorship of this poem is now discredited.

Siege of Melayne

A northern version of about 1400 which survives in B.M. Add. MS. 31042, dating from the mid fifteenth century. It was edited by S. J. Herrtage for the EETS ES 35 (1880).

The Siege of Thebes and of Troy

This is thought to be an epitomized version in prose of Guido's *Historia Destructionis Troiæ*, possibly refashioned from Lydgate's *Troy Book.* It has been edited (with a brief introduction) by F. Brie, *Archiv*, cxxx (1913), 269–85. In the unique manuscript (Bodl. Rawlinson Misc. D. 82) it is followed by the *Sege of Thebes*, also printed by Brie, op. cit. 40–52. *The Sege of Troy* was also edited and discussed by N. E. Griffin, *PMLA* xxii (1907), 157–200, while the origins of the poem are dealt with in 'A Middle-English Tale of Troy', *ES* xxix (1901), 1–26.

Sir Amadace

This romance, in about 800 lines of tail-rhyme stanzas apparently of north-Midland origin, is preserved in two late-fifteenth-century manuscripts which differ considerably in detail. It was first printed from National Library of Scotland MS. Advocates 19. 3. 1 by H. W. Weber in *Metrical Romances* (1810), then from the Ireland MS. by J. Robson in *Three Early English Metrical Romances*, Camden Soc. (1842). Both texts were printed by C. Brookhouse (Copenhagen, 1968).

Sir Cleges

This interesting minstrel's piece dates from the early fifteenth century, and consists of 570 lines in north-Midland dialect. There are two texts—Bodleian, Ashmole 61, and Nat. Libr. of Scotland, Advocates 19. 1. 11, both printed by A. Treichel in *Anglia*, xxii (1900), 374 ff. The Advocates text has also been edited by French and Hale, 877–95.

Sir Gowther

Composed early in the fifteenth century, this poem of 757 lines has survived in two manuscripts. It was written in the north or north-east Midlands and is taken from a Breton *lai*. It was edited from both manuscripts by K. Breul (Oppeln, 1886) and printed by E. V. Utterson in his *Early English Popular Poetry* (1817), i. 157 ff. from B.M. MS. Royal 17 B. xliii.

Sir Torrent of Portyngale

Composed early in the fifteenth century, this poem of 2,668 lines in the twelve-line stanza of the period has survived in one manuscript (Chetham 8009). It may have been taken down from recitation and has a strong ecclesiastical bias. It was edited by E. Adam for the EETS ES 51 (1887).

Sir Triamour

This romance was written in north-Midland dialect *c.* 1400 and consists of 1,719 lines in twelve-line stanzas. Two manuscripts have survived: the longer was printed by W. Copland (n.d.) and most recently edited by A. J. Erdman-Schmidt (Utrecht, 1939); the short version (1,539 lines) was edited by J. W. Hales and F. J. Furnivall in *Bishop Percy's Folio MS.* (4 vols., 1867–8), ii. 78–135.

The Song of Roland

This poem, a translation of a version of the *Chanson de Roland*, was composed in the east Midlands at the very end of the fourteenth century and exists in a fragmentary text only (B.M. Lansdowne 388). This dates from 1475 or later, and contains 1,049 lines in alliterative couplets. It has been edited by S. J. H. Herrtage for the EETS ES 35 (1880), 107–36.

The Sowdone of Babylone

This loose, condensed paraphrase of a French work has survived in one manuscript (Garrett 140). It was written in the east Midlands about 1400 and consists of 3,274 lines, mainly in quatrains. It was first edited by W. Nicol for the Roxburghe Club (1854), and later by E. Hausknecht for the EETS ES 38 (1881). Selections will be found in French and Hale, 239–84.

The Squire of Low Degree

This romance, composed in short couplets in an east-Midland dialect *c.* 1500, is probably a version of an earlier work. It was first printed by W. Copland (1550?). The text and a brief introduction are in French and Hale, 721–55, and there is an edition by W. E. Mead (Boston, 1904).

The Taill of Rauf Coilyear

Written in Scotland 1465–1500, this high-spirited work survives only in a print by R. Lekpreuik of St. Andrews, 1572. It has been several times edited: see D. Laing, *Select Remains of the Ancient Popular Poetry of Scotland* (1883); S. J. Herrtage, EETS ES 39 (1882); F. J. Amours in *Scottish Alliterative Poems*, STS 27 (1892); and W. H. Browne, *The Taill of Rauf Coilyear* (Baltimore, 1903).

The Tale of Beryn

This poem of uncertain date (after 1400) exists in a unique manuscript (Northumberland 55). It relates the adventures of the Canterbury Pilgrims on arriving at their destination, and adds a supplementary Tale. It was first published in Stow's *Chaucer* (1561), reprinted by Urry (1721) as Chaucer's *Merchant's Tale*, and reprinted several times before being edited by F. J. Furnivall for the Chaucer Society (1876–87) and again by the same editor and W. G. Stone for the EETS ES 105 (1909).

The Three Kings of Cologne

The *Historia Trium Regum* (*c.* 1370) was translated into English early in the fifteenth century from the Latin of J. de Hildesheim. It was first printed by W. de Worde (1496?; ii, 1499?), and has been edited by C. Horstmann for the EETS OS 85 (1886). The extant texts show at least three stages of revision.

The Three Kings' Sons

This has been edited from the unique manuscript (B.M. Harley 326) of about 1500 by F. J. Furnivall for the EETS ES 67 (1895). It is a translation from the French by an anonymous hand. The original is in part claimed by David Aubert in a text printed from the manuscript and published at Lyons (1501).

The Turke and Gowin

This romance in a late-fifteenth-century northern version consists of six-line stanzas with much alliteration. It survives, imperfectly, in the Percy Folio manuscript, and has been printed by Madden in his edition of *Syr Gawayne* for the Bannatyne Club (1839), 243–355, and by J. W. Hales and F. J. Furnivall in *Bishop Percy's Folio MS.* (4 vols., 1867–8), i. 88–102.

The Weddynge of Sir Gawen and Dame Ragnell

This work was written in the east Midlands in the mid fifteenth century, and originally consisted of 852 lines in six-line stanzas. It is preserved in Bodl. MS. Rawlinson C. 86. First edited by Sir F. Madden for the Bannatyne Club, *Syr Gawayne* (1839), 297–8, it was afterwards edited by L. Sumner in the *Smith College Studies in Modern Languages*, v, no. 4 (1924), and this text is also reproduced by B. J. Whiting in his study of the Wife of Bath's Tale in *Sources and Analogues of Chaucer's Canterbury Tales*, ed. by W. F. Bryan and Germaine Dempster (Chicago, 1941), 242–64.

INDEX

Many minor names and incidental references are necessarily omitted. Main entries are in bold figures. An asterisk indicates a biographical note. Topics and fifteenth-century authors and anonymous works in the bibliography are indexed.